The
Asian
Mystique

The
Asian
Mystique

Dragon Ladies,

Geisha Girls, &

Our Fantasies of

the Exotic Orient

To Carrie + Joan,

SHERIDAN PRASSO

*with best wishes
for happy travels —*

PublicAffairs
New York

Book design by Jane Raese

Library of Congress Cataloging-in-Publication Data
Prasso, Sheridan.
The Asian mystique: dragon ladies, geisha girls, & our fantasies of
the exotic Orient/Sheridan Prasso.—1st ed.
p. cm.
Includes bibliographical references and index.
ISBN 1-58648-214-9
1. Women—Asia—Social conditions. 2. Women—Asia—Public opinion.
3. Asia—foreign public opinion, Occidental. 4. Stereotype (Psychology).
5. East and West. I. Title.
HQ1726.P73   2005
305.48'895—dc22
2005043048

First Edition

2 4 6 8 10 9 7 5 3 1

For Priscilla Thayer Brandon,
who challenged me to see the world with new eyes

Contents

The Asian Mystique

Introduction

"The East is a University in which the scholar never takes his degree.
It is a temple where the suppliant adores but never catches sight
of the object of his devotion."

—LORD CURZON, Viceroy of India, 1899–1905

AN EXOTIC LAND OF GRACEFUL ALLURE, of swaying sugar palms
and soaring bamboo, of servants, silks, and sumptuous feasts. In the
mind's eye we can envision its mystical charms, its incense-shrouded
temples and opium dens; its appeal to the despot in all of us, lying on
a divan's satiny cushions, tended by beautifully beguiling Orientals. It
is sensual and decadent, enticing and thrilling in its forbidden temp-
tations. This has long been our Western fantasy of The Orient—antiquated, perhaps, but still shockingly influential.

We cannot easily escape its effect on the lenses we use to view Asia
and its people. We see through a constructed prism of our own making,
built from our experiences and from our knowledge acquired through
education and culture. Our perspectives are misshaped—contorted—
by centuries of misunderstandings built on mythologies, fantasies, fairy
tales, and fears. We in the West see the East through distorted eyes,
through an Orientalized filter of what I call "Asian Mystique."

In 1990, shortly after I had moved from Chicago to Asia as a news
correspondent, I became intrigued by a frequent visitor to my Mid-
levels neighborhood of Hong Kong, a man who shouted in a sing-
songy voice the same words over and over as he traversed the winding,
hilly streets. I lived in an apartment block in front of a concrete wall
holding back the mountainside, and to me this mass of concrete
seemed an affront to nature. I knew that the Cantonese people of
Hong Kong believe there are gods everywhere and in everything—in
the kitchen, the trees, the water, and the landscape. Could this man be

chanting to appease the mountain god who might be angered by this man-made desecration? I wanted to indulge the fantasy that I was witnessing the mystical Asia out the window of my concrete apartment block. I told my Chinese-speaking roommate about the man, and one day as I heard his cries I went running to get her. She stepped onto our small balcony, listed to his chant, and turned to me laughing, "I believe he is collecting scrap metal." I was never able to see Asia in the same way again.

Since then, in the fifteen years I have been writing about Asia, I found that the impressions I had brought from America didn't match what I was seeing with my own eyes. Travel writers and novelists described the mystical and exotic, the kind of Asia I was prepared to find in my scrap-metal collector's chant; instead, I experienced the normal and real. The true Asia, I found, was largely misrepresented by the dominant images we have in the West, where "the Orient" is often depicted with fantasy-fueled feminine adjectives.

The more I examined the implications, the more I realized how deep and far-reaching they are. These various aspects of the Asian Mystique, I believe, affect everything from international relations to business negotiations to cross-cultural relationships. In U.S. foreign policy, for example, Washington has focused paternal condescension toward our "little brown brothers," as former President William H. Taft once famously said, and has consistently underestimated military threats, most significantly in the Korean and Vietnam Wars, and now also from North Korea. In business, Western negotiators sometimes misread Confucian reserve as weakness, in part as a result of Western culture's portrayal of Asian men as vulnerable and emasculated. Asian women find themselves perceived as submissive, obedient, and obliging—or the opposite—but rarely as well-adjusted mothers and professionals. That "Asians" are hardly one homogenous mass—with thousands of ethnic groups among the nearly two billion people of the region—hardly seems to matter.

To determine why these perceptions exist, I knew I would have to dig deep into the history of West-East interaction: the thousands of years of trade and hundreds of years of colonial and military conquest, the experience of Asian immigrants in the West, and the pervasive and perpetuating images of literature and Hollywood.

Madame Butterfly modernized into the musical *Miss Saigon;* our own fable of Cinderella turned into the oddly unrealistic devotion of a young woman in *Memoirs of a Geisha;* the soft-spoken, servile Mrs. Livingston in *The Courtship of Eddie's Father;* the gentle and sexually uninhibited Mariko of the TV mini-series and novel *Shogun;* the quietly enigmatic Phuong in *The Quiet American;* the graceful Hana-ogi in *Sayonara;* the pouty prostitute in *The World of Suzie Wong;* the kick-ass dominatrix characters played by Lucy Liu. These depictions cause Asian woman to be perceived in Western culture as gentle geisha or China Dolls—servile, submissive, exotic, sexually available, mysterious, and guiding; or as Dragon Ladies—steely and as cold as Cruella de Vil, lacking in the emotions or the neuroses of real women. Characterizations of Asian men depict them as effeminate and emasculated on the one hand, but inscrutable, sneaky, stoic, and sometimes wise on the other. Combined with our history, these images play a role in creating a subconscious racism built on stereotypes—both positive and negative—that most of us don't realize we have.

We as a culture have come to realize the issues of patronizing racial cast in the character of Mammy in *Gone with the Wind,* for example. If our culture had stood static, content with such roles instead of demanding more equitable multi-dimensional ones for African-Americans, it could not have opened the way for the rich contributions of hundreds of women such as Oprah, Toni Morrison, Maya Angelou, and Halle Berry. We have not yet begun such scrutiny on behalf of Asians.

In Part I of this book, then, we examine the Asian Mystique and where it comes from—the history of contact between West and East; the images that have become entrenched in film, theater, fiction, and pop culture of the West as a result; and some of the implications for people, relationships (including the phenomenon of "Yellow Fever"), as well as East-West relations.

So who are "Asians" then, *a priori,* seen with unclouded, de-exoticized eyes? Part II seeks to shed light on that, taking a reality tour of Asia using the icons of our stereotypes—geisha, housewives, exotic Cathay Girls, China Dolls, Suzie Wongs, Madame Butterflies, powerful Dragon Ladies, martial arts mistresses, and the like. We examine the real complexities on both sides of the dual images and attempt to dismantle them, revealing the fully dimensional human beings beyond our usual perceptions.

THERE WILL BE A SENSE OF LOSS in this examination, in giving up our fantasies of exotic Orientals and accepting that cultures are ever-evolving. It is the same loss I felt upon understanding the scrap metal collector's call. It is the same loss that foreigners feel traveling to the American West when they don't find swaggering cowboys in chaps bursting through tavern doors ready to duel, or whooping Indians shooting arrows at bison on the plains. Or Al Capone–style shootouts on the streets of Chicago. The reward for giving up our fantasies of exotic difference will be a deeper, richer understanding, with more real and equitable cross-cultural interactions as a result. But just because it is easier to find Asians working in skyscrapers in modern cities instead of in conical hats tending rice fields, or that it is virtually impossible to find Japanese women tottering along three feet behind their husbands as they did a century ago, doesn't mean their "cultures" have disappeared. They have simply, as ours have, evolved.

This endeavor is the result of many years of observing, questioning, reading, and watching East-West interactions—and interviewing not only those we might view as the representations of our stereotypes, but hundreds of people who helped paint a more accurate picture of Asia. I talked with women from every class and education level, from as many possible diverse backgrounds and professions, in as many countries, and from as many ethnic groups in Asia as possible. I also talked with men—Asians, Blacks, and Caucasians. I talked with Asian-Americans, and Asian-origin immigrants in Europe and Australia. In almost every case, everyone I enlisted in this project was thrilled at the idea of a book that would, finally, try to lay bare the myths and fantasies Western culture holds about Asia, Asian women, and feminized perceptions of Asian men.

Many women took enormous amounts of time and trouble to welcome me into their lives, inviting me to their homes and businesses, introducing me to their friends, and helping me see a world that I simply could not have seen if I were a man. When I left to spend three months in Japan in early 2003, one of my former colleagues warned me that I would have trouble getting to know Japanese people. In his many years of reporting on the country, he told me, he had never once been invited into a Japanese home. As a woman, my experience was completely the opposite.

In Japan, the home is the domain of the woman, and Japanese women control it. (A Japanese man typically would have to ask his wife for permission before bringing home a foreigner.) Women there welcomed me in, offered me tea, allowed me to sit in while they talked about their concerns about parenting, their in-laws, and their sex lives, and to accompany them to the playground and when picking up their children from school. It was an opportunity I was granted, to the extent that I had the time and inclination, almost everywhere I have been in Asia.

The result is not a basic primer on "Asian cultures" or "Asian women," nor prostitution, women in the workforce, nor sexism in Asian societies, about which much has already been written. Rather, it is as much about us as it is about Asia.

It is about issues of race and sex, fantasy and power. It is about the nexus of misunderstanding where West meets East: our relationships and interactions, our misconceptions and stereotypes, our myths versus the realities, where our relations have been, and where they are going. I hope to strip away the romanticized idealism that clouds East-West relations and relationships. I hope to move us beyond the misty-eyed myths of exotic difference and into a realism that will shape our relations in future eras. Lord Curzon's words may have been all very well 100 years ago, when we could afford to luxuriate in idolizing the East and either revering or deploring its differences. But the exigencies of the modern world—where terrorism is as much a threat in Jakarta, Manila, and Tokyo as it is in New York and Madrid, where trade and globalization bring us all closer together—make distant adoration and well-intentioned fantasies not only impractical but perilous.

The stories I have chosen and the issues they represent are part of a larger paradigm. Polly the Chinese Communist, Berlinda the Filipina prostitute, Yumi the Japanese housewife, and the others we come to know through these pages, represent my attempts to portray a more multi-dimensional and thought-provoking picture of Asians and our Western fallacies.

Through them, and through the examination of our images of Asians throughout history and Hollywood, I hope to begin a discussion that few have begun before. I hope to examine and challenge the assumptions we hold on both sides, to examine ourselves while we look outward at others. I hope to challenge the "Mammy"-ism in depictions of Asians—and, consequently, also challenge the way we in the West have been viewing Asia and dealing with Asia for thousands of years. If this work can go even part way toward starting the inquiry, it will have been a success.

As I began my own journey through these complex issues, a moment sticks out in my mind: the night I saw *Miss Saigon* on Broadway. The musical was set to close in January 2001 after grossing more than $1.3 billion in worldwide ticket sales. It is the story, based on Puccini's *Madame Butterfly,* of an American soldier who has a love affair with a Vietnamese prostitute, fathers her child, returns to the United States, and marries an American. When the couple goes to Asia and meets the Vietnamese woman, she offers her son to them and then kills herself. Like every great operatic tragedy, and just as *Madame Butterfly* was before it, the final scenes are emotion-filled, heart-rending, and tearful.

As the curtain fell on one of the last Broadway performances, one of the audience members dabbing his eyes was a young man from the American Midwest. Blonde and freckled, no older than thirty-five, he told me he traveled frequently for his sales job and had decided to spend a free evening in New York City at the Broadway Theatre. As he turned to go, he volunteered how moved he was by the performance.

"That was especially hard for me to watch," he said. "My wife is Chinese."

Well actually, Chinese-American, he clarified. Born in the U.S.A. It took a few moments for his statement to resonate with me, but when it did, in one of those "you-only-think-of-a-response-after-the-moment-has-passed" moments, he had already disappeared out the mezzanine door. The story, of course, was about a poor Vietnamese woman, a prostitute and victim of American intervention. It was set in Vietnam, in a war that had little to do with a midwestern wife born of Chinese parentage, who knows how many generations removed. Most likely the origins of this wife's family were many thousands of miles from Saigon, as distant as Britain is to Italy, if not farther. To link them is like watching Carmen, another tragic opera which climaxes in the murder of a Spanish gypsy girl, and finding it difficult to watch because one's wife is of, say, French origin.

Spanish gypsy—French-origin American wife? We see the absurdity.

Vietnamese prostitute—Chinese-American wife? Not nearly so easily.

On some level, the wife of this midwestern salesman was not his unique partner, but the embodiment of an image that is interchangeable with all Asian women. She, *Miss Saigon,* and all individuals of Asian origin are wrapped up in this tangle of Asian Mystique. Let's unravel it.

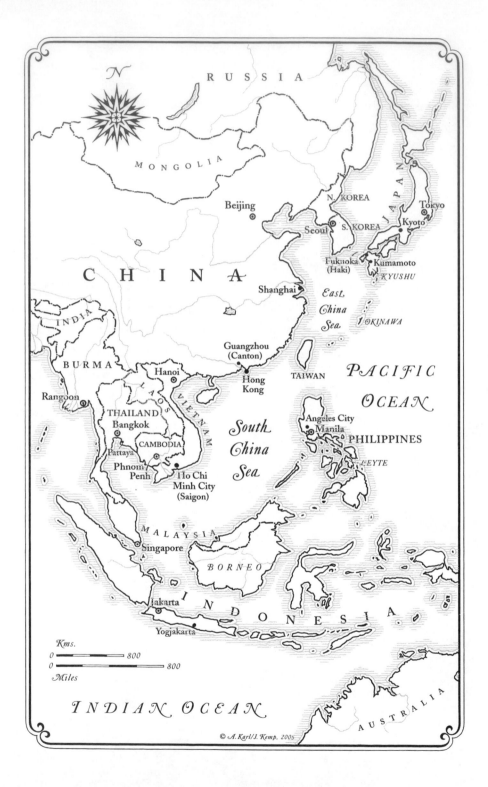

N

RUSSIA

MONGOLIA

Beijing

CHINA

N. KOREA

Seoul   S. KOREA

JAPAN

Tokyo
Kyoto

Fukuoka
(Haki)   Kumamoto

KYUSHU

Shanghai

East
China
Sea

OKINAWA

INDIA

BURMA

Guangzhou
(Canton)

Rangoon

Hanoi

LAOS

VIETNAM

Hong
Kong

TAIWAN

PACIFIC

OCEAN

THAILAND
Bangkok

CAMBODIA

Pattaya

Phnom
Penh

Ho Chi
Minh City
(Saigon)

South
China
Sea

Angeles City
Manila

PHILIPPINES

LEYTE

MALAYSIA

Singapore

BORNEO

Jakarta

INDONESIA

Yogjakarta

Kms.
0   800
0   800
Miles

INDIAN OCEAN

AUSTRALIA

© A. Karl/J. Kemp. 2005

PART ONE

The Asian Mystique

The Asian Mystique

AT A BAR CALLED SUPER PUSSY, in the heart of Asia's throbbing sex capital, Bangkok, a young woman in a white vinyl thong bikini, spreading her knees wide, is rubbing her crotch down a pole to the beat of AC/DC's "Back in Black." The stage is ringed with black lights, causing the enhanced contours of the dancer's vinyl-encased breasts and her gyrating triangle below to glow with eerie incandescence. Her face is a blur of anonymity. The luminous outlines of raw, accentuated flesh, a glow of lipstick, and a cascade of shiny black hair are all we are meant to see.

This is just the warm up. There is more on offer for a mere point to the menu card: "ping-pong-pussy show," "banana show," "whistling show," "smoking show," "birthday show," and "balloon-dart show," among others, for the equivalent of about $12 added to the bar tab. A waitress will take the order, and skilled women will come to the stage, strip off their bikini bottoms, and then propel these objects at the customers in the audience. The women blow whistles or horns, smoke cigarettes, expel air forcefully enough to blow out birthday candles, and shoot darts at balloons—all, astonishingly, from their exposed, well-practiced vaginas. There's more to be had, too, for a little negotiation. A girl for an hour. Or a night. Or a week. Or, for one you really like, for a lifetime.

It wasn't my first time in a Bangkok girlie bar. A decade before, a Thai friend had taken me around for a day, and his mini-tour included the usual sights for foreigners: the temple of the Emerald Buddha, a water taxi ride up the Chao Praya River, and these bars in the Patpong red-light district. Other cities of the world have similar forms of titillation. In fact, the strip clubs of New York's Times Square featured naked women and their cigarette-smoking-pussy and ping-pong-ball displays long before clubs in Thailand ever did. But usually such exhibitionism is hidden from view behind darkened doors, not on display at street level in prime view of tourists. The sexual entertainment of Bangkok is open and inviting, frivolous rather than seedy. Patpong is a must-see stop on the "Visit Thailand" tourist itinerary. A man from Adelaide or Kansas, or even someone like me—people who normally would never enter such realms in our own countries—feel few qualms about walking off the streets to see this display, yet another notch in the exotic Orient tour. My Thai host wanted to show me the sights of Bangkok. This was yet another.

What struck me that day was the incongruity with which women—and I as a woman—were viewed in each place, even in the same city, the same culture. At the temple, shorts were forbidden, much as they also would be inappropriate in a Christian church. I had worn a long skirt. But despite the humid, clinging, ninety-degree air, I was, like all similarly clad visitors and worshippers, required to put a scarf over my shoulders to cover my bare arms, or my cap-sleeved shirt would be taken as a show of sacrilege. And on the crowded water taxi, when a group of monks got on with their saffron-colored robes billowing in the light breeze, my friend warned me away from them, or the jostling of the boat might cause me to bump up against them. Women were not permitted to touch monks, he told me. Even a touch might contaminate them.

Yet, at the bars in Bangkok's red-light districts, it was as though nightfall turned the rules of the day upside down. No covered shoulders or long skirts here. No covered anything at all. And, here, it was the women who could not be touched—dancing and gyrating as they did on their pedestals above the bar. As a first-time visitor, I remember sitting in wide-eyed awe as the ping-pong balls flew, our heads craning upward toward the stage in much the same position as in gazing at the Buddha just hours before. This mock-worship, this setting apart of women to be both ogled and revered, struck me as a stark juxtaposition of sacred and profane. Whereas worshippers at the temple bent low to place their offerings of money and incense, here at the go-go bar they stretched out their arms to offer their tips.

So here, ten years later, I was watching Western men watch this representation of "the East," the naked women equally as exotic an image of Thailand in the mind of a tourist as the Emerald Buddha and a water-taxi trip up the Chao Praya River. For some of the men, these are among their first experiences of Asian women. Almost all the clientele at Super Pussy—and at Pussy Galore, Kiss Kiss Kiss, Lipstick, and dozens of others with similar names—are white, from Western countries. They are mostly Americans, Brits, Aussies, and Germans, but men from the rest of western and eastern Europe as well as Russia show up in these bars, too. Thai men hardly ever come. It is true that they—and Asian men throughout the region—are greater consumers of Asian women's sexual services than are Western men, by most measures. The red-light districts catering to Asian clientele are more extensive, prevalent, cheap, seedy, more the "wham bam thank you-ma'am," go-behind-a-curtain-and-get-it-over-with type—or, increasingly, the "sing karaoke songs at the club while you choose which doting girl to screw"–type. Asian men on business trips within Asia sometimes patronize the bars aimed at westerners, which play Western music, have English menus, and serve drinks and snacks familiar to the Western palate. Some Japanese-language bars in Bangkok, Pattaya, and Jakarta have sprung up to cater to Japanese (and increasingly Korean) preferences and tastes. Yet, for the most part, in the sex trade of Asians for Asians, there is little ogling of the female form, little mystique or fantasy. Primarily, it is straightforward, taboo-less, transactional sex.

But the sex industry catering to Westerners in Asia is different. Here, what is for sale is not only the flesh, but the mystique—the Asian Mystique—the fantasy of the exotic, indulging, decadent, sensual Oriental who will indulge you and delight you with the decadence and servility that no woman in your own culture could. It is built upon thousands of years of East-West interaction, and loaded with images, expectations, and misperceptions.

The men here, not surprisingly, are giddy, their eyes transfixed in a mixture of adulation, fascination, and lust. Some of them have come, like I did more than a decade before, out of mere curiosity. Some have come, to appreciate the flesh offered, to admire the kind of exotic beauty in the nudity that is taboo in their own cultures, as well as in this one. Because it is far from home, it is just part of the foreign experience. And some have come here to buy it. It is an easy purchase, this experience of Asia that is fantasy-indulging and, ultimately, "remasculating"—engendering feelings of masculinity or dominance which these Western men may have found diminished in their own cultures. No matter who these men are back home, here—in a developing country like Thailand—they are richer, better-educated, and desirable to large segments of the female population, particularly those women on lower economic and social rungs. No, not to all Asian women.

There are women in Bangkok and elsewhere in Asia who would never have anything to do with a foreigner. Among those who would, however, it's not only about economics. White skin is a status symbol and, for an Asian woman, the lighter her skin the more beautiful most Asian societies consider her to be. Having a light-skinned, mixed-race baby is now fashionable among certain sets in Thailand after several movie stars did it and the public deemed the photos of these biracial children in the media adorable. In Korea, where racial purity is valued and being of mixed race often carried the charged association of being the bastard child of a prostitute and a GI, popular biracial entertainers are breaking down those barriers. Several middle-class and elite women of Asia have told me that they want white boyfriends or husbands so that they can have cute white babies.

Even in a wealthy country like Japan, Western men frequently are considered more liberal than Japanese men, offering more personal freedoms and an entrée to a hip new world to those who feel less-than-conformist in their own society. The *koku-jo,* for example, are Japanese women who kink or cornrow their hair, visit tanning booths, listen to hip-hop music, and hang out near U.S. military bases in Okinawa to meet African-American Marines. These Western men are regarded as better able to appreciate darker skin, a bit of heftiness, or tomboyishness—qualities generally considered unattractive to Japanese men. For these women, getting breast and buttocks implants in order to better compete are a big business.

For Western men, this desirability among Asian women and the "remasculating" that accompanies it is potent therapy. It is something that cannot be purchased in the red-light districts of their own countries. Susan Faludi, in her 1999 book, *Stiffed: The Betrayal of the American Man,* wrote that American men were rebelling against a feeling of threatened masculinity, indeed emasculation, in a culture that broke its societal promises and stopped rewarding traditionally masculine roles.

CREDIT: Larry Rodney. Illustrated by Glen Schroeder.
© *Charisma Man 1998–2002 The Complete Collection*

But, in the bars of Bangkok and elsewhere in Asia, Western men who may find traditional notions of masculinity diminished by modern cultural expectations can find restitution. In their perceptions of their interactions with Asian women and Asian culture, they can experience feelings of dominance, wealth, power, and masculinity—at least temporarily. Here, any man can experience feeling attractive again—even loved. Old, fat, or ugly by Western standards, it doesn't matter. Anyone can be the Alpha Male and Lord Jim. Western men in Asia—all over Asia—compare it with feeling like a rock star, with women pursuing them everywhere they go, not just in bars, but in shopping malls, at restaurants, even when walking down the street.

A middle-aged oil worker from England, gleeful with drink at a club on a notorious Asian sex strip late one evening, put it best. I had asked him, simply, why he had come. "Here," he shouted, beer in hand, raising his arms over his head as if scoring a soccer victory before dancing off into a crowd of young beauties all vying to be the one he took home that night, "you can be KING!"

Every year, thousands of Western men partner with Asian women—if not ones from the bars of Asia, then others met in the workplace, through acquaintances, or just casually in a store or on a street corner. In the United States, Caucasian men and Asian-origin women marry more frequently than any other two groups. Thousands of men in the West every year send away for mail-order brides or meet Asian women through personal ads in the expatriate-aimed magazines of Asian capitals.

"Dirty Little Slut. 20 yrs, Chinese dirty girl seeking 20–35 yrs. Attractive white guys 4 sex. I have a nice body and good looking," said one ad in the personals of *Hong Kong Magazine.* "Gorgeous, good-looking 35 yr. old Caucasian seeks fun-loving Asian girl for discreet meetings of mutual pleasure. Relaxed and easy-going, I will please you, tease you and reward you," said a corresponding one from a male. Perhaps they found each other.

There are, of course, many thousands of wonderful, equitable relationships. A little mystique sometimes adds a lot to relationships, in very beneficial ways. But, of course, there are other such relationships that find their mutuality tested—and sometimes torn apart—by cultural differences and preconceived expectations.

Where do our expectations come from? Typically from the way that Asians have been depicted in Western culture. The image of the submissive, subservient, exotic Oriental is a pervasive one: the tea-serving geisha, the sex nymph, the weeping war victim, the heart-of-gold prostitute. And to deal with the disparity inherent in the fact that Asia has had long traditions of women in power—and to nod to the fact that Asian women may not be docile lotus flowers after all—we also have the opposing stereotype, that of Dragon Lady or Martial Arts Mistress.

Asia has had a long succession of female political rulers; it produced the world's first female prime minister, and has had more prominent women heads of government than any other region of the world. It has martial arts traditions developed by women; it is a region where women wield enormous economic clout in the home and in the marketplace, and matrilineal lines run strong in a number of Asian ethnic groups. There are fewer greater dichotomies than these—the submissive, servile Oriental and the Dragon Lady dominatrix.

The actress Anna May Wong once complained that in the sixty films in which she appeared beginning in 1919, she always had to play a slave, temptress, prostitute, or doomed lover; whose lines were in "Chinglish," who was forbidden to kiss a Western man (illegal until 1948 under California anti-miscegenation laws), and who always had

22 Aircon Rooms

Subic Nightlife Tours Personally Escorted by Blue Rock Management

24-HR Bar

Swim

All Wo

P.A.D.I

Daily Transport to and

Private

Interne

Internati

24-Hr

Baloy Beach, Bo. B.
Tel. No. 047-2249042
E-mail. bluerocksubic@hotmail.c
Tommo: 0919 556929

to die so that the woman with yellow hair could get the white man. When criticized for perpetuating stereotypes, she answered that actresses just starting out don't have much choice over their roles. More than eighty years later, the just-as-popular Lucy Liu, when criticized for perpetuating the opposing stereotype gave the same answer—that she did not have much choice, either.

It's not just Hollywood or Broadway or publisher's row; frequently these images are reinforced and exploited by Asians themselves, with a realization that playing to type frequently has been what plays to Western audiences. Witness just one example: tourist brochures for the Philippines showing sexy girls in bikinis or shoulder-less dress, inviting the male tourist to experience the sensual pleasures of the Orient. In short, as long as we willingly buy these exoticized, eroticized, sexualized images, there are Asians who will willingly sell them to us.

Western travelers to the "Orient" began selling these stereotypes and misperceptions back home centuries ago, as Edward Said famously wrote in his book *Orientalism,* published in 1978. Since the time of Marco Polo, and even as far back as the ancient Greeks who gave Western culture the sexual goddess Aphrodite as the first model of the "Oriental woman," he wrote, Western writers have painted Asia as inscrutable, romantic, decadent, dangerous, promising, and mysterious.

During the period of European colonialization of Asia and the French-Anglo experience with, first, the Middle East as "the Orient," then with the Asia that lay beyond, Europe gradually refined and narrowed the concept until it meant, more or less, the "Far East." Americans became the inheritors of those French-Anglo (and other European colonialist) cultural perspectives that had been forming since the beginning of East-West contact—which is why Americans still refer to Asia as the "East" or "Far East," when it is, in fact, only either of those when one is standing in Europe. The American colonial and war experiences in the Pacific reinforced those ancient perceptions inherited from Europe. Said's theory of "Orientalism" only goes so far in explaining this, concentrating primarily on the role of literature and scholarship in the earlier period of history, when European contact with the Near East and India constituted the "Orient." But in the last 100 years there has developed a factor far more influential in the formation of "Oriental" images, in which American dominance in the Pacific, combined with the Asian immigrant experience, were key: Hollywood. I believe that Hollywood became an incubator and a firing kiln for the Orientalized perceptions inherited from Europe. Bolstered and reinforced by American experience, Hollywood's images played a large role in re-exporting the reshaped perceptions back to Europe over the last century.

Asian women became the objects of an almost mystical sexual fascination during the rise of European colonial involvement in Asia. China's Empress Dowager was reputed to have "an abnormally large clitoris," according to a British scholar who claimed (falsely) to have had a love affair with her. A diary entry from the Siege of Peking in 1900, a period when Victorian beliefs dictated that white women participate in sex only out of marital duty but not enjoy it, records that a Manchu woman was "like a narcotic when a roar of fever still hangs in one's ears."[1] To this day, Korean feminists I know in Seoul snigger sarcastically of having horizontal vaginas, a myth that has persisted since the Korean War, if not long before.

EVEN NOW, centuries after the first mystical sexual fascination began, modern writers speak of being "seduced" by Asia. Many attribute their interest in the region to their interest, first of all, in Asian women and the lure of the exotic. Their very literal passion contributes to identifying Asia with "the feminine," and assigning the region and its people attributes that typically are associated with femininity in the West. Casting Asia as "feminine" causes the romanticization of it and—because women are "mysterious" to the opposite gender, no matter what their origin—contributes to its ineffability. Ian Buruma, one of the most profound European analysts of Asia in the modern era, writes in *The Missionary and the Libertine* that his fascination started in Amsterdam while watching "the imaginary East" in a magical theater performance. The stage was transformed into "a fantastic brothel, filled with girls, midgets, opium smokers, dandies, and drag queens. . . . If this is what Tokyo is like, I thought, I want to join the circus." Then Buruma "fell in love with a Japanese girl in the movies," a character in a François Truffaut film who was "mysterious and exotic," he writes, "as silent and as elusive as a ghost."[2] He, of course, then followed his heart to Japan, as have so many noted Western analysts on Asia before him and since. In his analyses of the East-West relationship, Buruma writes of Asia using the metaphor of a seductive geisha or, at other times, of beautiful native Filipinas being either raped by foreign conquerors or willingly offering to give them head. The images are sexualized, fantasized for the male imagination. With these views of Asia so pervasive, it is hard not to fall hard for them.

There have been attempts to dispel them, or to at least force us to examine them. Playwright David Henry Hwang's *M Butterfly* took the mother of all Asian stereotypes, *Madame Butterfly,* and turned it upside down. It started when he read a *New York Times* interview with the real-life French diplomat Bernard Bouriscot, who, when posted to China in the 1960s and enraptured with his own fantasies of exotic Asia, took a Chinese lover (who then spied on him). The relationship lasted, incredibly, for eighteen years without Bouriscot knowing his lover was a man. The Chinese man, Shi Pei Pu, was able to manipulate Bouriscot sexually—usually in the dark—into thinking he was a woman, and the Frenchman accepted the differences as "Oriental." (A medical examination conducted by French doctors during the espionage trial of the two in the 1980s determined that the Chinese man was able to retract his testicles into his body, tuck his penis back into the folds between his legs, and hold his thighs tightly together during sex so that Bouriscot believed their sex was intercourse, albeit different from that he had with Western women.³) The diplomat was quoted as saying, "I thought she was very modest. I thought it was a Chinese custom." It was evidence of his willingness to deceive himself to maintain his fantasy. Hwang wrote in the postscript to his screenplay:

> I am aware that this is not a Chinese custom, that Asian women are no more shy with their lovers than are women of the West. I am also aware, however, that Bouriscot's assumption was consistent with a certain stereotyped view of Asians as bowing, blushing flowers. I therefore concluded that the diplomat must have fallen in love, not with a person, but with a fantasy stereotype. I also inferred that, to the extent the Chinese spy encouraged these misperceptions, he must have played up to and exploited this image of the Oriental woman as demure and submissive.

Hwang continued

> . . . heterosexual Asians have long been aware of "Yellow Fever"— Caucasian men with a fetish for exotic Oriental women. I have often heard it said that "Oriental women make the best wives." (Rarely is this heard from the mouths of Asian men, incidentally.) This mythology is exploited by the Oriental mail-order bride trade which has flourished over the past decade. American men can now send away for catalogues of "obedient, domesticated" Asian women looking for husbands. Anyone who believes such stereotypes are a thing of the past need look no further than Manhattan cable television, which advertises call girls from "the exotic East, where men are king; obedient girls, trained in the art of pleasure." In these appeals, we see issues of racism and sexism intersect.⁴

Hwang's subversive play won a 1988 Tony Award, and the 1993 movie starring Jeremy Irons and John Lone was both moving and well-acclaimed.

But one drop of the dye of realism into an ocean of fantasy-driven images to the contrary cannot change its color. Fifteen years after Hwang wrote these words, travel brochures, personal ads, and ads selling "Geisha #1 Oriental Fun" and "Oriental Exotics" still take up

Village Voice escort service ads, 2004

pages in magazines and broadsheet newspapers in Manhattan as well as elsewhere in the United States and Europe. The trade in Asian mail-order brides has gone online, where more than 200 websites bring together some 4,000 to 6,000 couples a year who petition for immigration of the female spouse to the United States, according to the Immigration and Naturalization Service. The Philippines, along with the countries of the former Soviet bloc, supply the majority of these women.

LESS SEXUALIZED BUT EQUALLY ENIGMATIC Orientalized misperceptions have sprung up in modern times: the "Yellow Peril" scare
of Japan's economic might in the 1980s, with Michael Crichton's *Rising Sun* the foremost example; in academia, the Japan Revisionist
School of Chalmers Johnson, which holds that Japan's version of capi-
talism is fundamentally different from the West's; the West's willingness to accept the concept of "Asian Values," which patronizingly
argues that political freedoms do not suit the Oriental mind, espoused
by Singapore's former authoritarian leader Lee Kuan Yew as justifica-
tion for repressing dissent; and even the fervor with which Western in-
vestors bought into Asia's economic boom in the 1990s in the belief
that the "Asian Miracle" was somehow fundamentally different and
sustainable. Danger, exoticism, and inscrutability characterize most of
these ideas. With the exception of Yellow Peril, which has its origins
in the West's first experiences with job-seeking, strike-breaking Asian
immigrants at the turn of the century, all of these ideas were marketed
to the West by the vested interests of the East. They all, for the most
part, have been proved wrong. That we buy into them indicates our
continuing willingness to believe that Asia and Asian people are somehow fundamentally different—exotic, enigmatic, and inscrutable.

The Impact of Illusion

Over the centuries, much of the societal sexual curiosity has been satisfied and the misperceptions corrected: scholars have pulled back the
curtains of class, religion, and culture, as well as the philosophic traditions that had long kept Asia hidden from Western understanding.
Medical science has proved that all humans are, at essence, anatomi-
cally alike. Our recent Yellow Peril, Asian Values, and Asian Miracle
theories for understanding Asia have been proved wrong.

But our illusions about Asia remain. And they affect people, not
only Asians in their social, cultural, and business interactions with the
West, but those Westerners who marry, hire, befriend, and interact
with Asians. The range of consequences swings from geopolitical to
individual: On the one hand, you can see traces in state-to-state rela-

tions, diplomacy and foreign policy—as has been demonstrated in the issue of the U.S. military presence in the Pacific Rim, and historically in our colonial contact and war involvements in the region; on the other, you can find thousands of young backpackers setting off from Europe, Australia, and elsewhere every year seeking to experience the exotic, spiritual, sensuous East. They frequently return home disappointed that the Asians they'd met were just as practical, materialistic, and interested in making a buck as people back home. Yet the myths persist.

Asian-Americans and Asian residents of Britain and of the rest of Europe to varying extents feel misperceived and misrepresented— painted with the same homogenous brush of racism whether it is with the old negative epithets of "gooks," "Japs," and "Chinks," or its likewise individuality-robbing positive counterweight "model minority." (Sixty-eight percent of Americans hold negative attitudes about Chinese-Americans, according to a 2001 survey by the Committee of 100.)

In the United States and Europe, three, four, or even five generations of people of Asian descent already have been born. No matter, they still get the question, "Where are you from?" from their fellow citizens. Akron, or Yorkshire, or the 13th Arrondissement of Paris are not acceptable answers. "No, where are you *really* from?" they are asked, in a way that the descendants of European or African-origin peoples never are.

Asian-American women, in particular, report experiencing an increase in "fetishism" about them, fostered by Internet-connected communities that encourage the viewing of Asian women through an idyllic, sexual mystique. They feel expectations put upon them by American society. "Part of the staying power of the stereotype is that unfortunately people often think that kind of self-sacrifice and self-abnegation is part of who Asian-American women are," Traise Yamamoto, an associate professor at the University of California-Irvine has noted, adding that such misperceptions can "cripple careers" when bosses or colleagues expect an Asian woman to act demure, docile, or "nice" because of her ethnicity.

Asian-Americans find injustice in our justice system, with the erroneous targeting of falsely accused spy Wen Ho Lee being just one of

"Gay or Asian?" from *Details* magazine, April 2004

many miscarriages. (Nearly half of Americans (46 percent) in the Committee of 100 poll believe that Chinese-Americans passing secrets to the Chinese government is "a problem.") They are annoyed with expectations of superior academic performance when, in fact, Asian-American communities contain just plain average (and below-average) students as well; Southeast Asian immigrants in particular who still live in poor communities and work at menial jobs, as well as poor Chinese immigrants in inner cities, feel excluded from the "model minority" mindset, and feel the label prevents them from getting a leg up in American society. Some are so irked by the misperceptions and stereotypes—highlighted in just one example in April 2004, when *Details* magazine published a photo of a fashionable Asian-American male headlined "GAY OR ASIAN?"—that they vent their anger and exasperation on websites such as www.angryasianman.com, www.bigbad

chinesemama.com, www.alllooksame.com, and www.themodel minority.com. The level may not be that of pre-Rosa Parks segregated America, but this race-relations discontent—in the United States as well as Europe—is palpable for anyone interested in taking a measure of it.

Asian women who have achieved fame and standing in their own right are taken less seriously in Western circles than they might if no illusions of Asian Mystique existed. Dr. Pasuk Phongpaichit, for example, is among the most respected academics in Thailand. She is a Cambridge-trained economist and author of one of the most influential books ever published in Thailand. Frequently, she says, when she arrives to speak at a conference abroad with other economic experts, often in the company of her English writer husband, the experts from the same countries as those who have seen the girlie bars of Patpong shake the hand of her husband and begin addressing him first. "Oh, *you're* Professor Pasuk," they finally exclaim to her when corrected, without quite being able to hide their surprise that this soft-spoken, 5'2" Thai woman, not the tall British man next to her, is the economist. Even after delivering an important economic paper, she gets the impression, based on questions posed afterward, that they're hearing her words through a filter: as a woman first, as a Thai second, and only third as an economist and academic. (Of course, white and black women may have similar experiences, but they do not experience the additional complexity of the sexual imagery associated with Thai women.) In Thailand, however, it's a different story. Dr. Pasuk is famous and, in some circles, feared.

I first went to her Bangkok home on a rainy Thai New Year's Day in 1999, because it was the only time she was sure not to have a morning jammed with appointments. As we sat on wooden chairs on her back porch, drank tea, and watched the rain, she was so soft-spoken it was difficult at times even to hear her voice. But there was nothing soft about the book she had just written, *Guns, Girls, Gambling, Ganja: Thailand's Illegal Economy and Public Policy.* It had been out only a few months by then, and Thailand was changing in major ways as a result. A parliamentary committee had been set up to study how to control the illegal activities that she had exposed. The police force, formerly part of Thailand's powerful Interior Ministry, had been realigned to answer directly to the prime minister in an attempt to eliminate the improprieties she had uncovered. And Thailand's press—among the freest in Asia—had been emboldened to bring corruption into public debate, quoting Dr. Pasuk as their source.

Dr. Pasuk and her small research team at Chulalongkorn University, where she had taught economics for twenty-eight years, had documented what Thais themselves had long suspected: that many of their police, politicians, and businessmen were linked in an overwhelmingly corrupt web of self-interest. Dr. Pasuk found that many provincial politicians and businessmen had front businesses, such as construction, but generated most of their revenue from illegal sidelines. Their gambling dens, prostitution rings, and other illegal activities raked in billions of dollars, totaling 10 to 20 percent of Thailand's entire economic activity. After exposing this, she ducked death threats until the prime minister intervened with the police on her behalf. "We didn't realize we were cracking the rice pot of some local police," Dr. Pasuk told me that day on her porch. "We were a little bit naïve." It was hard to imagine this composed woman graying at the temples as being naïve. Rather, she seemed consumed with a quiet dedication to her cause. Whenever she leaves Thailand, however, she is once again reminded that she is viewed first as a Thai woman in the company of a white man, and only secondarily as an accomplished academic who has changed a nation.

Viewers and Viewees

Is it possible as a westerner to see Asia clearly? After all, as Said wrote, we cannot shed the filters that shape what we see. The "Orient" as a concept is defined only in its opposition to the "Occident," not because it has inherent, cohesive glue. "Never," he wrote, "has there been such a thing as a pure, or unconditional, Orient":

> For if it is true that no production of knowledge in the human sciences can ever ignore or disclaim its author's involvement as a human subject in his own circumstances, then it must also be true that for a European or American studying the Orient . . . he comes up against

the Orient as a European or American first, as an individual second. It meant and means being aware, however dimly, that one belongs to a power with definite interests in the Orient, and more important, that one belongs to a part of the earth with a definite history of involvement in the Orient almost since the time of Homer.[5]

To take Said's words to heart means that, as westerners, we need to maintain awareness of the filters on our perspectives while we try to see more clearly through them. As an American writing this book, I cannot escape being from a power with definite interests and a long history in the Orient. Educated in the tradition of scientific reason, I cannot avoid applying those methodologies in my observations. And as a Caucasian woman, I cannot eschew membership in a group that is not only held up, in the reverse stereotype, as aggressive and castrating in contrast to the stereotype of the docile, submissive, remasculating Asian woman, but also has been guilty of racist "sour-grapeism." (As the nameless Big Girl complains in James A. Michener's 1953 novel *Sayonara:* "It's no fun to be a State-side reject watching cute Japanese girls getting all the American men. . . . Damn them all!") The partial solution, as Said suggests, is awareness, and perhaps trying, as much as possible, to let the facts of history and the voices of Asians speak for themselves. Also, it sometimes takes an outsider to be able to describe what insiders cannot see.

I was reminded of that one afternoon in Yogjakarta, the cultural heart of central Indonesia on the island of Java. I was invited to the home of a Javanese woman who was the area leader of the women's branch of the country's second-largest Islamic civic organization, called the Muhammadiyah. The organization is a big deal in Indonesia. There's a competing one, called Nahdlatul Ulama, and the two, with a combined membership of about fifty million Indonesians, function as the social equivalent of church groups, Salvation Army-type charities, the Boy and Girl Scouts, YMCA/YWCAs, neighborhood watches, and community action groups. The women's branch, Aisyiyah, runs kindergartens, foster care, orphanages, homes for the elderly, as well as an increasing number of schools and universities. Aisyiyah also provides election education and encourages women to get out and vote— and vote their own consciences instead of their husbands'.

The Yogjakarta head of Aisyiyah, Kamamah Suratno, had granted me an audience. Heavy-set, jowly, and of an indeterminate older age, she spread herself onto her Javanese settee on the covered front portico of her gated home and motioned for me to take the visitor's chair while she held court for what was, presumably, one of thousands of times. It was too hot to sip the tea steaming from a glass on the table in front of me. Tropical fish swam languidly in a large tank to the side. It was about to thunderstorm. She spoke slowly, lauding the many activities of her group and the accomplishments of her life, chief among them, she said, was motherhood. I took notes politely and dabbed the sweat from my hairline before it could run too conspicuously down my temples. When she began to bring the discussion to a close without revealing much about herself, I decided to ask her to characterize her own personality and in what ways she viewed herself as typical or atypical of Javanese women.

"How could I do that?" she responded. "Just like the fish swimming here in the aquarium, how can it see itself? It is up to others to see it and to describe." Plus, she added, there is no such thing as a typical Javanese. Or a typical anybody. "Culture is always changing," she scolded. "I am a Javanese in the current of time. To say anything is 'typical' is static." She was right, of course, both about the need for caution in making generalizations about a people and their characters, and also about needing an outside perspective.

While conducting this research, I was interested in the images we have in the West of, say, the Japanese geisha bowing to her customers, the tea-pouring office lady bowing to her bosses, or the oppressed housewife bowing to her husband. Japan still has geisha, office ladies, and housewives, but I wanted to understand how those women viewed their own ability to exercise power in their own lives—or not. I wanted to know whether they felt misperceived by Western perceptions of submissiveness and societal subjugation—when, in fact we only see surface behavior. They did. "The old stereotypes are totally irrelevant to how Japanese women live today," the noted Japanese sociologist Mariko Fujiwara told me during the first five minutes of my first interview on my first full day of research in Japan. "It's very difficult to find a submissive woman in our society. If they are submissive, it's because they have a choice. Some people have a style of submissiveness, but that's the position they choose to be in rather than one they are put in." Cultural differences can be misleadingly superficial. So, I wondered, what does a modern portrait of Japanese women look like? Is it even possible to describe a people's national character?

One early summer Saturday afternoon spent among the young women outside the 109 fashion store in the trendy Shibuya section of Tokyo, I got something of an answer. Mayumi was a twenty-one-year-old dental hygienist from the wealthy Saitama suburbs. Her hair was dyed the light caramel color currently in fashion, styled impeccably "Jennifer Aniston," and hair-sprayed just below her shoulders. She carried a brown-with-gold patterned Louis Vuitton tote, wore a silver Bulgari hoop necklace and hoop earrings, and sported a Gucci watch. It goes without saying that her legs, arms, and torso were clothed in the latest denim attire as well, and she was on her way into the store with her friend Reiyu for a fashion update.

In many ways, Mayumi represented the type of young consumerist Japanese woman who spends thousands of dollars every month accessorizing herself, and that was why I had stopped her. Like many Japanese her age, she told me she had a boyfriend and that she hoped to marry by age twenty-four. (In Japan, twenty-four is traditionally the cutoff for being called the equivalent of "old maid" or "Christmas Cake," due to a perceived expiration date of the 25th—day in the case of Christmas and year in the case of women.) Then she would have children and quit working. It was, in Japanese society, what good girls are supposed to say. But, when I asked her whether her expectations of life were typical of Japanese women, she balked. "I disagree with stereotypes," she said, tossing her head. "*Junin toiro!*"

As she walked away, high heels clicking, my interpreter struggled to translate. "It's a Japanese expression that literally means, 'Ten people, ten colors,'" she explained. "Maybe you could translate it as, 'Many people, many minds'?" The profundity of this toss-away phrase from a twenty-one-year-old fashion queen began to sink in. What if, in fact, people were so diverse and unique that, even if they behaved in ways according to societal convention, they, like this fashionable young woman, defied characterization? Trained in the British tradition of social anthropology, I hesitated a long while before coming to such a conclusion. After all, anthropology is a time-tested discipline that originated with Englishmen hiding behind the bushes of colonial Africa and describing the practices of the "savages" they saw. By its very nature, it seeks to characterize people as a group by their behaviors.

But what if, in our modernized world that has created skyscrapers, middle classes, and office workers where only farmers or factory workers labored before, cultural practices now matter much less than individual character? With the world connected by Internet, TV, and telephone; with Toyota sedans in the middle-class driveways of Asia, Starbucks and TGI Friday's in Jakarta, Pret A Manger counters in Tokyo, Thai restaurants in Milwaukee and Raleigh, sushi in the American heartland, and McDonald's and KFCs absolutely everywhere, how different are we, really?

Instead of Japanese women or Chinese women or Javanese women or Thai women having unique characteristics along their own ethnic or national lines, it seems more accurate to say that there are types of women in every society, both East and West, who have more in common with each other than with their fellow countrywomen. There are those with mean streaks or altruistic tendencies; the flighty or the serious; those who are content to be good, nurturing mothers or those who would rather have high-flying careers. The list goes on. There may well be national characteristics as to how people in a culture behave as a group, but as an individual, the field is wide open. A young professional living in a high-rise apartment in Beijing has more in common with a young professional living in a high-rise in New York than with a Chinese farm worker on the outskirts of her own city. The Chinese women may speak the same language, share the same customs of respecting the elderly and preferring a male heir, enjoy the same kind of tofu and steamed buns, etc., but at heart, the hopes, needs, and desires of the urban, educated, ambitious resident of one modern city are much the same as in the next.

But the reason we have stereotypes is because they're partly true," I have been told, not just once but dozens of times by Western men with experiences in Asia. Yes, there are traditions in Asia, such as Confucianism, foot-binding, bride burning, and the like, that have helped form our notions of Asian women as "oppressed." To this day, societal factors such as lack of education, lack of affordable child care, and prejudice against women managers keep many Asian women from advancing in the work force. But, to be fair, women in the United States and Europe also face institutionalized sexism, as evidenced by the enormous class action suit by women refused advancement by Wal-Mart, or the multi-million-dollar sex discrimination settlements by large Wall Street firms that currently employ women in only one out of five executive management positions. In Asia, it's much the same story. Sex discrimination exists there, too. But Asian women also run major companies, as is shown later in these pages. They run more than half of all registered businesses in Thailand and the Philippines. Women in Asia who want successful careers—and who have the means for and access to education (and not all do, of course)—are able to have them. The Philippines has more women than men in the civil service, and it has more women elected to national public office than does the United States. Even Japan has close to the same ratio of women governors as the United States—four out of forty-seven, compared to six out of fifty. Thus, the stereotypes we still hold are based on old notions preserved, as if in aspic, by limited contact between East and West.

Then there is the issue of superficial cultural practices that contribute to the stereotypes, seen most clearly in interactions between Western men and Asian women. A number of Asian women say, explicitly, that their tactics (not their inner selves or core values) are different from Western women when it comes to male-female relations. It can be summed up, crudely, as something like, "Catch them first, reveal yourself later." Here is how a Japanese friend who had lived for a time in the United States explained it. We were having lunch one day in the top-floor restaurant of the Grand Hyatt Tokyo, enjoying the same view depicted in the bar scenes in the movie *Lost in Translation*. She told me that she would not disagree with a man for perhaps as long as three years into a relationship.

I know Western men who marry Asian women and later find out the woman is boss. They thought that the women were going to be serving them! If they go out with Asian women for a long period of time, maybe more than three years, they will start to know they [the women] have guts. They try to get some power, but not until then. Control takes time. The typical way that Western people perceive from looking outside is seeing only the superficial, the outside package of Japanese women. If you are a Western man and you go out with an Asian woman for maybe a month to six months, they wouldn't show themselves. You wouldn't know. They would be hiding. Really. It takes time for them to reveal. It's very cultural, I think. We are educated to have our opinion not to come to the front. We go with the group idea. On the surface, if you are an American man going out with Japanese women, I think you will feel, "She let me decide. Yeah, she let me do that. . . ." Maybe it's boring sometimes for some men. She wouldn't be too insistent on her ideas. So you feel, "Oh, how great. I can be a leader." But after a while, she is just human, same as all the American women. She will show whatever is inside, and that's when maybe the home conflict happens. Or that's when maybe they will think, "I had a different thought about Japanese women or about Asian women." But not until much later.

And it's not just the men who may end up disillusioned, as shown in subsequent chapters. Sometimes, Asian women who think they are marrying a "more liberal" Western man end up clashing with that Western man's expectations of having married a "more traditional" Asian woman. And marrying a Westerner—as desirable as it has been to hundreds of thousands of poor Asian women as their societies have strived to develop and modernize over the last century—is no longer as widespread a golden dream as it once was.

Once, at a Sichuan restaurant with a group of young professional Chinese in Guangzhou—a city of ten million that used to be called Canton and had several centuries of experience with Western settlers—the women expressed disdain at the idea of marrying an Englishman or American. After all, the urban standard of living is high in China now. Anybody who is anybody has domestic help. "If you marry a foreigner, you have to clean your own house and raise your children by yourself!" one of the women at dinner scoffed. "Only poor girls from the country are interested in foreigners." Plus, another woman interjected, white guys who hang around in China without real jobs looking all googly-eyed at Chinese women (she made a face with her eyes crossed and tongue sticking out) are really just "losers" back in their own countries anyway. Not surprisingly, even though several of these women had been educated in Britain and the United States, they chose Chinese men as husbands.

Some Asian women even believe the stereotypes to be reversed. Clara Chun Yu Ok, a famous Korean social commentator, author of eight books, and feminist, is one of them. She had lived in the United States as the first female Korean network TV correspondent posted abroad, and had formed an opinion while there. "I think Western women are far more submissive and more passive than Asian women," she told me when I met her in Seoul. "They work hard and have a strong will, but American culture is so conservative and family oriented. They are always thinking about what kind of man they have. That's what they talk about," she said. "For an Asian woman, her highest value in life is *not* a man, it is a child, or responsibility for family or society. But *not* a man. She's more independent than Western women in some sense. We have experienced tough things throughout history, so Asian women are tough."

"Orient" versus Asia

In geographic scope, "the Orient" has come to be defined through Western conception as the Asian countries of the Pacific Rim: East Asia (China, Japan, Korea, and Taiwan), and Southeast Asia (Vietnam, Thailand, Singapore, the Philippines, Malaysia, Laos, Indonesia, Cambodia, Burma, and Brunei). The ancient division of the world into East and West had previously defined "the Orient" as also including the Middle East, South Asia, and Central Asia, whose populations are predominantly Islamic and Hindu. It began to change in conventional parlance, more or less, after the nineteenth century, as a result of the Franco-British colonial expansion. Victorian England's tea, roses, and spices, which were imported from India, were Oriental. Later, the Biblical lands and India—because of their own unique religious and ethnic characters that we began to see as distinct through colonial contact—needed their own differentiations, narrowing the conception of "Oriental" to those cultures predominantly descended from Buddhist traditions.

Nonetheless, several countries remaining in the current conception of "Orient" do have Muslim populations. Indonesia, in fact, is the most populous Muslim-majority nation on earth, plus there's Muslim-majority Malaysia and Brunei. Parts of Thailand, the Philippines, Vietnam, China, and Cambodia all have Muslim communities, some of which continue to agitate for separatism. The Islam practiced in the Southeast Asian context is generally more liberal than that in the Arab world, and is influenced by more moderate cultural factors. There is one majority Christian nation as well, the Philippines, and there are large Christian minority groups wherever Catholic and Protestant missionaries did battle for converts in the colonial era: in Vietnam, Indonesia, Singapore, South Korea and, to some extent, China. Not to leave out Hinduism, plantation workers brought by British masters to colonial Malaya left ethnic Indian communities in the two countries that sprang from it, Malaysia and Singapore. The island of Bali, in the middle of the Indonesian island chain, is majority Hindu, too. If you look hard, you can find tiny communities of Jains, Jews, and Zoroasters in Asia's port cities, the descendants of merchant traders of long ago.

Because of this rich religious diversity, a more accurate way of dividing Asia would be into "Sinicized" and "Indianized"—influenced by the people of China and Buddhist/Confucian traditions, versus influenced by the people of India and Hindu/Buddhist/Muslim traditions. That would draw a dividing line, more less, between Vietnam (Sinicized) and every Asian country to its north, and Cambodia (Indianized) and every Asian country to its south and west, and including the Philippines. That means Japanese, Chinese, Vietnamese, and Korean people on one side, and Cambodian, Thai, Laotian, Burmese, Filipino, Indonesian, and Malay people on the other. Some scholars attribute the historical fractiousness of the Cambodian-Vietnamese border to this Sinicized Asia versus Indianized Asia division. Singapore, a tiny Sinicized piece of territory in an Indianized region, became a separate country after race riots due to this tension.

Such distinctions, however, came late to our concept of "Orient." Our Western construction puts a Thai woman into the same category as a Vietnamese, an Indonesian into the same category as a Filipina. In our eyes, no matter how different in religion or tradition, they are all "Oriental" or "Asian." And even that is not universal in the English language. "Asian" in Britain generally means someone of South Asian origin first (Indian, Pakistani, or Bangladeshi) and East Asian origin second; in the American context we tend to think of East Asians as "Asian" first before realizing that the word also includes South Asians as well.

It is only recently that Western cultures have begun to distinguish between Asian cultures at all. We were forced to in 1982 after the killing of Vincent Chin, a tragedy shocking in its lack of ethnic distinction. Chin, a Chinese-American, was beaten to death in Detroit by angry auto workers who shouted that "Japs" were taking all the jobs.

Now, the proliferation of sushi throughout the United States and western Europe in recent years has helped to increase the distinction between Japanese and Chinese food in the Western conception. Where the stomach goes first, the mind sometimes follows. The distinctions don't extend far, however, as this dialog on the Fox Network cartoon comedy *King of the Hill* illustrates.

HANK: So are ya Chineeese or Japaneeese
KAHN: I am from Laos, you stupid redneck!
HANK AND FRIENDS: (silence)
KAHN: You know, LAOS! East of Vietnam, north of Cambodia, west of Thailand.
HANK AND FRIENDS: (silence)
KAHN: I'm *Lay-Oh-Shun!*
HANK: OKAY! So are you Chineeese or Japaneeese?

On the other hand, the fact that this joke even exists may be evidence of changing perceptions. As we begin examining where our perceptions came from and why they are so firmly entrenched in our consciousness, it is useful to maintain an awareness of our constructed prisms—the ones we use to see Asian people as alike; the ones we use to make judgments about a Thai economist and her British husband;

the ones we use to insist that the stereotypes about Asian women are true; and the ones we use to indulge in wide-eyed exultations of "the East" through the dancers at the girlie bars of Bangkok. We will examine the facets of the Asian Mystique, and watch them slowly fade away. To do so requires that we start at the beginning, when West first met East.

Mystery, Sex, Fear, and Desire:

A Brief History

MYSTERY AND SEX, FEAR, AND DESIRE. It is how we have written about, thought about, and conceived of the East for much of our 2,500 years of recorded contact. The "Orient" has always meant lands far away, full of opulence and sensuality, danger, depravity, and opportunity. The West has sought to understand Asia within this context since the time of the ancient Greeks. Whether we know this history or not, we are all the recipients of received cultural perceptions that affect how we think, what we think, and what we think we know.

China's Empress Dowager was a victim of this perception—of one of the most extensive hoaxes, slander, and libel campaigns ever committed in the history of the world. It is worth examining her story because it is one of the clearest examples we have of how the Asian Mystique worked to distort history and how that distortion caused a ripple-effect of distortions forever after. It is because of the empress, Tzu Hsi, that we think "Dragon Lady" in association with Asian women who wield power. Her name means "Empress of the West," because she lived in the pavilions on the west side of the Forbidden City in Beijing. She is why the image of "Dragon Lady" even exists in our consciousness—and it is not even her fault.

In fact, historians writing after her death in 1908 determined that she was an admirable and sympathetic woman about five feet tall, slim, strikingly pretty and well-proportioned, with delicate hands, arched eyebrows, a high nose, full-well shaped lips, a stunning smile, and a "sweet feminine voice." She was fond of flattery, pretty clothes, Pekingese dogs, and chrysanthemums.[1] Solitary and pensive, Tzu Hsi's nature was to remain private. As a Buddhist, she consciously tried to emulate the Buddha's serene watchfulness. For this reason, the Chinese members of her court called her, with affection, "Old Buddha." She was, as Sterling Seagrave writes in his meticulously researched biography *Dragon Lady: The Life and Legend of the Last Empress of China,* much like Queen Victoria, who, while in power at the same time, earned none of the condemnation that was heaped on the Empress Dowager in the pages of history. Seagrave writes:

> Even now, [the] reptilian image of the Empress Dowager is difficult to shake because it provides a satisfying justification for Western actions in China during the nineteenth and early twentieth centuries, actions that otherwise look foolish or outrageous. . . . She lived in a world of conspiracy and poisonings and forced suicides, but a careful reexamination of the evidence shows that she did not commit any of them.

So, what happened? How did this pleasant, serene woman leave a ghastly legacy so evil and vicious that it affects our stereotypes and images of Asian women today?

The empress was a victim of not only political shenanigans, but of Western pornographic fiction passed off as fact by a charlatan. Invented accounts of her life written after her death were full of scandal, sex, and evil presented in convincing detail and held to be true for decades. When Oxford University Professor Hugh Trevor-Roper looked into the matter and exposed this deceit in 1974, even his unmasking referred to the empress in the same dark terms coined in the fictional works. "The con man had been exposed, but his counterfeit material was still bedrock scholarship," writes Seagrave. But Seagrave's own book, because of its *Dragon Lady* title, plays its part in keeping up the fiction, despite refuting the myth. Clearly, it's too late. The image of the Dragon Lady is indelible.

AT SIXTEEN, the pleasant and well-mannered woman, known then as Lady Yehenara, was chosen to be one of the many concubines of the Manchu Emperor. For a two-month period of her life, when she was twenty years old, she became his favorite concubine and then bore him a son. Even though he discarded her after that, being mother to an heir made her the most powerful member of the imperial household after the emperor's death. Because the Forbidden City was off limits to foreigners as well as to ordinary Chinese, we in the West knew almost nothing about the empress until 1898, when she was already sixty-three.

That year, the Empress Dowager—as any monarch would have—cracked down on a group of political reformers including a radical called Kang Yu-wei who escaped to Japan. Some British journalists who were based in Beijing were on friendly terms with Kang, whom history later judged a mere self-promoter with few ideas. The journalists, as well as a few missionary activists who believed Kang to be a proponent of American-style democracy, started promoting him as a hero.

From exile, Kang became an early twentieth-century Ahmed Chalabi, promoting his agenda to unseat the Manchu regime through the press, while having little evidence behind his assertions. He insisted that the empress was an "evil hag" who was keeping the young emperor imprisoned and plied with drugs and alcohol while she plotted to get rid of him. He said she looted the imperial treasury. And Kang also claimed that the chief imperial eunuch still had his "manhood," and was one of a multitude of lovers and co-conspirators. He called the empress a "depraved palace concubine," and a murderer.

Correspondents from the *Times* of London printed these assertions, and then began using words such as "that awful old harridan," accusing her of poisoning, strangling, beheading, or forcing the suicide of anyone who would challenge her rule.[2] In reality, the empress was simply avoiding needed reforms that she eventually was forced to implement anyway; and by the time she did, the Manchu Dynasty was so weakened that it was on the brink of collapse.

The terrible Boxer siege of the Peking foreign legion in 1900, during which foreigners were erroneously reported (by *The New York Times*) to have been boiled in oil as well as massacred en masse, was blamed on the empress.[3] But, in retrospect, "it was actually provoked by the bullying and hysterical behavior of Westerners who shot hundreds of Chinese civilians, imperial soldiers and mandarins *before* the siege began and brought the consequences down upon their own heads." One of those same *Times* of London correspondents reported a version of the siege—reprinted all over the world—that omitted these details, as well as worse acts perpetrated by foreigners and blamed on the Chinese; they were later found in his private diary.[4]

But that's not the full extent.

The next crime of history was carried out by the pornographic charlatan Edmund Blackhouse. He was a linguist, fluent in both Mandarin and Manchu, who teamed up with one of the *Times* of London correspondents to write two books, in 1910, two years after the death of Tzu Hsi, and in 1914, as the weakened post-empress regime was in collapse and civil war spread throughout the country. Blackhouse claimed to have uncovered court archives that confirmed that the empress was a wicked degenerate who disposed of rivals with poisoned cakes and kept false eunuchs behind the walls of the Forbidden City for her sexual pleasure, as the dissident Kang had falsely asserted.

In his subsequent memoirs in 1943, *Decadence Mandchoue,* Blackhouse went even further. He claimed to have had a six-year affair with the empress—when he was twenty-nine and she was already sixty-seven—and that it included perhaps 200 sexual encounters with her. He writes of accompanying her, in disguise, to a homosexual brothel where she commanded him to have sex with men, as he said he had boasted to her of doing innumerable times, for her amusement. On another occasion at the Summer Palace, he writes, the Grand Eunuch Li confided that the Dowager has

> an abnormally large clitoris, which she was in the habit of rubbing on the anus of her partner. . . . Li anointed my secret parts [with sandalwood oil, then] accompanied me to the phoenix couch, and the Empress exclaimed: "My bed is cold . . . now exhibit to me your genitals for I know I shall love them."

Blackhouse described being required to perform oral sex on the elderly woman, and of her inserting her fingers into his anus.[5]

England was just coming out of the Victorian era, after all, and libidinous conduct was still the stuff of forbidden fantasies. Blackhouse claimed that court eunuchs obtained sexual gratification from ducks, and that ladies of the court enjoyed having their private parts licked by dogs. He writes that the empress once told him, "You are now permitted to have me, but just before you are coming let me know. I want you to take your tool out and put it in my mouth, so that I may swallow the semen and thus enjoy a tonic." He claims that she said his semen tasted sour, adding, "Don't apologize. I like it and enjoy the tart flavor."[6]

Blackhouse's account gets more fantastical when he writes of a visit to the empress's tomb, after its looting by Nationalist Chinese troops in 1928 (twenty years after her death). He claims that he could see her "once beautiful pudenda [genitalia] which I had formerly, to her pleasure and my own, so playfully fondled . . . displayed before us in their full sacrilegious nudity, the pubic hair still abundant." Yes, twenty years after she died. He adds that he heroically "covered up Her Majesty's secret parts from the gaze of the vulgar."[7] The book was a sensation in England.

We didn't have to believe these fabrications. After the Boxer Rebellion of 1900, a number of books and magazine articles written by the women residents of Beijing appeared. American artist Katherine Carl, the missionary Sarah Conger, and the British First Secretary's wife Lady Susan Townley all had met the empress on more than one occasion, were favorably impressed, and recorded as much. But "the verdict of male reviewers has been that these appraisals were 'uninformed' and trivial," Seagrave concludes. The women's accounts were simply ignored, swept away by the fashion of casting the Empress Dowager as an evil relic of the depraved, imperial past in a country that was then, temporarily, a new republic. Historians of the early twentieth century instead relied on Blackhouse's falsified accounts, and then cited each other, creating a web of falsehood that passed as scholarship for decades.

The fall of the decadent Manchu empire had to be blamed on someone. While it was largely the fault of the feckless emperor, who indulged himself with various women of the palace and spent little time governing properly, Tzu Hsi was his last surviving wife or concubine, and she was guilty only of being resistant to change.

"What caught Western fancy was the idea that the emperor of China had been made witless by too much fornication, so any woman who participated must be depraved," Seagrave writes. "The sad truth is that [the emperor] needed no help falling apart." And the even sadder truth is that we made the reputation of the empress pay for it.

In yet another example of likely distorted history, Empress Wu Zetian made her rise to power in China by becoming the favorite concubine of a Tang Dynasty emperor at age fourteen. After he died, she became that of his married son, whose wife she then eliminated by accusing her (falsely) of killing her baby daughter. This empress created secret police to spy on her opposition and cruelly jailed or eliminated anyone in her way. But that's only the version of history we know now. As we can see from the fabrications of the Empress Dowager, who knows what really happened. The "official" histories of Empress Wu, many of which are conflicting, were not written until 300 years after her death—by Confucians who did not believe women had the right to rule. So, what we know of her in the West is selectively translated salacious commentary from the Confucians' works.

Additionally, as it turns out, eight women have occupied the Chrysanthemum Throne of Japan throughout history but, because their stories never resulted in widely translated tales of murder, sex, and intrigue, their names, unlike Empress Wu and the Empress Dowager of China, are unrecognizable to those in the West.

The myths have persisted because it is easy for the Western mind to imagine Asian women with power as decadent, sexually depraved, and fear-inspiring. We have been doing it ever since Aphrodite. Of course, powerful Western women do not easily escape "witch-ification" either, witness Margaret Thatcher and Hillary Clinton. But what is different about Asian women is the sexual component, and it is due to our history.

Aphrodite, the powerful goddess of the ancient Greeks, was modeled on the Whore of Babylon (her origins in the cults of Ishtar of the Assyrians and Babylonians, and Astarte of the Phoenicians)—making her of "Oriental" origin. The Greeks worshipped her as the goddess of love, beauty, sex appeal, and fertility, and depicted her naked or scantily clad (Botticelli's painting "The Birth of Venus" was inspired by the cult of Aphrodite, and technically the "Venus de Milo" statue in the Louvre museum also is Aphrodite); she sparked the Trojan War in order to win a beauty contest; she was the patron goddess of prostitutes. She was the first to transmit to the Europeans the "idea of the Orient as female, voluptuous, decadent, amoral—in short as dangerously seductive," writes Ian Buruma in *The Missionary and the Libertine*. "There has been a sensual, even erotic element in encounters—imaginary or real—between East and West since the ancient Greeks."

The merchants of ancient Rome discovered the sensual mysteries of luxury goods—fabrics, fragrances, and exotic spices—traded along the perilous Silk Route to ancient Cathay. Traders were mystified, for example, by the marvelously strong and luxurious cloth called silk until the eggs of the mulberry tree moth were smuggled back to Rome in the sixth century. The already precarious sea and land routes to China were by then becoming effectively barred to Western traders due to the rise of Islam and the violence that accompanied it; and in 878, China closed its doors to all foreigners, to remain secret and mysterious for centuries.[8]

It wasn't until the thirteenth century that trade resumed, and Marco Polo headed off, returning to Europe in 1295 with breathless, fantastical tales of a land of freely available sex. In households along the Silk Route, he reports, "They give positive orders to their wives, daughters, sisters, and other female relations, to indulge their guests every wish, whist they themselves leave their homes and retire into the city, and the stranger lives in the house with the females as if they were his own wives."[9]

In Beijing, where Kublai Khan was holding power, Polo writes, "the Great Khan sends thither his officers who collect for him 100 or more of the handsomest of the young women, according to the estimation of beauty communicated to them in their instructions." After being ranked according to beauty and having the less attractive women weeded out,

> they are divided into parties of five, each taking turn for three days and three nights, in his majesty's interior apartment, where they are to perform every service that is required of them, and he does with them as he likes. When this term is completed, they are relieved by another party, and in this manner successively, until the whole number have taken their turn; when the first five recommence their attendance.[10]

Outside the palace walls in Beijing, Polo writes, "The number of public women who prostitute themselves for money, reckoning those

in the new city as well as those in the suburbs of the old, is 25,000."
Of Kin-sai, south of Soochow, he writes:

> These women [courtesans] are accomplished and are perfect in the
> arts of caressing and fondling which they accompany with expres-
> sions adapted to every description of person. Strangers who have
> once tasted of their charms remain in a state of fascination and be-
> come so enchanted by their wanton arts, that they can never forget
> the impression. Thus intoxicated with sensual pleasures, when they
> return to their homes they report that they have been in Kin-Sai, or
> The Celestial City, and look forward to the time when they may be
> enabled to revisit this paradise.[11]

And of Tibet, he writes:

> A scandalous custom, which could only proceed from the blindness
> of idolatry, prevails amongst the people of these parts, who are dis-
> inclined to marry young women so long as they are in their virgin
> state, but require, on the contrary, that they should have had previ-
> ous commerce with many of the other sex. This, they assert, is
> pleasing to their deities and believe that a woman who has not had
> the company of men is worthless.[12]

Marco Polo leaves unclear whether he partook of any of this wanton
behavior himself—as, oddly, he never once noted that Chinese women
of the time had bound feet. It is likely that he met other travelers
along the Silk Route and, as traveler's tales have done from time im-
memorial, they recounted overstated, inflated versions that captured
the European's thirst for the exotic, sexual, and mysterious.

Polo's words had influence. Writers such as Chaucer and Dante
drew upon Polo's works to depict "ladies and damsels who dallied
with them to their hearts' content." After reading Polo's account,
Christopher Columbus jotted the words, "They do not want wives
save from among the women who have already had intercourse," and
that "men offer their wives and their daughters to passing travelers."[13]

It was from a Franciscan Friar, who spent three years in Beijing in
the early 1300s, that we learned of Chinese women binding their feet

and mandarins growing their fingernails to extravagant lengths. But in the middle of that century, the hugely popular *Travels,* by Sir John Mandeville, originally in French and translated into ten languages, "played a leading role in consolidating the fabulous myth of Cathay."[14] The tales were cobbled together from a variety of unreliable sources, and made such claims as that the Orient was at the center of an archipelago inhabited by sea monsters, some with ears down to their knees, some headless, and some with pendulous lips. Because the Far East closed again in 1368, during the xenophobic reign of the Ming Dynasty, no one was able to refute this nonsense. The peril-fraught *Travels,* along with Marco Polo's accounts of the sexually available women of Cathay, became the authoritative accounts of the East for the next 200 years of Renaissance Europe.[15]

Immorality and Condemnation

When the East opened again in the sixteenth century, traveling missionaries spreading Christianity added to the dual mystiques of sex and danger. The first missionaries to reach China were brutally tortured and executed, and some were persecuted in Japan as well, lending to the reputation of the savage East that had to be brought under Western influence and civilized. The Jesuit Matteo Ricci, the first Westerner to reach grudging acceptance by the Chinese and to really learn the language, set up in Macau and then Canton in the 1580s. He lauded foot-binding for keeping Chinese women chastely at home, and noted that the difficulties of learning classical Chinese curbed "youthful licentiousness" among Chinese men who, he said, were too much prone to homosexual practice. Elaborately dressed male prostitutes prowled the streets of Beijing, along with another 40,000 female prostitutes, he reported when he relocated there in 1601. "This people is really to be pitied rather than censured," he concludes.[16]

The Spanish, however, who had conquered the Philippines in 1565, did have censure in mind. Before they arrived, Philippine women had had the right to inherit property, keep their names upon marriage, and divorce for any reason. The pre-Christian Philippine creation myth held that men and women were created by splitting bamboo into two equal parts, assigning women neither physical nor intellectual weakness, nor inferiority. Women healers and priestesses, called Babaylan, held high positions of leadership in society, and they were deemed most powerful when they were both beautiful and sexually experienced.

The Spanish Civil Code instead gave husbands absolute authority over wives, banned women's property inheritance, and allowed divorce only if a husband abused his wife or if his adultery caused her public scandal or disgrace. (The Code also banned polygamy.) The Spanish denounced the powerful, sexual Babaylan women as witches, forcing them into nunneries where they had to sleep on their sides, covered, and facing the wall so that "the devil could not rape them," and bathe at least partially clothed at all times.[17] This attempt to bring the "immoral" women of the East into line with Christianity through more than 300 years of Spanish rule was not limited to the Babaylan. "Women, you ought to dress yourself in mourning or rags, representing yourself as a penitent bathed in tears, redeeming thus the fault of having ruined the human race," seventeenth-century Catholic priest Father Tertullian admonished all Philippine women. "You are the door of hell; you corrupt him whom the devil dare not approach."[18]

Perhaps that is because European explorers and traders were out discovering the carnal pleasures of Asia themselves. Dutch merchants on their way to Japan who landed in what is now southern Thailand—then the Islamic kingdom of Pattani, where an elderly water buffalo–hunting woman ruled as queen—found that unmarried young women were commonly offered to strangers to do household service by day "and other offices at night."[19] Upon reaching Japan, explorers found the kimono-clad prostitutes who boarded their ships offshore "very frollicke," but were not fond of the Japanese custom of women blackening their teeth as part of their beauty regimen.

English explorers attempted to charge through Thailand toward the remote kingdom of Luang Prabang (the old imperial capital of modern-day Laos)—"where they live like wild men and eat men's flesh and marke their bodies with hot iron"—according to Dutchman John Huyghen van Lindshoten, who was writing from Goa, in India, and who reported on these imagined dangers without ever having been there.

And, while those Englishmen never made it, Ralph Fitch among them did write in 1582 that the sexual customs of Siamese men in-volved sewing metal balls under the skin of their penises to give them a rough texture, and that "the women do desire" such a thing.[20] Men in Borneo, Bali, and the Philippines also inserted bone, metal, or bam-boo into holes pierced into their penises—to the preference of local women who inserted first one end of the spur and then the other while the penis was still limp and then could not withdraw until it was limp again—as the prudish Spanish were aghast to learn during close en-counters with Filipinas. The women were adamantly opposed to the reforms that Catholic missionaries tried to impose on their sexual practices. (The insertion of ball bearings under the skin of the penis is still practiced in the Philippines.) Colonialists all over Asia endeav-ored to stamp out the rural custom of older women who, past child-bearing age, were no longer considered sexual and went topless. (This practice continued for centuries, however. I observed an elderly Cam-bodian woman walking around her rural village topless in 1991. A friend reported seeing an elderly topless Chinese woman even in urban Beijing in 1985.)

As TRADERS, EXPLORERS, AND MISSIONARIES gave way to the European colonialists, sex was an important factor of East-West con-tact. William Adams, an Englishman shipwrecked in Japan in the early 1600s (and depicted in the novel and miniseries *Shogun*), became the first westerner ever to take a Japanese wife. He was the last for more than 200 years as the Japanese—fed up with scheming mission-aries whom they judged rightly to be the forebearers of colonialism—kicked out the Europeans entirely and barred them from coming ashore. Commodore Matthew Perry penetrated the isolated island again and forcibly opened it to trade in 1853. (Perry's sailors, like Dutch traders two centuries before, were provided with special "pleas-ure quarters" so that they would not contaminate the female popula-tion of Japan.) Syphilis—or "Canton sores"—was introduced to China in the 1640s via prostitutes who were then restricted to servicing white men in Canton (now Guangzhou), the port city of the Pearl River delta that served as the entryway to South China before there was a Hong Kong.

Ian Buruma writes:

People forget what a sexual, even sexy, enterprise colonialism was—
and I don't mean just metaphorically, in the sense of the virile West
penetrating the passive, feminine East. No, colonial life was quite
literally drenched in sex. . . . White men would enter the kampongs
and take their pleasure with native girls for a few coins, or even for
nothing if the men were cheap and caddish enough.[21]

Thus, for a young European man, heading out to the colonies provided a "sunny, pagan, hedonistic alternative to the cold, pinched and
dreary climate of the Christian, especially Protestant, West."[22]

The English discovered tea and roses in India in the 1700s, and
brought these Oriental items back home to a huge sensation. The far-
away exotic worlds imagined from little people and landscapes on lacquer screens and porcelain teacups brought from China captured the
imagination of all Europe, and chinoiserie became the fashion in the
eighteenth-century French court, where it blended with the decorative
Rococo, before spreading to England, Italy, and Russia as well. Enthusiasm for Chinese objects infused nearly every decorative art—furniture, tapestries, and wallpaper, decorated with fanciful motifs of tiny
gardens, human figures, pagodas, intricate lattices, and exotic birds
and flowers. Tending Chinese gardens and building replicas of tea
pavilions in the backyard (or at London's Kew Gardens) became all the
rage among the wealthy. The Orient had come to mean luxury, refinement, and abundance in the highest quarters of European society, and
the craze spread via the British to the American colonies, too.

When, in 1787, Monsignor Pierre Pigneau de Behaine returned to
France after extraordinary adventures in a remote land then known as
Cochinchina (now Vietnam), he dazzled the Louis XVI court at Ver-
sailles with Nguyen Canh, the seven-year-old son of a pretender to the
throne of Vietnam. Queen Marie Antoinette allowed the charming little prince, dressed in red and gold brocade, to play with the Dauphin,
the heir apparent. The missionary was lobbying for an ambitious
scheme—to create, under French auspices, a Christian empire in
Asia—and he propelled France toward its conquest of Indochina a

hundred years later.[23] With an adorable child dressed in prissy finery as its representation, Vietnam would seem an easy conquest.

In 1819, French writers characterizing Vietnam's Emperor Minh Mang (who spurned the first American trying to trade with Vietnam in 1820, fearing domination) called him "a gentle, almost effeminate scholar." French missionaries made great inroads into Vietnam under his reign. His successor, Tu Duc, in 1847, was "refined and distinguished," with "delicate hands" and black eyes of "remarkable profundity." His leniency toward Catholic missionaries and his tactics of avoiding confrontation led France to believe its military could conquer Vietnam should it invade. France did, and the defeated Tu Duc surrendered Vietnam to a French protectorate. This history set the stage for France's later colonial conception of "a sexualized and feminized Indochina"[24]—a grouping of the distinct cultures of Vietnam, Laos, and Cambodia that have virtually nothing in common except geography and the nominal practice of Buddhism (albeit in different forms)—that would continue even with the defeat at Dien Bien Phu.

As the colonial empires expanded, the mystique continued to grow even as colonial emissaries found their movements and contact with "the natives" limited.

> As the port of Canton is the only one at which the Outer Barbarians are permitted to trade, on no account can they be permitted to wander and visit other places in the Middle Kingdom.[25]
> —Imperial edict of 1836

Even within Canton, merchants were not permitted beyond the factories or allowed to live outside the small island of Shamian on the Pearl River, which was connected by bridge to the rest of Canton. The few Chinese permitted to deal with the Outer Barbarians were forbidden to teach them Chinese or have any unnecessarily dealings. A young American employed by the U.S. trading firm Russell & Co., reported being entranced by his first glimpse of a Chinese garden's artificial lakes, pavilions, and fruit trees, and when he caught a glimpse of women in one Chinese household "with their gowns of embroidered plum, pink and pea green silks" he recalled being impressed by their "black eyes, splendid eyebrows and teeth of ivory whiteness, and hair coiled and dressed with ornaments."[26]

The Opium Wars opened five treaty ports to European merchants and settlers in 1842, Amoy (Xiamen), Foochow (Fuzhou), Ningpo (Ningbo), Canton (Guangzhou), and Shanghai, and also ceded Hong Kong to Britain. The growing colonial expansion, in China, India, and throughout Southeast Asia, increased the availability of rose, jasmine, cinnamon, ylang ylang, chrysanthemum, bergamot, sandalwood, and other scents of the Orient at the same time that alchemy turned into chemistry and vapor distillation created bottling—resulting in the transformation of the French perfume industry into a large commercial enterprise. The discovery of musk from a Chinese deer sent the perfumery houses of Paris chasing up China's Yangtze River in search of exotic new flora and fauna.

At the same time, the Americans forcibly opened Japan, prompting a new Western fascination with "Japonisme" and geisha, much as chinoiserie had been all the rage a century before. The growing middle class in Paris eagerly bought up Japanese fans, lacquered boxes, hanging scrolls, ceramics, and other items from a curio ship called *Le Port Chinoise* that opened in 1862 near the Louvre, and these objects appeared as props in Impressionist paintings of the era. Claude Monet painted *La Japonaise,* a life-size portrait of his blonde wife in a lavish kimono and holding a fan in 1876; Japanese woodblock prints influenced the compositions of Henri de Toulouse Lautrec. Gilbert and Sullivan's *The Mikado,* which uses Japan as a backdrop, was inspired by a Japanese sword on the wall of Gilbert's study. The show opened just as a Japanese Village exposition was drawing crowds and causing an all-things-Japanese sensation in London. The antics of Nanki-poo, Ko-Ko, and Yum-Yum poking fun at pomposity played to packed houses in London in more than 1,000 performances over eleven years starting in 1885; by 1886 there were 170 separate performances being staged simultaneously across North America. A pin-up that same year of the show's popular American star Marie Lloyd showed her dressed in Western notions of "geisha" in a red long-sleeved kimono open like a coat, waving a fan, with pins in her hair and an enormous bow on her back. The chorus to her song was inscribed beneath the picture:

Every little Jappy chappie's gone upon the Geisha
Trickiest little Geisha ever seen in Asia!
I've made things hum a bit you, since I became a Geisha,
Japanesey, free and easy Tea house girl![27]

Japan's star geisha Madame Sadayakko toured Europe and the
United States to grand fascination in the late 1890s: Pablo Picasso
painted her in France; the Prince of Wales requested a command performance on a specially built Japanese stage inside Buckingham
Palace in England; and President William McKinley commandeered
box seats to see her in Washington, DC. Having Japan represented on
the world stage by a mere low-class actress and geisha, however, was a
big scandal back home in Tokyo.[28]

Worlds Apart, Bodies Together

Back in China, even newly allowed mingling between foreigners and
the "natives" did not necessarily ensure social intercourse; sexual intercourse was another matter entirely.

French and British residents of Shanghai dealt with Cantonese compradors who had moved north to set up in that city—which was becoming known as Asia's "Sin City" and "The Paris of the East."
Contact with any Chinese other than compradors was in the form of
houseboys, laundresses, stable hands, cooks, amahs, gardeners, waiters,
and porters. Europeans, then, had nothing to do with the life of everyday Shanghainese, with one exception: mistresses. Stella Dong, in the
marvelous account of *Shanghai: The Rise and Fall of a Decadent City*,
writes:

Shanghai at this time had so few European women that the ratio of
men to women in the Western colony never sank below ten to one.
It had yet to acquire the opulent bordellos specializing in recruits
from San Francisco that it would later boast, nor had it yet become a
happy hunting ground for unmarried Western women. . . . Owing
to the dearth of foreign females, many of the foreign bachelors—

and not a few married men with wives back home—took a Chinese mistress. Mistresses were often disguised as "maids," but were always young and attractive.

These sexual relationships across East-West lines were not ones of equals and only infrequently led to marriage. Dong also writes:

> When [marriages] did take place, the unions were regarded with horror by both whites and Chinese. To ensure that such marriages occurred as seldom as possible, nearly all British assistants had contracts that did not permit them to marry until after they had served five years in China. It became customary for these bachelors to find brides in England during a "home leave," and to send for them at the end of the five-year moratorium on marriage. So widespread was the practice of cohabiting with a Chinese mistress that even Sir Robert Hart, the inspector general of the Imperial Maritime Customs Service, had fathered three children with a Chinese woman when he was stationed in Ningpo and Canton in the 1840s and 1850s. He later acknowledged the arrangement was "a common practice for an unmarried Englishman resident in China at the time."

Upper-class "Celestial" women—as the Chinese were then called by Europeans—were kept at home, some of them still with bound feet (a practice just about to end among the elite of China after 900 years), and could be glimpsed along Bubbling Well Road (later Nanking Road West) in Shanghai, "decked out in the most gorgeous of silks and satins, glossy black hair, well-greased and heavily laden with gold pins, flowers, jade and kingfishers' feathers, fearful and wonderful paints and fans, bright red 'pants,' and invisible small feet."[29]

European men at social functions were regularly entertained by Chinese hostesses, or "sing-song girls" trained in the arts as well as in pouring men's drinks and making pleasant chit-chat. The highest ranking of these were like Japanese geisha, requiring serious cash outlays and time commitments if one wanted to court them. They worked out of courtesan houses on Foochow Road, with names such as "Temple of Supreme Happiness" and "Garden of Perfumed Flowers," and the most elegant of the establishments had silk curtains and an opulent luxury suited to kings and noblemen.[30]

But, as appealing as Chinese women were to the Europeans who glimpsed the mandarin classes on the street or interacted with the lower classes at courtesan houses, the social prohibition against marriage—exacerbated by Social Darwinism in the 1860s, which encouraged colonialism and missionary zeal in the form of educating the inferior races and saving the souls of the savages—was severe, and was in place for centuries. The early twentieth-century stories of British colonial novelist W. Somerset Maugham, mostly set in Malaya and Burma, repeated the common theme of tragedy befalling the white man who let himself fall for "native" women, and cast such males as weak in the face of desire, or "flagrantly unfaithful," sadly beguiled, or suicidal after a tempestuous end to the affairs. "He never forgot that he was an English gentleman, and he had no patience with the white men who yielded to native customs," Maugham writes in but one example of a man resisting temptation in his short story *The Outstation*. "He made no surrenders. And he did not imitate so many of the white men in taking a native woman, . . . for an intrigue of this nature, however sanctified by custom, seemed to him not only shocking but undignified."[31]

French writers also celebrated the forbidden sexual nature of East-West relations, the decadence of Oriental splendor, and the languor of easy opium. Gustave Flaubert's Oriental women characters exhibited sensuality, overt sexuality, and coarseness. His Egyptian dancer Kuchuk Hanem in *Salammbo* (1863)—representing "Oriental woman" in the French consciousness—becomes the model for the carnal female temptation to which his later Saint Anthony is subject. "The Oriental woman is no more than a machine," Flaubert writes. "She makes no distinction between one man and another man." Edward Said, writing in *Orientalism,* points out that Flaubert's dancer is "a disturbing symbol of fecundity, peculiarly Oriental in her luxuriant and seemingly unbounded sexuality. . . . Woven through all of Flaubert's Oriental experiences, exciting or disappointing, is an almost uniform association between the Orient and sex."[32] Said accuses Gerard de Nerval, who wrote *Voyage in Orient* in 1851, of the same. Nerval calls the Orient "countries of dreams and illusions," which conceal a deep, rich fund of female sexuality, Said notes. "The Oriental sky and the Ionian [Western] sea give each other the sacred kiss of love each morning," Nerval writes. When the writer returns to Europe, he is back in "the land of coldness and storms, where already the Orient is no more mine than one of the daydreams that soon comes to displace the boredoms of the day."

The exotic travel writer Pierre Loti came next, giving us the temporary wife from Japan who would serve as the model for *Madame Butterfly,* and tales of exotic China as well. "Virtually no European writer who wrote on or traveled to the Orient in the later period after 1800 exempted himself or herself from . . . [portraying] the Orient [as] a place where one could look for sexual experience unobtainable in Europe."[33] Let us also not forget the nineteenth-century French Orientalist painters, such as Eugene Delacroix, with their themes of harems and slave markets, and women lounging languidly in repose. In these depictions of the Orient, the exotic was never far removed from the sensual.

Victorian Ladies Never Move

The Victorian era (1839–1901), when proper Englishwomen were admonished not to enjoy the act of sex, and required that "ladies never move" while they performed their "sacrifice" for their husbands,[34] most certainly exacerbated the fantasies about Asian women—who, by comparison, were probably just engaging in what we might now consider normal sexual acts. "As one Victorian wrote with unfettered enthusiasm, it was the common belief that Oriental women 'understand in perfection all the arts and wiles of love, are capable of gratifying any tastes, and in face and figure they are unsurpassed by any women in the world,'" writes Diana Preston in *The Boxer Rebellion.*[35] "One of the siege [of Peking] diarists described an encounter with Manchu women that was 'like a narcotic when a roar of fever still hangs in one's ears.' Many men found local bed companions or 'sleeping dictionaries' an excellent and pleasurable way of learning the language."[36]

The sexual mystique of Asian women was perpetuated and enhanced by the teachings of Chinese sexology. Ancient texts on the sexual practices of Taoism, one of the three belief systems of China (along with

Buddhism and Confucianism), recommend various sexual positions (fifty-eight in all)—much like the *Kama Sutra* of India. The tenets are that males not ejaculate in order to preserve their *chi,* or body energy but instead seek to claim the "yin" essence of women. At the same time, women also try to claim the male's sexual energy, the "yang," through his ejaculation. Taoist manuals, including *The Art of the Bedchamber,* asserted that the Yellow Emperor, the founder of China according to legend, became immortal after having had sex with 1,200 women, and that sex with ten to twenty girls every night, particularly if they were virgins, was a way to ensure a long life. Chinese ginseng and opium grew renowned as aphrodisiacs. Chinese classical literature, as it began to be translated into English and more widely known, gave flowery imagery to sex, calling women's vaginal secretions "clouds," men's semen "rain," women's genitalia "peach" and men's "jade dragon." While the rich literature of Chinese sexology and erotica was known to the Victorian colonialists, the actual texts remained a mystery. The most famous work, *The Golden Lotus,* said to be Mao Zedong's favorite pleasure reading (along with the equally racy *Secret Methods of the Plain Girl*), wasn't translated into English until much later, in 1939. (Its first edition contained fifty prurient passages rendered in Latin by prudish translators.) Later, the English divorcée Wallis Simpson would be accused in rumor of seducing the Duke of Windsor with sexology techniques she had picked up in a Shanghai brothel.

Europeans discovered the erotica of Japan in this period as well, as it was customary for newlyweds to be given a "pillow book"—an illustrated guide to sexual positions. Those with more intellectual pursuits could read the writings of Lafcadio Hearn, a half-Irish, half-Greek journalist and adventurer, who arrived in Japan in 1890, became infatuated, overcame social prohibitions against taking a Japanese bride, and eventually became a Japanese citizen. For fifteen years his writings were monumental in forming an image of the Japanese in the West, particularly his *Japan, an Attempt at Interpretation* in 1904. He not only lauds Japanese beauty, he extols Japan as a land of charming, graceful, and complacent women: "The most wonderful aesthetic products of Japan are not its ivories, nor its bronzes, nor its porcelains, nor its swords, nor any of its marvels in metal and lacquer—but its women." Japanese women succeed in "winning affection by gentleness, obedience, kindliness," he writes, virtues that "only a society in which all self-assertion was repressed, and self-sacrifice made a universal obligation" could have produced. Hearn was the first of a long line of Western male experts to observe Japanese society with the help of Japanese wives, mistresses, girlfriends, consorts, and even male lovers. A substantial number of the Tokyo diplomatic corps still do today, as do the staff of U.S. embassies all over Asia.

There was another sensational exception to the East-West marriage prohibition in the same year that Hearn published his first book: that of the relationship between George D. Morgan, the nephew of millionaire financier J.P. Morgan, and the Kyoto geisha Oyuki. The young Morgan, who then was just thirty-one, had gone to Kyoto to watch the Cherry Dances and fell in love with the twenty-one-year-old geisha on the stage. He courted her; she resisted icily. The story of the fabulously rich, lovelorn foreigner and the cold-hearted geisha became big news. Newspapers started reporting that Oyuki demanded money and that Morgan went to New York to raise it, inspiring a stage play titled "A Single Night's Dream for 40,000 Yen." Although both Morgan and Oyuki's family denied it, U.S. newspapers reported that Morgan paid Oyuki's family $25,000 (equivalent to $440,000 in modern currency) "according to Japanese tradition."[37] Morgan finally won his bride and they married in Japan before setting sail for America; it was the year that the Puccini opera *Madame Butterfly* debuted in Milan.

The couple did not receive a happy welcome in New York. While quaint tea pavilions in the back garden were a fine pursuit for the wealthy, the idea of mixing with Asians in the salon was not. "The prodigal son and his Madame Butterfly bride who could barely speak a word of English found themselves ostracized not only by the Morgans but by all of New York polite society," Lesley Downer writes in *Women of the Pleasure Quarters*. "There were no invitations to Mrs. Astor's balls or to soirees with the Vanderbilts. After a few uncomfortable months, the couple set sail for Paris. But by 1906 they were back in Japan with the intention of settling there." Not welcome there either, they returned to Paris where they spent a decade until Morgan suffered a heart attack, leaving Oyuki a widow at age thirty-four.

Legend has it that Oyuki returned to New York bearing her husband's ashes and was welcomed much more warmly. But in truth,

Downer reports, letters written by Oyuki and uncovered in Japan reveal that she stayed on in Paris and took up with a French legionnaire. He had been sending her love letters while Morgan took many business trips to New York alone, and that far from being a Madame Butterfly waiting devotedly for her husband's return, Oyuki had complained of being "a widow" long before her husband's death.

America's Sexual Century

The Americans who began taking over Europe's dominant role in the Pacific in the early 1900s created and entrenched their own myths of mystery, sex, desire, and fear. Spain ceded the Philippines to the United States after more than 300 years of colonial rule, and William H. Taft, who later became president, arrived as governor in 1901. At first the Americans were reluctant colonialists. Taft was famous for his patronizing categorization of the Filipinos as our "little brown brothers" who needed to be educated and brought up in the image of America, and Rudyard Kipling admonished the Americans to remember "The White Man's Burden" in his famous poem that calls the Filipinos "your new-caught sullen peoples, half-devil and half-child."[38]

The first thing America did was launch its first Pacific war to quash the Philippine independence movement. The U.S. military sent about three-quarters of the standing army at that time, roughly 75,000 troops, and suffered 6,000 dead and wounded. The Philippine side suffered 20,000 military casualties and hundreds of thousands of civilian ones. Afterwards, new laws passed under American patronage returned some of the rights of women and of access to education that the Spanish had taken away. As a result, Philippine women were the first in Asia with the right to vote, which they did for the first time in parliamentary elections in 1937.

The flamboyantly egotistical General Douglas MacArthur, who took over as governor in the 1930s and commanded the Philippine Armed Forces, publicly extolled the virtues of Christian morality. But, after his first marriage ended in divorce, he took up with an exquisite Eurasian-Filipina actress and vaudeville star who was in her early twenties, Isabel Rosario Cooper, or "Dimples" as she was known by her thousands of fans in Manila. MacArthur was so smitten with the young woman that, at a toast at the Manila Hotel about five months after he met her, he lauded the Philippines by noting "the moonbeam delicacy its women." The love letters he wrote her never have been published, but according to journalist and historian Stanley Karnow who saw them, they "bear the imprint of an impassioned schoolboy— or worse yet, the infatuation of a man of middle years for a beauty half his age. Blushing with references to hearts and flowers, kisses and undying love, the passages read like greeting cards."[39]

MacArthur brought "Dimples" to Washington, DC, and kept her in a suite at the Hotel Chastleton at 1701 16th Street for four years, buying her black-lace lingerie and bedroom gowns, but no street clothes. She didn't need them, he told her; her duty lay in bed.[40] When she grew bored of being a caged bird, sneaking out at night for other affairs with prominent men, demanding to attend law school, and threatening to expose the general, the relationship ended. Even though he was fifty-four-years old, MacArthur did not want his mother to find out about his mixed-race young mistress. MacArthur's friend Admiral William Leahy later remarked: "He was a bachelor. All he had to do was look everybody in the face and say 'So what? Cunt can make you look awful silly at times.'"[41] But instead, MacArthur tried to send "Dimples" discreetly back to Manila in 1934. She re- fused, and eventually pitched up in Hollywood, taking small-time movie roles and trying to tell her story. Nobody listened. MacArthur married for the second time in 1937, to Jean Marie Faircloth, a mem- ber of the Daughters of the American Revolution and Daughters of the Confederacy. "Dimples," whose death certificate listed her as a "freelance actress," later killed herself.[42]

It was MacArthur, of course, who led U.S. forces in the Pacific in World War II and then presided over the seven-year occupation of Japan. The experiences that American soldiers encountered there, and their impact as portrayed through Hollywood, would go a long way toward solidifying the American public's association of the East with sexual availability, sensual pleasure, and danger, much as the experi- ences of British, French, and Dutch colonialists had done for the Euro- pean public for centuries before. "Unlike Germany, this vanquished enemy represented an exotic, alien society to its conquerors: nonwhite, non-Western, non-Christian. Yellow, Asian, pagan Japan, supine and vulnerable, provoked an ethnocentric missionary zeal inconceivable vis-à-vis Germany," writes John Dower in *Embracing Defeat: Japan in the Wake of World War II*. "To American reformers, much of the almost sensual excitement involved in promoting their democratic revolution from above derived from the feeling that this involved denaturing an Oriental adversary."[43] Whereas Germany was divided into U.S., British, French, and Soviet-administered zones, Japan was militarily subservient to MacArthur and the Americans. MacArthur famously likened the Japanese to "a boy of twelve" in relative terms of modern civilization, and "old Japan hands" argued that follow-the-leader Japanese couldn't handle the grown-up responsibility of democracy.

In addition to this "sensual excitement" of denaturing and re-creating that Dower cites, there was the actual sexual excitement as well, as hundreds of thousands of U.S. servicemen descended on Japan. Urban families sent their women to the countryside fearing rape and pillage at the hands of the enemy; those that remained where they might encounter Americans at first continued to wear the baggy pants of the war years rather than feminine attire, and young girls were cautioned not to appear friendly. On the other hand, the government Home Ministry discreetly told police throughout the country to set up "comfort facilities" with female volunteers to service the Americans and thereby ensure the chastity of the "good" women of Japan—just as had been done for the Dutch traders and Perry's sailors 300 years and 100 years before. But professional prostitutes were reluctant to sign up, fearing that the scary Americans portrayed in war-time propaganda would have enormous sex organs. So, in the Ginza district of downtown Tokyo, comfort facility organizers recruited ordinary women with a sign that read: "As part of urgent national facilities to deal with the postwar, we are seeking the active cooperation of new Japanese women to participate in the great task of comforting the occupation force. . . . "[44] Within a month, 1,360 women in Tokyo had enlisted in the R.A.A., or Recreation and Amusement Association, pledging "to defend and nurture the purity of our race . . . [by] offering ourselves for the defense of the national polity."[45]

What happened next was ghastly. Several hundred GIs on the first day the facility opened on August 27, 1945, found their way to the

R.A.A. in Tokyo's Omori district, where a small number of mostly in-experienced recruits had gathered, Dower reports. Neither beds, fu-tons, nor room partitions were yet available, and fornication took place—without privacy—everywhere, even in the corridors. "Later Japanese accounts speak of shameless 'animalistic intercourse' that showed the 'true colors' of so-called American civilization," Dower writes. "By one estimate, R.A.A. women engaged between 15 and 60 G.I.s a day. A 19-year-old who had previously been a typist commit-ted suicide almost immediately. Some women broke down or deserted. By mid-September, however, this grotesque exercise in 'people's diplo-macy' had become more or less routine."[46] The price for one visit was fifteen yen, about the price of half a pack of cigarettes on the black market, Dower reports, and initially the Japanese women segregated for use by black soldiers were said to have been horrified—until they discovered that many black GIs perhaps in kinship with fellow non-whites, treated the women more kindly than white GIs did.

This wasn't to last, however. An alarming rise in venereal disease among the troops prompted authorities to cancel the R.A.A. program after just five months; some 90 percent of the women tested positive for infection. The number of reported rapes then rose in Japan, from about forty per day while the R.A.A. was operating, to 330 per day af-ter it closed.[47]

Servicemen then took up the company of "panpan" and "geesha girls," false geisha who may or may not have dressed in kimono in-stead of modern dress, but who prostituted themselves for GIs. They gave Americans an incorrect impression of the real geisha world, where geisha means "arts person" trained in music and dance, not in the art of sexual pleasure. Because of the war, the number of real geisha had declined to 1,695 in Tokyo, down from a peak of 80,000 in the 1920s.[48] But the number of prostitutes—"geesha" and "pan-pan"—approached 70,000 when the trade was formally legalized in December 1946. They thronged by the hundreds around the railway arches of Ginza near General MacArthur's headquarters, pulling GIs into the shadows and begging for cigarettes, gum, or even food. "Gee-sha girl" became a term for anyone of dubious morality, from bar host-esses to streetwalkers.[49] They were "tough, vulnerable figures remembered for their bright lipstick, nail polish, sharp clothes, and sometimes enviable material positions," Dower writes.

> Among G.I.s the term provoked ridicule, pity, compassion, exoticism and plain eroticism. . . . [Among Japanese] the panpan became associated with the liberation of repressed sensuality—a world of erotic indulgence that had found earlier expression not merely in the pleasure quarters of the late feudal period, but in the bawdy relationships and amorous dalliances celebrated in popular tales and courtly romances of ancient times. Their self-indulgent carnality was as sharp a repudiation as could be imagined of the stultifying austerity and discipline the [wartime] militarists had demanded.[50]

Soon, bright lipstick, bright clothes, and a GI boyfriend were a part of the new Japanese woman's fashionable, newly Americanized cultural identity. "More strikingly," Dower writes,

> the defeated country itself was feminized in the minds of the Americans who poured in. The enemy was transformed with a startling suddenness from a bestial people fit to be annihilated into receptive exotics to be handled and enjoyed. That enjoyment was palpable—the panpan personified this. Japan—only yesterday a menacing, masculine threat—had been transformed, almost in a blink of an eye, into a compliant feminine body on which the white victors could impose their will.[51]

The promiscuity led the Japanese government to start promoting the image of Japanese women as devoted wives and mothers, according to several Japanese scholars of the period. The notion that a "panpan" girl or "geesha girl" personified Japanese womanhood suggested that Japanese society was morally and culturally inferior to the West. To counter this, the government emphasized the social mores of the Samurai, who had repressed widespread sexual rights that women had enjoyed in the previous Heian period, and asked women to be loyal, subordinate, and self-sacrificing keepers of the moral code.

It was in the interests of the American government, however, to encourage cross-cultural liaisons. "In 1947, in the face of widespread criticism of his first year as leader of the occupation of Japan, General Douglas MacArthur and his staff actively began to issue statements and encourage press coverage of the United States' presence in Japan as a partnership of complementary opposites," writes Caroline Chung Simpson in the feminist journal *Differences*. Occupation romance became the manifestation of this new U.S.-Japan political partnership.

> As long as interracial occupation romances remained a distant metaphor for the inevitability of U.S. dominance in Asia, they could serve a stabilizing function by casting the American mission in Japan as benevolent. But when these romances ended in marriage and the Japanese woman came home, as it were, her presence in America provoked palpable discomfort.[52]

The discomfort in American society was indeed palpable. Between the end of World War II and the end of the Vietnam War, nearly 172,000 Asian women came to the United States as "war brides"— 66,681 Japanese, 51,747 Filipinas, 28,205 Koreans, 11,166 Thais, 8,040 Vietnamese, and at least 6,000 Chinese, according to the U.S. Immigration and Naturalization Service. Media articles cast them as "Madame Butterflies" who would have a hard time adapting to middle-class American life.[53] Some states kept laws banning Caucasians from marrying other races on the books until the U.S. Supreme Court declared them unconstitutional in 1967.

As evidence of the reprobation that mixed-race couples continued to face, Yoko Ono took much of the blame for the 1970 breakup of the Beatles after her marriage to John Lennon. Beatles fans called her Dragon Lady and made her the world's most reviled rock-star wife until Courtney Love. Most likely, the fact that Ono was twice-divorced, seven years older, and had said, during the couple's public "bed-in" war protest in which they invited reporters to their Montreal honeymoon bed, that she could have prevented World War II if Adolf Hitler had only spent ten days in bed with her, didn't help. The writer David Sheff, who interviewed the couple for *Playboy* magazine in 1980, expressed surprise when he finally met her.

Ono is one of the most misunderstood women in the public eye. Her mysterious image is based on some accurate and some warped accounts of her philosophies and her art statements, and on the fact that she never smiles. It is also based—perhaps unfairly—on resentment of her as the sorceress/Svengali who controls the very existence of John Lennon.

"The enigma called Yoko Ono became accessible as the hard exterior broke down . . . with that giggle she became vulnerable and cute and shy, not at all the creature that came from the Orient to brainwash John Lennon," Sheff wrote. It seems that Ono could not have had as much control as her detractors asserted; the couple broke up in 1973 for eighteen months when Lennon took up with his Chinese assistant May Pang. But later accounts credited Ono with orchestrating that, of course, as well as his return to her embrace.

THE AMERICAN MILITARY EXPERIENCES continued in Korea and Southeast Asia as the United States battled Communism in the Pacific throughout the Cold War. To a large extent, the U.S. forces exerted themselves, collectively and metaphorically, as the masculine force of paternal dominance over compliant, feminized peoples who might otherwise succumb to the evil lure of Communism. When viewed with this perspective, there seems little coincidence that American descriptions of Asian leaders almost always note feminine qualities: Mao Zedong, before he took power in China, had "a feminine quality in him" embodied in "a high pitched voice," "long, sensitive woman's hands" and a "feminine mouth."[54] And so, on the eve of the formation of the People's Republic of China in 1949, Central Intelligence Agency reports discussed the probable "issue of subservience to Moscow" by China's new Communist leadership.[55] As we now know from history, rather than subservience, Mao deftly managed a prickly distance from Caucasian communists and instead developed his own independent model of Communism. Likewise, Vietnam's leader Ho Chi Minh, who frequently advocated non-violence as his preferred method of resolving conflict, was "small and frail . . . earnest yet gentile."[56] Ngo Dien Diem, the prime minister of South Vietnam while President Lyndon Johnson significantly escalated the American troop presence, was, "as fragile as porcelain, with delicate features and ivory skin."[57] President Johnson called him "boy." And later, President Ferdinand Marcos of the Philippines would be "America's boy," too, a term not far removed from "little brown brothers" of a half-century before. An American Lieutenant Colonel in Vietnam, John Paul Vann, once told David Halberstam of *The New York Times,* in a statement that seemed to reflect how his up-close-and-personal experiences with the Vietnamese people perhaps clouded his professional ones: "These people may be the world's greatest lovers, but they're not the world's greatest fighters. But they're good people, and they can win a war if someone shows them how."[58] If Americans underestimated the tenacity and fierce fighting skills of the North Vietnamese side, it's not hard to see why.

> *Hey Joe, try taking a little excursion*
> *You'll feel good from a little perversion*
> *Massage requiring total immersion*
> *Some strange positions they say are Persian*
> —Vietnam War–era ditty

American GIs did not bring prostitution to Asia. It has thrived in almost every country for centuries. But wherever there are single men with money, prostitution is sure to follow. And so, a sex industry catering mainly to American GIs exploded with the rise of the U.S. military presence in Asia. Many of these spots still thrive today, drawing in foreign men and Asian girls from everywhere. The U-Tapao air base in Thailand fostered the growth of the notorious sex-and-sand resort Pattaya. The Patpong sex strip of Bangkok was created as a sexual playland to draw GIs on R&R, or Rest and Relaxation, from Vietnam (or rather, as they called it, I&I—Intoxication and Intercourse). In Seoul, the Itaewon district, or "America in Seoul" with its seedy strip clubs on "Hooker Hill," expanded to meet the needs of GIs from the 8th U.S. Army Headquarters nearby. "The Gate" outside Gate 2 of Kadena Air Base in Okinawa, Japan, as well as a few other strips near the bases, still do a hopping sex trade. In the Philippines, the sex strip on Fields Avenue outside the old Clark Air Base in Angeles City remains infamous, even though U.S. bases in the Philippines closed in the early 1990s. The streets of Saigon, teeming with prostitutes servicing GIs in the early 1970s, have started to purr with prurient nightlife again in recent years following a Communism-imposed hiatus that lasted into the 1990s.

LOSING THE VIETNAM WAR gave Americans a new perspective on the assumption of paternal dominance over the placid peoples of the Pacific, but it did not change the overarching association of Asia with the sexual, seductive, and dangerous. The misty, water-colored "Indochine" of the French imagination and the whole set of exotic, seductive, and dangerous images that accompanied the colonial period simply gave way to a new American concept, "'Nam," with its new set of exotic, seductive, and dangerous images.

"Saigon . . . shit" utters Martin Sheen's reckless character in the first two words of Francis Ford Coppola's epic film *Apocalypse Now*. Michael Cimino's *Deer Hunter* also portrays this aspect of the Vietnam War, with the character played by Christopher Walken drawn by Saigon's vices into the depths of an insanity that finally claims him. Vietnam is thus "a wicked swamp of iniquity waiting to suck Westerners into its rotting depths. Saigon was glamorous and corrupt, destroyed by the white man, and destroyer of white men," writes Ian Buruma. "It might have been shit, but it was seductive shit."

As a result of these contrasting images of old "Indochine" and wartime "'Nam," there have been two distinct categories of tourist wandering through modern Vietnam, neither looking to fully see the true country that is there but to glimpse images that satisfy their preconceptions: the wistful French in search of quaint peasants in conical hats tending the rice fields, who tsk-tsk over the run-down state of the colonial-built buildings, relish the vestiges of French cuisine, and chat up old men in cafes to determine if they still speak French and are longing for the days of colonial rule; and the Americans, thousands of them men who fought in the war, chasing their ghosts and memories of how they escaped both the death and seduction.

The Servility Factor: U.S. Immigration

Even before the U.S. military forces took over power in the Pacific, there was a peculiarly North American phenomenon going on that significantly affected the formation of stereotypes of Asians as sexual and servile: immigration. These stereotypes were reinforced by the simultaneous European colonial experiences in Asia in which Americans also took a small role, such as in Shanghai which had an American Concession as well as British and French ones. As we have seen, Chinese were mere servants or mistresses to the Europeans and Americans. As America was forming its national identity in the 1800s, they were serving more or less the same function in America, too.

Afong Moy was the first recorded Chinese woman in America, and she came to New York City in 1834 at age sixteen as an exhibit. Museums in New York and Brooklyn displayed her on an oriental latticework chair, wearing a silk gown and four-inch-long slippers on her bound feet. Audiences watched with fascination as she ate with chopsticks, counted in Chinese, and did computations on an abacus. A few years later, P.T. Barnum brought the second Chinese-woman exhibit, and the circus featuring her attracted 20,000 spectators in only six days.[59]

The first three "Celestials" arriving to seek employment in San Francisco landed in 1848; the first Chinese restaurant "Canton" opened in 1849.[60] But it wasn't until the Gold Rush of the 1850s that Chinese immigrants from Canton headed by the thousands to California and up to Canada. When golden opportunity began to dry up, the former "Celestial" prospectors—a long queue of hair braided down their backs in Qing dynasty fashion—took up what was known as "women's work" in San Francisco because, at the time, there were few women on the frontier. They became cooks and nannies for the wealthy, and they opened up laundries, restaurants, and curio shops. By 1886, nine out of ten farm workers in California were Chinese. Because the typical immigrant was from the poor southern province of Canton, he was no Yao Ming (the basketball player, who is a tall northerner). In those days, Chinese laborers averaged just 4'10" and 120 lbs.[61]

Due to the dearth of women, "Celestials" began importing Chinese women from home as wives and as prostitutes. "Although California was not officially a slave state, it tolerated the sale of female flesh during the antebellum period; slave auctions of Chinese women were held openly and brazenly on the docks before large audiences that included police officers," writes Iris Chang in *The Chinese in America*.

> By the 1860s, however, a stricter code of morality disapproved of such public transactions. The auctions didn't stop but simply moved to Chinatown and then indoors—for instance to a Chinese theater or even a Chinese temple. . . . Most girls ended up in low-class brothels, or "cribs," tiny shacks no larger than 12 x 14 feet, facing dim, narrow alleys and sparsely furnished with a washbowl, a bamboo chair, and a bed. These *loungei* ("woman always holding up her legs") were forced to service, often in rapid succession, laborers, sailors and drunks for as little as 25 cents each, drawing in customers with their plaintive chants: "Two bittee lookee, flo bittee feelee, six bittee doee!"

The most successful courtesan of San Francisco was Ah Toy, who, at her peak, drew lines for blocks of white men and Chinese alike.[62] Americans paid $0.50, more than twice what dinner cost at a nearby restaurant, for entry to a Chinatown "lookie show" to satisfy their curiosity about whether Chinese women's genitalia differed, as rumored, from those of white women.[63]

Then the acrimony started. In 1870, seventy-five Chinese immigrants brought from San Francisco arrived in Massachusetts as shoe factory strikebreakers, and "Yellow Peril" was born. The fear of an infinite supply of servile workers ready to take white men's jobs caused hysteria, and "Chinamen" quickly replaced "Celestials" as the epithet to describe the immigrants. Writer Bret Harte published a poem that became the most popular of the 1870s, "The Heathen Chinee," which recounts a fictional card game between "Ah Sin" and an Irishman. Even though the Irishman blatantly cheats with cards stuffed up his sleeves, he keeps losing. Finally he shouts, "We are ruined by Chinese cheap labor!" and then assaults Ah Sin, knocking hidden cards out of the Chinese man's sleeve. The poem was set to music, as well as reprinted in virtually every newspaper in America, and Harte collaborated with Mark Twain to bring the story to stage.[64] While

Congress granted civil rights to Chinese, it still denied them U.S. citizenship.

By 1880, cheap Chinese labor was a presidential campaign issue, and so the 1882 Chinese Exclusion Act became the first legislation to bar immigrants that was based on race. Previous immigration restrictions had been only for prostitutes, lepers, and "morons." Now all Chinese "idiots," "lunatics," and "laborers" were also excluded. Canada followed suit in 1885.

The restrictions kept the ratio of Chinese men to women extremely high, at more than twenty-to-one. From 1906 to 1924, only 150 Chinese women were allowed to enter the United States, and then for the next six years not a single one.[65] This, of course, kept the popularity of prostitutes high among Chinese men who could not find wives (and were barred from marrying any other races under California anti-miscegenation laws in place from 1880 until 1948), and it kept the ratio of Chinese men doing "women's work" high as well. The most popular business was laundry, which required little start-up capital and wasn't a threat to organized labor. According to the 1920 census, almost 30 percent of all 45,614 Chinese employed in the United States worked in laundries.[66]

With so many Asians in the services and sex trades, it wasn't hard for our stereotypes to develop—and just in time for the advent of the movie screen to entrench these ideas forevermore.

The Crossover: From Hollywood to Europe Again

Britain, which also had restricted Asian immigration, counted just 1,934 Chinese in the entire kingdom in the 1930 census, half also working as launderers, and the other half as seamen. When a British journalist went to interview the Chinese-American stage and screen sensation Anna May Wong at the Park Lane Hotel in London, he colored his prose with Asian Mystique to the extent that he could. A "spectacular Chinese servant" ushered him into the sitting room of Wong's suite where he was mildly disappointed not to find "the opulence of the East." After all, it was a London hotel. Still, he noted Chinese vases (a leftover from Britain's chinoiserie period?) and easy chairs near the fire. She offered him a Player's cigarette "from a hand which should have held a gold case inlaid with jade."[67] But it didn't. The writer just couldn't get around the plain fact that he was meeting an American in a London hotel suite.

In a movie review in the Portuguese magazine *Cinefilo,* the writer noted that after seeing Wong, audiences will "long for the Chinese, dreaming of Oriental scenes, full of opium smokers and peaceful faces," and want to write her "mysterious notes in strange characters, copied from crates of tea."[68] As one of the few personified representations of "the East" in the West, Wong also beguiled the Germans (with only thirty Chinese women resident in the country in the 1925 census) and the Austrians, who depicted her on a poster with a topless gypsy costume, her skin yellow and legs and posterior larger than life to emphasize her exoticism.[69] French cinema, too, took from Wong an intoxication with Asian bodies, and with portraying in Oriental representations the melancholy languor of a lost, opulent past that more closely mirrored France's own colonial experiences than the realities of Asia.

Thus, while Americans were originally the inheritors of European notions of an opulent, sexual, and dangerous Orient, Hollywood codified these ideas, and then sent them back to Europe where they resonated with a new-found strength based on the immigrant and historical experience there.

Hollywood, Burbank, and the
Resulting Imaginings

I never saw Asian people on television or movies so my dreams were somewhat
limited. I'd dream, "Maybe someday . . . I could be an extra on M.A.S.H.*"*
"Maybe someday . . . I could play Arnold's girlfriend on Happy Days.*"*
"Maybe someday . . . I could play a hooker in something."
I'd be looking in the mirror, "SUCKY FUCKY, TWO DOLLAH!"
"ME LOVE YOU LONG TIME!"

— MARGARET CHO, *Notorious C.H.O.* (2002)

MARGARET CHO is one of the most talented comedians in America
and, as an unkempt and brash, trash-talking Asian-American, she
makes her living in part by making a joke of the absurdities of the
stereotypes about Asian women. In the promotional posters and
DVD/video cover for her *Notorious C.H.O.,* a film compilation of her
stage routines, she appears in low-cut, high-cleavage black leather, her
hair blown back model-style, her face in full makeup, her lip snarled
and right hand curled into a cat-like claw—a send up of the image of
the Asian sexual tigress. When the film starts, she clomps out onto
the stage makeup-less, in dumpy unmatched clothes and clunky
shoes—the opposite of the image on the posters and promo pictures.
She talks—bawdily and crudely in jokes riddled with expletives—
about sex, while at the same time projecting an image that is anything
but sexy.

What she means is that there weren't any *real* Asian characters on
television when she was growing up in the 1970s. Because network
television didn't begin broadcasting until 1947—and the 1950s and
'60s TV gave us only one Asian woman in a brief role[1]—it wasn't until the 1970s that the American, and subsequently worldwide, view-

ing public got their first impressions of Asian women on TV. Combined with Hollywood movies, these extremely limited images are how we in the West first get to see—and come to understand—Asia and Asian women. (Because the portrayal of Asian men on Western screens deserves its own discussion, that is examined separately.)

Hollywood movies have given only a slightly more multi-dimensional view, as we examine later, but in many ways, television has been a more important medium in this regard. Television places images into our homes, directly into our living rooms and bedrooms, where one's guard is down. And, unlike the act of going out to see a movie in which we consciously suspend our disbelief for two hours as the theater darkens and the projection begins, images on TV are more believably integrated into the fabric of our lives. We develop an affinity for our television characters, and sitcom viewers week after week tune in to see our adult versions of imaginary "friends," whether it's Lucy and Ricky; Hawkeye and Trapper John; Sam and Diane; Jerry, George, and Elaine; or Rachel and Ross.

The Asian extras on *M.A.S.H.* (ostensibly set in Korea but in reality mirroring the U.S. involvement in Vietnam) took in the officers' laundry and sold trinkets and the occasional few drinks to members of the 4077 Mobile Army Surgical Hospital from the early days of the series beginning in 1972. Sometimes we saw them as war casualties or, yes, as hookers. It wasn't until the final season of the CBS series that a recurring Asian female character was introduced to the show. It was the Korean war bride of Corporal Max Klinger, Soon-lee. In an ironic twist to an eleven-year-long plot line of a man who would do anything, including wearing dresses and acting loopy, to be sent home, Klinger announced he was staying in Korea to help Soon-lee find her family. She was a war victim; he was an American man to the rescue. It was typical Hollywood. They married in the series finale on February 28, 1983, in a show that drew 105 million viewers, a still-unbeaten record for the largest audience for a series finale in television history.[2] Klinger and his bride then took up their own series, *After M.A.S.H.*, which lasted only one season.

On *Happy Days,* the girlfriend of the owner of Arnold's drive-in appeared only briefly. She was a long-distance love interest, and the two had met, not so originally, by exchanging pictures through the mail.

Momo, it seems, was either a mail-order bride or a "picture bride" arranged by a matchmaker. "Arnold," played by Japanese-American Pat Morita, was only around for one ABC season initially, in 1975–76, and his season-finale marriage to Momo gave him the excuse for leaving the show—to star in the short-lived sitcom *Mr. T and Tina,* about a Japanese inventor transferred from Tokyo to Chicago. It was cancelled after one season, as well. Morita returned to *Happy Days* for another season in 1983, just before the series ended.

"Arnold" wasn't exactly the *Happy Days* character's name. The story was that a Japanese-American businessman had bought a drive-in called Arnold's and, to save money by not having to change the sign, he decided to keep it as is. Rather than learn his difficult Asian name, Matsuo Takahashi, the kids from Jefferson High School who hung out there (Richie, Potsie, Fonzie, and the gang) just called him Arnold. "Sign cost money!" he said in one episode. "You know how many letter in Takahashi?!" Because in real life Morita had been born in California (and spent World War II in a Japanese-American internment camp), his accent on *Happy Days* (and subsequent *Karate Kid* movies) was a fake.

There was another well-known war bride from that television era— Mrs. Livingston, the housekeeper on *The Courtship of Eddie's Father.* Like *M.A.S.H.,* this show was a movie turned into a TV series, running on ABC from 1969 to 1972. Mrs. Livingston's accent was real. She was born Miyoshi Umeki in Japan in 1929 before coming to America. Always soft-spoken, demure, unassuming, dependable, philosophical, and wise in the ways of child care, Mrs. Livingston also was confused about American customs and in need of guidance. Her constantly repeated line, spoken softly in highly accented English, was the ever-obedient, sing-song toned, "Yes, Mr. Eddie's Father." Although the series never explicitly stated so, it left viewers to infer that, because of her age, Anglo surname, and seemingly widowed status, she had been a war bride not from the previous two American conflicts in the Pacific but the one before that, World War II. An accomplished Hollywood actress who had won an Oscar for her role in *Sayonara* (1957), Umeki brought a dignity to Mrs. Livingston that subtly subverted her typecasting.

THUS, THE TELEVISION SITCOMS of the 1970s gave us images of Asian women in the form of brides and servants. They were docile and obedient, portrayed as dignified but still needing help and guidance from their husbands or masters. Additionally, the reality of the war in Vietnam during that period in history added another dimension to our perceptions, that of war victim. As the first "television war" in U.S. history, images of that conflict—of tearful women, watching as their villages burned or sobbing over news of killed relatives, or bicycling serenely in their silky *ao dai* through the streets of Saigon—also reached into U.S. living rooms and affected American perceptions. Famous photographs on newspaper front pages, such as the one of the nine-year-old girl, Kim Phuc, running, burned and naked, from the napalm attack on June 8, 1972, were seared indelibly into the Western consciousness. As Susan Sontag wrote in her 1977 book on the power of imagery, *On Photography,* "Photographs may be more memorable than moving images because they are a neat slice of time, not a flow." The image of a naked, violated, preadolescent Asian girl cannot be erased from how we have conceived of Vietnam and its people ever since.

Perhaps the only humorously subversive relief came in the form of a television commercial for Calgon laundry additive that debuted in 1972 and ran throughout the decade. Just about any American watching television in the 1970s saw it. While still playing off the stereotypes of Asians in the service trade as tricky and inscrutable, this one has the Asian woman trumping both her secretive husband and their white customer.

CUSTOMER: How do you get your shirts so clean, Mr. Lee?

MR. LEE: Ancient Chinese secret.

MRS. LEE (to camera): My husband, some hot shot. Here's his ancient Chinese secret, Calgon. Calgon's two water softeners soften wash waters so detergents clean better. In hardest water, Calgon helps detergents get laundry up to thirty percent cleaner.

MRS. LEE (shouting to husband): WE NEED MORE CALGON!

CUSTOMER: Ancient Chinese secret, huh?

1980s TV: Sexual Servitude, Anti-Feminism, and Absence

Shogun, the twelve-hour, five-part 1980 epic miniseries, was based on the best-selling novel by Australian-born, British-educated, former World War II Japanese POW and then Hollywood screenwriter-turned-author James Clavell, who had a hands-on role in the production. His novel, when it came out in 1975, sold more than seven million copies and made *konnichi-wa* and *arigato* household words among the literary set. When the miniseries aired on NBC in 1980, it was seen by an enormous viewing audience—an estimated 130 million people.

A number of commentators at the time attributed an increase in the popularity of things Japanese—Benihana restaurants in America, tourist travel to Japan—to *Shogun*'s enormous impact in American society. *Cosmopolitan* magazine called it "an Oriental *Gone with the Wind*" because of the forbidden love affair in 1600s Japan between the beautiful wife of a Japanese Samurai and John Blackthorne, a shipwrecked English navigator. Indeed, as James Clavell had begun his post-British military career in Hollywood, that also is likely what he intended, at least for the TV portrayal. The book and the TV version explore the culture clash between a Renaissance European and Shogunate Japan, with each side becoming more "civilized" in the others' eyes as they come to know each others' customs.

There was some historical truth behind the story, which contributed to its appeal. Traders from Portugal, the Netherlands, England, and Spain had been arriving in the Japan islands since a Portuguese ship, blown off its course to China, landed there in 1542. By the time an English navigator named William Adams was shipwrecked there with his Dutch fleet in 1600, Japan was overrun with missionaries seeking to convert the islands' inhabitants and bring them under European power. Initially imprisoned along with his crew on suspicion of being a pirate, Adams managed to impress one of the Shoguns with his worldly knowledge. He was made an honorary Samurai, granted a large estate, and allowed to marry and father two children with the daughter of a highway collection official—even though he already had a wife and children back in England.[3]

Traders from the East India Company, arriving in Japan in 1613, enlisted Adams to help them set up the first British trading post in Japan before he died in 1620. Later, Japan's Shoguns, fed up with European attempts at exploitation, expelled all westerners and kept them off Japan's shores for more than 200 years (except for limited contact at the remote port of Nagasaki) until American Commodore Matthew Perry and his Black Ships forced the country to open again to trade in 1853.

Two hundred years was plenty of time to allow the legend of the first Western Samurai in Japan to grow in the European imagination. (Hollywood's 2003 version of a romanticized portrayal of this world, in the form of Tom Cruise as *The Last Samurai,* is set in 1876, after Japan reopened again and the Samurai were ending their rule.)

BASED ON HIS CONTACTS with the Japanese, *Shogun*'s fictional Blackthorne believes the Japanese to be cruel, brutal savages, although the political intrigues, murders, and betrayals of the period weren't much different from what went on among the merchant princes of Europe in the same time period. Nonetheless, "six faced and three hearted" is what one of the Portuguese Jesuit characters in the series calls the Japanese and, indeed, the series makes a point that their noble actions are punctuated by treachery and the use of ninja assassins. Yet Blackthorne's first images of Japan after being shipwrecked (and our first images as viewers) are of waking up on a comfortable palette, food set out awaiting his consciousness, and a female servant on the other side of the shoji screen, waiting to slide it back and to cater to his needs. When the servant brings him his cleaned, pressed clothes, she bows in extreme deference, touching her head to the floor three times. As he leaves, having dressed and eaten, the women and girls in the courtyard bow to him, too. The Japanese, unable to pronounce "Blackthorne" call him "Anjin," meaning "Pilot" (as the real-life Adams also was called).

The servitude, which was appropriate for an honored guest in that era of Japan but unlikely to have been extended to a man arrested and held in prison on suspicion of being a pirate, continues as he meets Lady Toda Buntaro (Mariko) and she is assigned to look after him as his interpreter of Japanese language as well as customs. In his logbook the real-life Adams reported fearing the executioner every day during his first several months in Japan. Given that, the slavish obedience to the needs of the visiting white man, as the following dialog demonstrates, does seem a bit over the top.

ASA-SAN (one of three young women keeping Anjin company): In pillowing, how do you compare your women with ours?

JOHN BLACKTHORNE (Anjin): Pillowing? I don't understand.

MARIKO: Pillowing is a way of referring to the physical joining of men and women.

ANJIN: (Pauses, speechless) I have nothing to base the comparison on.

MARIKO: You haven't pillowed since you have been here?

ANJIN: No.

MARIKO: You must be feeling very constricted, ne? One of these [three] ladies will be delighted to pillow with you, Anjin-san, or all of them, if you wish.

ANJIN: All?

ASA-SAN: [They giggle.] Certainly.

MARIKO: But if you don't want any of them, there is no need to worry. They would not be offended. Just tell me the sort of lady you would like and we shall make all the arrangements.

ANJIN: Thank you, but, umm, perhaps later.

MARIKO: Are you sure? Please excuse me, but my master has given specific instructions that your health is to be protected and improved. How can you be healthy without pillowing? It is very important for a man, yes?

ANJIN: Thank you, but, I, uh . . . not now.

MARIKO: Or maybe you would prefer a boy?

ANJIN: A boy?!

MARIKO: Only if you wish it.

ANJIN: I do NOT wish it! Do I look like a God-cursed Sodomite?[4]

MARIKO: Please forgive me. I've made a terrible mistake. I was only trying to please, but I have never known an Englishman before, so I have no way of knowing your intimate customs.

ANJIN: Well, Lady, my intimate customs do not include boys!

MARIKO: Please forgive me for offending you. It was entirely *my* fault, due to my stupidity and ignorance.
(She bows deeply, then all three girls bow.)

When Anjin sets up in a coastal village to learn Japanese, with the aid of Mariko, he spends his first day walking around. When he returns, Mariko offers, "Please sit down, you must be tired. Would you like some sake or a bath? The water is hot." He agrees. Mariko then takes off her clothes and slips into the bath naked in front him. (The original series did show the frontal nudity—deemed acceptable, it appears, for depicting exotic Oriental practices even if it was not otherwise permitted for Caucasians on prime time TV.) Then Mariko offers him a "consort," a beautiful young village widow, to take care of his needs—laundry, bathing, and otherwise.[5]

That night, Mariko slips into Anjin's bedchamber after he refuses the consort. In the morning, Anjin declares his love for her. Mariko tells him not to speak of it:

MARIKO: That would not be seemly, Anjin-san. It is our custom to make life simple; we admire simplicity, so men and women can take pillowing for what it is.
ANJIN: Then, nothing is to be said between us?
MARIKO: Nothing. That is wise.

Ah, a woman who offers sex without commitment and doesn't want to have a relationship discussion in the morning. How refreshing. Mariko, according to a posting about the series on an online review site, is "the perfect woman," and another in an Amazon.com review of the DVD calls her "the picture of Oriental womanhood." She is perfectly deferential at all times, always referring to Lord Toranaga (her husband) as "my master." (In fairness, this was the direct translation of the term in Japanese used for "husband" in a previous era, though it now has fallen into disuse.) Making her more acceptable to a westerner, she is a converted Christian and wears a cross on a necklace outside her pink kimono. "Yes," she says, "I am a Christian, but first I am Japanese." When she places herself between Blackthorne and a Samurai who wants to shoot him, he calls her "brave" and "beautiful." Yes, the perfect woman, indeed.

The Mariko character, played by Yoko Shimada, was loosely based on Hosokawa Gracia, a real-life Christian convert and wife of a noble Hosokawa-clan Samurai. Her assisted suicide during a fiery attack on her Osaka residence where she was held in seclusion (for her protection from the warlords' battles depicted in *Shogun*) came on July 17, 1600, three months after the real William Adams was shipwrecked in another part of Japan. According to his logbook, he was held in prison for a period of at least two months before being banished to his ship off the coast for the duration of the period in which Lady Gracia was alive. He never mentions Lady Gracia in his logs, and it is virtually impossible that the two could have met (she didn't speak English). Any sort of romance between Lady Gracia and any foreigner likely was a concoction of fiction, as Jesuit records of the time laud her extreme devotion and report that she prayed fervently in her final hours until she ordered a servant to end her life rather than let her fall into the hands of her husband's rival—unlike in the miniseries when she dies fighting heroically with the adoring Blackthorne at her side. She was canonized by the Roman Catholic Church in 1862.

In the novel, the fictional romance with Anjin is only a side story to the political intrigue of the era. In Hollywood, of course, it became a central focus. Clavell stressed in interviews that he was writing historical fiction, not fact. But does fact even matter when the American viewing public devours such stories?

As clearly shown by this example, history, first rewritten as fiction, then recast on screen, takes the image of Asian woman and distorts and sexualizes her—even one as pious as Saint Gracia—to conform to our Western perceptions. If, after all this television watching, you came away with the impression that Asian women were sexual fantasy-catering, obedient servants, who could blame you?

Mariko's character also came at a time when the full in-your-face thrust of the women's movement was being felt in the United States. The 1970s brought derisive snickers about "Women's Lib." The pitched battles to amend the Constitution to add the Equal Rights Amendment waged for the entire decade.

In 1975 we got *The Stepford Wives* and, unlike the 2004 comedic remake, the original was much more sinister. In a community with bland, boorish husbands and beautiful, dutiful women, it turns out the wives had been eliminated and in their place were robots built by the men to service their desires—bake perfect cupcakes in the kitchen, act like sex kittens in the bedroom. The original novel by Ira Levin was meant as satire, a feminist statement against male chauvinism. But the result of the movie was a message that men were fed up with feminism and wanted the happy homemakers of the 1950s, not the bra-discarding equal rights seekers of the 1970s. In this environment for the American male, the Mariko of 1980 must have seemed an exotic and comfortingly retrograde relief.

For the remainder of the 1980s, the prominence of Asian women on television was scaled back. TV shows continued giving Asian women bit parts in their usual roles. The United States continued its search as a nation to reconcile its involvement in Vietnam, and most of that reckoning took place in the string of Vietnam movies coming out of Hollywood. On TV, the portrayal of Asians as wives, as caregivers, and in need of a guiding hand continued in *After M.A.S.H.* (1983–84), and *China Beach* (1988–91), which depicted the personal lives of personnel at a U.S. military base in Vietnam. *China Beach* portrayed a few Vietnamese women in bit parts: employed as a nanny and in a beauty salon; lost and befriended by an American soldier. Episodes of *Miami Vice, Tour of Duty,* and *Magnum P.I.* used as plot devices crimes against Asian women or societal acceptance of interracial coupling. But, for the most part, people who grew up watching television in the 1980s didn't get many impressions about Asian women at all.

1990s TV: Enter the Dragon Lady

Television started to change in the 1990s. Female Asian characters, suddenly empowered—sexually, in the workplace, and otherwise—appeared on American TV screens. Margaret Cho got her own crack at the first sitcom to feature an all-Asian-American cast, *American Girl.* It told the story of a second-generation Korean-American rebelling against her strict, old-country parents. But it was canceled in 1995 after just one season. The show's producers had forced Cho to lose weight so drastically that she suffered kidney failure. She jokes about it in her stage routines, saying that she was hired to play a TV version of herself, but then was told to lose weight and act "more Asian," and then, several episodes later, instructed to act "less Asian." By all accounts, the writing was terrible, the jokes were bad, and the show never could figure out whether it wanted to be authentic or ridiculous.

A sci-fi show, *Forever Knight,* about an 800-year-old Vampire working as a police detective, gave us one season (1994–95) of actress Natsuko Ohama ordering detectives around a Toronto police squadron, although her character was named Captain Amanda Cohen. *Beverly Hills 90210,* which ran for the entire decade, gave us the character Janet Sosna, a Japanese-American magazine assistant who, in one episode, got locked in a refrigerator with her boyfriend while investigating a haunted house. In the new era of sexually empowered Asian women on TV, the two have sex, of course. When later in the series they marry, Sosna's stern Japanese parents don't approve, relenting only after they see their biracial grandchild.

Then, the emergency-room drama *ER* gave us Dr. Deb Chen (Ming-Na, who in real life was born in Macau, grew up in Queens, and got her break in the 1993 movie *The Joy Luck Club*). She appeared for one season on *ER* in 1995, and then returned to the show in 2000. Finally there was a tough, somewhat bitchy recurring Asian character on a TV series. After moving through relationships with a number of fellow medical residents (not unusual on the show), she becomes pregnant by an African-American as the result of a brief fling. The conflict over telling her conservative Chinese mother about the biracial baby, and giving it up for adoption, was featured in several episodes. Later in the series, Dr. Chen insisted that her colleagues begin calling her by her Chinese name, "Jing-Mei," instead of "Deb," and in some scenes was shown speaking Mandarin.

This would have been a first on prime time TV, too, if it weren't for the most memorable Asian TV character of the 1990s, Ling Woo of the Fox Network's sitcom *Ally McBeal* (1998–2002). Played by Lucy Liu, Ling was an icy, abrasive Chinese-American lawyer who also spoke Mandarin. Unlike the 1970s depictions of docile Japanese and Korean women on TV, Ling's character was the stark opposite—the classic stereotype of Dragon Lady.

Early in the show, Ling made her entrance in an episode to the theme music that accompanied the Wicked Witch of the West in *The Wizard of Oz*. Depicted as a sexual predator who nonetheless "doesn't much like sex; it's messy," Ling did like to suck fingers and give "hair" during sex (dragging her long black hair over her partner's body). She spouted such lines as: "A woman hasn't got true control of a man until her hand is on the dumb stick," and, "There's nothing I enjoy more than seeing a happy couple and coming between them." Her liaisons are with white men, of course, but not only with men. Famously, in a dream sequence of Ally McBeal's in which the two of them go on a date, they kiss on screen—yet another Hollywood first. The scene was considered so racy that the episode was banned from being shown in Singapore.

Liu started to make a career out of her icy TV-screen demeanor. Her role as Ling led to being cast as Pearl, the sadistic dominatrix hooker in Mel Gibson's 1999 movie *Payback*. The movie was based on the novel *The Hunter* by veteran crime writer Donald E. Westlake (writing under a pseudonym). (It also was the basis for a 1967 film, *Point Blank,* starring Lee Marvin and Angie Dickinson, but including no Asian dominatrix.) *Payback* was full of the startlingly anachronistic racism of an earlier decade's pulp film. "They don't feel pain the same way we do," Gibson's partner, Val, says of the Chinese triad members who are portrayed as incompetent as they bumble to their violent deaths under Pearl's orders and at the hands of the two white guys. Pearl and Val beat each other bloody as foreplay in the bedroom scenes. "The thing about killing Chows," he says, "is that an hour later you want to do it again."

Liu moved on to the role of icy Princess Pei Pei who hooks up with Jackie Chan's white sidekick in *Shanghai Noon* (2000). But it was her role in *Charlie's Angels* that gave her screen prominence a global reach. Liu played the role of Alex Munday, bikini-waxer and private investi- gator, in the 2000 remake of the 1970s television show *Charlie's Angels* and its sequel in 2003. In the role she was no more vixen-ish or kick- ass than either of the other crime-fighting Angels (a blonde and a red- head), but perhaps that is because of the revelation we get in a surprising scene at the end of the sequel: Liu's character with her white father, making it clear that Alex Munday—finally a character of equality with her co-stars—isn't fully Asian.

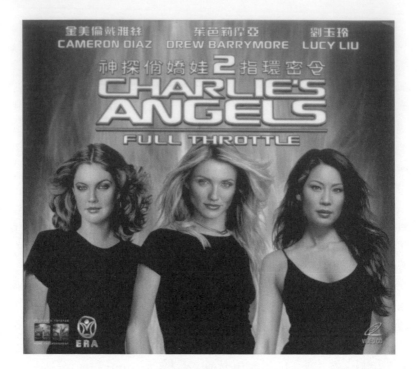

But it is interesting to look at the promo posters and DVD/video covers for *Charlie's Angels: Full Throttle* [*Charlie's Angels 2*]. In them, Liu is dressed more provocatively than the other two. Shown from the front, Liu is the only one in a low-cut top. Shown from the back, she is the only one in spaghetti straps revealing a bare upper back. The other two wear high-necked, short-sleeved T-shirts. The movies also make use of sexual imagery imported from China—not for Liu's character but for one of the raven-haired villains, played by Demi Moore— falsely elongated, pointy fingernails once favored in the court of the Chinese Empress Dowager, from whom the origin of the Dragon Lady myth derives.

When asked in an interview how she felt about perpetuating the Dragon Lady/Vixen stereotypes, Liu replied, "I don't have many options now."[6] There may well have been truth in that. In between the *Angels* movies, Liu tried her own top billing, as an FBI agent co-starring with Antonio Banderas in the strangely titled *Ballistic: Ecks vs. Sever* (2002). The role was still a continuation of her kick-ass fighter persona, but it also was her first attempt to prove she could draw a crowd as a leading lady. She didn't, however, and it flopped at the box office. The movie-going public, it seemed, wasn't yet ready for a kick-ass Asian woman in a leading role.

It was ready for a white woman in that role, however: Uma Thurman's blonde, blue-eyed Bride—in *Kill Bill Vol. 1* (2003). Liu again played the secondary part of evil foil in yet another pulp movie, and her character, O-Ren Iishi, is at her cruelest and most sadistic yet. Wearing black, she whacks off (with a plop) the head of a Japanese man who questions her authority, among other acts of spatter and splatter barbarism. We also get an evil Japanese schoolgirl, taken from the Japanese *manga-anime* (cartoon-animation) world and readily adaptable to Western stereotypes. And, yes, we get the recurring theme of white person vanquishing a phalanx of incompetent Asian fighter guys, yet again, who cry *Eeeee yaaaaaa* just before meeting their deaths. The hierarchy of competency goes white woman, Asian woman, Asian girl, and lastly, Asian men. "Silly Caucasian girl likes to play with Samurai swords," Lucy Liu says before Uma slices off her cranium and exposes her brain. Just imagine trying to reverse the roles—Lucy Liu in the avenging-heroine role, taking out a room full of incompetent white guys, and killing a blonde evil Dragon Lady. The icons are a pervasive part of our cognizance.

It is hardly coincidence that the 1990s gave us the image of Asian women as cold, bitchy Dragon Ladies. It coincided with the rise of a prominent Chinese-American newscaster, Connie Chung, who rose to fame as a national network correspondent throughout the 1980s. A 1999 Salon.com profile called her "America's Most Bitchin' Broadcaster," and that's not an understatement. She was the first Asian-American to co-anchor an evening news broadcast, *The CBS Evening News with Connie Chung and Dan Rather* (with top billing, no less), and her own weekly magazine show, *Eye to Eye with Connie Chung.*

Millions of Americans watched her play hard-ball as she built up a reputation for her aggressive pursuit of interviews—both to line up her subjects and on camera after she secured them. Chung's assertion during an interview with Microsoft Chairman Bill Gates that his tactics against competitors were "like a knife fight" caused him to storm off the set, and her bullying questions to figure skater Tonya Harding made her cry. Also, Chung went public in the early 1990s with news that she was trying unsuccessfully to have a baby with husband Maury

Povich, an admission that added to her caustic public persona. Chung cited the need to take "a very aggressive approach" to having a baby, according to a press release cited in the Salon.com article—as if it were like securing yet another interview.

Connie Chung finally went too far in the eyes of the public, however. In an interview in January 1995 with House Speaker Newt Gingrich's mother, Chung asked her what her son really thought of Hillary Clinton. Mrs. Gingrich wouldn't say. Chung kept asking, leaning over with a conspiratorial, "Why don't you whisper it, just between you and me." Finally, the sixty-eight-year-old Mrs. Gingrich answered "Bitch!" Except that it wasn't just between the House Speaker's mother and Connie Chung. CBS broadcast the response to millions of viewers and hyped it to the hilt.

Chung had to be aggressive to get to that level of network news—anyone did—but to a public accustomed to seeing Asian women on TV as war brides, war victims, and "Yes, master" servants for the previous thirty years, Connie Chung must have come as something of a shock. Within months she was fired from the anchor's chair at the *CBS Evening News,* leaving Dan Rather alone again, and CBS chopped the "with Connie Chung" off *Eye to Eye* as well. Despite briefly resurfacing on her own show on CNN in 2002, Chung has more or less disappeared. She left us a legacy, however, in the form of kick-ass Dragon Ladies on the screens of America.

Not only that, but Asian women as newscasters have almost become a stereotype in their own right since Chung. Particularly on the West Coast of the United States, an older white man/younger Asian woman co-anchor pairing is the norm, thanks in part to affirmative action hiring plans of the 1990s. In one newscast I watched regularly over the last several years, KING 5 News in Seattle, not only was the older white man/younger Asian woman pairing the regular feature of the anchor desk, but all the correspondents broadcasting from the field were either older white men or younger Asian women. Somehow, after the omnipresence of Connie Chung in the realm of early 1990s TV news and her path-breaking pairing with Dan Rather, it didn't look all that unusual.

TV of the 2000s:
Opposing Stereotypes' Uneasy Coexistence

In American serial television of the 2000s, the Dragon Lady and the servile, sex-offering Asian now co-exist as equal TV counterparts. HBO's series *Sex and the City* (1998–2004) once depicted an Asian woman with a heavy, fake accent as a sadistic maid (although both Margaret Cho and Lucy Liu have made cameo appearances), and the same network's *The Mind of the Married Man* (2001) gave us a lead character who, while married to a smart, gorgeous blonde, leaves his wife waiting at home and gets massages from an Asian masseuse who was often topless and eager to offer sex—and, as viewers find out, put on a fake Chinese accent to cater to her clients' expectations. ABC's *Dharma & Greg* (1997–2002) once portrayed an insensitive portrait of an Asian woman cast as a mail-order bride. These are just bit parts, and there are the occasional non-stereotyped TV roles for Asian women as well that don't stand out enough to get noticed. But, with the exception of the still somewhat bitchy and promiscuous Dr. Chen on *ER* (who was created in the emerging Dragon Lady period of 1990s TV), American television as of mid-2000s had yet to create a smart, non-stereotyped, lasting, and recognizable Asian woman character on prime-time TV.

But lest we think that the Hollywood image of bitchy Dragon Lady originated in the newscasts and TV shows of the 1990s, we need to go back in time. Connie Chung may have paved the way for the resurgence of this image, but she certainly didn't start it all. For that, we have to look back to 1930s Hollywood and the screen image of Anna May Wong.

1930s–1940s Hollywood:
Enter the Dragon Lady

Until Lucy Liu, Anna May Wong had been the most famous Chinese-American actress in the world. She appeared in approximately sixty films from 1919 to 1960, most of them made in Hollywood, but also in Germany, France, and England—where she became an exotic stage and screen sensation as well. Wong started out playing slave girls, prostitutes, temptresses, and doomed lovers, and carried on those roles in dozens of films throughout her career. But it is from her charisma and cold-cunning on the black-and-white screen that we take our images of the Dragon Lady. Of course Wong didn't originate the stereotype either, but her on-screen representations of it helped make the image an indelible part of Western consciousness.

Three of Wong's notable films clearly show the Dragon Lady image: *Daughter of the Dragon* (1931), *Shanghai Express* (1932), and *Limehouse Blues* (1934). While her roles back then were more nuanced than the modern ones of Lucy Liu, and in them Wong's characters loved and lost and felt pain and rejection, nonetheless she played a scheming, murderous, other-worldly beauty who killed coldly and without remorse. The *Daughter of the Dragon* role was based on the *Daughter of Fu Manchu* novel by Sax Rohmer, the pen name of British author Arthur Ward. Rohmer/Ward, an eccentric Egyptologist, was assigned by a magazine editor in London to write about London's former Chinatown, known as Limehouse. Based on several sit-down discussions with an old Chinese man whose words Rohmer/Ward embellished to fit already-formed English notions of the intrigue, dangers, and wonders of the East, his thirteen books (starting in 1911) centered around the diabolical Dr. Fu Manchu, "the great and evil man who dreamed of Europe and America under Chinese rule . . . whose existence was a menace to the entire white race." Rohmer/Ward later said he knew nothing about the Chinese but something about Chinatown.[7]

This kind of villainous Yellow Peril played well in Hollywood, and just in time for the first "talkie" films to start reaching wider audiences. Interest in China was high in the 1920s and '30s, as the carnage and chaos of the civil war in China—where Nationalist forces battled the Communists of Mao Zedong—made daily newspaper headlines. The Great Depression made the opulence and adventure of the Orient all the more intriguing among the unemployed, despairing, and downtrodden.

Because Hollywood has dominated the world's film industry since its inception, American images are global images. Films from France and Germany imitated American styles and stereotypes. The French, in particular, wrote of how American filmmakers portrayed "a cheap world of Dr. Fu Manchu and *Madame Butterfly* and the world of crimes and kidnappings . . . [where] blonde young girls were held captive in secret rooms below laundries." But still, France's own Asian starlets— "Miss Moonlight," "Miss Weeping Lily" "Miss Ivory Legs"—did little to dispel any of Hollywood's stereotypes[8]—and, in fact, French film's idealized portrayal of colonial Indochina served to enhance the mystique of the Orient. Wong herself was just as famous in Europe as in the United States, having learned both French and German to land more roles on stage and screen there.

In *Daughter of the Dragon,* Wong plays a stage performer, dressed Peking Opera style, who sets out to avenge the death of her wicked father, Dr. Fu Manchu. But she has fallen in love with the white man deemed responsible—who has seen her on stage and is beguiled as well—even though he is betrothed to someone else. Once, they nearly kiss but do not. (Anti-miscegenation laws prohibiting marriage, cohabitation, or sexual relations between Caucasians and members of other races were not lifted in California until 1948, so the Motion Picture Code did not allow scenes of interracial relationships.) Despite her love, Wong's character, nonetheless, plots to kill him. She drugs the wine and ties up her love interest and his fiancée, but is thwarted by Scotland Yard which bursts in and kills her, leaving the white couple to live happily ever after.

In her next movie, *Shanghai Express,* Wong's character does escalate to murder, and she does it coldly and rationally. The director, Josef von Sternberg, was known to have a taste for things Eastern and exotic. He has Wong and Marlene Dietrich playing prostitutes with elegant gowns, sharing a first-class compartment on a train to Shanghai, which is hijacked by rebels during the Chinese civil war (an event loosely based on the news). Their leader, the half-Chinese General Chang (Warner Oland, who also starred opposite Wong in *Daughter of the Dragon* and who later played Charlie Chan), is kidnapping the train's occupants. The scenes of the train passing through China are exotic and atmospheric, lending to the mystique. General Chang attempts to rape Dietrich's character, Shanghai Lily, then settles for raping Wong's character instead. We see Wong, the next day, hair disheveled and face ashen. She unsheathes a steel blade, which she uses to stab him to death in retribution. "You'd better get her out of there," she warns Dietrich's on-screen love interest. "I just killed Chang."

"I don't know whether I should be grateful to you or not," Dietrich's character says.

"It is of no consequence. I didn't do it for you," Wong answers coldly. "Death cancelled [the General's] debt to me."

In the end, Wong's character walks away alone, while the white couple embraces on the platform. It is the first time, in the ten years since she started in Hollywood, that one of Wong's characters survives to the end of a film. The emergence of the Dragon Lady of the Hollywood screen is complete. The Chinese government banned the film, calling it a disgrace to China.

In Wong's subsequent film, *Limehouse Blues* (about London's China-town), she dances in a serpentine style on a nightclub stage wearing a Chinese *qipao* dress with a dragon motif. Graham Russell Gao Hodges observes in *Anna May Wong: From Laundryman's Daughter to Hollywood Legend* that "from a Chinese perspective, Anna May's body, her dress and the ceiling decoration accentuate the power of the dragon as a symbol of China. From a Western viewpoint, the elements signify the dreaded Dragon Lady." Some observers believe that director von Sternberg (*Shanghai Express*) had a behind-the-scenes role, even though he was contracted to another production studio at the time. In the end, yet again, a young white couple escapes to happiness while the Chinese suffer violent deaths. The Chinese government didn't like this film either, which the Chinese press said "again disgraces China."[1]

Wong's roles—particularly as Dr. Fu Manchu's daughter in *Daughter of the Dragon*—were partly the inspiration for the "Dragon Lady" in the 1934 Chicago Tribune Syndicate cartoon series *Terry and the Pirates*. The cartoon's creator, Milton Caniff, may have coined the term "Dragon Lady." He drew her as the villainous ringleader of a gang of pirates, capable of seducing, humiliating, and attempting to murder the strip's heroes. It proved so popular that in 1937 it became a radio series, in 1940 was brought to the big screen, and in 1952 ran as a TV series. Another of Caniff's inspirations may have been a 1930 book by Aleko E. Lilius, *I Sailed with Pirates,* in which the female Chinese pirate, Lai Choi San, is "Queen of the Pirates." Even though Yellow Peril and the vilification of the Empress Dowager originated the concept

Anna May Wong
CREDIT: courtesy Paramount Pictures

that led to the popularization of such characters and to Wong's on-screen roles, it wasn't until the cartoon series that the image had a name. Like Lucy Liu, when Wong was criticized for perpetuating stereotypes, she responded that when you are just starting out, you don't have much choice about the roles you get to play.

Director von Sternberg must have liked the Dragon Lady image he helped complete, because he uses it again in the 1941 film *The Shanghai Gesture*. This time, his lead characters are all Caucasians dressed as Asians, a long-standing practice in Hollywood that helped studios steer clear of the mixed-race couple laws. Mother Gin Sling (Ona Munson) is the owner of a vice-ridden casino in colonial Shanghai and "the warlord of the Chinese underworld." Her description before she enters the scene, by Victor Mature playing the smarmy "Arabian" Dr. Omar, leaves no room to mistake any act of kindness for mere generosity. Rather, her every thought and gesture is a clever, calculated ploy. "The real boss is a remarkable lady, the most cold-blooded dragon you'll ever meet," Omar says. "She'll devour you as a cat swallows a mouse." To complete the image, Mother Gin Sling wears a long silk robe, her hair braided and looped crown-like back to her head in large circles that grow ever larger with each scene in tandem with her treachery. While she hardly looks Asian, she does convincingly pull off an inscrutable, exotic mystique. "My people are Manchus," she pronounces coldly, just like the Empress Dowager of China. Her every order to subordinates is punctuated by the words, "chop, chop." We know she is capable of murder, and she does not disappoint us, killing in cold blood the husband who once abandoned her.

Not every role of the 1930s and '40s portrayed Asian women in a villainous pall, or as the slaves or temptresses of Wong's earlier career. Wong herself starred in *Lady From Chungking* (1942), playing a guerrilla fighter leading the uprising against the Japanese occupation of China. It was a particularly welcome portrayal at the time, as the United States then was at war with Japan. Prior to that, the 1937 film adaptation of the Pearl S. Buck novel *The Good Earth* held up Chinese peasants returning to the land as a dignified image of noble primitivism. While it seemed progressive in its day and had stunning special effects in the form of a swarm of locusts, it featured the Asian wife as long-suffering, obedient, and loyal in the face of her husband's infidelity.

Wong had wanted to play the role of leading lady O-lan, but the studio gave it to Austrian-born Luise Rainer, who won an Oscar for Best Actress for a somewhat (by modern standards) overacted, stage-like performance. Because the leading man, Paul Muni, also born in Austria but later the product of the Yiddish Art Theater in New York, was Caucasian, under the Motion Picture Code both had to be the same race. To see the film now in a modern context, with overwrought Rainer's Austrian accent and Muni's heavy "New Yorkese," they make an odd pair. Wong was asked to read for the only bad-girl role in the film—the flighty call girl who tries to break up the peasants' marriage. Wong was incredulous and refused. "You're asking me—with my Chinese blood—to do the only unsympathetic role in the picture, featuring an all-American cast portraying Chinese characters?"[10] The studio found someone else, of course, another Chinese-American would-be starlet long-since forgotten. (She, Mary Wong, committed suicide three years later, at age twenty-five.)

THE 1930S ALSO GAVE RISE to a type of Hollywood glamour focused on the image of the exotic Oriental that coincided with the take-off of the cosmetics industry. By wearing Oriental make-up and clothing, Western women could present themselves as a combination of (white) virtue and (nonwhite) sexuality.[11] An advertisement in *Vogue* in 1935 declared it fashionable to look like a "Balinese maiden," and advised:

> If you are wearing a swathed Oriental evening frock . . . your makeup should be as glamorous as possible—deep mysterious eye shadows, with perhaps a touch of gold or silver. This is the moment to use mascara on your lashes, and even indulge in kohl, and to make yourself, in general, as exotic as you possibly can.[12]

Another 1936 ad for Helena Rubenstein's lipstick and blush in "Chinese Red" offered more opportunity to exoticize: "It is vivid, young—with lots of red for flattery and just a hint of gold to give you a touch of the exotic. To pallid skin it lends a lovely glow."[13] The same year, Elizabeth Arden introduced a summer line of "Chinese and Copper" makeup, with the foundation an "amber tone that makes you look like a Manchu princess," dark eye pencil, and blue-green "Eye-Sha-do."[14]

1920s Hollywood: The Submissive Is Born

Long before she created so effectively the screen image of Dragon Lady, Anna May Wong gained her early stardom playing the opposing stereotype: the submissive Asian girl, sometimes referred to as "Lotus

Flower," the name of Wong's character in *The Toll of the Sea* (1922)— her first major screen appearance at the age of seventeen. The movie was a reworking of the *Madame Butterfly* story set in China, where the peasant girl Lotus Flower is loved and abandoned by a shipwrecked American sailor who fathers her child.

Madame Butterfly has been made and remade again by Hollywood over the years. Mary Pickford played in the role of abandoned Japanese wife in a 1915 silent version. Next, Cary Grant played the lead in a 1932 version, changed somewhat from the Puccini opera. The 1954 and 1995 film versions were screen adaptations of the opera, and there are numerous European opera company performances available on video and DVD as well. In short, it is a story that has stuck with us for more than 100 years in several dozen interpretations on stage and screen. It was inevitable, then, that when Asian actresses first began appearing in the first creations of the Hollywood film industry, that's where they would have ended up. In addition to these five films, several other works have adapted or reinterpreted the *Madame Butterfly* story, either with men or Vietnamese women cast as the doomed lovers, including: *Limehouse Blues; China Gate* (1957) starring Angie Dickinson and set in Vietnam; the made-for-TV movie *The Lady From Yesterday* (1985) in which a Vietnamese woman shows up to her former GI boyfriend's home in America and delivers their child; *M Butterfly* (1993), which makes the lovers both men; and, of course, the musical *Miss Saigon,* which transports the setting to the Vietnam War.

It is worth recounting the origins of the *Butterfly* story to show, yet again, how a loose interpretation of historical fact, rewritten as fiction, and then transformed onto stage and screen, takes the image of Asian woman and distorts her to Western fantasies.

Giacomo Puccini's original 1904 opera *Madame Butterfly* was based on a play Puccini had seen in London in 1900 that was adapted from an 1898 *American Century* magazine short story that was, itself, adapted in a sort of half-truth from an 1887 French novel called *Madame Chrysantheme* by Pierre Loti (real name Julien Viaud), which was loosely based on encounters he had on a visit to Japan. In it, main character Loti lands at the Japanese treaty port of Nagasaki with the twin objectives of getting a tattoo and acquiring a temporary wife, "a little yellow-skinned woman with black hair and cat's eyes. She must be pretty. Not much bigger than a doll."

Here is the factual part: In Japan at that time, girls from poor families were hired or sold to traders as temporary wives. Foreigners were able to look them over, make a selection, and negotiate a price. For the most part, it was a straight commercial transaction with no romance. The "wife" was more or less a long-term prostitute with housekeeping duties for as long as the trader was in port.

In the novel, Loti acquires Miss Chrysanthemum, but quickly finds her tiresome. He makes disparaging remarks about the Japanese in general, and he is glad to be rid of her as he prepares to leave Japan. She makes a big scene of crying and begging him not to leave. Later, having forgotten something, Loti returns to find Miss Chrysanthemum happily counting the money he had given her and awaiting her next "husband."

That story was made into an 1893 opera and ballet and enjoyed moderate success.[15] Seven years later, the American writer John Luther Long wrote a short story for *American Century* magazine graduating Miss Chrysanthemum to Madame Butterfly. Long said that his sister had been to Nagasaki and had met the offspring of one of these unions between a visiting sailor and temporary wife. The offspring, a son, recounted that his mother had tried unsuccessfully to commit suicide. Long's fictional story keeps the transactional side of the temporary wife arrangement, and makes the protagonist an American naval officer. The officer in his story returns to Japan with his American wife but does not go see the Japanese woman. The American wife does, and when she discovers the Japanese woman has the child of her husband, she claims him as her own. Because the Americans have taken away her child and left her with nothing, the Japanese woman attempts suicide but fails.

By the time playwright David Belasco adapted it to the stage in a one-act play, and then Puccini saw it in London and felt inspired to create the most successful opera of the early twentieth century, *Madame Butterfly* had evolved again, and would once more. Puccini's opera depicted his Butterfly and Lieutenant B.F. Pinkerton in somewhat coarse terms, akin to prostitute and cad. But after initial less-than-rave reviews of the debut at La Scala in Milan, Puccini made the characters more sympathetic, transforming *Madame Butterfly* into the story we know today: a Japanese woman with loyal, undying love for the officer who abandoned her and left her pining for his return, who willingly gives up her son and commits suicide (successfully) so that her son can be raised in America and have a better life. It took more than seventeen years to transform the story of a tiresome, money-counting prostitute into the story of a pining, suicidal lover. And it is Puccini's final portrayal of Asian woman as a delicate, fluttery, bewitching butterfly that has endured, affecting so many of the images of Asian women since.

LT. PINKERTON: Almost transparently fragile and slender, dainty in stature, a quaint little figure seems to have stepped down straight from a screen. But from her background of varnish and lacquer, suddenly light as a feather she flutters. And like a butterfly, hovers and settles with so much charm, such seductive graces that to run after her, a wild wish seized me. Though in the quest her frail wings be broken . . . .

To think that pretty plaything is my wife. My wife! But her charm is so alluring. My heart is beating madly with passionate longing.

Child from whose eyes witchery is shining, now you are all my own. You are clad all in lily white raiment. How sweet are your tresses of brown in your snowy garment.

CHO-CHO (Butterfly): I am like the moon's little goddess. The little Moon Goddess who comes down by night from her bridge in the star-lit sky.

LT. PINKERTON: Bewitching all mortals.

Examining a bit of dialog from David Henry Hwang's play and film *M Butterfly* (1993) provides insight into how silly we might think this story would be if placed in another context. This conversation is between the French diplomat pseudonymously named Réné Gallimard and the Chinese opera singer he falls for (who turns out to be a man) after watching her/his performance in *Madame Butterfly*:

GALLIMARD: It's a very beautiful story . . .

SONG LILING: It's one of your favorite fantasies, isn't it? The submissive Oriental woman and the cruel white man. . . . Consider it this way: what would you say if a blonde homecoming queen fell in love with a short Japanese businessman? He treats her cruelly, then goes home for three years, during which time she prays to his picture and turns down marriage from a young Kennedy. Then, when she learns he has remarried, she kills herself. Now, I believe you would consider this girl to be a deranged idiot, correct? But because it's an Oriental who kills herself for a Westerner—ah!—you find it beautiful.

Not just beautiful—archetypal. The West has a continual appetite for the image of sweet, gentle Japanese child-women; the *Memoirs of a Geisha,* which again took aspects of real truth and fictionalized them in what has now become a century-old tradition of Western men writing fiction about Japanese women, sold more than seven million copies after it was published in 1997. A 2005 production by Steven Spielberg, directed by Rob Marshall, promises us yet another permutation of a child-like, pining, devoted Japanese woman on screen in the form of that book's heroine geisha, Sauryi.

Stereotypes of Asian Women on Screen

Submissive (desired)	Dominant (feared)
Geisha Girl/Lotus Flower/Servant/ China Doll: Submissive, docile, obedient, reverential (including Asian men as effeminate, servile)	Dragon Lady: Wily, clever, and calculating; powerful but lacking empathy or maternal instinct
Vixen/Sex Nymph: Sexy, coquettish, manipulative; tendency toward disloyalty or opportunism	Dominatrix: Sexually dominating, icy, emotionless
Prostitute/Victim of Sex Trade/War/ Oppression: Helpless, in need of assistance or rescue; good-natured at heart.	Martial Arts Mistress (or Master): Cold, distant, steely, capable, with emotions kept in check
Enigmatic Oriental: Inscrutable, unpredictable, unknowable, with mysterious and sometimes wise ways	

1950s Hollywood:
Devoted Wives, Girlfriends, and Back-scrubbers

The 1950s marked a reversal of all the gains the image of Asian women had made on screen in the 1940s. Reflecting the real-life experiences of soldiers from World War II and Korea returning to America with war brides—as well as those of soldiers who experienced the licentious prostitution of post-war Japan in the form of "panpan" or "geesha girls"—the image of Asian woman as devoted wife or girlfriend became a big theme of Hollywood as America tried to grapple with issues of biracial couples and racism, as well as with humanizing the Japanese following the demonizing of the war.

We saw this change in image in *Japanese War Bride* (1952), *The Barbarian and the Geisha* (1958), *China Doll* (1958), *South Pacific* (1958), and, in one of the most famous movies of the decade, *Sayonara* (1957). (There was no shortage of devoted wives to the King of Siam in the Rodgers & Hammerstein musical *The King and I* (1956), *Anna & the King of Siam* (1946), or the 1999 remake, *Anna and the King,* all of which have been banned in Thailand for being historically inaccurate and disrespectful of the monarchy.)

Like *Shogun* before it, *Sayonara* was a best-selling novel before it hit the bit screen. Marlon Brando starred, and the movie garnered Oscars for its best supporting actor (Red Buttons) and supporting actress (Miyoshi Umeki, who later became Mrs. Livingston on TV); Brando lost the best actor title that year to Alec Guinness for *The Bridge on the River Kwai*. The movie version more or less adhered to James A. Michener's book, in which American servicemen stationed in Japan during the Korean War fall in love with Japanese women despite the racist attitudes of their fellow Americans and strict U.S. military regulations against it. It presented Japanese women as romanticized and idealized—delicate, doll-like creatures who wish for nothing more than to scrub their husbands' backs. In part, this seems an attempt to humanize the Japanese in the years following the war, to show their admirable strengths in times of adversity, and go beyond calling Japanese women ugly, "slant-eyed runts" as occurs in the beginning of the film. Thus, the Brando character (Major Lloyd "Ace" Gruver) is sent off to Japan to "tango with the . . . dolls." After arriving, he breaks off his engagement to girl-back-home Eileen Webster (the daughter of a general and his bossy wife) who, despite having "an enormous capacity to fill a bathing suit," nonetheless "thinks too much." Ace comes to this realization in a discussion with fellow officer Capt. Mike Bailey.

BAILEY: Are you afraid of American women?

ACE GRUVER: I hadn't thought of it.

BAILEY: I've been over here a long time, what with one thing and another. I've watched lots of our men go for these Japanese girls. . . . Hell, I won't be superior about it. I do myself. Frankly and all kidding aside, Ace, I'd a damned sight rather marry Fumiko-san than Eileen. But I just wondered why you felt that way?

GRUVER: I don't feel that way. At least if I do I don't know about it. But why do you?

BAILEY: With me it's very clear. On thing explains it all. You ever had your back scrubbed by a Japanese girl . . . a girl who really loved you?

GRUVER: What's back scrubbing got to do with it?

BAILEY: Ace, either you understand or you don't. . . . Can you imagine Eileen Webster scrubbing your back?[16]

Gruver then admits to his "great fear that Eileen Webster would not be able or willing to do that for her man." So instead, Gruver falls for stage actress Hana-ogi.

[She] looked at me in a quiet, submissive Japanese way which betrayed no emotion but which dared me to budge her one inch. . . . Long after she had gone I recalled the graceful way she bent down by the doors to put on her *zori,* the rare delicacy with which she arranged her kimono, so in spite of persistent apprehension that I was headed for trouble, I determined that no matter what she thought of Americans, no matter what order Camp Kobe handed down regarding Japanese girls, I was going to see her again.

Another World War II reconciliation movie which came out the following year, the *Barbarian and the Geisha* (1958), starring John

John Wayne in *The Barbarian and the Geisha,* 1958
CREDIT: courtesy Jerry Ohlinger's Movie Material Store

Wayne, didn't do much better for the image of Japanese women. Filmed in Japan and directed by John Huston, it purports to tell the story of Townsend Harris, sent by President Franklin Pierce to serve as the first U.S. Consul-General to Japan, and Harris's devoted Japanese consort, Okichi.

The *Barbarian and the Geisha* is yet a third example of Western writers taking splices of historical fact and turning them into the fiction of an idealized Japanese woman. Townsend Harris and Okichi were real-life people. But a very different Japanese version of what happened goes like this:

The American who turned up on the shores of Shimoda in 1856 really was a barbarian—the Japanese ate no meat or dairy in those days and referred to foreigners as *bataa kusai,* "stinking of butter." Okichi was a very popular geisha and town elders ordered her to take up with Harris, who had asked about her after seeing her walk down the street. Three days after Okichi arrived at his home, Harris discovered that she had a suspicious skin eruption and told her not to visit again until it was cured. But even after the sore had disappeared, whenever the subject of a visit from Okichi was broached, Harris always declared himself unwell. Two and a half months later, he terminated the contract. Okichi had had to sleep with an old, repugnant man, had had to abrogate her right as a geisha to choose her customers, and then she had been publicly humiliated and found wanting. Now, she was ruined. She became a beggar and years later drowned herself. Today, there is a shrine at Shimoda (and a museum of sex) dedicated to Okichi's memory.[17]

Here's the Hollywood version.

Okichi takes up willingly with the dashing John Wayne as Harris. When he tells her that he must return to America, she breaks down in tears.

OKICHI: America so far away!
HARRIS: Not so far away that I'll forget you. Every time I see a woman with ornaments in her hair, I'll think of Okichi and her yellow combs.

Later, there is another exchange.

HARRIS: I'm coming back to you, Okichi. And that's the last we'll ever be separated. (He points to a hot spring and suggests they build a house.) Would you be happy in a house like that?
OKICHI: It is written, fortunate is the woman who rises in morning to cook her husband's rice.
HARRIS: Fortunate is the man.

They part, she again breaks down in tears over having to part with her beloved. In the final scene she wears black (inaccurately, as Japanese wear white for mourning) and we hear Okichi's words: "He passed into our history and from my sight, but never from my heart."

Quite revealingly different, isn't it? But because of the enduring power of images, and because "all film creates the illusion of documentary reality," notes Terry Teachout,[18] drama critic for *The Wall Street Journal,* we take the Hollywood version to be fact. We can document this by watching the A&E Television Network special *The Secret Life of Geisha* (1999). The A&E supposed documentary splices in scenes from the Hollywood movie, retelling as fact the invented grand love affair between Harris and Okichi, and other misinterpretations from the movie such as John Wayne's lines that the "Shogun's palace [was] lavish beyond words" at a time when Japanese simplicity of design may have been a more apt description. Lavish, seductive Orient and adoring Asian women are what we have come to expect from Asia after so many centuries. We invent these fictions, imprint them in film, and then recount them as fact over and over again.

For a time, the geisha world became a fascination of Hollywood. We also saw geisha in *Teahouse of the August Moon* (1956), *Cry for Happy* (1961), and *My Geisha* (1962). As Gina Marchetti points out in her 1993 book, *Romance and the "Yellow Peril: Race, Sex, and Discursive Strategies in Hollywood Fiction,* geisha appeared to be Hollywood's "chief emblem of postwar reconciliation. Although on the surface she might appear cool, distant, mysterious, or morally suspect, underneath she was seen as docile, eager to please, malleable, child-like, and vulnerable. Metaphorically, a bellicose Japan, through the figure of a geisha, became a yielding and dependent nation." Moreover, Marchetti writes:

> As part of a general reaction to the emergence of women as an economic and social force during the wartime absence of men on the home front, these geisha tales could also very conveniently serve as postwar moral fables for independently minded American women. The point being made is quite clear: white American women should put aside their own interests to return to the prewar male-dominated order that their geisha sisters accept as the "natural" way of the world.

This was reinforced through the quiet servility of Phuong in *The Quiet American* (1958, remade more authentically in 2002). Based upon the brilliant novel by Graham Greene about an innocent abroad, it depicted a British journalist and an American intelligence agent competing for the heart of an enigmatic Oriental, the Vietnamese dance-hall girl Phuong. But while both the main characters—Fowler, the self-tormenting Brit, and Pyle, the brashly naïve American—are strongly developed, Phuong's image is of a somewhat flat, objectified frailty. Her function is to be a beauty to behold, to be desired and taken care of—and by whichever of these men it does not seem to matter. Neither of them truly understands her or her switching alliances. Phuong, of course, is a metaphor for Vietnam, for a country that neither Fowler (representing declining British empire) nor Pyle (representing rising America)—nor the author Greene, who confessed as much later—quite understood. As Fowler says of the American, "Saving the country and saving a woman would be the same thing to a man like that."

Another 1950s movie gave us a model for Chinese women that same year, *China Doll* (1958). An American pilot fighting the Japanese in China finds himself the unintentional "owner" of a Chinese housekeeper, Shu-Jen, whom he has purchased during a drunken evening. They fall in love, but, disappointed by the pilot's late nights in bars, Shu-Jen leaves. When he finds out she is carrying his child, he finds her and marries her in a traditional Chinese ceremony. The family is happy together and Shu-Jen is devoted, until the base comes under attack by Japanese bombers, making for a tragic end.

It is fitting, then, that the end of the 1950s would offer viewing audiences the merger of both the images of the docile Lotus Flower/China Doll that typified the decade and the Dragon Lady from the decades before in the screen adaptation of the long-running Broadway musical *South Pacific* (1958). This was another adaptation of an adaptation—of yet another James A. Michener tale. The original Rodgers & Hammerstein Broadway production had begun its run in 1949. It was the musical that gave us the classics "I'm Gonna Wash That Man Right Outta My Hair," "Some Enchanted Evening," "Bali Ha'i," and "There's Nothin' Like a Dame."

Hollywood at the time still was struggling with America's tension over biracial couples, and even though California had lifted its laws banning them, not all states did until a ruling by the U.S. Supreme Court in 1967. *South Pacific,* in a relief from the relentless Asian-woman-as-devotee theme of the decade, kept true to its origins of an earlier decade and gave us the old image of Dragon Lady yet again.

While the setting might have been the South Pacific islands, the characters are Asian, described as "Tonkinese." The stout African-American singer Juanita Hall played "Bloody Mary" (after Anna May Wong dropped out due to declining health); the surprisingly juxtaposed France Nuyen, with her small-boned delicate physique, played her sexually available daughter.

Our first encounter with Bloody Mary finds her offering ten dollars to a soldier trying to sell her a load of grass skirts for eighty dollars. "Now see here, Dragon Lady," he says, dispelling any doubt about her role. Then she offers her daughter in marriage to the lieutenant. As soon as the girl is introduced, with only a few moments' hesitation, she rushes into his arms and they embrace. Then, following a cheesy cutaway to a sunset, we are back in their bedroom in what is obviously post-coital nightfall. He is shirtless, and her now-disheveled hair has been taken down from its bun. In contrast, when the French plantation owner tries merely to kiss the story's heroine, played by Mitzi Gaynor, she rejects him and runs away. The message, seemingly, is of the sexual availability of the submissive young Asian girl versus the propriety of the white woman. In the end, the proper white woman gets her man; the promiscuous Asian girl doesn't. The transition to the image of Asian-woman-as-prostitute/sex-vixen that would typify the 1960s had begun.

1960s Hollywood: Prostitute and Vixen

Next came *The World of Suzie Wong* (1960). This was the Paramount Pictures adaptation of the popular 1957 Richard Mason novel. Unusually, the screen adaptation was more progressive than the book, which was written in the patronizingly British tone of cultural superiority over the uneducated, "dirty yum-yum girls" of Hong Kong's red-light district.

The book tells the tale of Robert Lomax, an English artist who—by sketching Asian women—finds himself stirred in primal, sexual ways—ways that English women had never moved him. In the movie, he is played by William Holden and becomes an American with more slightly progressive ideas who pitches up in Hong Kong and meets his

China Doll—Suzie, played by Nancy Kwan. The film version depicts almost none of the blatant sexual racism of the book. Suzie is an illiterate, orphaned prostitute. He hires her to model for him, then finds himself first pitying her and then falling in love with her when she persistently keeps butting into his life. After she enjoins him to help save her illegitimate child, who dies in a flood, he becomes her white knight, saving her from the sordid world of prostitution.

Lomax, in the book, ruminates: "I tried to explain why I wanted to marry Suzie. . . . All the reasons that I had given her sounded superficial, and I felt sure that I left out the most important reason of all. Yet I did not know myself what it was." Finally he settles on it: escapism. If he married an English girl who offered to get him a cushy job in a bank, he reasons, he would be trapped, confined, in his own little social circle. By rescuing his China Doll, he could escape the confines of his own world—and find the exotic realm of the Oriental.

James Bond added to the Asian-woman-as-prostitute/sex vixen stereotype, for in the 1960s he departed from the usual phalanx of blondes, brunettes, and redheads and added an Asian to the collection of Bond girls. There was a new dimension to this, however, drawing on the ancient notions of Orient as dangerous: if you succumb to the temptation, you risk death. In *You Only Live Twice* (1967) (when Bond was still Sean Connery), our hero finds himself in Hong Kong, in bed with a Chinese woman with long black hair. He kisses her, saying:

BOND: Why is it that Chinese girls taste different from all other girls?

CHINESE GIRL: You think Chinese better, huh?

BOND: Not better, just different—the way Peking duck is different from Russian caviar. But I love them both.

CHINESE GIRL: Dah-ling, I give you very best duck.

She then jumps out of bed, aware that two men with machine guns are about to burst in. Bond escapes, of course. Subsequently, he is lured by a Japanese woman who tricks him into chasing her straight into a trap. She stops, turns around. He thinks he has caught her and takes a step forward. Then, a trap door opens and he falls through. Bond also—strikingly—marries a Japanese woman and "becomes"

Japanese with the help of make up. Of course, his wife is killed by a ninja who drops poison into her mouth while the couple is sleeping.

At the end of the movie, we return to the image of Japanese women scrubbing the backs of their men. Chief Tanaka, sitting in the bath alongside Bond, remarks: "Your English girls would never perform this service."

By the close of the 1960s, Hollywood had run the full spectrum of popular stereotypes, from submissive Lotus Flower to Dragon Lady to devoted wife/girlfriend to sex vixen.

There was something of an exception: *The Flower Drum Song* (1961). Based on the 1958 Rodgers & Hammerstein Broadway musical loosely based on the first novel written by a Chinese-American (C.Y. Lee) to reach the best-seller list, it was the first Hollywood release about (and starring) Asians. By today's standards it appears dated, telling the story of a Chinese woman, Mei Li, (played by Myoshi Umeki, the future Mrs. Livingston), and her father, who arrive in San Francisco as stowaways. Mei Li is coming for an arranged marriage to her unseen fiancé, who prefers his girlfriend (played by Nancy Kwan). Mei Li also falls in love with someone else. While Mei Li, as a fresh-off-the-boat Chinese girl, appears on the surface to be seemingly servile, she turns out to be full of pluck in her own way.

We would not see such nuances in Asian women characters on screen again until the 1990s brought to Hollywood the Asian directors and actors who scored commercial successes in Hong Kong and Taiwan.

1970s–1980s Hollywood: Dehumanized, Prostituted, and Conquered

The late 1970s and 1980s, when America was reconciling the war in Vietnam on screen, brought another regression—a much more dehumanized view of Asian women seen through the viewpoint of the GIs who served there. As prostitutes and war victims were largely how these men encountered the women of Vietnam, and subsequently how we saw them through their eyes in the series of Vietnam War–reckoning movies: *Deer Hunter* (1978), *Apocalypse Now* (1979), *Platoon* (1986), and *Full Metal Jacket* (1987), among others.

One Vietnam movie was an exception, *Good Morning, Vietnam* (1987) in which Robin Williams playing a zany, rebellious DJ for Armed Forces Radio falls for a proper Vietnamese woman who, much like the enigmatic Phuong from *The Quiet American,* is depicted with shifting allegiances, revealed in her case through family connections to the Viet Cong.

In most of the Vietnam films, however, Asian women are shown as war victims sobbing with children in their arms as their villages burned, or in streams of war refugee convoys—or wielding automatic weapons on the side of the Viet Cong. Typical were the scenes from Stanley Kubrick's *Full Metal Jacket* that incensed an Asian-American community just starting to find its voice in American public life. In the movie, our first glimpse of Vietnam comes with a hooker in high heels walking down a street in Saigon to the tune of Nancy Sinatra's "These Boots Are Made for Walkin'" and encountering two soldiers at a café.

HOOKER: Hi baby, you got girlfriend Vietnam?

SOLDIER: Not just this minute.

HOOKER: Well, baby, me so horny, me so horny. Me love you long time. You party?

SOLDIER: Yeah, we might party. How much?

HOOKER: Fifteen dollar.

SOLDIER: Fifteen dollars for both of us.

HOOKER: No, each you fifteen dollar. Me love you long time. Me so horny.

SOLDIER: Fifteen dollars too *beaucoup*. Five dollars each.

HOOKER: Me sucky sucky. Me love you too much.

SOLDIER: Five dollars is all my Mom allows me to spend.

HOOKER: Okay, ten dollar each.

SOLDIER: What do we get for ten dollars?

HOOKER: Everything you want.

SOLDIER: Everything?

HOOKER: Ev-erything.

When the soldier gets up to have his photo taken with the hooker, who lifts her skirt to flash her behind to the camera, he says to his buddy, "You know, half these gook whores are serving officers in the

Viet Cong. The other half have got TB. Make sure you only fuck the ones that cough [first]."

Just to make sure we get the point, there is another exchange later. This time, a South Vietnamese officer rides up on his motorbike with a hooker in sunglasses on the back and presents the girl, her hands provocatively on her hips, to the assembled unit.

> GIs: Good morning, little schoolgirl. I'm a little schoolboy, too. Woo!
> OFFICER: Do you want Number One fucky? (The men howl and make jokes.)
> GI: Me want sucky.
> OFFICER: Sucky, fucky, smoke cigarette in the pussy. She give you everything you want, long time.
> GIs: How much there, chief?
> OFFICER: Fifteen dollah, each.
> GIs: Uh uh. Fifteen dollars *beaucoup* money. Five dollars each.
> OFFICER: Come on, she love you good. Boom boom long time.
> GIs: Five dollars.
> OFFICER: No. Ten dollah . . . . Okay, five dollah. Give it to me.

The third and last Vietnamese woman we see in the movie is a uniformed Viet Cong, her hair in schoolgirl-like braids, firing an automatic weapon. She is the sniper who killed several men in the unit. Our protagonist, Joker, shoots her in a firefight, then looks over her supine body and shoots her again as she draws her last breaths and pleads for a quick death. "No more boom boom for this baby-san," a fellow soldier says. Fighter or prostitute, it hardly matters.

The 1985 film *Year of the Dragon,* its screenplay written by *Deer Hunter* director Michael Cimino and *Platoon* writer/director Oliver Stone, also caused outrage in the Asian-American community. Stanley White, a Vietnam-veteran cop played by Mickey Rourke, goes to clean up Chinatown, which, since the days of Fu Manchu years seventy years before, consistently has been portrayed in films as exotic, criminal, and dangerous. After Asian-Americans organized boycotts and picketed theaters at the movie's release, MGM-UA added this disclaimer to the opening scene:

Mickey Rourke and John Lone in *Year of the Dragon*, 1985
CREDIT: courtesy MGM/UA Entertainment Co.

This film does not intend to demean or ignore the many positive features of Asian-Americans and specifically Chinese-American communities. Any similarity between the depiction in this film and any association, organization, individual or Chinatown that exists in real life is accidental.

When viewing the movie, however, with its scenes set clearly in New York's Chinatown, it's a little hard to suspend disbelief. Detective White becomes involved with the character of Tracy Tzu, a TV newswoman with a short, sassy haircut and a professional lifestyle modeled on Connie Chung, who at the time was still a national news correspondent and not yet an anchor. (Tzu as in Tzu Hsi, the Empress Dowager and Dragon Lady of China.) While positioned as a classic, exotic seductress of the married Mr. White (whose wife is at home with a wrench fixing the sink and accuses him of "breaking my balls"), Tracy is also independent and career-minded. But White dominates her as their relationship progresses. He rips her clothes; she slaps him; he threatens to rape her. He moves in with her, verbally and physically abuses her, tells her how to do her job, and takes away her independence. We see scenes of her walking around naked or topless. White's dominance over Asian woman as a representation of foreign and feminist threat (and at the same time over the Chinese kingpin played by John Lone, who, in a sexually charged final scene in a supine position under White, submits to his dominance, too) is legitimated throughout the movie. Tracy is forcibly transformed from Dragon Lady to submissive China Doll by the power of Mr. White in the course of two hours. Lest there be any doubt that Tracy, while Chinese-American, well-off, and well-educated, is a representation of "Asia" that must submit to the dominance of White, we hear these lines from Stanley, the anger for having lost Vietnam transferred to a modern Chinese-American woman born a world away:

> It's the same thing as in 'Nam. We lost because *you* were smarter than us.
>   The first time I saw you, I hated your guts. I think that I hated you even before I met you. I hated you on TV. I hated you in Vietnam. . . . So why do I want to fuck you so bad?

1990s *Hollywood and Beyond:* Less Sex, More Kick-Ass

It is not until the 1990s that we get a more-nuanced and less-sexualized portrayal of Asian women—and their Chinese-American daughters—in the adaptation of the best-selling novel by Amy Tan, *The Joy Luck Club* (1993). Directed by Hong Kong–born Wayne Wang, the movie marked the beginning of a wave of Asians into Hollywood that has served to take the harder edges off the stereotypes. Another was *Crouching Tiger, Hidden Dragon* (2000). The joint U.S.-Chinese production with Chinese writers behind it, directed by Taiwan-born Ang Lee and starring Chinese-Malaysian martial arts actress Michelle Yeoh, was designed as a tribute to martial arts films. Yeoh, after building her name as an Asian action superstar, has stated publicly that she only wants to appear in non-stereotyped roles that serve to better the depictions of Asian women in Hollywood movies.

She also did that in her role as not just the typical Bond girl but a Chinese secret agent with both brains and martial arts talent in the James Bond flick *Tomorrow Never Dies* (1997). While in both these roles, Yeoh is cool, steely, ethereal, professional, and in control of her emotions, her portrayal of an unrequited love interest in *Crouching Tiger* gives her some room for nuanced expression at the end of the movie to a degree not typically seen in Hollywood films.

One issue, however, is that in the Hollywood movies of the early 2000s in which Asian women play prominent and more equitable roles, they attain that power through martial arts ability. Yeoh, Liu, and others, while fearsomely proficient and technically skillful in the art of self-defense, ultimately are limited by those roles as well. The interest of directors Quentin Tarantino and Sofia Coppola in Asian film and imagery provides a possibility of their expansion. It remains to be seen how they develop those interests.

Yes, but what about the dignity, strength, and grace under adversity portrayed so remarkably by so many of the Asian actresses of Hollywood over the years? Haven't they shown us, in many ways, attributes to be admired, and created a stellar image of Asian woman as graceful femininity that we can hold in high esteem? After all, devoted housewives can be seen as virtuous; Dragon Ladies can be seen as strong; and at the very least, prostitutes and vixens are sexy. Virtue, strength, and sex appeal are valued in Western culture, right?

This debate is not dissimilar to the "good nigger" roles for blacks in the early days of Hollywood. We have only to think of Annie the maid in *It's a Wonderful Life* (1946), or Mammy the maid in *Gone With the Wind* (1939). As Mammy, Hattie McDaniel was the first African-American to win an Academy Award, for Best Actress in a Supporting Role, just as Miyoshi Umeki would become the first Asian to do so in her role as the devoted wife Katsumi Kelly in *Sayonara*. McDaniel's portrayals of maids, in which she specialized and played over and over again, are a world away from the much more complex and nuanced characters played by Pam Grier, Whoopi Goldberg, and Halle Berry in modern Hollywood. Nothing comparable exists for Asians. No Asian-origin woman has won an Oscar for acting since 1957. (The non-Asian Linda Hunt won a Best Supporting Actress Oscar for portraying an Indonesian man in *The Year of Living Dangerously* (1982), yet more evidence of the emasculated portrayal of Asian men on screen.) As the African-American actors of a half century ago found, the members of the Academy have been kindest to Asian women in roles that kept them "in their place"—as wisdom-dispensing house-keepers and back-scrubbing wives. Which is, of course, not very kind treatment at all.

Matters of Men and Country:
The Incredible Lightness
of Being Portrayed

If there are some admirable aspects of the portrayals of Asian women in Hollywood and on TV, it's hard to say the same of the portrayals of Asian men. Rarely have they been depicted with traditionally masculine traits. With a few exceptions, Asian men on screen have been small, sneaky, and threatening—or spineless, emasculated wimps, or incompetents who may well be technically proficient in martial arts, but impotent when faced with white man's superior strength or firepower. Lacking machismo, they almost never get the girl.

In the thirty years since the end of the Vietnam War, there have been just two on-screen romances between a white woman and an Asian man—one British-made, and the other French (and in neither do these "transgressions" end happily). But not in Hollywood. There, the Asian action star usually walks away alone, Zen-like. Or, more typically, the Asian man is an evil incompetent who dies at the hands of a superior (white) force. For the most part, what we see of Asian male sexuality is the assertion of a stronger Western virility at the expense of Asian masculinity. In short, the imagery takes Asian men lightly, as less-serious competitors for women, and less-competent fighters.

Outside the theater, we transfer these perceptions of Asian men to Asian countries. If Asian men on screen are to be easily vanquished, so are Asian male leaders in real state-to-state relations. Even, as *Fortune* columnist Stanley Bing writes in the title of his book, Sun Tzu is "a sissy." This "lightness of being portrayed" can be seen historically in the descriptions of Asian male leaders such as Ho Chi Minh and Mao Zedong, and now even of Kim Jong Il. It seeks to minimize the Asian male as a threat—and, I argue, quite possibly leads to serious repercussions.

It is easier to see the progression by starting with some of the more recent examples out of Hollywood. Chinese kung fu action hero Jet Li in *Romeo Must Die* (2000), for example, risks his life to save the girl. The families disapprove of any romance between them, hence he's nominally Romeo; she's Juliet. (And, in an unusual twist to such action movies, she is black—played by the now-deceased actress and singer Aaliyah.) But, while there's lots of chemistry, they never even kiss. He saves her father, avenges her brother—she gives him a nice, big hug.

It's the same thing—but worse—in *Kiss of the Dragon* (2001). This time, Jet Li saves the American farm girl in Paris (Bridget Fonda) and her daughter from a corrupt French cop, who has kidnapped the daughter and is forcing Fonda's character to work as a hooker. Li kills the bad guy with a single needle jab to the neck that causes a terrible, eye-poppingly bloody death. The grateful Fonda, reunited with her daughter, grabs Li's hand and gives the back of it a fond kiss.

Hong Kong's screen hunk Chow Yun-Fat doesn't even get that in *The Replacement Killers* (1998). He may be one of the hottest sex symbols in Asia but, on the Hollywood screen, he doesn't get the girl either. There seems to be chemistry between Mira Sorvino and Chow and, for a time, it appears that she kind of wants to "get got"—or, at the very least, wants to give him the obligatory pat of affection that Chinese action stars get from American girls after saving their lives. But, at the airport, ending, as Chow prepares to return to China, she simply says goodbye. Chow turns around and walks to the jet way alone.

When playing the King of Siam in *Anna and the King* (1999), Chow never gets to kiss Anna, either. Of course, that has never been in the plot of the story of the English schoolmistress in the court of Siam, based on a 1944 novel that was based on the mostly self-inflated and fictionalized recollections of the real, scandal-ridden English teacher Anna Leon Owens in her memoirs, *The Romance of the Harem,* published in 1872. Her book contained no romantic fantasies of the king, merely their clash over her Victorian values and his practice of having many wives. Nonetheless, the story was cast as a sexual-tension-filled,

Sessue Hayakawa in *The Cheat,* 1915
CREDIT: courtesy Jerry Ohlinger's Movie Material Store

unrequited love story on screen in 1946 with Rex Harrison and then
with Yul Brynner, its Broadway-turned-screen star of the musical, *The
King and I* (1956). As we know, Hollywood doesn't stick to historical
truth, so an on-screen kiss would have been exactly the way screen romances between white guys and Asian women have been portrayed
over the decades. But as Hollywood hunks playing Asian men,[1] they
never got the girl either.

So, do they ever? Well, forcing the matter doesn't yield a good result. One of the first Hollywood movies to depict the Asian man as a
ruthless, sneaky, sexual predator was *The Cheat* (1915). In the silent
black and white, punctuated by such lines as the Rudyard Kipling
verse "East is East and West is West, and never the twain shall meet,"
a Burmese ivory king (Sessue Hayakawa) tries to force Mrs. Edith
Handy, a member of the Long Island smart set, to have sex with him
after he loans her money. She refuses; he tries to overpower her, then
brands her with a fire poker. She shoots him, leaving him emasculated

and fallen, but alive. Her husband takes the rap, and is put on trial and exonerated to great cheer.

The evil, sexless Asian already was entrenched in Western consciousness due to the historical events we have examined so far, and to Hollywood's gradual build up of the depiction of Chinese as an evil threat: An 1894 silent film, *Chinese Laundry Scene,* had a Chinese character eluding an Irish cop; in *The Fatal Hour* (1908), a Chinese villain is aided by cleaver-wielding Chinese thugs who kidnap and enslave innocent white girls.[2] These images set the stage for the villainous plots of nearly a dozen Fu Manchu films in Hollywood history that still have echoes today in such evil Chinese triad leader roles as John Lone in *Year of the Dragon* (1985), and Jet Li, yet again, in *Lethal Weapon 4* (1998), among many others. The forces of good always triumph; evil Chinese men are always outsmarted by the white (and black) cops.

A few largely forgotten or not-widely seen exceptions have come out of Hollywood over the years: *The Bitter Tea of General Yen* (1933), in which an American missionary in China fantasizes about kissing the general and ends up holding his hand and resting her head on his lap as he dies; *The Inn of the Sixth Happiness* (1958), in which Ingrid Bergman as another missionary engages in cautious romance with a half-Chinese army officer; the BBC miniseries *The Ginger Tree* (1989), the story of a married Scottish woman who falls for a Japanese nobleman and has his son; and *The Crimson Kimono* (1959) in which two Los Angeles detectives, one of them Japanese-American (James Shigeta), fall for the same crime-scene witness and she falls for the sensitive, poetic nature of the Japanese guy; James Shigeta appeared again in *Bridge to the Sun* (1961) as a Japanese diplomat who marries a southern belle and moves her to Tokyo just before the attack on Pearl Harbor. It is one of the only—yet obscure—true, on-screen romances, based on an autobiographical novel, between a Caucasian woman and an Asian man. Another example is Mae West, as mistress of a Chinese gangster in *Klondike Annie* (1936), who sings, "I'm an Occidental Lady in an Oriental Mood for Love."

All of this is tame stuff, however, as compared to the work of French writer Marguerite Duras. The French film, *L'Amant* (*The Lover*) (1992), based on her novel, is in a class all its own as an explicit depiction of requited lust. The story is also based on true-life events—

Duras's semi-autobiographical account of a love affair with a Chinese man in French colonial Saigon, where she was born. (Duras's other work, the black-and-white film *Hiroshima Mon Amour* (1957), is about a French peace activist spending the night with a Japanese man.) *The Lover* is filled with racial tensions; an interracial Lolita punctuated with graphic sexual intercourse between a pubescent French girl exploring her sexuality and her Chinese lover. As the lover of an underage white girl, however, the Chinese man must pay; the girl tortures him with childish scorn and refuses to love him, even though she realizes—after her return to France much later—that she does. In Duras's book, which sold three million copies, the French girl reunites with her Chinese lover later in life. Not in the movie version, however. In a tragic end typical of Asian man–white woman romance, he succumbs to a loveless arranged marriage, and to opium. Still, if it weren't for white women relating their real-life stories, it seems Hollywood would have depicted no such stories at all.

Western Firepower Trumps Kung Fu—and Karate, Too

The trumping of Asian masculinity by Western virility is clear in this exchange between Jackie Chan and co-star Chris Tucker in *RushHour 2* (2001), a Hollywood movie that Chan fans in Asia disliked. Both men are comedic actors in these roles, but in no way does Tucker view Chan as a credible rival for the affections of a beautiful white woman.

> TUCKER: She picked me because I'm tall, dark and handsome, and you're Third World ugly.
> CHAN: Women like me. They think I'm cute, like Snoopy.
> TUCKER: Snoopy is six inches taller than you.

The joke resonated in Hollywood because Chan, 5'10", had presented the 1996 Academy Award for short films standing next to 7'10" Kareem Abdul-Jabbar (who had studied martial arts under Bruce Lee). The American press noted that Chan was "half" his size. The press in Hong Kong, Chan's hometown, was indignant, but Chan later told *GQ* magazine that it was his idea. The pairing was done for comic effect, but it appeared to some degree to be a metaphor for Chan's comparative masculine stature in Hollywood as well.

In Asia, Chan is legendary for his martial arts skills and his ability to perform all of his stunts himself; and he is one of the biggest regional symbols of masculinity. In movies he makes for Asian audiences, he is macho, strong, indomitable. Women go wild at the sight of him. In the romantic comedy *Gorgeous* (1999), which was not released outside of Asia, he starred as a dashing leading man who sings a love song at the end. He almost kisses the girl, but Chan decided to cut the scene and add it to the outtakes at the end, asking audiences for feedback. Reportedly there were suicides in South Korea by fans distraught with jealousy. Although it is hard to verify this, undoubtedly the movie was a huge success in Asia. It would not have been successful for Western audiences, however, where Chan's character does a 180-degree reversal into cute, comic asexuality.

Chan has said publicly that he wants to change that image, and to be cast as a dashing leading man in Hollywood. He told Jay Leno on *The Tonight Show* in July 2004 that he wants "a love story, drama, no action," "kissing Sharon Stone on the beach." He did have one on-screen kiss with a white woman, Claire Forlani, in yet another action comedy, *The Medallion* (2003). The fact that Chan kissed a white woman on screen also was big news back in Hong Kong. But not many people in the West saw it; that scene and the whole movie were panned by Western critics for its "stupid, pathetic" version of "kung fu lite" and its "goofy-nice guy charm."

Chan didn't help his image in the West by keeping his hair long. After a 1986 stunt mishap that nearly killed him, Chan said his producers told him not to cut his hair short or, like ancient Samson, he might lose his strength and be prone to injury. So Chan has at various times throughout his career worn his hair past his shoulders—even as far back as 1973, when Bruce Lee grabs him by it in *Enter the Dragon*. Distractingly, Chan changed hair length in the middle of *The Medallion*.

In the movie *Shanghai Knights* (2003), Chan, playing Chon Wang (John Wayne, get it?), is the only man in 1880s Carson City, Nevada, with long hair, and he wears wide-bottom pants that almost look like a skirt when he is walking. He takes a bubble bath in a rooming house/brothel and emerges wrapped in a towel, his long wet locks cascading over his shoulders and down his back. (If this was an attempt at authenticity—because the Chinese in America didn't cut their queues until the end of the Qing Dynasty in 1911—Chan would have had to have worn it both long and braided.)

It's clear from Hollywood's treatment that, despite Chan's mastery of kung fu (and his predecessor Bruce Lee's powerful displays of *wing chun,* which he developed into his own *jeet kune do*), martial arts are regarded by Hollywood more as an "art" form, valued for their almost ballet-like beauty, grace, and self-discipline, than as a serious method of perpetrating violence. Yes, they are impressive, requiring not only skill but mastery. But victims of high kicks don't necessarily die in Hollywood movies—perpetrators emerge with barely a scratch.

Indeed, the primary goal of martial arts is to disable your opponent, not to kill him, unless there is absolutely no other choice. This is not the manly choice in a Hollywood movie, which does not value as "masculine" the self-discipline and years of monastic-like training required, and the ability to inflict violence using only one's hands. Additionally, with the popularity of women across racial lines making martial arts stunts ubiquitous (Michelle Yeoh and Zhang Ziyi in *Crouching Tiger, Hidden Dragon,* Lucy Liu and Uma Thurman in *Kill Bill,* and Halle Berry in *Catwoman,* just to name a few), mastery of martial arts techniques is no longer an exclusively male domain and has instead become a seductive female attribute.

No, far from being regarded as masculine, martial arts masters are sometimes portrayed as impotent when confronted with Western firepower. No matter how masterful or powerful, the fastest of Eastern hands or most skillful Asian swordplay still can be trumped by the power of a gun. In *Raiders of the Lost Ark* (1981), Harrison Ford as Indiana Jones demonstrates this in one of the most resonating examples to come out of Hollywood. The setting is "the Orient"—Cairo, "paradise on Earth," a narrator tells us. "Indy" and "Marion," played by Karen Allen, are in an Oriental bazaar. A phalanx of dim-witted attackers wearing white robes (the traditional dishdasha attire of the Middle East), their faces obscured with black scarves wrapped around their heads, come at the couple. The incompetent fighters swish at Indiana Jones with knives, he ducks and punches them out, one by one.

He cracks his bullwhip a few times. A dozen attackers are vanquished, seemingly without much effort at all. Even Marion outsmarts one who is chasing her with a knife, by ducking into an open doorway and then clunking him on the head with a frying pan.

Finally, after all this silly horseplay, Indiana Jones is confronted by a "ninja" wearing black, a wide red sash around his skirted waist, an image imported and adapted from ancient Japan. This final assassin represents an escalation from white-robed incompetent attackers to the ultimate force of threat from "the East." The ninja wields the largest knife of all, a sword which he twists in a figure eight in front of his body with a menacing laugh. The crowd parts, leaving East and West to duel. Indiana Jones, clearly exasperated, merely takes his gun from his holster and blows the man away. Later, when interviewed about the scene, Harrison Ford said that it wasn't in the script, that he merely was tired and didn't want to do yet another fight scene in the hot sun, so he improvised. The director loved it. It captured the essence of Western firepower blowing away the stylized, weaker threat from the East.

The phalanxes of inept Asian male fighting forces are a prevalent theme in Hollywood. Undoubtedly, this image came from the kung fu genre of Asian cinema, but it adapted easily to Hollywood action flicks where the white guys (and girls) are the heroes. The incompetent fighters losing to Mel Gibson in *Payback* and even to Uma Thurman in *Kill Bill* are just a couple of examples. Long before that, James Bond defeated a roomful of karate and kung fu experts with mere kicks and cross-punches, and later with the help of two Thai-Chinese girls in school uniforms, in *The Man with the Golden Gun* (1974). Bond had protectively ordered them to "stand back, girls." (The movie, released during the Vietnam War, also treats us to GI slang, with a southern-accented Sheriff J.W. Pepper, along with Bond for the ride, referring to Thais as "little pointy heads" and "Goddamn little brown water hogs," epithets that never would have been tolerated if directed, for example, against blacks.) Even Jackie Chan played a bumbling, inept Japanese in *Cannonball Run* (1981), his first role in an American production.

Ineptitude, weakness, and emasculation go together, and if we don't quite get the picture, there are plenty of movie scenes to point it out. In an earlier 007 film, *You Only Live Twice* (1967), Japanese intelligence chief "Tiger" Tanaka—who in Ian Fleming's book is a huge man, the size of a sumo wrestler, with a gregarious personality—is cast in the movie as a slight character who looks more like a bank clerk. When he meets James Bond, he sits small in his low chair, at the same level as Miss Moneypenny. Bond asks for the secret password for the mission, "I love you," and while looking up at Bond, Tanaka is forced to utter the words. There's little doubt who is dominant. Bond attends ninja training school and masters the techniques of a lifetime of study in just three days (though hardly convincingly). In the final scenes, after 007 has teamed up with some Japanese Bond girls, fought off all the incompetent ninjas, and saved the world from annihilation, Bond and Tanaka are shown having their backs scrubbed in the bath by beautiful Japanese women. Tanaka tells him the women are intrigued by his hairy chest. One of the women remarks, "Japan men all have beautiful bare skin." Bond, his chest hair exposed, replies: "Japanese proverb say, bird never make nest in bare tree." It would be hard for any man to compete with Sean Connery, but this line asserts that the entire Japanese race can't even come close.

There's another stereotype of weak Asian male in Hollywood—that of the geek. Many Asian-Americans recall gasping in horror while watching *Sixteen Candles* (1984). This movie featured a greasy-haired Chinese exchange student, "Long Duk Dong," who mortified Molly Ringwald with his foreign nerdiness, and whose entry into scenes was punctuated by the clash of a gong. Her grandparents call him a "Chinaman," the old epithet from a century before; the filmmakers have him get drunk, trash the car, jump out of a tree yelling "banzai," and end up face-down on the front lawn. He does get a girl, but only for the comedic contrast of her being a weight lifter—taller, stronger, and sturdier than he—with enormous breasts. Yes, it's comedy, and it's a teen genre movie. But just think of the outcry if, for example, an African-American actor was depicted eating watermelon, being called by an epithet, and performing other stereotypically racist conduct. We wouldn't think it was funny. It would be so unconscionable that no Hollywood director would even dare do so.

Bringing New Meaning to Supporting Roles

That same actor, Japanese-American Gedde Wantanabe, turned up in the role of the only prominent male nurse, "Yosh," on the emergency room drama *ER* in 1997. Running for more than seven years, the show has added a Chinese-American woman and an Indian woman as medical residents, but kept the only Asian-American male in a nursing role. Asian men get a lot of these types of "supporting" roles on television.

At least the *Law & Order* spin-off *Special Victims Unit* has given us the ongoing character played by B.D. Wong, a doctor of sorts, in the role of a forensic psychiatrist occasionally dispensing wisdom about the criminal mind to help out the squad detectives. He's the only recognizable recurring Asian male actor on early 2000s television. Before that, there was Sam, the loyal assistant to the medical examiner on the TV series *Quincy* (1976–1983), who made notoriously bad coffee. Detective Yamada, played by Jack Soo (nee Suzuki), on Barney Miller (1975–1982) made bad coffee, too, but he didn't do much else. Before that, there was Arnold serving his customers on *Happy Days,* as well as the extras on *M.A.S.H.* who mostly took in laundry and sold trinkets. Lieutenant Sulu on *Star Trek* (1966–1969), played by George Takei, got one episode where he jumped around the ship shirtless and brandishing a sword. But for the most part, he spent his time on the bridge following orders with an "Aye, Captain" (as opposed to the Scotsman and the good ol' doctor who were continually bucking them), or was shown watering his aspidistras. Still, it was most the progressive role yet for an Asian man on TV. Bruce Lee played the faithful Japanese houseboy, Kato, who incongruously knew the Chinese martial art of kung fu (1966–67) on *The Green Hornet.* There was Hop Sing, the hot-tempered Chinese cook who worked for the Cartwright family on *Bonanza* (1959–1973), who would shout, "You listen Hop Sing! Hop Sing 'A Number One' cook. Will cook whatever you like."

The entire genre of *Charlie Chan,* in the detective novels of 1925–32, movies of the 1930s and '40s, and TV series of 1957, could be viewed as a slight exception. But Chan, whose deductive reasoning always cracked the case, was not only half sage, he was half buffoon, rambling off proverbs like fortune cookie messages with a personality reduced to a Chinese takeout menu. As a white cop once tells him: "You're all right. Just like chop suey. A mystery, but a swell dish."[3] Chan was played by a long list of non-Chinese actors in yellow face, a practice that led to caricaturing the Chinese. Chan's son, Barry, bumbling and always at risk of fumbling the case, was played by a real Asian-American, James Hong.

Perhaps Detective Chan's moral rectitude was meant to counter the image of the evil Asian male in *The Adventures of Fu Manchu* (1955–56), the television adaptation of the many screen versions of Chinese evil. Mustachioed and elegantly gowned, Dr. Fu Manchu (also played by a white guy in yellow face, Glen Gordon), was an Oriental scientific genius operating out of the exotic locale of Macau, and his nefarious goals included the destruction of Western democracy. Fu Manchu was no new character; he was based on the series of novels by Sax Rohmer from the early 1900s that played on fears of Chinamen taking away the jobs of whites and the resulting Yellow Peril of the 1870s. The revived Yellow Peril in the 1980s, caused by the perceived threat of the burgeoning Japanese economy, gave us the movie *Rising Sun,* with all manner of evil Japanese characters intending to take over the U.S. computer industry, based on the 1992 novel by Michael Crichton. "For a Japanese, consistent behavior is not possible," a Los Angeles police detective informs us. Why for Japanese more so than for anybody else?

When Asian males have been portrayed in competent, morally upright roles—such as Charlie Chan, or the wise Oriental master Mr. Miyagi (played by Pat Morita) of the *Karate Kid* movies of the 1980s, or David Carradine's aesthetic Shaolin monk Kwai Chang Caine in the 1970s television series *Kung Fu*—they dispense wisdom, but remain asexual. Carradine got the role over Bruce Lee, who had helped develop it. Lee, apparently, looked "too Chinese" for prime-time, although he was of one-quarter German descent. The image of Caine walking away at the end of an episode—as Jet Li and Chow Yun-Fat remind us—shows us over and over again that the true nature of the wise, competent Asian man is, at essence, alone.

The Role of History and the Deception of Appearances

It is worth examining history to see where these images came from, why we have them, and why they continue to resonate through Western culture. As we know, since the time of the Romans, travel to "the Orient" was dangerous and meant traversing perilous mountain paths and sea routes fraught with danger from, if not the sea monsters of the medieval bestseller *Travels,* a lack of proper navigating instruments and the typhoons that plague the tropics to this day.

Marco Polo's tales describe rulers who kept harems or who had their pick of palace concubines at any moment of desire. The first British travelers to China and to Siam recounted the many wives and concubines of the emperors and kings they encountered. The decadence and opulence associated with that time in history has remained with us. Surely, men who had so many women at their beck and call did not have to pound their chests with masculine vigor to get them—or even to demonstrate Western notions of masculinity at all. All was opulently provided to the Oriental despot, who, clothed in finery and draped in jewels, had only to sit back and enjoy the sensual pleasures provided to him.

Asian attire did not help this perception. Apart from the opulent jewelry and silks worn in the royal courts of Indian, central Asian, and Southeast Asian kingdoms, in China before the twentieth century, Chinese men wore dresses—in the form of long, flowing silk mandarin robes. Of the Great Khan ruling China in the 1200s, Polo wrote

> [T]wenty thousand nobles and military officers are clad by him in dresses similar to his own in point of color and form; but the materials are not equally rich. They are, however, of silk, and the color of gold; and along with the vest they likewise receive a girdle of chamois leather, curiously worked with gold and silver thread, and also a pair of boots. Some of the dresses are ornamented with precious stones and pearls to the value of ten thousand bezants of gold.[4]

Even the senior members of the Shanghai underworld in the early twentieth century wore long gowns, leaving the top button undone and the sleeves rolled up, ungentlemanly, to show their knuckles.

It was the women of China who wore pants. When the progressive Shanghainese invented a dress called the *qipao* in Mandarin, or *cheongsam* in Cantonese, in the flapper era of the 1920s, it was in fact an adaptation of a man's gown—a long tunic with a side slit that was worn over trousers. Progressive women adapted it to fit their figures, and suddenly they were dressing like Chinese men, only form-fitted. They liked the look so much that a season later, they slit both sides to mid-thigh level. Eventually they shortened the whole dress to above the knee and stuffed their feet, finally unbound after more than 900 years, into high-heeled shoes.[5]

Chinese mandarins wore their hair far longer than Europeans—in a queue, a long braided strand down the back. Short hair became the fashion of Europe and the Americas in the later seventeenth century; the Puritans of England had asserted that long hair was an example of royal decadence and a sin against God, and their progeny in the Plymouth Bay Colony of Massachusetts banned long hair for men in 1634, setting a style for the Americas in contrast to the long-haired native Americans. But at that exact same period in history, ordinary Chinese men started to wear their hair in the long queue in a sign of Qing (Manchu) Dynasty fidelity that would last until 1911.

Chinese men wore their hair that way for sixty years after they had first started immigrating to California and elsewhere in the West, and many continued to wear the mandarin's gown, giving Americans a rather feminized view of the "Celestials" in their midst. As late as 1906, the Hollywood silent film *The Terrible Kids* depicted a group of mischievous boys attacking a Chinese man and yanking his long queue. The perceptions of femininity were not aided by the men's height—averaging 4'10"—and slight builds, and the fact that they took up "women's work" on the frontier. At first, the 6' Irish foreman in charge of hiring laborers to build the transcontinental railway across America resisted hiring Chinese. "They couldn't possibly do the work," James Strobridge had said. At the time, Chinese men, with "delicate hands, hairless faces and long braided hair" were constantly compared with white women in the American press. But Strobridge finally relented and allowed fifty Chinese men to work on a trial basis in 1865, after it was pointed out to him that it was the Chinese who had built the Great Wall. A month later, Strobridge admitted that his Chinese workers had performed superbly, proving to be among the strongest and most diligent workers on the rails, and so he hired more.[6]

When you consider that American society's first contact with Chinese on a large scale was with slight men with long braided hair—some in long silk gowns—tending to laundry, cooking, and childcare, the origins of Hollywood's feminized image of the Asian male become easier to understand. Had northern Chinese been the first immigrants to America instead of the Cantonese, the perception of Asian men as small, 120-pound weaklings would have been different. The basketball player Yao Ming is an aberration at 7'6", but his countrymen in northern China are typically taller than their Cantonese and southern Chinese counterparts. There's no data available for same time period, but an inflammatory 1941 *Life* magazine article, "How to Tell Japs from the Chinese," reported the average height of northern Chinese to be 5'7" and sometimes exceeding 6'. That would have been more on par with Caucasian American immigrants: a seventeenth-century Englishman was about 5'7" and a modern American man averages 5'9". Frequent famines in China certainly played a role in producing smaller men, but that has changed considerably. Today, the average male in Beijing is still 5'7", with men exceeding 6' not at all unusual; Cantonese men average 5'5½".[7]

During the colonial period in China, every foreigner, no matter how poor, had a "boy," a manservant dressed in the ubiquitous long-sleeved blue gown and black cap and devoted to making his master's life as carefree as possible. "Whether laying out the master's morning clothes, cleaning, or replenishing stock in the liquor cabinet, the servant performed his tasks so well that he usually became indispensable to his employers," writes Stella Dong in *Shanghai: The Rise and Fall of a Decadent City*. A travel guide of the period noted that a foreigner returning "to lands less well supplied with servants, will often long for the long-gowned boy of the China coast."[8]

Chinese compradors who arranged the business contacts of foreigners or who joined the civil service grew their fingernails to extravagant lengths, a sign that they were cultured and did not have to work as laborers. Even today, men all over Asia—in China and in Southeast Asia as well—leave their pinkie nails long, about an inch or even two, to signify their non-working-class status. And if they are wealthy, they can appear to boast a more showy kind of masculinity than in the West, of gold-buttoned blazers, expensive cigarettes, constant cell phone chatter, and fat wads of cash carried in purse-like leather totes under their arms.

Other superficial aspects of modern Asian masculinity still serve to contribute to the old stereotypes. They involve the industry of sexual potency elixirs, in the form of energy drinks, rhinoceros horns and other rare animal parts—and taking a mistress or two to put the concoctions to good use. Chinese men spend $6 billion to $7.2 billion on sex potions every year.[9] There's also a burgeoning multi-billion-dollar industry of men's grooming products and creams. Most Asian male politicians over the age of fifty dye their hair jet black. Now, there's makeup, too: Korean men spent $4 million on "Colour Lotion" foundation in the six months after its 2002 launch; Japanese cosmetic maker Shiseido was predicting 2004 sales of $3 million for its "Shiseido Men" line. Probing what constitutes modern Asian masculinity, however, is a new, rich subject that has yet to be explored in depth.

The stage is another realm that historically has confused the masculine identity and image of the Asian male. Actors on the Chinese stage traditionally were men. In Japan, young men used to be geisha, too, and those typically younger than age fifteen performed in the kabuki theaters, after women were banned in 1628 because men started fighting over the members of a women's troupe that had started twenty years before. (The banned women went on to become geisha—which means "practitioner of the arts"—in private Samurai households.[10]) Men played on the Elizabethan stages of England in the sixteenth century as well, but then they often were obviously in drag. In Asia, actors were so skillful in female impersonation that one writer in China at the time noted, "It is hard for a stranger to believe that they are, in fact, male actors." (Today, some of the most taut, shapely strippers in Bangkok's red light districts are transvestites.)

Along with this conflation of roles, the stage has long been a well-known realm of homosexual practice. In China, being an actor—often a boy sold by destitute parents and then schooled in the erotic arts—meant giving sexual favors to male patrons. Far from being considered deviant, homosexuality—or at least bisexuality—had a long tradition among the Chinese aristocracy.[11] Men having sex with men did not lead them to a self-identity as "gay" or "homosexual." Rather, it was merely another sexual option, a variation on sexual heterosexual practices, without loaded moral strictures or connotations of deviance or "sin." The act may be homosexual but the man was not. As long as it did not interfere with the imperative to father a child and keep up the bloodline, homosexual practice had no social stigma.

In a famous Japanese novel written 1,000 years ago, *The Tale of Genji,* a prince retiring to his room late one evening—after failing in a quest of female seduction—passes by the chamber of a teenage boy and decides that he'll do as a substitute. Christian missionaries had long noted the practice with disdain, in China as well as in Japan. A fact that may shock westerners in search of the mystical, spiritual East is that monks in Buddhist temples of both countries commonly had homosexual relations with novices, and during the Edo period of Japan, homosexual brothels proliferated near Buddhist temples for the service of monks.[12]

Among the Samurai, *nanshoku,* or male passion, was not a perversion but a lofty ideal. Indeed, phallic worship is one of the oldest aspects of religion in Japan (and parts of Indonesia) for both men and women; much as the Meiji Restoration endeavoring to Westernize Japan tried to wipe out such worship, there are still phallic festivals of fertility at shrines dedicated to the penis in Japan today.[13] In Japan in particular, the desire to modernize and Westernize meant a societal condemnation of homosexual acts beginning in the twentieth century.

Homosexuality was sometimes linked with power in Asia, not only among Samurai, but among Chinese emperors who kept male lovers openly in their court, and promoted them to important positions. Power meant sexual conquest, and the gender on the receiving end was not always relevant. The most feared warlord in China of the 1920s, the rapacious "Shantung monster" Chang Tsung-Chang, not only maintained a harem of three dozen Chinese and foreign beauties, but once, between courses at a riotous dinner party, bent over a male entertainer and sodomized him in front of guests, servants, and the city's most expensive sing-song girls.[14]

In addition to theater, other Oriental art forms also lent to the Western perception of femininity of the Asian male—as well as the entirety of Asian culture itself. Reading the great works of Japanese literature, the British-born Indian writer Pico Iyer notes:

> I was struck again and again by how much Japanese writing was touched with a decidedly feminine lilt and fragrance, a kind of delicacy and a lyricism that I associated, however unfairly, with the female principle. This softness was apparent not just in the watercolor wistfulness of Japanese poems, but also in the very themes and moods that enveloped them—loneliness, abandonment, romance. . . . Even gangsters, at their deaths, wrote poems to the seasons.

It may be because, as Iyer was not the first to point out, the squiggly characters of Japanese writing that constitute an alphabet of sounds—as distinct from the Chinese characters used by men in official script—used to be the almost exclusive domain of women. (Both character sets, along with a third that denotes foreign sounds, make up the complicated mélange of written Japanese used by both genders today.) Iyer writes:

> As a result, perhaps, early Japanese poetry was all love poetry (where its model in China dealt more often with friendship.) And by the tenth and eleventh centuries, and the great cultural flowering of the Heian period, the Japanese alphabet was so much a woman's domain that men actually pretended to be women if they wanted to use native script, and even fit themselves into the conventions and emotions of women.

The Tale of Genji and *The Pillow Book,* the two most famous works of Japanese literature from the period, were written by women.

Iyer finds that "poetry and femininity seemed almost interchangeable in Japan, as they never would be" in the West, its charm felt through "its girlishness, its womanly refinement, its sensitivity to nature and to the lights and shades of relationships. Here was the poetry of the paper screen—of delicate walls and sliding panels of shadows and suspicions, of secrecy and stealth."[15] To this day, scholars of China and Japan—of their languages, literature, and cultures—read these works and are taught to recite the lilting poetry of gardens, flowers, trees, lovers, and moonlight.

But what about the Samurai? By the time the West was allowed back into Japan, after Commodore Perry forced open the island to trade in 1853, Samurai rule was waning. The way of the sword was being displaced by the drive toward "enlightenment" by Japan's Meiji Restoration. Whereas Japan was a dangerous land ruled by warriors for the prior 200 years, this gruff, masculine, Samurai strength came to be regarded by the West as a relic of Japan's quaint and noble past.

And even though the Samurai period maintains a masculine reputation in the West (as in 2003 movie *The Last Samurai*), things were a bit more nuanced than that, as is shown by the Samurai practice of loving boys. A famous eighteenth-century Japanese document, for example, advised young followers of *Bushido,* or The Way of the Samurai, always to "carry rouge and powder" for "after rising in the morning, or after sobering up, we sometimes find that we do not look very good. In such a case we should take out the rouge and put it on." This was especially important when going to do battle, for one must be beautiful even in death.[16]

The earnest new rulers of Japan wanted to emulate what they regarded as the superiority of Western culture and philosophy, pitting the Japanese as the new pupil of European and American masters. And, as Perry so clearly demonstrated long before Indiana Jones, the way of the sword was easily trumped by the power of the Western gun.

IN THE MOST FORMATIVE YEARS of East-West contact, it seems clear that Western perceptions of Asian masculinity were formed based on slight-of-build men clothed in silk dresses and jewels, who wore their fingernails long and their long hair braided, who rouged their cheeks, who engaged in homosexual acts, who had only to recline and be tended to by harems of doting women rather than having to fight to win their affections, who wrote lyrical poems about love and the beauty of nature, who had men dress up convincingly as women on their stages, and who—when they immigrated to the West—took up women's work in the areas of cooking, laundering, and nanny services. They came from countries that traded in exotic flowers and teas, silks, and spices, the fine porcelains and screens of the chinoiserie and Japonisme periods, and the enchanting scents used in French perfumes. When Hollywood started entrenching images of the Asian male on screen, these "feminine" aspects of Asia and the "feminine" roles taken up by Asian male immigrants in the West became part of the portrayal.

There is one more issue that must be addressed in the discussion of Asian men and issues of femininity and masculinity, because it comes up so often in terms of white and black men asserting superior sexual potency: the issue of penis size or, in slang terms, the "Hong Kong dong." And it's not just men. I once attended a dinner party where a Chinese-American woman mocked her ex-boyfriend from Beijing by holding up her pinkie finger and wiggling it. The topic comes up not only in this type of locker-room banter, but also in film: in the name "Long Duk Dong" in *Sixteen Candles;* and perhaps more famously in the scene in *Full Metal Jacket* when a Vietnamese prostitute refuses to service an African-American soldier because she declares him "too big," in comparison with Vietnamese or white men. He unzips his fly and takes out his "package" to show her before she relents.

Although medical researchers say that a flaccid penis has little to do with its size when erect, findings do indicate that these jokes are based in fact. According to research published by the University of California–Santa Barbara, following are average penis sizes when erect:

Asian	4"–5" length, 1.24" diameter
Caucasian	5.5"–6" length, 1.5" diameter
Black	6.26"–8" length, 2" diameter

Presumably, nutritional and height issues should be taken into account, but the research does not select out that criteria nor say where or how the measurements were taken. However, four separate studies of male penis length conducted in South Korea between 1971 and 1999 all found an average close to 5", with the shortest average 4.7" and the longest 5.3".

Up Close and Personal

What does it matter? If we underestimate and mis-portray, emasculate, and feminize the Asian male and Asian culture, does it make any difference—apart from to the poor Asian guys who feel slighted by it all?

I argue that it does—and that it is at our societies' expense. We have noted dating and marriage patterns as being significantly higher among Caucasian men and Asian women than among Asian men and Caucasian women in the United States. We have examined some possible reasons being Asian women's status consciousness and their view of Caucasians as perhaps more liberal or progressive choices than Asian males, as well as the preferences and fetishes of Caucasian men. Beyond that, Asian-American men complain that their portrayal as wimps, geeks, and emasculated asexuals in Western culture hurts their image and status with Asian women as well as among themselves.

"There is a level of self-imposed discrimination that Asian men put on themselves. It would be hard to argue that Asian men are not at all affected by the way in which they are portrayed by Western popular culture," writes an Asian male columnist trying to deconstruct the disparity on www.modelminority.com, in a view that represents the sentiments of thousands of Asian and Asian-American men. "What manifests is an inferiority complex . . . and the fear of dating non-Asian women." He continues:

> I have often been praised by non-Asian women for "not acting Asian." But what is that supposed to mean? To praise someone for "not acting Asian" concedes that there is some predetermined mode of "acting Asian" or else it would not have been said. I therefore politely ask them to clarify. Apparently being extroverted, playing the guitar, having a great smile, and nice arms, are all qualities that make me non-Asian. So the contra-positive dictates that Asian men are *introverted, untalented* and *physically unattractive,* in that order. This is nothing short of a pat on the head, which comes at the sacrifice of my Asian brethren.

The result has been many Asian guys having a tough time in the dating world of America. An exception, possibly, is in France. Postings to a geocities.com-hosted discussion group on interracial dating reported that the popularity of the book and film *The Lover*, along with resulting magazine and popular press articles about why Asian men are "great lovers" increased the cachet of Asian males, at least among French women. "It is widely known in the Asian male community that, for differing reasons, French women seem to *like* Asian men," writes "Herman" in one message board posting.

A Canadian actor named "Ed" who was scouting modeling opportunities in Europe, reported that

> Asian men are somewhat popular in Scandinavian countries, where they are considered to be "cultured" and "refined." Maybe you should add rich to that list. When I was over in Paris I noticed posters featuring Asian men. . . . I also garnered stares from women in France. It was very unusual but very flattering to receive all this attention from white women overseas, but it was welcome just the same. I get attention from women here (in Edmonton) too, just not as much.

In France, the Franco-Asiatique has had somewhat of an easier time at assimilation into French society anyway—so successful, in fact, that you rarely hear a hyphenated term like that. Instead, if they were born in France and speak French as their native tongue, they usually are called "French" no matter their ethnic origin, unlike the Arabs or Jews in France who are referred to as religiously or ethnically distinct. This is primarily because the descendants of the Vietnamese community and smaller Cambodian and Lao groups there have come from the educated French colonial-trained administrators and elites from the former Indochinese colony, rather than the poor job seekers of the first wave of Chinese immigration in America. (Later immigrant Asian groups to the United States have included the educated elite of the Kuomintang fleeing Communist China after 1949, U.S. military allies of South Vietnam and Laos in 1975, and later poor refugees and boatpeople resulting from the end of those conflicts.)

Britain experienced only a few thousand Chinese job-seekers at the same time that tens of thousands flooded America's West Coast in the mid-1800s, and managed to hold the number of Chinese at below

2,000 by 1930. France and England had imported 100,000 Chinese laborers from Shandong province in World War I. The men built barracks and roads and made ammunition, and 2,000 of them died in the war and are buried in Europe. But most went back to China; only 3,000 remained, mostly as metallurgists, into the 1920s.[17] Thus, Europe never experienced the same level of racial tensions with job-seeking immigrants that America did—at least with East Asians. Britain's immigration problems largely stemmed from a flood of immigrants from South Asia, and France's from North Africa.

EVERY NOW AND AGAIN, an article pops up in mainstream American media that claims Asian men are the hot topic *du jour*. In February 2000, just before *Crouching Tiger, Hidden Dragon* won best picture in Hollywood, *Newsweek* reporter Esther Pan wrote an article titled "Why Asian Guys Are on a Roll." The article said that stars such as Jet Li and Chow Yun-Fat demonstrate that Asian men can be objects of lust. (The article did not point out that they never get to kiss the girl.) It noted that men like Jerry Yang of Yahoo! are changing the image of Asian males as "son of a laborer or laundryman" to "future Internet millionaire," and cited a marriage statistic that 19 percent of Asian-American men born in the United States and living in California have married white women. One article interviewee even joked that Asian men are the next "trophy boyfriends" and his Caucasian wife agreed: "It's almost like Asian boyfriends are the fashion accessory of the moment."

A vision of Asian males as masculine makes news because it is the exception. Such media moments, however, fail to counter decades of entrenched stereotypes and perceptions. After all, white women threw themselves at Sessue Hayakawa, the sexual predator star of *The Cheat* as well as the Japanese colonel in *Bridge on the River Kwai,* in Hollywood's earlier era—including one woman who chased him through a theater, naked except for her coat. No one remembers what a sex symbol Hayakawa once was, except for a few aficionados of Hollywood lore and the director Martin Scorsese, who once told the story at the Asia Society in New York.

THE IMPACT OF IMAGES is not only felt in relationships. It affects Asian men in their occupations as well, where "model minority" stereotypes of being mathematically inclined, for example, can keep men with creative talent from opportunities, where silence can be interpreted as Confucian reserve, and reserve interpreted as weakness. Over the years, I have been surprised by the number of Western businessmen who have told me how "tough" their negotiations with Asian business partners had been, as if their expectations were that their Asian counterparts would roll over easily.

Imagine this situation, only the circumstances and actors changed, in thousands of business transactions across East-West borders over the decades: Edward Han, a Chinese-American born and raised in New York and an attorney at a prestigious Washington, DC, law firm, walks into a conference room to take a deposition. As usual, there is a witness present, as well as the opposing counsel. Looking Han up and down, the other attorney makes a determination about the strength of his adversary and, if he is an older white man, that assessment is often of weakness. He probably has seen a lot of movies over the years, the ones where Asian girls are submissive and servile, and Asian guys are wimps—and even if they have wisdom it is of the fortune-cookie variety. He's thinking, "wuss," Han recalls. He can tell from the other man's eyes, his manner of superiority. "Like, 'I can push this guy around.'"

Han had encountered this before, numerous times. Maybe it was how such men acted around all young lawyers, says Han. But on second thought, he didn't think so. "I certainly felt like it was accentuated because I was Asian," he says. "I guess my personal style is a little more subdued, which they may have interpreted as being submissive."

But it wasn't. And so he waits, letting the other lawyer think he can get the best of him, letting him overplay his hand. Soon enough, his guard will go down, and Han will move in. "At some point, you can put something in the record that makes them very vulnerable," he says. This was in the days, early in Han's career, before anyone had read *The Art of War,* the ancient Chinese military text now tucked under the arms of hurried business people in airports around the globe.

Han hadn't read it then either. It just seemed, logically, like the best way to get the better of anyone who would underestimate him.

> Use humility to make them haughty.
> Attack when they are unprepared.
> Make your move when they do not expect it.
> —Sun Tzu, *The Art of War*

Han is a partner in his law firm now, and this doesn't happen to him anymore. Nobody, not even an older white man afflicted by the blinding power of stereotypes, would underestimate a partner, even if the partner happens to be Chinese.

The Global Significance

The larger implication, on a global scale, is much harder to measure and more difficult to prove. We have seen a glimpse of how Lt. Col. Vann underestimated the threat of the fighting force he encountered in Vietnam in his casual remark that the Vietnamese were better lovers than fighters. How the perception of the threat from the "small and frail . . . earnest and gentle" Ho Chi Minh and the tiny blip of a country called Vietnam resonated in the mind of President Lyndon Johnson, who significantly escalated U.S. involvement there, is a matter to be studied by historians. (The writer Frances FitzGerald, for one, wrote in *Fire in the Lake,* that "The idea that the United States could not master the problems of a country as small and underdeveloped as Vietnam did not occur to Johnson as a possibility.") It is, however, worth examining a few possible aspects of these perceptions in light of the Asian Mystique.

We have seen previously how the United States, as a country, has cast Asian leaders and people on our side and under our tutelage as our "little brown brothers" and our "boys." And how we have depicted in feminine terms many Asian leaders who stood in opposition to the United States (as well as the most pliable ones on Washington's side).

In place of a masculine Asia dominated by strong male leaders, Soong Mei-ling—the wife of General Chiang Kai-shek—became the modern face of pre-Communist China in America when she became a media darling, gracing virtually every U.S. newspaper and magazine in the 1940s, and was the second woman ever invited to address the U.S. Congress, during the repeal of the Chinese Exclusion Act in 1943. She graced the cover of *Time* as "Dragon Lady," meant in the most complimentary, lauding-of-her-power way. Madame Nhu, the sister-in-law of Ngo Dien Diem, after assuming the role of First Lady of Vietnam in the 1950s, came to represent the "Dragon Lady" face of Vietnam in Washington, too. The extravagant Imelda Marcos and the more pious Corazon Aquino of the Philippines would also become as famous—or more so—in the West than their husbands.

Let's cast forward to today. Now, articles that seek to probe the motives of North Korean leader Kim Jong Il typically have categorized him as a goofball playboy in platform shoes and a bouffant hairdo— the archetype of feminized Asian despot, a modern villainous Fu Manchu who ultimately can be defeated by the forces of good. Yet, as of early 2005, he posed one of the most significant threats to the security of Asia and the world. Is it possible that the West, with its focus on Iraq during a time when Kim's regime has most likely developed a nuclear weapon, was not taking the nuclear threat posed by North Korea seriously enough? The North Korean leader certainly thinks so. He keeps demanding more economic aid, and threatening to test a nuclear weapon if he doesn't get it—in short, to be taken as seriously as the threat he poses.

The United States continues to view itself as the protector of Japan and South Korea, ensuring their security by keeping 58,500 troops in Japan and 37,000 troops South Korea—a presence that was renegotiated in early 2004 to be reduced 10 percent by 2007 and relocated out of downtown Seoul. Those countries also view the United States as their protector. But it is illuminating to read the coverage by newspapers in Seoul to see a slightly different perspective that doesn't make this patron-dependent relationship quite as stark as we might think.

Articles written by Western reporters depicted U.S. Defense Secretary Donald Rumsfeld, on a trip to Korea to negotiate troop relocations, as giving the Koreans the equivalent of a reassuring, parental pat on the head, and a little push out the door of self-sufficiency.

RUMSFELD: S. KOREA MUST CUT U.S. RELIANCE

OSAN AIR BASE, South Korea (AP)—The United States and South Korea agree the time has come, 50 years after the Korean War, for the economically vibrant Asian country to lessen its dependence on the American military, Defense Secretary Donald H. Rumsfeld said Tuesday.

"It is time for them to set a goal for becoming somewhat more self-reliant," Rumsfeld said during a question-and-answer session with several hundred U.S. troops at Osan Air Base. Banners lining the hangar where he spoke highlighted the immediacy of the North Korean military threat felt by 37,000 American troops stationed here and around the country.

(11/18/03)

RUMSFELD ASSURES S. KOREA ON U.S. TROOP OVERHAUL

SEOUL (Reuters)—Defense Secretary Donald Rumsfeld assured South Korean leaders Monday that plans to reposition U.S. forces in this country would not diminish the American ability or commitment to deter communist North Korea.

Rumsfeld and South Korean Defense Minister Cho Young-kil endorsed plans to reposition the 37,000 U.S. troops stationed in the South, and urged North Korea to scrap its nuclear arms program and to stop making and selling weapons of mass destruction.

(11/17/03)

The Koreans, however, saw in the same event primarily the inability of the United States to agree with Korea's relocation demands. They cast their articles completely differently. The following example is from the English-language *Korea Herald,* but the rest of the Korean-language papers reported the story in much the same way. The primary issue for the Koreans was how many troops South Korea would agree to send to Iraq to help out U.S. forces there and how quickly U.S. troops would get out of downtown Seoul, as the beginning of this article reveals:

KOREA-U.S. FAIL TO AGREE ON TROOPS

(SEOUL)—Top defense policymakers of Korea and the United States failed yesterday to find clear breakthroughs on the two major pending issues—Seoul's plan to dispatch additional troops to Iraq and relocation of the U.S. military headquarters out of Seoul.

Defense Minister Cho Young-kil and visiting U.S. Defense Secretary Donald Rumsfeld held the 35th annual Security Consultative Meeting in Seoul but reconfirmed their previous basic policy principles on the composition of any additional deployment of Korean troops in Iraq.

Just before Rumsfeld's arrival, South Korea decided to limit the size of its planned additional troop dispatch to Iraq to 3,000, possibly noncombatants, despite Washington's desire for some 5,000 infantry troops from Korea.

(11/17/03)

It seems possible, from this kind of exchange, that the Koreans are not in as much need of head-patting reassurance as Rumsfeld might think. The Korean newspapers never even reported his comments. Immediately after the final agreement was reached in May 2004, and the United States agreed to pull troops out of the location in downtown Seoul that they had occupied since the 1950s, some 250,000 potential buyers plunked down a total of $6 billion in deposits hoping to get part of the hottest real estate land grab in Korean memory.[18] The 800-acre area is almost as big as New York's Central Park, and the primary concern of most Koreans involved is real estate development, not U.S. patronage or protection.

Of course, the Koreans find it convenient to point to the presence of big bad America as a deterrent to North Korea, and the U.S. presence makes it a lot less expensive to Seoul's national budget and far less status quo–endangering to a border that has been tense since the Korean War armistice in 1953. Keeping things as they are, in that context, is a sign of prudence rather than weakness and dependence, despite American rhetoric. Yes, the rhetoric is partly to pressure the Koreans into acceding to U.S. demands, but the U.S. side is playing on long-standing Western perceptions of Asian weakness and dependency to further its negotiating position.

There is no doubt that the perceptions continue to hackle our Asian partners at a time when cooperation to counter the world terrorist threats is critical. In just one example of what is a continual, multi-faceted feature of U.S.-Pacific relations, a December 26, 2003 *Washington Post* editorial discussing cooperation on exactly that issue with Thailand, where a long-running Islamic insurgency is forging new ties with Middle East terrorist networks, featured the headline "Our Man in Bangkok." This characterization is not out of keeping at all with Washington's perception of that ally and did not raise an eyebrow in America. It most certainly did in Thailand. It prompted this angry letter to the editor from the Thai ambassador to the United States, Sakthip Krairiksh:

> Prime Minister Thaksin is not anyone's man in Bangkok but a highly independent and forward thinking leader of a country who is working hard to resolve all his nation's problems. At the same time, though, we are a dependable friend and partner of the United States, as we work together not only to deepen our cooperative endeavors, but also to address the many common threats and challenges confronting us.

He is right. Thaksin is a billionaire businessman who owns many major business interests in Thailand, a sort of Donald Trump, Jack Welch, Bill Gates, and Warren Buffett combined, with power that comes from his enormous stakes in media and the very infrastructure of the country. This prime minister has presided over the government during the mass killings of hundreds of Islamic separatists, as well as the killing of thousands of suspected drug dealers—whom police shot and killed rather than arrest, in one of the most considerable modern human rights violations in Asia. Thaksin is beholden to no one, not in his own country and certainly not in Washington, DC.

Historically, Thailand has proved itself as the most diplomatically shrewd country in Asia—alone among its neighbors in managing to escape being colonized by a Western power. Thailand is much more similar to, say, Italy, than to a small Asian country dependent on the

United States. The editorial editors at *The Washington Post* would never think to refer to Silvio Berlusconi—who in many ways is Thaksin's political and businessman equivalent—as "our man in Rome."

A KIND OF CROTCH-FORWARD, chest-out triumphalism has been an aspect of America's dealings with the world for the last century. The danger, however, is that macho swagger paints other nations—the nations of Asia—with a dismissive and paternalistic brush that obscures not only threat but acumen. As these countries continue their economic rise, with it will come a power that challenges the long-standing position of U.S. dominance and paternalism in the Pacific— and challenges the West to see Asian countries with unclouded eyes focused not on the feminized weaknesses of our dependent "boys," "little brown brothers," or modern-day Fu Manchus, but on equal partnerships or rivalries in which Asian leaders do not feel challenged to test their manhood or mantle by standing up to America.

While the leaders of Asia will be delighted finally to be regarded more equitably, it is America's own best interests and the interests of the stability of the Pacific Rim to do so. The United States has consistently underestimated military threat from Asian men and their armed forces: in the surprising ferocity of Philippine fighters resulting in 6,000 American casualties in that war a century ago; in the surprise bombing of Pearl Harbor; in the surprise pushback of American forces to the tip of the peninsula in Korea; and, of course, in the surprising loss to the tenacious guerrilla fighters of Vietnam. Do we really need to keep being so surprised?

"Race-ism," Fetish, and Fever

Jerry: Hellooo?? Who is this? Donna Chang? Oh, I'm sorry,

    I musta dialed the wrong number.

Elaine: Donna Chang?

Jerry: (redialing) I shoulda talked to her; I love Chinese women.

Elaine: Isn't that a little racist?

Jerry: If I like their race, how can that be racist?

JERRY SEINFELD IS TRYING TO CALL his friend George in this episode of *Seinfeld,* "The Chinese Woman," which first aired on October 13, 1994. But every time Jerry calls, the phone lines are crossed and a woman named Donna Chang answers. She likes Chinese food, teaches acupuncture, and misspeaks the word "ridiculous" as "ridicrulus." Jerry asks her for a date. "My first date ever with the Pacific Rim," Jerry declares to Elaine. "I'm *very* excited." When George's mother also reaches Donna Chang when trying to call her son, they talk for an hour and Donna talks her out of divorcing Mr. Costanza.

But when Donna arrives for the date, she is a blonde; she tells Jerry that her real name is Changstein. Jerry later complains to Elaine of feeling cheated. Mrs. Costanza feels cheated, too. "Well, then, that changes everything!" she shrieks. "I thought I was getting advice from a Chinese woman. She's not Chinese. I was duped. I'm not taking advice from some girl from Long Island."

IF HE LIKES THEIR RACE, how can that be racist?

It is not an idle question. Asian-Americans and Asians coming into contact with westerners think about it all the time. Like or dislike, a judgment about someone—how he or she might behave, think, appear, perform academically, be able to dispense advice, or anything else—according to his or her race, *is* a kind of racism. Most dictionary definitions have two entries for racism, one that says racism is this type of characterization, and another that makes discrimination, antagonism, or prejudice a factor in the definition. Because of our history of experiences with slavery and the civil rights movement, however, Americans tend to associate racism with only the latter negative definition without being aware that it is also the former. Here's the *Oxford English Dictionary* on the subject:

> 1 the belief that there are characteristics, abilities, or qualities specific to each race. 2 discrimination against or antagonism towards other races.

Perhaps, then, we need to hyphenate the word to show its distinctions, "racism" as negative, and "race-ism" as neutral or positive. Of course, trying to classify people according to groups and characteristics is part of human nature; it helps us understand who we are and how to interact. But when those classifications—in the form of prejudgments or prejudices—affect our cross-cultural expectations and interactions, it is of concern to Asians and the Asian-American (Asian-Pacific Islander American, or APIA) community.

Asian immigrants have long experienced overt racism in their contacts with the West: starting with the Gold Rush in the 1850s; the 1882 Chinese Exclusion Act; the World War II internment of Japanese-Americans in the 1940s; the 1982 killing of Vincent Chin; attacks on Korean shopkeepers in South Central during the Los Angeles race riots of 1992; and the false accusations of spying against Wen Ho Lee in the late 1990s. The British government, famous for its posting of a No Dogs or Chinese Allowed[1] sign in China, in the British Concession of colonial-era Shanghai, also has had immigration laws designed to keep out the perceived Asian hordes, despite maintaining colonies in Burma and Malaya until the 1960s, and in Hong Kong until 1997; as did France, with its colony Indochina that lasted until the 1950s.

And overt racism is still with us. In but one example, in October 2003, women's golf pro and former LPGA glamour girl Jan Stephenson, referring to the sudden prominence of talented Korean women golfers such as Se Ri Pak and Grace Park on the LPGA tour, told *Golf*

Magazine, "They've taken it over. This is probably going to get me into trouble, but the Asians are killing our tour, absolutely killing it—their lack of emotion, their refusal to speak English when they can speak English. They rarely speak." If people like Jan Stephenson are the only choice of people to talk to, then it would be hard to blame them.

Any prominent Asian woman can be a target, as evidenced by this January 17, 2004, posting to a fan message board for San Francisco–born Korean-American comedienne Margaret Cho: "F*ck you, you oriental cu*t. you are not even an american. You are soooo stupid. Go f*ck yourself and go back to Asia you slanted eye who*e."

Yet Asians and Asian-Americans find that, on the whole, negative "racism" slowly has been changing to neutral or positive "race-ism" over the years. Particularly, as academics such as Keith Osajima have noted, the label "model minority" was coined (during the racial tensions of the 1960s) partly as a way, for the white-majority society to hold up the example of Asians as untroublesome minorities compared to blacks and Latinos.

Our growing frequency of cross-cultural relations has helped, too. The number of Asians in the United States is steadily increasing: up by 9 percent from 2000 to 13.1 million in 2004 (4 percent of the U.S. population), and to a projected 33.4 million—or 8 percent of the total population—by 2050. The result has been, and will be, more frequent and widespread interracial interactions.

FEW TOPICS BRING OUT RACISM—or "race-ism"—more than romantic relationships across racial or ethnic lines. About 5 percent of U.S. marriages are interracial, compared to 3 percent twenty years ago, according to an analysis of 1998 census results by *American Demographics*. The researchers found that one-third of all married Asian-Americans between the ages of fifteen and twenty-four married outside theie ethnic groups (compared to only about one-tenth of married blacks). They also primarily married whites. Almost every high-profile Asian-American woman in America—including, for example, authors Amy Tan and Maxine Hong Kingston, and newscaster Connie Chung—married a Caucasian.[2]

Other statistics, cited on www.modelminority.com, show that 50 percent of women of Asian-origin living in the United States married white men. *The San Francisco Examiner* reported in 1990 that such marriages in the San Francisco area outnumbered Asian male/Caucasian female marriages by a 4-to-1 ratio and in the Sacramento area by an 8-to-1 ratio. (The marriage announcements in *The New York Times* indicate a significantly greater ratio in the northeast.) A researcher at Indiana University concluded that the ratio may appear higher because of dating couples. Based upon observation, the researcher estimates a ratio of between ten to one and twenty to one.[3]

Among those Asian women living in their native countries who marry foreigners, Americans are a popular choice. For Japanese women who took foreign husbands (7,755 out of 799,999 total marriages in Japan in 2001), Japanese government figures record Americans as the second most popular, at 1,416 marriages, behind Koreans at 2,477. (Japanese men married 175 American women in 2001.) British men were the fourth-most-popular choice, at 267 marriages, behind Chinese at 793. (Chinese wives are the most popular group for Japanese men, at 13,936 in 2001, followed by Filipinas at 7,160, Koreans at 6,188, and Thais at 1,840.) These trends have held steady in Japan, for the most part, since 1975.

The numbers are increasing in Europe. In Germany, for example, the number of German men marrying Asian women more than doubled between 1992 and 2002—from 3,192 to 6,609, according to government statistics. There were only twenty-five Asian wives in Germany back in 1960, the first year for which statistics are available, and 1,278 by 1980. While the government counts women from the Middle East and Central Asian republics as Asian, as well, more than 75 percent of the marriages are with East and Southeast Asians, and the highest number—42 percent or 2,775—are with Thai women,[4] perhaps a reflection of the growing number of German tour groups traveling to Thailand over the last fifteen years.

It is difficult to pinpoint exactly why rates of marriage between Caucasian men and Asian women are higher than for any other combination of racial groups in the United States, but several academics have tried to examine the question. It may be the result of "hiergamy," according to Professor Larry Shinagawa of Sonoma State University, where people "try to maximize their status opportunities, and their sense of wholeness, in the context of a society that's stratified by race, class and gender." In other words, he means that Asian and Asian-American women are seeking a bettering of their social status by choosing white men over Asian men in societies where white men hold power.[5]

The Indiana University researcher Tanaka Tomoyuki also noted that for Caucasian males, "there is something a bit adventurous about dating or marrying out of one's race. White males are more adventurous (less cautious) than Asian males [who feel pressured to carry on the family name along racial lines]. This contributes to the disparity" as does, according to Tomoyuki, societal support for dating Asian women—support that is not demonstrated for Asian male/Caucasian female couples.

When Caucasian or other non-Asian males are attracted to Asians with more intensity or frequency than is shown for other groups of women, Asian-Americans refer to this as "Yellow Fever" or "fetish"; nicknames for those who exhibit such behavior include "Fetish guys," or "Rice Kings," or "Rice Queens."

"Rice King definitely has that kind of master-subject connotation," says Reina Mizuno. She grew up in Nagoya, Japan, went to Georgetown University as an undergraduate, went back to Tokyo to work for three years, then returned to the United States to get her M.B.A. at Harvard University (at age twenty-seven). Mizuno was so motivated by what she felt was an increase in the "Asian fetish" phenomenon on American campuses since she returned to the States for graduate school that she wrote an article for the February 2, 2004, Harvard Business School's student newspaper, *Harbus,* headlined "Sex and the Campus: Attack of Yellow Fever."

> As an Asian person, I can immediately sense when someone has an Asian fetish. You spot someone staring at you from afar and the next moment coming to talk to you at a crowded [mostly white] party. You see a guy walking down the street, hand-in-hand with another Asian girl, and he still checks you out as you walk by him. Undergraduate majors of any East Asian language or East Asian Studies, or post-college work as an English teacher in any Asian country, are

easy giveaways. Back in the day (circa late '90s), these Asian Studies types were the only people with Asian fetish, but now, they seem to be everywhere, and their Asian fetish is not restricted to any one particular Asian [group]! . . . I can't help but think that some of it is men's chauvinistic fantasy about petite, reserved, submissive women. Is this about American men, tired of Anglo-Saxon feminists, seeking more traditional Asian women who would be dependent on them and make them feel good about themselves? Others would argue that the fetish has developed due to the increased exposure of beautiful Asian celebrities (*e.g.*, Lucy Liu from Charlie's Angels). Regardless of the rationale behind it, as an Asian woman myself, I have mixed feelings about this phenomenon. While I am glad that Asian women are getting the attention they deserve, I feel uncomfortable about men who are attracted to a woman just because she is Asian. On the other hand, I also feel that Asian fetish has positive social effects. As more people engage in interracial relationships, perhaps the color of your partner won't matter so much.

In her personal experiences of men with Asian preferences, Mizuno told me, she frequently felt typified and categorized by expectations of the behavior she "should" exhibit as an Asian woman. Now she has a Caucasian boyfriend with whom she has what she considers a normal relationship, but it took a while to find someone she felt comfortable with.

"I had this experience in college of men hitting on me very aggressively, and when I found out about one guy, that all his previous girlfriends were Asians, I was like, 'This is a fetish guy. I don't want to deal with that,'" Mizuno said. She continued:

It would involve putting me in the box of what he imagines Asian women to be, being vulnerable, naïve, submissive, reserved, all the classic stereotypes. I would also be concerned about other people's perceptions, that Reina is just being used because she's Asian.

I couldn't figure out whether it's an exotic thing or a smallness thing. Asian women are slimmer and skinnier than American women. I find they project the image that they're more vulnerable and feminine, and these American guys who were used to strong, assertive American women felt more comfortable dating these seemingly more vulnerable and naïve women.

When I was in Japan dating white guys, I got comments like, you're very Americanized, very outspoken for a Japanese girl. They had expected me to be less outgoing. Some people definitely choose to be submissive and don't care about careers in Japan, just because it's more comfortable and they're lazy. But, especially my generation of Japanese women, we are more focused on career, getting more education. So it's somewhat offensive when non-Japanese people think Japanese women stay at home. That's old-fashioned.

These attitudes aren't merely held toward Japanese women—even though, as we have seen, it has been primarily Japanese women who have been portrayed in the stereotypes Mizuno talked about, in *Madame Butterfly, Sayonara, Shogun,* and as geisha, loyal wives, and obedient housekeepers. Virtually all Asian-Americans (Chinese, Korean, Vietnamese, etc.), as well as Asians born in Asia, find that Western societies perceive of and stereotype Asian woman in the same ways.

Mizuno's Harvard Business School classmate Debbie Liao, a twenty-five-year-old Taiwanese-American, was born in Richmond, Virginia, moved to Taiwan at age eight, and then returned to the United States to study first at Amherst College and then at Stanford University. Even though she lived in the geographic opposite end of the country from Mizuno, she reported the same experiences, regardless of birth place or distinct ethnic origin. Said Liao,

This Asian fetish, whatever you want to call it, this whole trend, has become more prevalent in our current generation. It makes sense because more and more Asian-Americans are living in integrated communities as opposed to our parents' generation when there wasn't as much mobility. Shifting migration patterns cause more interracial couples. But the celebrities portrayed on TV or movies in America tend to be very fetishized, of a very particular type. Lucy Liu, for example, has small, slanty Asian eyes. The definition of beauty in Taiwan is different from the definition of beauty for Asians in the U.S. There, it is large eyes, instead of small eyes, and a thin, small nose. They tend to have fairly defined facial structure, and are more Western looking, whereas the celebrities in the U.S. are very "Asian" looking. Lucy Liu, people in Taiwan look up to her because she's been able to break into Hollywood, but they wouldn't have necessarily thought she was a beautiful Asian woman. Asian fashion models they use in the U.S. tend to have the same small, almond-shaped eyes, whereas in Asia, in Hong Kong, China, Korea and Taiwan, they want large eyes, and they have eyelid surgery to get it.

I had a Caucasian boyfriend for five years. When we first started dating, I was very concerned that he had an Asian fetish. I didn't want someone who was interested in me or attracted to me because I was Asian. It took him a lot of persuasion to overcome that, to prove he was interested in me because I was a person, not an Asian. A lot of my girlfriends claim they can tell right away if someone has an Asian fetish—if he has had a string of Asian girlfriends, that indicates he probably has an Asian fetish. For most Asian women it *does* bother them, for so many reasons. You're seen as an object, because you have black hair or prominent cheekbones or whatever, and not for who you are. A lot of us ask ourselves why the preference and where the line is. Some guys prefer blondes or big butts, so it's really hard to draw that line. It's more than attraction, though, it's the way they act or treat you. Is it racism? When you think about it emotionally, no, but logically, it does make sense to say that racism is any type of categorizing or stereotyping.

Beth Kwon, a second-generation Korean-American writer living in New York, draws the line even closer. "Some people think that an Asian fetish is no different from a propensity to seek out women with, say, red hair, big breasts, or a nice, round butt," she wrote in a 2001 column for *Time Out New York*.[6]

I don't buy it. Preference for Asians is not merely aesthetic. Apparently my black hair and olive complexion scream out "I'm great in bed!" or "I'll pour your tea and massage your feet"—the point being, of course, that we Asian women are all submissive, demure, and extremely skilled in the sack. When these guys look at me, they don't see me, they see a geisha in modern clothing. The perfectly charming guy I'll meet at a party will seem normal until one of the telltale signs of the affliction creeps into his conversation, such as the loser who actually told me, "I really like your people!" Men think they'll woo me by declaring, with a triumphant look, that they've been to Flushing or have eaten in Chinatown, as if [that] should earn them a medal.

But, Kwon told me, not all her Asian-American friends feel the same way. "I have known countless Asian women who say things like 'My boyfriend likes Asian women' as if they are LUCKY that a white man deigns to date them. Among people I've known, women often make the distinction of 'I only date white guys' or 'I don't like dating Asian guys,'" she said, some of which she attributes to a kind of ironic Asian-American feminism that denounces the patriarchal traditions of Asia and casts white men as more liberal alternatives to sexist Asian men. "Some of them also believe that the reason their boyfriend or husband prefers Asian women is because they are not difficult like white women supposedly are. They are proud that they can be good mates. It's like, 'White men like me because I'm obedient. I treat my man right and I'm not willful like white women,'" Kwon said. "Sometimes white men who date Asian women think they're doing them a favor—like that they are accepting them and they are the superior race."

Not all men, of course. It is worth stating yet again that there are many thousands of normal, healthy, wonderful relationships between Caucasian men and Asian women. I am not attempting to draw a definitive line between right and wrong, good relationships and bad. The most innocuous dictionary definition of fetish is an "unusually obsessive preoccupation or attachment; a fixation." When it comes to interpreting what that means in a relationship sense, clearly much of it is subjective and dependant upon the individuals involved.

The issue of fetishism and preference, however, is so prevalent, so pervasive in relations between East and West, that even healthy, normal relationships often are tarnished by the accusation. Sometimes, the men either doubt themselves or feel defensive, even when there is no

objective reason. If they're analytical or self-reflective, they find themselves examining their own motives and motivations for their attrac-
tions, in part to justify them against the stigma attached to fetishism
and "Yellow Fever." They may believe their attraction has to do with
an indefinable exoticism, the mystique built up over our history of
East-West interaction and perpetuated in Hollywood and mass media.

Sometimes, they say, it is a clearly stated rejection of Western
women or Western cultural norms when it comes to dating and marriage. Sometimes, some men admit, it has to do with body type—an
attraction to a more pubescent look of smaller breasts, straighter
waist-to-hip lines, and less body hair. Sometimes it has to do with being able to feel masculine or dominant because of the way Asian or
Asian-American women act or treat them. Or feeling like they somehow are saving the women—from sexism, discrimination, victimiza-
tion, prostitution, heathenism, poorer economic circumstances, etc.
And sometimes men just don't know why Asians give them more
erotic charge than other women. And if they do, many say, so what?

"You like what you like. If we all can find more ways of liking each
other in this world, what's wrong with that?" said a friend of mine, a
Caucasian who had lived in Asia for many years, married an Asian, and
argued—in a way typical of Western men in Asia—that he saw preferences as normal. He is right: preferences in sexual attraction are
normal.

What isn't normal, however, is when preference crosses the invisible
line, when Asian and Asian-American women on the receiving end
feel—as Liao and Kwon say—objectified and valued not for who they
are as people, but for their race or perceptions of the culture they come
from. While there is a joke-perpetuated stereotype that blondes are
ditzy, there would not necessarily be an expectation that a woman
would behave that way just because she is blonde. We easily see
through its transparency. It can be very different for Asians, however,
who find frequently that men's expectations of certain behaviors are
strongly attached to the preference, even before they cross the line into
"Yellow Fever" or fetishism. "Race-ism," then, can be just as uncomfortable as "racism." Not that there are clear definitions, anyway.
Women of Asian origin try to look for indicators, such as a string of

previous Asian girlfriends, to figure out if a man falls into the category of fetishist. But that's not always reliable, either. The line is not a clear one; drawing it is up to the person on the receiving end.

A FORTY-ONE-YEAR-OLD AMERICAN WRITER I met in China who had married a Chinese runway model who is about his height and is nineteen years his junior, had thought a lot about his preferences and whether he could justify them to himself. As I spoke with him at length about his choices, I came to admire his candor and capacity for self-analysis. We sat in a café in the old French Concession of Shanghai, and he told me his story of first taking a temporary job in South Korea—in part to escape a relationship with an American woman that he didn't have the courage to break off—and then subsequently moving to China.

> You know that passage that Michael Caine says in *The Quiet American*? "At first I was promiscuous, then I fell in love." That happened to me. All of a sudden I arrived in Korea. It was like a dream come true. You have all these gorgeous women throwing themselves at you. Korean women are incredible—beautiful, very darling, very sweet as well, not how they're portrayed as passive. They can be quite manipulative and strong. It was like they cast a spell on me. I was entranced.
>
> I hate the name they've given this syndrome, "Yellow Fever." I came down with a bad case of that. I just couldn't even imagine being with Caucasian or African-American women after that. Soft skin, dark hair and dark eyes, and the mystique, and they were wonderful lovers.

When he went home to the United States for his first visit he said, a neighborhood friend from childhood asked him whether it was true that Asian women had horizontal vaginas. "He was the first, but by no means the last, American male to ask me that offensive and patently idiotic question," the writer said. "In terms of origin, it probably has some correlation to the 'slitty' eyes—the lack of an epicanthic fold? I'm not sure." But he did experience at least one different sexual practice. Among the many Asian women he encountered, he said, 99 percent did not enjoy anal intercourse, much the same proportion as he found among American women. "On the other hand, ass licking, female to male, was something I hadn't encountered until I moved to Asia."

I had a bad experience in Korea, an American woman who accused me of being racist, that I used Asian women for sex. My "defense," although I don't need to defend myself, is that people have preferences. I've read biographies about men who have an obsession with obese women. I look on, I wouldn't say my "obsession," but my passion for Asian women, as my personal preference. It was quite upsetting [to be accused]. It was never a one-way street. There was always reciprocity. I was very frank, like, "Is this what *you* want to do?"

He also told me that, in Shanghai at least, Chinese women have extremely high standards when it comes to finding a mate, either Western or Chinese. "What you have in Shanghai is a certain hierarchy or strata where professional women tend to look for men who are earning as much or more than they are," he said.

They have certain standards in looking for husband. My wife is very unique. She knew that I was a writer and didn't make a lot of money. She simply believed you marry for love and not for money. We lived together for two to three years before getting married. We got together in November 1999, when she was eighteen, and I was thirty-seven. She told me she was twenty-three because she thought I wouldn't be interested in her otherwise. She's a relatively new phenomenon in China. She's a career girl, excuse me, career woman.

When I first met her I was just hypnotized by her beauty. Her eyes sparkled. She had this great laugh, great smile. It was flattering for me for this young beautiful woman to show an interest in me.

He was at a bar one evening and had spotted the willowy Chinese woman talking with a friend. He didn't have the courage to go up and meet her right away and, soon after, the two women left. He panicked and dashed outside, where they happened to be lingering. The tall Chinese woman told him she was a model. He invited the women to get a bite to eat nearby, and they accepted. He was delighted that the young woman's English turned out to be proficient. Later that night, he called her to make sure she got home safely. Before long, they were dating. Soon after, she moved in.

> I think there's a bit of a superficial streak in me, although I don't know why I'm being hard on myself. Most people like to be with attractive people. In the States, I had been with women my age, university-educated, and those relationships didn't work. There was something about [my wife] that was so refreshing. I knew we were really going to have to work at it, to be understanding of each others' cultures. I said it wasn't going to be a cake walk, that we were going to have to work at this.

Chinese men, he said, were reluctant to date a woman as tall as his now-wife (she is 5'10"). And they don't treat her particularly well in the modeling profession, he continued. There is protectiveness in his voice, and a note of pleasure rooted in being able to save his wife from the worst aspects of her own culture.

> There was an incident once when someone reached out and grabbed her breast, so I kind of had to defend her. I had to beat him up. She was wearing a padded bra and he wanted to see if she was real. She's very flat-chested, and I don't have a problem with it, and she doesn't have a problem with it, even though there is kind of a big tit sensation going on in China now.

It's true. A more Western aesthetic of beauty has taken hold in Asia, where—as Liao had noted—women with big, wide eyes, high cheekbones, pointy noses, and very light skin are considered more beautiful than ones with almond eyes, round faces, broad, flat noses, and darker skin. Hundreds of thousands of Chinese women undergo cosmetic surgery every year and slather their bodies in whitening cream every day to achieve this look. Large breasts are considered part of the beauty aesthetic as well, with billboards and advertisements everywhere starting to feature buxom Chinese models selling cognac, and breast implants. Curvy, light-skinned, wide-eyed Chinese women are in. That is not the aesthetic that interests this man, however. He, of course, thinks his thin, flat-chested wife with almond eyes is the most beautiful woman in the world, and her success as a runway model attests to her beauty regardless of the shifting tastes in consumer marketing patterns. He has spent a lot of time thinking about why, and he thinks he may have found something of an answer.

My father is an attorney in Philadelphia. Because he had low self-esteem, I think he projected it on to me. My mother suffered from depression and struggled all her life. My wife has a lot of self-esteem. I wish I had her confidence. Mom was involved with war victims from Vietnam. A lot of our coffee table books had graphic scenes from the Vietnam War, including the one of that girl burned by the napalm. We had napalm victims stay at our house during medical treatment. There was this aura of gratitude to my mother for what she had done. I think in a subconscious way that may have planted the seed for my attraction to Asian women. I don't think I have a savior complex or anything, and I haven't thought it out to the extent that I probably should, but that's the only connection I can make, that both my parents were involved in the anti-war movement. All that said, there is an aspect there of why do I prefer Asian women, why do I think the Asian aesthetic is more appealing than others.

More than one Caucasian man describing his attraction to Asian women has noted characteristics more aptly describing the photo of the thin, naked girl running down the road to escape a napalm attack. A 1998 Salon.com article, "Tiny, flat-chested and hairless! A white man extols the wonders of Asian women," quoted a "bona fide yuppie" named Ted living in San Francisco with a six-figure annual income from a job as a financial consultant. His story, and the sudden revelation of the interviewer, goes like this:

I remember when I was an adolescent boy, watching ABC's *Wide World of Sports,* and those cute little Chinese gymnasts with their small breasts. I remember being so excited by them. I don't like large breasts. They're so sloppy, or something.

There is something more exotic about Asian women. The physical is part of my attraction, the sexual part of it, too. . . . Asian women, they don't have any sexual hang-ups. They'll do anything, and I think it's because their culture wasn't based in Christianity, with all the guilt and repercussions. They tend to be more experienced sexually and anticipate what you want. . . . I hate body hair . . . They have beautiful, smooth skin. They age way, way better than Western women. And of course the problem with large breasts, which Western women tend to have, is that they never stay firm. . . .

The interviewer asks: "How about the rumor that Asian women are, well, tighter, because they're smaller?"

"No. And I lament over that, I really do," Ted says.

"I just have to say one thing," the interviewer concludes after looking over her notes. "Likes no hair. Small breasts. Tiny stature. Smooth skin. Ages well. Doesn't that sound like the description of, well, a ten year old? Do you think something in your sexual psyche is connected to pedophilia?"

"Maybe," he says cheerfully. "I've never thought about it, but I suppose it does sound like that."

A Chinese-American woman I know broke off her engagement to a white man after realizing with horror that it was her very girlish figure, quite literally, that attracted him. She is a size zero, if she can find clothes in that size, and otherwise shops in children's departments. After dating him for a year, she suspected pedophilia.

Other white men admit openly that it is fear of and intimidation by white women that drives them to their preference. A 1990 pullout section in *The San Francisco Examiner* quoted a Bay Area resident, Tom Knight, as saying, "there's a fear there with women I feel too much equality with. I see something of a feminist backlash in it. I don't really understand it, but I know I feel less threatened by Asian women." After traveling in China, he said, he started thinking of white women as "big, overweight Amazonians, with no bra, frizzy hair and lots of freckles. It made me feel kind of ugly myself." But a relationship with a Japanese-American woman, which lasted six years, ultimately did not culminate in marriage.

> She did a lot for me. She had tea ready when I came home; she scrubbed me in the bathtub. I liked it—you probably would, too. My friends thought it was sick, but it made me happy. . . . [But] there's such a thing as too much "otherness." We couldn't communicate. We weren't mental equals. Her whole world was her relationship with me.

It would have been interesting to find out, if Knight had married her, whether that would have remained the case.

The article quoted another man as well, Mike Arnold, who, it said, suffered from low self-esteem because of being sexually abused as a child. "I get some breaks from Asian women. Their standards are lower," he said.

> It's a Darwinistic world, dating-wise, and I have an inferiority complex with white women. Most of them have a big chip on their shoulder, and I don't care how liberated they say they are, they're not interested in someone who doesn't make much money. I eventually realized that being white, I could make it with an Asian women who's more physically attractive than I am, just because she's got a cultural inferiority complex.

Other men, feeling judged or invalidated by their societies, have joined a growing online community of membership websites, Usenet discussions, message boards, and blogs that seeks to explain and justify these preferences, and to persuade others.

The Communities and Fetishes of the Net

The growth of the Internet has fostered the proliferation of websites and cyberspace communities dedicated to the promotion of Asian women as objects of either pornographic fantasy, of fetish, or simply of wonder. The sexual fascination with Asian women, far greater than for any other "category" of women, is clear when you look at the numbers. A Google search of sexual content websites that can be classified as catering to Asian women fetishes finds approximately 3.55 million websites with names such as www.AsianFetish.com and www.asian licking.com, (with a large number in German as well as in English); there is even a website dedicated to the unusual "fetish of Japanese women's farts." By comparison, a comparable search for blonde fetishes turns up 3.21 million sites; 2.28 million for feet fetishes; and 2.08 million for black women fetishes.

Additionally, the Internet has given power to interconnected communities where only individuals existed before, and has emboldened those individuals in the primacy of their beliefs. "If you get likeminded people in constant touch with each other, then they get more energized and more committed, and more outraged and more extreme," Cass R. Sunstein, who wrote about the social impact of the Internet in his book *Republic.com,* told *The New York Times* in February 2004. Sunstein was speaking about how the intensity of grassroots support for Democratic presidential candidate Howard Dean came less from his own personal efforts than from the fact that Dean supporters were in contact with each other via the Internet. Geography would normally isolate them and spread them out into a less-powerful force; the Internet made them strong and united.

IT IS INTERESTING, then, to apply this analysis to the proliferation of websites promoting Asian women as perfect partners, sexually or otherwise, as well as those seeking to sell either the images of them or, quite literally, the women themselves via matchmaking services. While I am not advocating these websites, nor encouraging their viewing (and, in fact, some sites transmit computer viruses to visitors), their content is enhanced and made more truthful by the anonymity of their postings coupled with this feeling of an emboldened community.

As a result, the sites reveal more about the thinking behind "Yellow Fever" or fetishes than any interview might reveal and more than has ever been available before. While they may appear to be a few individuals going to extremes, the postings go to the core of "Yellow Fever," representing feelings that may be felt to a lesser degree by large numbers of men. It is for that reason that I include, in depth, the contents of a number of these sites.

Some men, such as the originator of asianwhite.org—"dedicated to improving race relations between Asians and Caucasians"—are seeking to clear up misunderstandings. His "Asiaphile homepage" refutes the idea that Caucasian men are merely seeking submissive women as an alternative to whites:

> The Asian features, black hair, slender builds, golden skin and Asian eyes are extremely appealing to me. I don't know why I have always liked the way Asian women look. Does any man know why he finds certain looks attractive? . . . When an Asian woman looks at me with attraction it fills me with a great sense of being a handsome man. I have never figured out if a disproportionate number of Asian women find me attractive, or if the ones that do simply express it in a way that I can understand and appreciate.

He also includes these refutations:

THINGS WHITE PEOPLE SAY[7]

It is amazing some of the things white people say when they see an Asian "girl" with a white man. Their response shows just how deep our racial stereotypes go.

1. "She must be a wildcat in bed!"
This perception of the Asian woman as a sex toy probably comes from GI Joes who see nothing but prostitutes and women in desperate conditions when they travel overseas. In fact, some Asian women are sexually active, many are not. Just like Caucasian women, it depends on the person.

2. "Oh, isn't she the most sweet and innocent little doll!"
Movies, plays, and books perpetuate this image of Asian women. Many Asian women play this role, and play it well, but many do not. Asian women, like anyone else, can be career driven, independent, and even downright aggressive.

3. "He must like those submissive types."

This is a cut on both the white man and the Asian woman. The thinking is (usually started by a white woman) that the man wants to go back to an era where he is boss. It implies that Asian women are all a bunch of submissive slaves. Asian women and white men have complex relationships, depending on their cultural background. She may have chosen him because he is an East Coast liberal who recognizes women's equality. Sometimes the white man is the leader, but I haven't known many Asian women who don't get their way.

4. "He must have some kind of weird fetish."

When a white man dates only white women he is never accused of having a fetish. Men may find blondes attractive, or women who are petite, or older women, or. . . . well, you get the idea. Some men have an attraction to Asian QUALITIES. Less healthy men have a fetish for Asian women as OBJECTS.

5. Silence

If you have ever crossed the racial divide, you have met the awkward pause. Some people have never met an Asian before; they just don't know how to act.

6. "Asian girls that date white men are ugly by our standards."

An Asian woman once told me this. Ironically she was very beautiful by any country's standards, and was dating a white man (in secret).

7. "She's sleeping her way to a Green Card"

I had a girlfriend that cried for hours when she heard someone labeled her a green card seeker. No doubt some women have used white men as their ticket to America; to imply that every Asian woman is a prostitute for the price of papers is demeaning to the couple.

8. "He is dumb"

A white friend of mine with a 4.0 GPA was studying with his Korean girlfriend (GPA 3.1) when one of her friends dropped by; in the course of conversation she made a comment that it was good of her "to be helping him with his chemistry." In fact, the situation was reversed.

To make sure he is not misunderstood, the author posts a large yellow-tinted box with the words, "What's wrong with white women? Nothing, in fact many white women have qualities I describe above . . . My attraction to Asian women has Nothing to do with White Women, and Everything to do with Asian Women."

BUT FEAR OF OR DISGUST with white women and the backlash against feminism are well-articulated in so many other examples in cyberspace that they clearly are a major factor of fetishism or "Yellow Fever." The website "Young Dudes' Guide to Japan" is an ostensible online travel guide written by Kris Foxton, a twenty-four-year-old Briton who was an English teacher in Japan (available at http://kawama.tzo.com:1023/kris/index.html).

> Wouldn't it be great if you could just find girls who weren't all '90's modern woman, and female supremist, talking like a guy and about their right to have the best orgasm they can, reading books about the 100 top ways to achieve their career aims, and crushing the men on their way to the top. Wouldn't it be nice just to find a kind, po-lite girl, who wasn't actually that worked up about women's state in society, just didn't really mind that the world is pretty much male-dominated, and actually quite enjoyed simply getting on with it, getting the most out of whatever life offers them. Someone who is ultra-feminine, of the surfer-chick mentality, and sexy as well. . . . Well, that's Japanese girls, dude! Most of them anyhow. And on top of that they come in pineapple, vanilla and mint-choc chip flavors! *joke*. I'm not saying there's anything wrong with the other type of birds, but those '90's career mistresses are just not my cup of tea, and probably not yours either if you're here reading this. . . . [In Japan] women have a set place in male-dominated society. Are they happy about it? I think so. . . . Japanese chicks are like Disney cartoon characters.

Of course, anybody who's been in a long-term relationship with a Japanese broad will know that they're not the tepid little flowers of the East that people envision them to be, but real women who know how to bitch when the bitching's good. But what they don't do is smoke more than you do, they don't drink you under the table, and they aren't filthy-mouthed she-men, like the ones that you might find down your local nightclub. A dude's gotta feel like a dude at the end of the day, gotta feel like he can come home to someone who needs him around. To tender, reciprocal love of the kind that you can see in old 50's Hollywood movies, and what is slowly becoming a myth in today's Western bigger better deal society. Let's face it, since us guys can't all be Brad Pitt, we tend to take the path of least resistance and go for the type of women whose expectations are just a little lower than modern day Western woman's.

The monologue continues for thousands of words and many pages. It includes the grouping of Japanese women by "type" and advice on how to bed each. The site also contains narratives about Foxton's hot pursuits of various Japanese women, and one Chinese. By the end of the affairs—and ironically, given his monologue—he ends up labeling all the women "BITCH!" The narrative concludes with his return to England and creating a website that has allowed him to remain in contact with like-minded people.

I woke up one day wanting to create a place where I could bring together people like myself, people who had woken up. And surely I wasn't the only guy in the world who thought Japan was the most magical place there is?? Anyway (cue *Star Wars* style narration), so I started this dirty little page. And through it I've met quite a nice community of diiirty little Asian-babe lovers. From the darkness, from the shadows, you see, we're out there.. multiplying.. festering away. Assimilating into the workforce, we keep our enemies close to ourselves in preparation for the day when we rise.. waiting.. Who is a member, how can you know that your closest and dearest isn't secretly one of us? The man behind the check-out.. the postman.. the fireman.. the hillbilly.. how do you know they don't have an Asian female tucked away at home? A nod and a brief smile is all it takes for one to recognise his brothers, for they are there in their multitudes, they *are* there, rising, infesting women of the Orient with their WHITE DEMON SEED!! GUWAA HAHAHAH AAAAAA AAAAAA! (echoing laugh into the darkness).

Other sites are more overtly sexual, such as worldsexguide.org. On it, men extol the sexual virtues of Asian women and how to meet and bed them in every big city in Asia (as well as women of other nationalities elsewhere in the world). Its entries are "reviews" written by contributors, kind of like a *Zagat's Guide* to sex, as though each nationality could be sampled like a flavor at Baskin Robbins. One reviewer wrote of Angeles City, Philippines:

The women are beautiful, Oriental and enthusiastic. . . . Although the girls in Thailand are more beautiful and tend to be slimmer, the Filipina women are a lot more friendly and extremely affectionate. Filipina girls generally speak really good English, which means they can chat and joke with you, which adds to your general enjoyment of their company. They quickly get attached to their lover and tend to be really loyal. At the end of the day, they hope to meet the man of their dreams who will sweep them magically to a land far away from the poverty they are used to. So if you're looking for a wife, then the Philippines is your dream destination.

Another wrote: "I fucked most of the girls in the Philippines at least three times during the night, in addition to the blowjob and massage they willingly administered." For 600 pesos (US$10.90), "this has got to be the best deal on earth."

You can also find out that the massage girl sent to your room at the Mandarin Oriental Hotel in Manila can be paid to stay the night, the Shangri-la's will give you a hand job for 1,000 pesos (US$18.20), and room service will send up condoms upon request.

In the Thai beach town of Pattaya, yet another reviewer writes that

typical girls are small, sexy, cute, uneducated MONEY-starved girls between the ages of 18–40. . . . Many girls prefer older men, as they tend to dote on their "girlfriend" and thus spend more money.

What do you expect—imagine what you'd do if you could land a drop-dead beautiful 18 year old who'll suck and fuck you as often as you asked—even though you're 52 years old and ugly as hell?

Enthusiasts for Thai women in particular have their own online communities, such as that created by a German resident of Thailand, Serge Kreutz, who encourages Western men to come experience their pleasures through his www.asialove.org and www.sextourism.org:

> I actually believe that sex tourism is a natural social phenomenon. If we assume that striving for sexual satisfaction is a primary motivator in people's life, than it is understandable if men hunt where they can find easier prey.
>
> Now, to the coalition of those who oppose sex tourism, allegedly out of moral concern: The women in the countries from where male sex tourists hail are usually strongly against sex tourism. No wonder. Their biological interest is that "their" men stay at home and compete for the females of their own societies, and do not go abroad for easier, younger, and more attractive women. They have reason to be jealous. The women sought by male sex tourists in Third World countries are their immediate competitors. . . . More than anything else, anti-Americanism is based on the fact that the U.S. is so eager to export its feminist moral standards and the norms by which it regulates the interactions of the sexes. For Asian men, this smucks [sic] of virtual castration. And Asian wives fear that by Americanized rules, they would have to separate from womanizing husbands who nevertheless are good providers, family men, and fathers, thus ending up as losers anyway. American ideology educates women that it breaks their heart if their men have sex with other females. . . .
>
> Come-on! Asian adults don't have to be treated as immature children. And they are adult enough to engage in sexual relationships with foreigners if they so desire. It is the primary aim of this site to provide some guidelines to Western visitors on how to go about it in various countries. Some of the information is available publicly; additional honest and straight-forward recommendations are reserved for site subscribers. . . . Asia is a fantastic sexual playing ground—for locals and even more so for Western visitors.

For self-described advocates of "Thai pussy" on the site bkktonite. com (BKK is the airport code for Bangkok) who make contact via a message board and meet up together in Thailand, there are hundreds of postings from men everywhere in the world. Following are just a few:[8]

—Posted by Peter, 1:20 AM on Mar. 2, 2002
Well, I am 48 years of age, German, now live in Italy.

Used to works in Peking for a couple of years and went whenever possible to Thailand—just for the smile in the faces, first. Soon investigated Patpong and got wholly involved!

From then on (some 7 years ago), whenever I am traveling and looking for some nice company after work, I focus on Thai girls. Luckily you find them about everywhere. My experience was made in different places in Germany, also Denmark and Italy. Generally Thai girls abroad keep up with the high standards of gentle and kind, open and warm charme. Only some, who are really too professional (they all are, I know), tend to follow the exemple of their local colleagues and become unhospitabel, doing just the job and out you go.

By the way: Hamburg has a wonderfull place, run by someone like us, where great girls and women give massage and soft excitement—100% recommendable, so sweet. Anybody around that part of the world, be in touch.

—Posted by mysteryman, 2:22 AM on Mar. 23, 2002
[W]ell I am 27 years old . . . I was born to Italian father and New Zealand mother with greek russian ancestory, so I look, well, Italian Greek, I guess. have only been to LOS [Land of Sex] once, went to Phuket with my wife and daughter. . . . been married to a Korean woman for 5 years, I have also been living in and out of Korea for 5 years.

I have my own company in Korea, love Asian woman, the first one I nailed I married, no, no, that's not true I shagged a few in college, but never a korean . . . have had chinese, japanese, cambodian, all were different, still am a LOS virgin, but that's all going to change when I come down in July with my friend for 2 weeks of shagging and partying. IM tired of Korean girls. I cheat on my wife because I have yellow fever BAD!!

and living here doesn't help it one bit, hahahahaha.

I am real looking forward to having my first thai girl and reporting to you all on this board.

—Posted by BigDUSA, 1:46 PM on May 29, 2002

Hi, I'm 55, retired and have a lot of free time on my hands. I'm from Philadelphia, PA. I've been to Thailand 6 times over the last 2 years and would move their if I didn't have a young child living with me. I'm a disabled Vietnam vet who found out I love Asian women when I was stationed in Vietnam. I have lots of different interests and enjoy life. I hope to attend a roundtable in late July/ August. Hope to meet some the guys who are on here.

—Posted by pbd714, 3:19 PM on Sept. 16, 2002

I agree 100%. There just is no substitute for a Thai girl. I think blue jeans were made for them and their delicious butts. Oh yea I almost forgot one point. Ever notice how good a Thai girl walks. So smooth the way that ass just glides from side to side. Not like an american woman walking like a horse!

—Posted by sukhumvit boy, 2:49 AM on Sept. 18, 2002

I am 40 year old guy from London, England. First went to LOS in 1990 and have been back 11 times since (in November it will be 12). I fell in love with the country and the girls from that first time and now I wouldn't ever think about going with any other girl apart from Thai (a few exceptions). I love everything about them and that's why I have to keep going back.

This is such a large community that there is an entire publishing industry in Thailand devoted to it. Books with titles such as *Money Number One: The Single Man's Survival Guide to Pattaya; Sex, Lies and Bar Girls: The ABC's of Bar Fines and Short Times;* and *Love, $ex & Trust: Romantic Adventures in Thailand* are written by Western men who, after years of experience patronizing bar girls in Thailand, offer advice on how not to get swindled or heartbroken. The books are available

"Sleazy, disgusting, politically incorrect and shockingly insensitive; I loved it!" - Nury Vittachi, HK Standard.

HARDSHIP POSTING
True tales of expat misadventure in Asia.

VOLUME 1

Compiled & Edited by **Stuart Lloyd**

BEST SELLER IN ASIA - Over 20,000 copies sold!

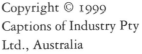

Copyright © 1999
Captions of Industry Pty
Ltd., Australia

where the intended audience is likely to be—in the various English-language bookstores in Bangkok, and on Jomtien Beach in Pattaya. Other books such as *Hello My Big Big Honey: Love Letters to Bangkok Bar Girls and Their Revealing Interviews* as well as *Hardship Posting: True Tales of Expat Misadventure in Asia* seek to capitalize on the regularity and commonality of such experiences by Western men in Asia, or point out the more poignant or comical aspects of the transactions. Judging by the success of the latter book, which has spun off into four editions, there is no shortage of material or audience.

Mail-Order Brides and International Introductions

With such a proliferation of white male enthusiasts for Asian women, it's no wonder that the world of selling Asian women—or at least selling introductions with them—has moved online as well. A 1999 U.S. Immigration and Naturalization Service report to Congress on mail-order brides reported the practice "growing rapidly" and that there were 200 sites operating in the United States. It noted 4,000 to 6,000 couples matched through the sites annually in which the brides applied for U.S. immigration, the large majority from the Philippines as well as from the former Soviet Union. According to Philippine government statistics, 150,000 Filipinas left the country between 1989 and 1998 to be brides in foreign countries, primarily in North America, Australia, and Europe.

Before the Internet, the mail-order bride business was mostly conducted via catalogs and brochures. In 1974, Cherry Blossoms, which claims to be the "world's first picture personals" service, started publishing a magazine of color photos. It subsequently moved operations online, to www.cherry-blossoms.com, and its "About" page claims to have matched more than 50,000 couples. Cherry Blossoms anticipated matching another 2,000 couples in 2004.

The sites offer introductions, primarily with Filipinas: www.goodwife.com (the "Mail Order Bride Warehouse" with an "Asian" page and 12.9 million page views since 1997); manilahotties.com; www.eastwestmatch.com; www.1000brides.com; and www.sweetsingles.com (also offering "4,500 lovely Thai ladies"). Another site, My KoreanBride.com, specializes in "sincere and honest Christian Korean brides."

Some sites, such as www.asian-women.com run out of Hawaii, insist that they are not mail-order bride services, but rather merely introduction agencies. In other words, if men want to marry the women to whom they are introduced, then it happens outside the scope of the service; the website merely provides an introduction. This is because the Philippines banned mail-order bride services, so companies get around the ban by operating around the rules. The site's FAQ page reads:

Q. Are you a "mail-order bride company"?
A. Absolutely not! A "mail-order bride company" sells marital slaves. If your "bride" is not submissive enough you can return her within 30 days for a prompt refund or exchange her for another bride. "Mail-order bride companies" exist only in the minds of

biased critics and the imaginations of portions of the media. There is no such thing as a "mail-order bride" or "mail-order bride company!" In reality, it is the ladies who do the choosing by selecting which men they wish to respond back to. Sunshine International is a correspondence/penpal service which promotes friendship. We respect our lady members and present them in a wholesome manner such as befits them. The only "exploitation" of Asian ladies comes from biased critics who portray them as prostitutes trying to escape desperate circumstances.

Q. I've heard that the Philippine government has banned "mail-order bride companies." Does this affect your company or me marrying a Filipino lady?

A. No. On July 24, 1989, the former Philippine government passed a law prohibiting "mail-order bride" companies from operating in the Philippines. The law also prohibits tour operators from bringing groups of foreign men to the Philippines to meet Filipino ladies with the intentions of marriage. The law does not, however, deprive the ladies from corresponding with or marrying a foreigner. We do not solicit the ladies to join us, nor do we operate in the Philippines.

The www.manilabeauty.com site out of Rockford, IL, advises:

I know many of you are tired of the U.S. or Canadian singles scene like I was. You know . . . insincere girls who like to play games or expect constant material gifts. But these Asian ladies are honest, faithful, rarely lose their figures as they age, are extremely supportive, and care more about your heart than your wallet. For them, nice guys finish first! I know that is a new concept to many who are reading this. I know it was for me. Don't settle for a demanding and unappreciative woman.

It refers interested men to its "How to Order" section and the requires a credit card number to start sending profiles.

If you think about it, this service is really no different than any other domestic singles, dating and matchmaking service. "Mail Or-

"Lucky Men from Denmark" from www.sweetsingles.com
(The woman at left decided not to marry him, according to a later
site update which showed a replacement.)

der Brides" is a term that means slavery and servitude. While true
in the past and in illegal underground sex trade operations today, it
is no longer a normal part of the foreign introduction industry.
. . . If you are very successful and are in good shape (not overweight)
you may find a lady as many as 30 years your junior to accept you.

Sites make a selling point of saying that the women fit well with
men with "traditional" beliefs unappreciated by modern Western
women. "These beautiful Filipina girls speak fluent English and are
surprisingly modern in their attitudes and education, but still hold a
conservative, religious, and traditional outlook about the world and
concept of family," according to manilahotties.com. A number of sites
post photographs as proof of successful matches.

THERE IS NO EVIDENCE that mail-order or international-introduc-
tion matches are any happier or unhappier than any others, or that
they result in more or less spousal abuse than do any other marriages.

Len & Mai, England, from
www.sweetsingles.com

An autobiography written by Wanwadee Larsen, a mail-order bride
from Thailand herself, offers a rare glimpse from the other side. She
reports that, on the whole, her marriage was happy; although she
chronicles her quiet, incessant pressure on her husband for years to get
him to quit smoking pot. She makes a point of noting the acceptabil-
ity of such marriages to the brides who sign up for them.

> Yes, far from being "kitchen appliances with sex organs," Asian-
> American women are as full of questions about life as anyone else.
> We do indeed have egos, flickering candles capable of flame. If you
> divide and sub-divide people by race and gender, there is hardly a
> slice of humanity as diminutive in stature and all-but-invisible as
> Oriental women. I am not so much complaining as calculating here:
> As no one else does, the Asian woman acts upon her root belief that
> in softness and in silence there is enormous strength. . . .
>   It is not at all unusual for marriages in the Orient to be arranged
> by contract, usually between neighboring families. It is of course
> more unusual for those marriages to be between complete strangers

who live thousands of miles apart and are from totally different cultures. . . . Although some stigma is attached to the practice in the West, in the East it is one of several acceptable means by which a young lady may find an appropriate mate.[9]

A March 2000, study of mail-order brides in Canada conducted by the Philippine Women's Center of British Columbia in Vancouver found that the Canadian husbands primarily were aged forty to sixty, had been married previously, lived in rural areas, and had "antiquated ideas of marriage." (Twenty percent of the brides had been previously married and 83 percent came from rural areas in the Philippines.) Of the husbands, 79 percent were college-educated and another 16 percent had vocational training; more than half of the couples (52 percent) had an age difference of more than ten years between them.

According to the study, the men regarded their spouses as "meek docile slaves, Oriental beauties with shady pasts, as passive and manipulable, but also predatory, with 'traditional' values." It said that women chose such marriages because of a perceived increase in status by marrying a white man, the social pressure to marry particularly for older women, and more chance for economic stability. Marriages as a group could neither be termed successful nor abusive, the study concluded, but instead, like most marriages that are not arranged, ran the spectrum in between. Nonetheless,

the presence of Filipina women performing domestic work for twenty years in Canada has constructed an objectified, slave-like ideal of Filipino women, pushing them further into the margins of exploitation and abuse within Canadian society. Filipina women are considered better marriage material not because of the principled virtues they possess, but because of the belief that Filipina women are obedient, docile, subservient and old-fashioned. Thus, the dividing line between servant and wife is bridged by mail-order brides.

One statistic the study cited was that, of a total 20,000 Filipina mail-order brides in Australia, since 1980 twenty-two had been murdered or had disappeared. The INS report said that in 1998, 3,300 battered spouses complained of abuse through INS channels, up from

2,500 in 1997. While it is unclear whether the complaints came from mail-order brides, the petitioners were recent immigrants to the United States seeking legal residency on their own, apart from their abusive husbands.

Anti-feminist rhetoric is part of the mail-order bride business as well, beyond the veiled references to finding "traditional" "ladies" and "girls" instead of "demanding unappreciative" "women" posted on the sites themselves. The report from the INS, which had solicited public comments in 1997 on proposed regulations governing immigration of mail-order brides, included this one:

> The overwhelming majority of the men who use such services are sincerely wanting to find a woman with old-fashioned values to love and cherish. . . . The proposed regulations are obviously a ploy of the feminists to eventually abolish such services. The feminists do not want to see men happy. The INS should not be the puppet to the feminists' strings. Until the day women in America can understand and accept the true meaning of feminism there will be a continuing flood of American men who will look overseas to find that "real" woman.

Beyond INS attempts at regulation and the Philippines' outright ban, there's has been yet another method of confronting the mail-order bride phenomenon. It comes from a former student at UCLA, Kristina

Wong, a Chinese-American who designed as a student project www.big badchinesemama.com. Her site contains key words such as "mail-order bride" and "horny Asian women" to try to intercept men who might be searching online for Asian wives or Asian porn. When they click on bigbadchinesemama.com, they are

"Loyal, gentle, and sweet. Like any good Asian wife." From www.bigbadchinese mama.com

greeted with pictures meant to spoof the online photos of mail-order bride sites by showing beautiful Asian women on, say, a toilet seat, or with six eyes, and notices such as "You are the 35,864th pervert to come to our site." At its height of popularity in 2000, the site popped up on the front page of the Google search engine page as one of the top ten listings for mail-order brides, and drew hundreds of thousands of hits.

"I hate cooking. I hate cleaning," the twenty-five-year-old Wong, now a performance artist and activist, said when I asked her to discuss the site. She had taken to dressing as "Fanny Wong, former Miss Chinatown Second Runner Up," wearing a vintage dress, sporting a cigar, and walking around Los Angeles' Chinatown posing for tourists. "Now I want to challenge the idea of positive icon," she said.

"At one point I woke up every day overcome with rage at the white man. 'I'm NOT this, and I'm NOT that. You can't put me in this box,'" Wong said. "I think you can have fun with the way you challenge oppression." Wong later grew bored with dealing with the thousands of hate postings and vitriol she got as a result, and eventually took down her online "guestbook." The postings were about 70 percent attacks written by white men and the remainder comments by Asian-American activists in-fighting over whether such a confrontational approach was a good idea, Wong said. Plus, it was taking up too much bandwidth. "People would write, 'Well, I traveled all through Asia and found women to be submissive' or whatever. It's the same old shit. It's so obviously ignorant," she said. "Can we even *begin* to subvert the idea of race and imperialism?"

PART TWO

Ten People, Ten Colors

Ten People, Ten Colors

BEFORE SHE LEFT THEIR ATLANTA HOME for Tokyo he confronted her. "I want you to listen to me," Chris said. That's how he often started his sentences. "Listen to me. I want you to listen to me." This time it was about car seats for the children. "Your parents are bad drivers. I want you to buy car seats for the kids as soon as you get there so they'll be safe driving around." It was how he had talked to Yukie throughout their twelve years of marriage, giving orders, demanding that she listen. But Alex was seven already, and Ian was five.[1] They had outgrown the need for car seats. Imagine, Yukie thought, getting into Narita airport at the equivalent of the middle of the night Atlanta time, then taking two cranky children after a seventeen-hour flight to buy car seats on the way to her parents' house from the airport. "Listen, just buy the car seats," Chris said. Yukie didn't answer him. She heard him, but she wasn't going to listen.

Chris had more admonitions. "Listen, don't let the children play outside by themselves. It's dangerous," he said. But Japan wasn't dangerous at all by American standards, and definitely not the nice neighborhood on the outskirts of Tokyo where her parents lived. Chris's words were just an effort to exert control over a situation in which he had long ago lost control.

Listen.

Listen to me.

I am the boss in this house.

YUKIE WAS LEAVING FOR JAPAN for two weeks to take her children to see their grandparents, as she did every summer. Chris wasn't going. Yukie couldn't wait for a few weeks of peace, couldn't wait to speak her own, native language, without the hectoring and the fighting.

Although he didn't know it yet, Chris was going to be served divorce papers while Yukie was gone. When she came back, she hoped, Chris would be resigned to it, and they could part amicably, finally, after more than a decade. They had discussed divorce for a long time now, and for the last two years they had lived in separate bedrooms of their house, more like roommates than spouses. For the sake of the children, they said.

But the children were growing up learning more about tensions than about love between parents; they were surprised to learn that the parents of their friends slept in the same bedrooms. Even when Chris and Yukie were just talking, the children would plead with them, pleeeease, to stop fighting. But they weren't fighting, exactly. Neither raised their voices. But the tension was so thick, it often seemed that way.

"Grow up," Chris would tell her. This is what marriage and children and responsibility are all about. But Yukie *had* grown up. That was the problem. She had grown into a mature, professional woman who didn't want this man bossing her around, telling her what to do, telling her to listen. She spoke English well now. She wanted a clean break. She wanted to be on her own. Chris was in denial. He never thought his wife would actually do it, file for divorce. He thought she needed him.

YUKIE, FOR A BRIEF TIME, was a career woman and professional in Tokyo. But when her husband insisted on returning to Atlanta, with or without her, she felt that she needed to follow him, to give the marriage one last chance. She did not want an international custody battle over her children. So she gave up her career. On the day she had met me, she was still working, pondering that decision she would later make. She strode out of her downtown Tokyo office building a portrait in confidence. Tall for a Japanese, Yukie was a rarity in many ways in Japan—a country where only 11.3 percent of corporate managers are women[2] (compared to 32 percent in the United States), and 13 percent of Japanese companies have no women on career tracks at all. I didn't ask Yukie her salary, but fewer than 3 percent of women make more than the equivalent of $58,000 a year, while 24 percent of males do. My guess, from her stylish clothes and the fact that she worked for a company headquartered in California, was that she probably was one of them.

Yukie had grown up in a very traditional Tokyo home, with what she calls a "very traditional" father. In the family dynamic, her mother didn't appear to have any power, at least in front of the kids. She just seemed to go along with whatever decisions were made by her husband. He voiced the family decisions, and she did everything for him—cooking, cleaning, laundry, taking care of the household. He wasn't around much; he ran his own business and worked all the time. So when he did come home, he expected full-service treatment and he got it. Like most Japanese men of his generation, he went to bars and clubs after work to socialize with his colleagues—a mandatory part of climbing the corporate ladder in Japan—and had affairs with the hostesses there. This kind of marriage was the only kind of partnership Yukie knew growing up.

At age sixteen, Yukie went to Los Angeles as a high school exchange student, an experience that opened her eyes to a whole new kind of family dynamic, one that seemed to be based on a more mutual, affectionate relationship. Driving in the car, the American wife would touch her husband's leg, and they would exchange smiling glances. Yukie admired this surprising display of affection between a couple after twenty years of marriage. This American husband seemed devoted to his wife. Yukie couldn't imagine him cheating like her own father did. Rather than the distant, formal relationship her parents had, Yukie wanted one just like this.

When Yukie convinced her father to let her return to study at California Tech a few years later, she had never even had a Japanese boyfriend. Shy and quiet, she stuck to her girlfriends at school. But once she was in the States, she was different. She would keep her distance from the type of American guy who would tell her how much he liked "Asian girls," or insist on taking her to Little Tokyo, the type who, she says, has self-esteem issues with American women and likes to feel dominant around less-aggressive Asian women. There was so much about American culture she wanted to learn. She wanted to go to hamburger places; she wanted to reach into a pizza box and practice pulling off a piece without losing the toppings—not watch an American guy try to impress her with his ability to use chopsticks in Little Tokyo.

Yukie loved the American lifestyle, where behavior seemed so much more free than back home. That's how she met her husband-to-be in a bar while celebrating the end of finals. He liked her for who she was as a person, she thought, not for her being Asian. He didn't even like Asian things. And he hated Asian food. Yukie loved that about him. He preferred pizza and hamburgers to sushi. At that time in her life, Yukie did, too. They married at twenty-three, moved to Atlanta, and had two kids.

Chris worked in real estate, but he was never very successful at it. He liked spending time with the kids in the park. It was Yukie who had a successful career at a Web design firm. They decided it made sense that she would be the one to make the money and he would be the one to stay home while the kids were small. As a Japanese woman, she felt a little uncomfortable with this reversal of her own tradition. It made her husband seem less masculine to her, but it seemed to be the best situation for the family. Her career continued to go so well that she was offered a six-month stint in her company's expanding Tokyo office, with the option to stay on and be promoted through the managerial ranks. After all, she spoke the language, knew the culture. It was a great opportunity. How could she pass it up?

I HAD MET YUKIE while she was on her Tokyo assignment. And over our lunch that day—a set-menu *bento* of grilled fish, seaweed salad, and pickles in a compartmentalized box—she pondered her future. Her husband had gone back to Atlanta after less than three months, leaving her and the kids with the instruction to join him as soon as her assignment was over. He didn't much like Japan, living as they did with two young children at the home of Yukie's parents. While Yukie went to work in the morning, her husband, speaking no Japanese, stayed at home, in the domain of his mother-in-law. He wanted to help care for the children during the day. After all, that was his job back in Atlanta. Women's work, his mother-in-law said. Her disapproval was obvious, and the silence between them, exacerbated by the language barrier, did not help. They enrolled Chris in Japanese language courses at the university. He wouldn't go. And when his mother-in-law made dinner for the family every night, he had a hard time eating it. He didn't like fish, or soy sauce. Yukie had known that since they first met, but she had hoped that this achingly American husband of hers would try to adapt for the sake of the family. Instead, he asked Yukie to make him separate dinners of lasagna, fried chicken, and steak. In Japan, the man she had married had become as helpless a child, but worse. At least her children could speak Japanese. Getting her husband to change was doomed, and Yukie knew it. His immovable American-ness was what first attracted her to him. Now it was what was tearing their marriage apart.

But there was an even bigger problem. Yukie's husband had decided after their children were born that they should all share a family religion. He was raised a Baptist, but he had rejected the religion in his teens. After trying out various Protestant denominations, her husband decided they would all convert to Greek Orthodoxy. Yukie, like 99 percent of Japanese, had been raised nominally Buddhist. Her family had practiced Shinto ceremonies on holidays and important occasions, and kept an altar in the family home in remembrance of the family patriarch, her grandfather. She believed in God. But most people in Japan weren't religious by American standards. Yukie wasn't either. Now, however, her husband asked her to believe in Jesus Christ. As she told me about it, she was heartbroken. The man she had married for his open-minded "American-ness," his flexibility, who provided an alternative to the rigid traditional Japanese marriage in which the husband makes the family decisions, had now decided something for her that was fundamental to her being—her religion, and what she should believe. He said that she, as his wife, should honor his decision. She respected Christianity, she said, and found a lot about the religion appealing. But this belief in Christ was not inside her. Yukie tried, but she could not feel it. It was not part of her upbringing; it was not who she was. Her husband was not sympathetic. She would realize it someday, he said. Someday she would accept Jesus Christ as her savior—but by then it would be too late.

And now she was slowly beginning to understand more clearly why her husband had chosen her. As a Japanese woman, Yukie said, she appeared non-aggressive, non-threatening, as someone who would respect her husband's wishes, as someone who would follow along—be traditional, deferential, and obedient. Was she, to him, supposed to fulfill some sort of idealized role of Asian wife, like a geisha he had perhaps seen in a movie somewhere? She wondered it aloud as she prodded her grilled fish lunch.

Traditional and obedient was not how she was. It was not how any Japanese women she knew were. It was not why she had come to America to study, and had decided to marry an American man. And it didn't make sense given the untraditional roles she and her husband had assumed when it came to bread-winning and childcare. She did not understand why her husband did not understand her after all these years. Now, with her husband back in Atlanta, Yukie had to decide whether to give up her job and return to him, or to remain with her parents in Tokyo and fight to keep their children in Japan.

Reflecting about the choices she had made in life, Yukie had begun to reconsider her youthful rejection of a Japanese marriage. No longer did she believe Japanese men don't make suitable husbands. There are many Japanese men who have traveled, she said, who are flexible and open-minded.

During the same time frame in which Yukie was telling me her story, the possibility of naming a female empress was being debated openly in Japan for the first time in 200 years; the first woman to hold the post of foreign minister was about to be booted out of office—despite her popularity among the public—and replaced by another woman; and Japan was on its way to electing three women governors—a first in modern Japan. Eight women had held the position of empress in Japanese history, but centuries of Samurai rule had considerably weakened the rights of women in what was formerly a matriarchal society—where women freely chose sexual partners and had more personal freedoms 1,000 years ago than they had during the past 100 years.

Japan has been changing again since the economic boom of the early 1990s went bust. The society has begun to accept that the way to recover the economy is to allow women to take up a greater role in the workforce; that, by putting pressure on women to quit and stay home to raise children, half the brainpower of the country was disappearing into the households of Japan just when it otherwise could be at its

most creative. But women had always occupied an equal if not dominant role in the Japanese household, one that traded the husband's
breadwinning ability for the wife's domesticity in an equitable but
very static quid pro quo. When Yukie's father came home from work,
he handed his pay to his wife, and she gave him back spending money
as an allowance. It has long been the tradition in Japan, and still is today in 75 to 80 percent of Japanese households.[3] Even direct deposit
hasn't put much dent in the practice. On the 25th day of the month—
payday in many Japanese corporations—housewives can be seen lining
up at ATMs to withdraw the monthly household funds along with
their husbands' allowances. Often, the breadwinner himself doesn't
have an ATM card. And if he does, it is only to withdraw his salary to
then hand it over to his wife so that she can give him back a small
amount.

Not so in Yukie's home in Atlanta, however. Her husband didn't
want her to be in charge of the money. He was the husband. He was in
charge. She put the money she earned into their joint account, and he
spent it. Observing her mother now as an adult, Yukie began to reconsider what she used to think about her parents' marriage, and about
who was the boss in that house.

Her mother, Yukie now believed, held power in her own way. Even
though she seemed passive and agreeable in front of the children—
because harmony is an important value in a Japanese household—she
would save her ammunition until she and her husband were in private
quarters. Her words were soft, but they were powerful. If her mother
disagreed with any decision affecting her or the family, she persuaded
her husband to change his mind—always, as far as Yukie could now
determine.

And there were other ways her mother exerted power, Yukie said,
like through the knowledge that her husband was dependent on her
for his quality of life once he passed through the doorway into her domain, that without her, for example, he couldn't have a hot meal. Another was through her almost complete control in the raising of the
children. Fathers are sometimes called "Sunday friends" in Japan—the
only day of the week in which they spend time with their children, as
they frequently get home on weeknights after the children have gone
to bed and sometimes even leave in the morning before the children

wake up. For the most part, then, children's personalities, morals and characters are shaped by their mother. Yukie now admitted, sadly, that she had realized this dynamic was a lot more complicated than the way she saw it when she was a teenager. And, sadly, unlike for her mother, Yukie's quiet words uttered in private held no sway with her American husband. The irony was, she believed, in seeking more power in her own marriage than her mother had in hers, she had ended up with even less.

Yukie did quit her job to follow her husband back to Atlanta. She couldn't get her old job back. He tried to be the breadwinner for a time while she stayed at home or took other, part-time positions. But it just wasn't working. Yukie resented giving up her career; Chris resented the fact that his wife never seemed to listen to him. By the time of Yukie's trip to Japan to visit her parents two years later, Yukie had decided to end it, to be free of a man who wanted what he thought would be a nice, obedient Asian wife instead of a person who wanted freedom from the constraints of tradition. Yukie sees her own mother now in ways that only a woman who has become a wife and mother herself can see. With the benefit of hindsight, she sees the situation as being a lot more complex than she had realized.

It was this type of complexity that brought me to Japan, to try to examine the contradictions between the true, hidden realities and the outward appearances that affect how Western cultures view the East, and how the resulting misperceptions affect our relations and relationships. As an outsider, there is much that I would never know about the inner realities of Japanese households and husband-wife relationships. There would be contradictions in the lives and expectations of the women I had met that I would never resolve. Unlike the United States, where openness is a prized societal value, Japan is a society where true feelings are hidden. But, what I could see was that a lot of what we think we know in Western culture about what constitutes being an "Asian wife" comes from misrepresentations in Western culture—of, for example, Madame Butterfly, of images of geisha and devoted wives in Hollywood movies, and of press coverage in the West that has frequently presented Japanese women as victims of sexism and discrimination. The reality was clearly more complex and sometimes contradictory.

There is an old joke in Japan that goes: A Japanese man bows slightly to his colleagues, fifteen degrees to his boss, and ninety degrees to his wife. "It's true!" Japanese women always exclaim when I ask them about it. But the idea that foreigners might picture Japanese wives perched on the bathtub scrubbing their husbands' backs when not rushing around serving them tea is what really makes women laugh. Japanese men sometimes indulge in such bathing luxuries in the red-light districts—in the popular "soap lands," as massage parlors are called, where a bath comes with fellatio or more—but wives think it strange to be associated with the practice.

Japanese women also think the old Western joke about the perfect wife being Japanese is strange, if not somewhat flattering. It goes: Heaven is an American salary, a Chinese cook, an English house, and Japanese wife. Hell is a Chinese salary, an English cook, a Japanese house, and an American wife. After all, in Japan, *kaka denka*—henpecked husband—is a common term used by Japanese men, as are wives' terms for husbands who suddenly start hanging around the house after retirement, *nure ochiba* (wet leaves) or *sodai gomi* (oversized trash).[4] There's even the term *kitaku kyofusho,* a phobic fear of going home and being confronted with one's wife, which was said to have afflicted Japanese salarymen in the 1990s, and perhaps still does today. Seemingly, only foreigners think the institution of marriage in Japan is a grass-is-greener place. Perhaps this is partly because of the wide gap between prescribed public behavior and private reality. As Ian Buruma, who married a Japanese woman, wrote in *Behind the Mask* in 1984:

Foreigners, who see how meek Japanese housewives are bossed around by loud-mouthed husbands incapable or at least unwilling to do anything for themselves, often draw the conclusion that men are very much in command in Japan. In many cases, the meek, housewifely exterior is the public façade of a tough, steely wife and mother who is very much in control at home, while Dad's growling boorishness hides a helpless man clinging to his masculine privilege. The slave and sergeant-major are public roles that have little to do with actual strength of the individual. The wife shows respect for her husband in public because it is expected of her, but it is a respect for his role, rather than for the man himself. What happens in private is quite a different matter.

Even the public displays have been changing among the younger generation. Men under the age of fifty[5] don't expect their wives to be obedient followers. No Japanese woman would refer to her own husband as *shujin,* or "master," anymore, although it remains the polite term used to inquire about someone else's husband. There's one exception, a Japanese wife told me—getting rid of door-to-door salesmen by saying, "I'm sorry, I must ask my *shujin.*" Instead, women commonly use the legal term, *otto,* or spouse.

Also, in another indication of the growing self-actualization of the Japanese housewife, the once-popular genre of "housewife magazines," had mostly disappeared by 1995, replaced by "lifestyle magazines" that feature fashion trends, shopping guides, gossip, and sex.[6] "Ladies comics" are popular, too, for featuring not only romance but explicit pornography. Even X-rated ones are available at convenience stores and serve as a form of sex education for teenage girls in Japan. Unlike in the West where girls pass around steamy romance novels between friends or watch racy teen dating shows, Japanese girls read pornographic *manga,* some of which depict rape fantasies and all of which progress to full nudity and explicit intercourse within the first few pages.

A television commercial for mothballs aired some years ago with the slogan "The best husband stays healthy and away from home," and the saying became as popular with Japanese housewives as "You've come a long way, baby," or "Takes a licking and keeps on ticking," or "Have it Your Way" in America. It's not that Japanese women don't love their husbands; it's that housewives in Japan relish the personal freedom of living lives apart. They meet their friends for long lunches while their husbands are at work and children are in school. They pursue hobbies such as dance lessons, pastry-making, or calligraphy. Many Japanese women I talked with told me that if they want to go out in the evenings, they don't feel the need to ask their husbands. Much of the time, the men aren't home in the evenings to ask, anyway.

From *Aya,* a Japanese "ladies comic."

Generally, in Japan women and men live segregated social lives. Men go out together, particularly after work, to socialize and cement office camaraderie at restaurants, karaoke bars, and hostess clubs. Women also go out together in groups—girls' night out all the time. They go to public baths and health clubs, to lectures, out to eat, to theater performances, and to all manner of other events, without asking their husbands or expecting that their husbands would want to join them.

Westerners working and living in Japan are almost always surprised to find that when they invite a male colleague over, he will not want to bring his wife. I have heard westerners point to this as an example of sexism; but not one Japanese woman I have met would ever want to go one of her husband's work-related events. "Boring!" they say. And if they ever are pressed into attendance, they count the minutes until they can leave. When women have the time to socialize—between domestic chores and child-rearing—they would much rather do so with their female friends; it is infinitely more interesting.

When one housewife I had met, Yumi, held an outdoor barbecue for her neighbors one Sunday, in an imitation of American tradition, only two husbands showed up out of a nearly a dozen families invited. Most of the husbands had thought it would be a woman's event—and instead they either stayed home or had work outings to attend, usually on the golf course, in the company of other men.

I had met Yumi and a fellow housewife, Kumi, through a Chinese-American, Karen Ma, who grew up in Hong Kong, married an American, lived in Tokyo, and had written a book called *The Modern Madame Butterfly,* about cross-cultural issues in relationships between Asian women and Western men. These friends of hers are married to Japanese men, however, and she knew them because their children attended school together.

Yumi is shy, soft-spoken, and somewhat tomboyish. She wears her hair short and wears no makeup. She sometimes plays in a basketball league on the weekends. Kumi is pretty, fashionable, and gregarious, and you can tell she was in the popular crowd at school. She speaks quickly and animatedly. Her passion is modern dance. Both these women had lived in the United States—Kumi studied travel and tourism in Boston, Yumi had accompanied her husband on a two-year assignment to Delaware—and so they were more aware of cultural differences than Japanese women who had never left Japan. That made them ideal observers of cross-cultural misperceptions, women who had taken the time to reflect on their own lives because of the differences they observed while abroad. And they, too, were more representative of women with the class and education levels typically marrying foreign men, although they themselves had not. When I had talked (through an interpreter) with Japanese women who had spent all their lives in Japan and did not speak English, I often found them to be somewhat lacking in self-awareness, self-conscious that a foreigner would want to know about them, and inclined to cover up problems in their relationships or perceived imperfections in their lives out of embarrassment at airing dirty laundry in front of someone outside of the culture. That's why I wanted to talk to Kumi and Yumi, in the hope that they would provide insights into both cross-cultural mis-perceptions and the realities.

Both had quit their jobs to raise children and neither of them regret-ted it. After all, women have little chance for advancement in the workplace anyway. Actually, women can advance if they are willing to put in the late-night hours required of men—but it is extremely diffi-cult to do if women also want to raise a family. The result is that 67.4 percent of Japanese women quit working upon the birth of their first child, a unique phenomenon in the developed world rivaled only by South Korea[7]—even though companies are required by law to give one year's maternity leave with 40 percent pay. It turns out, in practice, that new mothers don't want to inconvenience their colleagues by mak-ing them take on their workload while they are out of the office. And if the mothers don't feel sufficiently embarrassed by giving others this burden, office gossip informing them that quitting would be more proper and respectful of their colleagues quickly reaches their ears.

Quitting is a modern phenomenon as well. In the poor, pre-industrialized Japan of 1910, 64 percent of Japanese women worked full-time outside the home (only 26 percent of American women, and only 10 percent of British women, did in the same year).[8] Japanese women's participation in the workforce has been continually dropping since then, except for a brief rise during World War II, to 49 percent in 2003 (60 percent in the United States, and 55 percent in Britain).[9]

By the time women do quit, however, it usually comes as a relief. Many Japanese women consider the long hours that men are required to spend in the office just to get a promotion to be an appalling waste of time anyway. And that the Western woman's constant striving to be everything—wife, mother, and career woman—is a losing battle that is, itself, oppressive.

Among Japanese women themselves and Japanese society as a whole, motherhood as a woman's career choice is more highly affirmed than working hard like a man. (Ma's book finds that Western house-wives living in Japan report feeling more valued by Japanese society than their own for this reason.[10]) For more than a century in Japan, the term *Ryōsai Kenbo* (good wife, wise mother), has been held up as the ideal for womanhood. In part this was a Meji Restoration endeavor to Westernize Japan into the "nuclear family" model, using nineteenth-century Germanic code. In the Tokugawa period of Samurais and Shoguns in the eighteenth and nineteenth centuries, the divorce rate in northeast Japan had been higher than in the United States today, according to Ochiai Emiko, a sociologist at Kyoto University.

Thus, the strong nuclear family is purely a modern invention in Japan—a result of Japan's attempts to be more like the West. There is nothing "traditional" about it. The "Good Wife, Wise Mother" role model for women was reinforced and promoted by the Japanese government after World War II, when the country embarked on nation rebuilding and—much like America of the 1950s—needed women at home raising families in order to do it. Pointing to Japanese women as model housewives, too, was a way for the Japanese government to bring societal pressure against the wanton sexual behavior of the Allied Occupation period, of "panpan" and "geesha girls" and GIs, under control, and to counter the resulting Western images of Japanese promiscuity.

As a result, in today's Japan, a woman who quits work to raise a young child is continually praised for that decision. A woman who chooses going back to work over staying home with a young child is continually asked to justify her choice—by her friends, relatives, and fellow mothers. If she calls it a financial decision, she is looked down upon as an object of pity, that her husband doesn't make enough money to support her. It's embarrassing. If she calls it a professional decision, she is considered selfish. That's embarrassing, too. Even if women want to deviate from this prescription for their lives, the overwhelming peer pressure of Japanese society makes it extremely unrewarding.

A morning television drama on NHK airing daily at 8:15–8:30 AM, extremely popular with housewives after their husbands leave for work, reinforces the "Good Wife, Wise Mother" ideal; mothers picking up their children from school talk about what happened in that morning's episode. Schools also make it difficult for women to work by requiring attendance at daytime activities. For example, when one working mother I know sent her husband, a musician with a more flexible day-time schedule, to help out at a school's fundraising sale after the school insisted on parental attendance, he was sent away. Only mothers were required.

While I was living in Japan, I was struck by the revealing nature of the press coverage of an incident where a grade-school child walking to school was splashed with gasoline and set on fire. Newspaper articles insinuated that the fault lay not with the arsonist attacker but instead with the mother for letting the child walk alone. Police were quoted as saying that they were investigating why the mother was not walking the child to school—despite the fact that it is common practice in Japan for children to walk alone.

The pressure to have a child starts soon after a couple marries, and women who stay single are derided in the Japanese press as selfish, as "parasite singles" who refuse to grow up and, instead, live off their parents while working go-nowhere jobs to earn money to lavish upon themselves. Even former Prime Minister Yoshiro Mori said as recently as 2003 that women who don't have children don't deserve social security. "It is really strange [to say] that women who enjoy a liberated life, not having any children, and later grow old, should get help through taxpayer money," he said.[11] His remarks caused a public outcry, but many Japanese agree.

Given the pressure women come under to have children, give up working, and devote their lives to family from the moment they get married, it's not hard to see why Japanese women keep putting it off. The average age at which women marry and the average age at which women give birth both have been rising steadily in Japan for years, to today's all-time high of 27.4 years for marriage (compared to 25.1 years in the United States), and 28.3 years for motherhood. This postponement means the total number of births is declining in Japan as well, to the lowest-ever rate of 1.32 per woman. This has alarmed the government into launching motherhood-encouragement campaigns and opening more daycare centers for extended hours to try to offer women who prefer to work the choice of motherhood, too. There seemed to be a contradiction in the fact that Japanese society as a whole seems to value freeing women from the severe constraints of the workplace just to saddle them with the constraints of motherhood. The compensation, some Japanese women I have met say, is the freedom they have with the rest of their time, especially once their kids reach school age.

So, HAVING ACCOMPLISHED the requisite feat of Japanese womanhood by having children that were now approaching school age, Kumi
and Yumi were considering doing something else. Japanese women
consider the ages three and five to be liberation milestones, of a sort.
By then, the unremitting vigilance of childcare has abated somewhat,
and walking, talking three year olds can be left with parents, with
babysitters, or in day care; after age five children can go to school all
day. Three-fourths of Japanese women return to work after their children reach this age, but by then it is often too late to resume a career
track, and the women end up in part-time jobs, as retail clerks or in
other non-professional positions. Japan's tax structure imposes penal-
ties on spouses making more than about $12,700 per year (1.3 million
yen; up to that amount is tax-free). Until the tax code is revised, wives
find it hard to justify making more than that anyway. Both Kumi and
Yumi wanted to resume working part-time. Kumi was considering
opening a dance studio. Yumi loves the English language and wanted
to conduct small English classes in her home. We discussed it one day
over lunch at a trendy Tokyo café.

> KUMI: Most of our generation wants to spend time with their kids
> until they are three or four years old. After that, it's not too late
> to start something new. My mother's generation didn't have
> much money, and now they have curiosity. My mother helps my
> father with his gold-plating business—doing the accounting.
> But now she's really blossoming. She really loves traveling.
>
> YUMI: That's the same as my mom. She is teaching paper cutting
> and drawing now. She refuses to watch my brother's kids. My
> sister-in-law is so surprised! She did everything at home, laundry,
> food, took care of my father's mother. Now it's her turn.
>
> KUMI: But your fifties and sixties are too late! We have to do
> something now!
>
> YUMI: If we just had a preschool for kids below three years old!
> There's a place you can leave your kids for two or three hours, but
> mostly just for emergencies.
>
> KUMI: Yeah, but my son cried for three hours there. That place was
> so awful.

Kumi lives what she thinks is a somewhat typical life. She gets up at seven every morning to bake fish for breakfast and make lunches for her husband and children—and put on her makeup before her husband wakes up. They eat breakfast together every day at eight because her husband leaves shortly afterward and works until midnight at a television production studio. She only cooks dinner for him once a week—on Saturday. He cooks on Sundays so she can go to dance class. Their relationship had started as an office affair. She got pregnant, he left his wife, and then she had to quit her secretarial job or risk causing an office scandal. Now they have two sons, who, typical of Japanese children until age five, both sleep in the bed with their parents.

Kumi does her best to keep herself attractive, and to not let the routines of motherhood overwhelm romance.

> I try to be a lady, not like a mother. It's hard to wear makeup in the house. But I try not to be like a mother with sloppy hair. I try to go out with my husband on weekends. I keep up with magazines so we can talk about things. When the kids are around he calls me "Mama," but I never call him "Papa," even in front of the kids.

When I ask her about maintaining a sex life when there are small children in the bed, she laughs. "Well, there's the bathroom," she says, "and the kitchen, and the sofa . . . "

Yumi, Kumi, and Karen have plenty of opinions about interracial relationships, based on the experiences of friends or on interactions they had heard about secondhand.

> KUMI: I heard that once American or Western guys find Asian girls, they never go back to Western girls.
> YUMI: They like it that a lot of Japanese girls obey. They just say, "Yes, yes." So the men think they are the stronger ones. Just until they get married, right?
> KAREN: They say the exotic is erotic.
> KUMI: They like the structure of the body. It's different, smaller.

At this point I interject. Personally, I am smaller than most Japanese women, and I point out that not all Western women are big. But that isn't exactly what Kumi had in mind. "No, you know!" she said, and started to spell with an index finger on the palm of her hand and mouthing the letters of a word she wasn't sure how to spell in English.

> KUMI: I think it's P-U-S-S-Y, is that right? The hips are bigger on Western ladies. Asian women are more narrow.
>
> KAREN: Guys do talk like that.
>
> YUMI: My husband and I always say that it's a certain type; they cannot talk with strong American women. They are very soft. Most Asian girls don't say their opinions very strongly.
>
> KAREN: Asians try to avoid confrontation. Men find that very comforting. They like to be agreed with.

That's what my Japanese friend Akiko, who had lived in the United States, had told me during a previous discussion at a long, leisurely lunch, where the other tables were filled with women lunching together, just as we were doing, well into the late afternoon. In her case, Akiko said, she wouldn't disagree with a man for three years into a relationship, until she felt that she had power over her man. Control takes time, she said. In her view, which seemed to be a consensus among the dozens of people I spoke with in Tokyo, Western men get a mistaken impression of Japanese women, which they then transfer to all Asian women by association, because of this tendency to avoid confrontation.

> For example, you go shopping at the mall. American women will not hesitate to fight with the boyfriend or husband, "I want to do this, I want to go there. I want to . . ." whatever the topic is. She is not afraid about the impression of other people. You wouldn't see that in Japan. We keep it inside, which isn't very healthy, I think. I like American women being so expressive and open with their emotions. It's easy to understand. They will tell you, usually, if they have a problem with something. They are more likely to say something directly to you. If I am talking to my Japanese women friends, I have to think, "Are they really thinking that way?" I have to double make sure, "Are you sure this is okay?" like twice, to find out the truth of their feelings. So it's kind of hidden.

As proof, she said, look at older women in Japan. Women over fifty are called *obasan,* which means "Auntie." They tend to have short, curly gray hair, and wield large purses as a weapon. Who hasn't been elbowed out of the way by one? she asked. After years of acting deferential in public, they're done with the façade—fed up. "They don't hesitate to grab whatever they want, get whatever they want. Like on the bus, in a public space, in the supermarket, they get in the line in front of you, like 'Go away!' Have you seen that?" Akiko said. "That's the truth coming out. When they're younger, they're still attracting the men, but when all is said and done, the truth reveals itself."

To me, the most interesting part about this phenomena was that whenever I tried to ask the *obasan* about their behavior—whether, after years of bowing and acting deferential, they felt entitled to get their own way—their hell-bent, get-out-of-the-way demeanors transformed instantly into that of sweet, polite old ladies. They only wanted the best for society or for their families, they said, not for themselves. It was what they were supposed to say to a foreigner, while smiling sweetly and bowing slightly.

But, more than once in Japan, with my petite stature and my natural hair color that is a popular shade of dye for young, trendy Japanese women, I was mistaken from behind for a Japanese. Once, in front of a confection counter in the basement of a department store, I apparently was blocking the view of two older women who wanted to buy some sweets. Wham! A strong nudge of a large purse in the small of my back quickly got me out of the way. All of us were women—me, the two *obasan,* and the woman behind the counter, not a man in sight. When they realized I was a foreigner, they bowed and smiled and asked me to excuse them. In no other situation could the façade of Japanese women's public behavior and the inner reality be more clear.

"My husband says it's scary, all these schemes of women," Akiko continued.

Of course, there is true romance and true love; there are many couples like that. But all women are smart. They're thinking to find someone like Richard Gere, in *Pretty Woman.* They have some sort of fantasy how it's so nice, the poor girl becomes rich. Rich guy picks poor lady up, makes her beautiful. We adore this story. That movie became a big hit in Japan.

In her own marriage, Akiko had rejected an American boyfriend—the rebellious son of a Chicago doctor—in favor of a Japanese. Most marriages in Japan, which as recently as 1949 were arranged by parents or matchmakers 65 percent of the time,[12] are now "love matches" as in the West. Like Yukie, Akiko also wanted the freedom that came with attending school abroad and pestered her parents until they relented.

I didn't like the uniforms in high school. At that age, I started thinking "Why do I have to wear this uniform?" And teachers come up to you and say, "Did you dye your hair? What's the matter with you?" Like in junior high school, they will tell you what color your socks have to be.

I remember the old Japanese traditional saying, the nail that sticks out gets hammered down. I felt like everything in Japan felt like that. And the society was too restricted. People were still wearing the same "uniform" after graduating high school, like men's suits, all the same. It kind of made me sick. I don't know why. I felt like it was very important to have your own thing, your own ideals and ideas, own inspiration; you don't have to go along with other people. That's why I went to Australia. I wanted to go to America. I had an image of America being a free country. But my father thought America was too scary, with guns and crime. So he sent me to Australia. That's how it started.

Eventually, Akiko did go to the United States to attend college in the Midwest, but she found societal strictures there, too. "There is a kind of stereotype about America being a free country, but it's kind of a tough life there," she said.

Everybody has their own culture. In America, you'd be called a loser if you lived with your parents after high school or college, which is normal for Japanese people. So everyone's not totally free there. There's a way that society expects you to live anywhere you are.

Women are expected to do a lot more in America. In Japan, women can come out to [this restaurant], have lunch all day, then go home and cook dinner, that's all they do, and that's okay. In the U.S., that's not allowed.

Plus, it's too dangerous in many areas for a woman to be out alone at night, which also impinges personal freedom, she said.

It's really not as easy living as I thought; you have to be so protective. Secondly, it is very important in the U.S. to make a good living, make good money. It is the topic that American women spoke of when meeting a man. It was like, "Oh is he rich?" and has an expensive car, or his occupation, or how he dressed, etcetera. I guess all women in the world like money. Hey, that's what it takes to live! And getting kicked out of your parents' house so early, again it means making money to live is a big issue. Life is so tough for Americans.

She liked dating American men. They would cook for her, make pancakes on the weekends. "They take you out very often. They try to entertain you. They get all the beers ready and try to prepare. Don't you think? They try to make it nice for you." One of her friends, she said, went overboard in making it "nice" for her American boyfriend. Akiko said,

My girlfriend from the north part of Japan, she met this black guy from Minneapolis. But he slept around; she knows he does. But he never stops. They were living in Minneapolis. He was having affairs; he had pictures of naked women in the bed. She was so nice, she forgives him. Maybe that's sort of typical Japanese woman. No, of course not! She came back to Japan, so he followed her here and was working as a teacher. Of course! He has the best deal! I mean, he goes out, fucks around, or fucks at home, and this girl forgives him. Of course he will come chasing after her!

He talks about her to his [American] friends, so everybody thinks she is the stereotype, that Japanese women are paradise for them. She would cook, she would vacuum, she would clean up the house. She would do everything. She says she loves him. She came from a really strict family, so maybe that's liberation for her. The north part of Japan is a strict part, more countryside.

Akiko didn't like anything about that type of relationship, and she didn't like that her own American boyfriend was jealous when she spent time with her friends instead of with him. As a Japanese woman, she expected to spend a lot of her social time in the company of girlfriends, not as part of a couple, and she had male friends she liked to see, too. She was independent. He expected her to be more, well, devoted. "I didn't expect American men to be like that," she said—either the way her jealous boyfriend acted, or the way her friend's boyfriend behaved.

When it came time to marry, Akiko chose a man back home who'd had a crush on her since elementary school. They have been together for seven years. Akiko's husband is slightly "feminine," she said, "not very manly." He was popular with girls in school who like the "cute" look—the preference among Japanese girls that makes Leonardo Di-Caprio one of the hottest American idols in Japan. More importantly he was flexible. He was willing to do the household accounting, because Akiko hates numbers and did not want to balance the checkbook. He does half the housework—vacuuming and taking care of garbage. Even though they fight openly sometimes, which is unusual among Japanese couples, they usually come to a compromise. Sometimes he backs down; sometimes she does. "I hate men who are bossy, who have a stiff brain, like stones," she said.

Her husband liked that Akiko did not want to quit working—as a yoga instructor—when they had children. "He thinks just staying home watching children grow up is not cool. That makes women dependent on their children and husband, which is not a good thing," she said. That they both make the same amount of money means they have an equal marriage, she says. They live with Akiko's parents on the outskirts of Tokyo, and her mother helps out with childcare, giving Akiko not only the freedom to set her own work schedule but to have all-afternoon lunches, and to take belly-dancing lessons. In all, Akiko believes she lives a happy, fulfilling life, far freer and easier than that of American women she knows. It was hard to know whether

Akiko's husband was typical of the "new man" in Japanese society, but certainly there were a lot more men like him now than there were when her mother was young.

Like Yukie, Akiko wonders how much the model of her parents had to do with her choices. Her father is what is known as a "Kyushu danji"—a man from the southern island of Japan called Kyushu. It is closer to Korea than to Tokyo; many people there are of mixed Korean descent, and patrilineal tendencies influenced by Confucianism run strong. Within Japan, Kyushu men are known as macho and tough—picture grunting Samurai rather than Tokyo salaryman. Women have a reputation for being tough as well. (Once, on a visit to that island, I asked a female Kumamoto city official working in the government's Office of Gender Equality about the reputation. Her response, accompanied by a smile, was, "Who says Kyushu women are strong?" an unusually confrontational response for Japan, which amounted to an answer in itself.)

Akiko's mother was an assistant at Sumitomo Bank, and she quit working for seven years to have children. When she went back to work, it was to help out her husband in his business ventures—a scuba diving shop, and an Italian restaurant. Akiko says,

My Dad cooks sometimes. He used to be a very Japanese kind of man. He wouldn't have dinner at home. He was working all the time. Half a year he was away [working]. When he was younger, his hair turned grey early. Now it's black. He didn't dye it. It just grew back black, at age fifty-nine, after he stopped working so hard. He tried to be macho, I think. Inside, maybe there are roles Japanese men try to play, like there's peer pressure on them. People from Kyushu, you have to be strong if you are a man. My mother, she is strong. She's a fighter. Maybe my father changed because of her.

But when her mother saw Akiko fighting with her husband, she said, "'Are you crazy? Can't you shut up?' She would tell me to just 'receive it,' let him get it all out, and don't be so stupid by reacting to it. Let him go on. She says she always did that."

When Akiko was young, she watched how her mother drew the power in the relationship, not by fighting back but by leaving.

"Maybe once a year my parents would have a big fight and she would leave and not come home for like a month," Akiko said. In the end, her father would always apologize so that her mother would come home. And not the little kind of "excuse me" apology that one hears often in everyday interactions in Japan. It was a full-blown, deeply meant apology, a *gomen nasai,* in front of the children. Her mother never apologized. "So maybe she was more empowered. Maybe that's her character. Maybe that's the era, too."

Not every Japanese wife has Akiko's good fortune of in-home child-care, particularly if her parents don't live in Tokyo. Yumi, for example—the tomboy mother who plays basketball—comes from Yamagata Prefecture, in northern Japan, where her parents still live. She came to Tokyo to study English, took a job as a clerk at a foreign exchange company, married, had children, and stayed. When she and her husband went on his two-year assignment to Delaware, she quit working and concentrated on raising her children. Now they live in a two-bedroom apartment in Naka-Meguro, an upper-middle-class residential neighborhood of Tokyo—akin to the Upper West Side of Manhattan, Lincoln Park of Chicago, or Pacific Heights of San Francisco —where Japanese civil servants, foreigners, and other professionals live within an easy fifteen-minute subway ride to central government office buildings.

I WAS INTERESTED IN SEEING the everyday life of a housewife in Japan, so one day Yumi invited me to her home. When I arrive at the subway stop, Yumi is waiting for me outside the turnstiles, carrying her son, Ken, who has just turned two. Japanese are taught always to be ten minutes early so as not to inconvenience the other person by being late. That means meetings often start more than ten minutes before the appointed time, because, knowing that the other party will be ten minutes early, the first person arrives ten minutes earlier than that. In all the times I showed up early to appointments in Tokyo to be the first one there, I only rarely succeeded.

We walk to Yumi's bicycle, which has two child seats, one for little Ken and the other for five-year-old Akira (who had just started her first day of school), and head to a parking garage near Yumi's apartment block, about fifteen minutes away. We leave the bike there and switch to the car, a red Volkswagen Golf hatchback, and drive up the hill. On the way, we exchange logistics and pleasantries—who was going to join us for lunch, what we had done over the summer since the last time we had met—and we talk a little bit about happiness, whether it is attainable or whether it just keeps slightly out of reach so that you always feel like you are striving for it.

Yumi had a friend who wasn't happy and she had called Yumi in tears that morning to cancel lunch with us. She did not want to have to talk about her impending divorce. Not knowing how to comfort her, Yumi instead took on some of her despair. Last year, the friend had asked Yumi if, ten years into her marriage, she and her husband still had sex. Yumi was surprised at the question; she and her husband did, of course. Apparently, it had been many years for the friend and her husband and, shortly after her question to Yumi, she decided to divorce.

This was Yumi's third friend to seek a divorce and in all three cases the wife was the instigator—in one instance simply because the wife deemed the husband quiet, unambitious, and, well, boring. Divorce rates have doubled in Japan since the 1970s, to an all-time high rate of 2.3 per 1,000 marriages in 2002. (This rate is lower than the 4.0 rate in the United States, and 2.6 in Britain, but higher than the average 1.9 rate for the European Union.[13]) It's not that marriages have suddenly become unhappy but instead that, previously in Japan, unhappily married husbands and wives often kept up the façade of marriage long after they no longer slept together or had any kind of companionship. Appearances were maintained for the sake of his job, her financial dependence, and the couple's fear of being viewed as social failures. There's even an expression for it, *kateinai rikon,* or in-family divorce. With divorce becoming more socially acceptable in recent years, however, many wives who think that they can make it on their own financially have decided to rid themselves of the obligation to cook and clean for men they do not love.

But Yumi and her husband still have what they consider a romantic relationship that is spurred on by the affection they witnessed between American couples when they were living in the States. Imitating them, they try to hold hands in public places, and he opens doors for her, a chivalry that is not part of Japanese tradition. He doesn't go out drinking with his colleagues in the evenings, and he deliberately chose his job with a foreign company in Tokyo so that he would not have to.

Even so, like most Japanese men, her husband gets home after Yumi and the kids have eaten, and he eats—by himself—a dinner that Yumi has left for him. But he is home early enough to help out occasionally with household chores and he sometimes does the ironing. "He's great!" Yumi says, when it comes to sharing the housework. Most Japanese husbands refuse, or come home too late anyway. (Working husbands in Japan spend twenty-six minutes a day on childcare or chores, compared to more than seven hours a day for housewives.14)

But, in some ways, Yumi's husband isn't her ideal. Always a bit of a tomboy, she likes to play sports, particularly basketball. Her husband sometimes plays, too, but mostly he likes to sit in the shade. She likes excitement, and has traveled on her own to Southeast Asia and to Europe. Once she took the kids to Brazil by herself, just because she wanted to see it. Her husband prefers to stay home. She considers her marriage a coupling of opposites. "I met a lot of men, and he was the safest," she says. "He's Mr. Safety, Mr. Healthy. Sometimes it's boring." If she had it to do over again, she says, flexing her biceps, she would marry an American muscle man.

"No, no," Yumi says, she's just joking. She loves her husband, and they have a good marriage. But she gives the impression of always looking over her shoulder to make sure that unhappiness isn't gaining on her too quickly. She wistfully thinks about travel, about living in the States again, about returning to her country town in Yamagata. She had suggested to her husband that they live separate, commuting lifestyles. Yamagata is a fifty-minute flight away, and he could come on the weekends. She would be close to her family, have someone to help out with child-rearing.

In Tokyo, Yumi is unable to go out or to see friends without taking her son along with her, because there is no one to watch him, and no childcare in her neighborhood for kids under age three. She had bided her time and, then when the family went to visit her parents and it looked like her husband was in a good mood, Yumi gingerly broached the idea of moving permanently. But her husband works in marketing and there weren't any marketing jobs in Yamagata. Few, if any, companies were headquartered there. What would he do for a living? Teach maybe? Their income level would drop considerably. Then, she asked, how about commuting? He didn't want to do that either. The family would stay in Tokyo.

Yumi feels isolated in Tokyo, and all the more so because she is a bit of a loner. She doesn't like the group ethic of the playground where all the mothers phone each other and arrange to meet at the same time every day; they stand around at the park, drinking iced coffee and gossiping with their friends, and then leave en masse. Yumi likes to go to the park when she feels like it and to leave when she feels like it. For that reason, she doesn't always go to Komabano Park with the other mothers from Komaba Kindergarten. Sometimes she gets on her bicycle, puts her son in the child seat, and takes off for the other small parks nearby—where she can keep her own schedule. It is perhaps for this reason that I have the opportunity to witness her lifestyle, and even though Yumi herself is not typical of her peer group, through her I can glimpse those who are.

WE PARK THE CAR and go upstairs to her third-floor apartment. It is small by the standards of American houses, but not bad for Tokyo. Bunk beds and toys fill the kids' bedroom; but the children don't sleep there. They both sleep with their parents on the big, king-size mattress that Yumi and her husband thought was one of the great things about America. They brought it back from the States with them. The bed is so large that it takes up the entire master bedroom, leaving space only for a wall of bureaus lined up next to each other and a small aisle in between.

The toilet and bathing areas are across the hall from each other. The toilet room is large by Japan's standards, and the bathing area has a full-size American bathtub, with a shower head perched outside so you can shower first and soak afterward. The apartment has a small foyer for the Japanese custom of taking off one's shoes and leaving them at the door. The kitchen is narrow, big enough to fit only two people side by side; the stove has a small gas grill, instead of an oven, and there also is room for microwave and rice cooker. The living room is dominated by a large wood slab table, with plank benches on both sides, and a large TV. The carpet is beige and the colors, mostly, are neutral; but Yumi bought two bright red vinyl loveseats and placed them opposite each other. Red makes her happy. The room is so narrow that if you sit on one of the loveseats and stretch your legs out in front of you, you just barely miss touching the other.

Yumi apologizes for the small size, and I tell her that we live in small apartments in New York, too. Yeah, she says, but she has a family of four. She shows me pictures of her friends in the States which she has tacked onto her refrigerator, and tells me about them. One is an African-American woman she met in Delaware. She had told Yumi she wants her family to have perfect manners, and is attracted to the prescribed rituals of Japan. The two of them had taught each other the perfect table manners of their respective cultures.

"Is it correct that you have to eat with your left hand on your lap at all times?" Yumi asks me. I respond that I didn't think we were as formal as that, and that mostly we keep both forearms resting against the table edge, with the only prohibition being against putting elbows on the table. But then it occurs to me that I had learned only by convention, not from a rule book, and perhaps I don't know. She pulls out some photo albums to show me more of her life in the States, and as she points out her friends and memories, it is clear that she misses America. Soon we have to go pick up Akira from kindergarten.

School normally ends at 2 PM, but because it is the first day of the September term, the children are ready to be picked up starting at 11:30 AM. This was Akira's third year at kindergarten—children go for three years starting at age three—and she would start first grade the following year. At this age, children mostly are taught group socialization, creative arts, and how to play nicely. Because the apartment is so small, rather than keeping all the art projects that Akira brings home, Yumi takes photos of them and then throws them away. It makes her sad. Recently, for the Tanabata festival on July 7 (the celebration of two stars coming together in the form of a prince and princess; to celebrate, children write down a wish and hang the paper on a bamboo tree) Akira brought home a tree with wishes on it. Yumi let it die so that she wouldn't feel bad about having to throw it away. She just didn't have space in that small apartment, even for wishes.

ON THE WAY TO SCHOOL, I ask Yumi about meeting her husband. She had met him playing basketball on a company-sponsored co-ed league. A friend had got her playing again—Yumi had played in high school and college and thought that it was good exercise. At first, Yumi wasn't attracted. She was twenty-three at the time and had just broken up with a boyfriend, which had soured her on men. She'd decided not to even look at men again until she was thirty. But this man persisted in calling her. Eventually she began to regard him as a friend, and quickly adds that, after ten years of marriage, that's what marriage is anyway—more like a good friendship—so why not start out that way? She could afford to be cool to him, she says, and that only increased his desire.

WHEN WE OPEN THE BRIGHT PURPLE GATE of the playground, all the other mothers are already there, milling around and chatting. Yumi tells me this is called *ido bata kaigi*, "around water meeting," and that it is important to Japanese social life. The phrase comes from the old days when women would gather at the well and exchange news. Yumi has never liked it. She says hello to a few moms but is not the social butterfly that a lot of them are, going around glad-handing almost politician-like. Kumi, the pretty, gregarious mom who spelled P-U-S-S-Y on her palm, is one of them, handing out flyers thanking moms for some project they helped out on previously. I recall that mothers in Japan are expected to help out at school whenever needed, and it seems that those who work and can't do it are judged harshly by this crowd.

The children are all wearing straw hats with a navy ribbon. They were supposed to have lined up in formation for their mothers to claim them, but instead several are running around the sand-covered playground taking turns catching a chicken and a rooster that don't seem to mind; others are collecting the moltings of crickets and putting them in jars. The school itself has playrooms set up for crafts, with tiny toddler-sized woven rattan chairs, and a communal sink with soaps hanging from netting so that they dangle above the faucets. If mothers have an appointment and want extended child care after 2 PM, then the kids can stay until 4 PM That's great for stay-at-home moms and their long lunches, but it doesn't help working moms, who must arrange for someone to pick up their children and take them to daycare or elsewhere.

We invite one of the other, quieter moms to lunch with us, and set off with Ken, Akira, and the other mom's kids. The other mother, Koto, had spent two years in Germany with her husband, who works for the Transport Ministry. They live in government-subsidized housing—rows of humanity-suppressing apartment blocks that look only marginally better than what are called housing projects in the United States and council estates in England.

Koto says that when she lived in Germany, she learned to be more outspoken about her opinions when voicing them in German, which she learned to speak while living there. That's what women do in Germany, she says. When they returned to Japan, her husband asked her to adopt a deferential, more-Japanese attitude toward him, at least outside of the home. After all, they live in government housing and the neighbors are the wives of his colleagues. A loose tongue in front of others could affect his career, he tells her. It could convey a challenge to his public image of masculinity and dominance that could prove damaging in the office environment. She agrees with him. Public appearance is important. It is hard to know whether she really agrees, deep-down, or if she has simply decided that she must for the sake of her marriage. Yumi doesn't directly contradict her friend, but says in front of her—in what amounts to a challenge—that she believes that Japanese women should be encouraged to be more outspoken about their opinions. Later, Yumi makes a face when she talks about it. "If my husband had told me that, I wouldn't be here," she says, frowning.

KOTO'S APARTMENT is even smaller than Yumi's, about the size of a trailer home, and she has a family of four, too. There is a *tatami* room where the adults sleep, a two-person kitchen, a six-by-six-foot living room with a small round dining table, a miniscule bathroom, and a small sleeping room for the two kids near the front door. There is no bedding visible; it gets folded up and put away every morning so that the family can make use of the floor space during the day. A full wall in the kitchen holds racks of audio-visual equipment, and another is of racks of opera CDs, including *Madame Butterfly*. Her husband is the opera fan, Koto says, not her. The corner holds a large television. There no room for any other furniture, not even a loveseat. We leave little Ken to play at Koto's and take Akira to the park.

On the way, we meet a woman who Yumi introduces as a doctor on maternity leave. She tells me she specializes in internal medicine, specifically kidney disease, and that she had practiced for two years at the Mayo Clinic, where she had met her husband, also a Japanese doctor. This is their third child, a boy, after having two girls.

The hospital where she works has a generous attitude toward maternity leave. The doctor can go back in three months, but she wants to investigate returning only part-time. It's a conflict for her. She loves medicine, but feels like she's falling behind her colleagues by taking time off. At the same time, your kids are only kids once—and for a brief time, she says; she doesn't want to miss it. She is relieved that Japanese society, unlike American society, will not judge her harshly if she decides not to keep chasing her career so aggressively. There is a lot to keep up on in medicine, she says. There is a lot to keep up on in children, too.

The rest of the mothers at the park are a highly educated, highly privileged group. Kumi is here again, and she introduces me to a tall, darker-skinned woman with a high-bridged nose who she says used to be a famous model in TV commercials and magazines. The children take turns climbing up and sliding down a slide, and pushing each other on a merry-go-round. The women gather around and tell me how strange it is that westerners think of them as being submissive to their husbands. Somehow, they are vaguely aware of Western perceptions, perhaps through Hollywood films or Japanese media. "Do they really think we are like geisha?" one of them asks when I tell them what I am doing in Japan. After all, Japanese women are more free than American women, they say. Look at the freedoms we have to come to the park all day where it is safe. Or to go out at night with our friends as long as someone is looking after the children. Or not to have to work if we don't want to. Japanese society values motherhood, they say, and they're happy about that. "We just are who we are, that's all," the doctor says. The mothers quickly get bored of the topic and turn to each other to catch up on their news—whose husband got a promotion, whose in-laws or parents are becoming increasingly dependent in their old age, whose child got a good grade in school. Two of the mothers offer to go buy iced coffees for the rest. They'll be here for another hour or two, like always, before they each go their separate ways to get dinner started.

As Yumi and I turn to leave, I remember the saying that the trendy girl at the Shibuya fashion shop had tossed out, "*Junin toiro!*" Ten people, ten colors. Many people, many minds. There are at least ten mothers here, with at least ten different kinds of relationships with their husbands, ten different ways of leading their lives. What they have in common is the sorority of motherhood, the prescribed behaviors of being Japanese that are required for polite society, the independence of their relationships, and coming to this park together in the afternoons.

YUKIE, the woman married to the American, returned to their Atlanta home after her two weeks visiting Japan eager to find out whether Chris had been served his divorce papers. She found him still in denial. He pretended nothing was wrong. He didn't change any of his behavior. He had thought Yukie would forget the whole idea. So she had him served papers again, and this time she was home to see his reaction. Finally, she got an emotion—rage. He tore up the papers in front of the courier and started screaming. "It was kind of a scary moment, of course," she says.

Finally, Chris consented. The divorce was finalized in December 2003. Yukie got the house, and Chris went to live a couple blocks away at the home of a friend, although it took him another four agonizing months to finally move out. Yukie brings the boys to school in the morning, and Chris picks them up every afternoon. They swap the kids again at night, but they rarely see each other. Yukie calls and the kids come out, or he just drops the kids off at Yukie's door and they ring the bell. "As much as possible, I don't want to deal with him," she says. But sometimes she can't help it, like when he called recently to tell her that even though he has court-appointed financial responsibilities and it's his turn to pay for soccer league, he can't come up with the money. Yukie landed another position in Web design that pays even better than the job she gave up for Chris. Even so, there have been many times when she thought of taking the boys with her to Japan for good. "I wasn't sure I could make it here," she says. "But if I do that, I couldn't come back. And also I have to consider what is fair for my boys." Yukie's mother has been philosophical about her daughter's marriage to an American. Anybody can have love, she told Yukie, but marriage is a business partnership. If love is all you have, it won't survive long.

"My future is little by little," Yukie says. "I feel sad sometimes, of course. I would like to have a family, normal family, although I don't know what is called normal anymore. Love again? Yes, of course. I think I'll be interested again. But you need to repair first." Yukie has thought a lot about whether she should give up on American men entirely and seek out a Japanese instead. "I'm not quite sure. Time will tell me, I think. The right person, it probably doesn't matter who they are, Japanese or American." Men, she says, are just men.

The Real Memoirs of Geisha

A RAINY NIGHT HAD FALLEN ON KYŌTO, Japan, and on the restaurant-lined Pontochō-dori—the thin wisp of a passageway where paper lanterns reflected in pools of yellow light on the wet ground. I had come to see geisha, the real-live geisha who still live and work in this unusual but declining profession.

There are perhaps 5,000 geisha left in modern Japan, and that estimate, given by the Secretary General of the Asakusa union of geisha in Tokyo, may be high. The numbers have declined significantly from a peak of 80,000 in the 1920s; but there have been ebbs and flows in the number of women joining the "flower and willow world" since it began back in the mid-1800s. Their ranks had fallen to zero during World War II, when all the geisha houses were closed and some 2,500 geisha, who returned to the profession by 1947, had to go work in factories. The numbers surged in 1960s, declined in the 1970s, surged again in the go-go '80s, and fell off again during the recession of the 1990s into the 2000s. Most Japanese people have never met a geisha. A noted Japanese sociologist once told me that they are regarded in Japanese society in a similar way that westerners might think of, say, circus clowns.

Unlike the perception that GIs may have derived from their interactions with "geesha girls" in Japan after World War II, real geisha aren't prostitutes or sexually available to westerners. Traditionally, they are "arts people" trained in dance, music, and song. Historically, they were free to operate outside the confines of marriage tradition, taking lovers as they pleased—sometimes married men—and having children out of wedlock if they chose. Or, if they desired, they married and continued to practice their profession, or left it if they preferred a traditional marriage. The point is that they had choice. As glamorous entertainers, they were permitted to practice a century ago what is the norm in modern Western (and Japanese) urban societies today—the practice of women choosing their sexual partners without societal condemnation or the constraints of marriage.

I was hoping to catch a glimpse of their modern incarnations rushing off to parties and appointments in the early evening. But after a few hours of trying, I gave up and started down the major thoroughfare. The colors reflected on the wet pavement suddenly changed. Gone was the quiet, lantern-illuminated yellow quaintness of Ponto-chō-dori. It was loud and red—from the tail lights of stopped traffic, the entrances to the garish pachinko parlors and gaming rooms, and the signs above brightly lit restaurants. Garrulous men fell against each other, tipsy and red-faced from drink, as they walked toward the train station. Young couples bought ice cream cones under a pink neon sign.

Suddenly, just in front of me, a black taxi pulled out from an alleyway to turn onto the main road. I stopped short as the sedan waited for a break in traffic, putting me almost face-to-face with the occupants of the back seat. They were two apprentice geisha, known as *maiko* in the Kyoto dialect, in full white facial makeup, kimonos with red collars, coiffed black hair, and hairpins. These were the first apprentices I had ever seen, and one had a cell phone pressed to her ear.

The following morning I went to see the real Sayuri. It was the real reason for my trip, to meet the woman who served as the real-life inspiration for the character in the 1997 novel by Arthur Golden, *Memoirs of a Geisha*. Her name is Mineko Iwasaki, and she still lives in Kyoto, the heart of the geisha world. Initially she was suspicious of my request to meet her. All foreigners misunderstand the geisha world, she had told my intermediary from the Japan Society, even those (and especially those) who study it and believe they have come away with an understanding after only a brief time. It takes more than ten years for a Japanese girl living in "the flower and willow world" to know and appreciate the inner workings of Kyoto's main geisha communities, Pontocho and Gion. How could a foreigner even begin to grasp at understanding? In *Memoir*'s Acknowledgments, Golden calls Miss Iwasaki a good friend and credits her with correcting "my every misconception about the life of a geisha." But the end result was a book that still distorted the truth, Miss Iwasaki said. She sued him for misrepresenting her character.

Liza Dalby, an American who wrote *Geisha* in 1983 after spending a year in Pontochō and, for her Ph.D. thesis, becoming the only Western geisha; and Lesley Downer, an Englishwoman who spent several months in Gion and wrote *Women of the Pleasure Quarters* in 2001, had distorted the facts, too, Miss Iwasaki said. They came in with preconceived ideas, and set out to build a case around their notions in order to prove them, she said. In her opinion, these investigations were not deep or thorough enough. Foreigners were hopeless and could never understand. They equated geisha with prostitutes, spread falsehoods and misimpressions, and refused to grasp the nuances of very sophisticated, very adult relationships. So why talk to me? I would just misunderstand everything, too.

But, after several rounds of explanation through my patient intermediary and a request that I write an essay for her explaining my understandings of the geisha world, Miss Iwasaki began to have a clearer picture of my motives. If foreigners always misunderstand, then I wanted her to help me to understand. If there were mistakes in what had been written by others, then I wanted her to help me correct them. But most importantly, I wanted to understand Mineko Iwasaki as a person, not as the muse for the fictional, undeveloped, child-like devotee of one man as presented in the character of Sayuri.

Memoirs is a lovely, Cinderella-like love story, but hardly representative of true emotions. In one example of a scene from the book, Sayuri as a young girl meets The Chairman and he buys her an ice cream cone, sparking a devotion that she carries on until his dying day.

> I watched him walk away with a sickness in my heart—though it was a pleasing kind of sickness, if such a thing exists . . . In that brief encounter with the Chairman, I had changed from a lost girl facing a lifetime of emptiness to a girl with a purpose in her life.
>
> He was looking at me as a musician might look at his instrument just before he begins to play, with understanding and mastery. I felt that he could see into me as though I were part of him. How I would have loved to be the instrument he played! . . . With my eyes squeezed tightly shut and my hands together, I prayed that [the gods] permit me to become a geisha somehow. I would suffer

through training, bear up under any hardship, for a chance to attract the notice of a man like the Chairman again.

Forty years later, The Chairman is married with children. Sayuri
tells him, just before he gives her her first-ever kiss (at a time in
Japan's history when kissing in public would have been offensive and
indecent, although it was an esoteric technique in an experienced
geisha's arsenal, to be used only in private—rather than an act initi-
ated by a man[1]):

Every step I have taken in my life since I was a child in Gion, I have
taken in the hope of bringing myself closer to you.

In the foolish hopes that had been so dear to me since girlhood,
I'd always imagined my life would be perfect if I ever became The
Chairman's mistress. It's a childish thought, and yet I'd carried it
with me even as an adult.

The reality of geisha life was different, I knew. I wanted others to
see it, too.

Geisha with Starbucks bag,
Kyoto 2003

Mineko Iwasaki (*left*) in the 1970s . . .
CREDIT: Fukui Asahido Co., Ltd.

I arrive at Miss Iwasaki's traditional wooden-frame home slightly before the appointed time of 10 AM. I am surprised that she answers the door herself. Based on the degree of formality required to arrange the meeting, I had expected a servant to answer the door and for her to make a grand entrance in kimono. Instead, she greets me warmly, wearing a *kantan* simple kimono, gray with a white bamboo-leaf pattern and lined with mauve. It looks like cotton but it is polyester, two pieces with elastic waist around the pants. It is the Japanese equivalent of a Tommy Hilfiger sweat suit. At age fifty-three, with her hair cut short, and wearing no make up, jewelry, or other adornment, she has a type of beauty that verges on cute. She introduces me to her German Shepherd as big as a small bear, and to her husband, Jin, a well-known artist in Kyoto, who also has come to the foyer to greet me.

I had expected we would have tea, then perhaps lunch, and that I would leave by early afternoon. Yet, at 10:30 PM—long after tea, a lunch of udon noodles, more tea, late-afternoon coffee, a sushi-delivery dinner, candies, and more tea—she was still talking, still relating her stories, happy to have an audience for her reminiscences of the old days and for her thoughts on Japanese womanhood. Other topics came up,

. . . and in 2003.

too: Middle East peace, religion, art, the state of the Japanese royal family and what it has done to the poor princess, the institution of marriage, whether Hillary Clinton would ever run for president, young people today, and who would win at Wimbledon, among other things. Well-read and cosmopolitan, she had strong opinions about them all. Miss Iwasaki smoked long, filtered cigarettes, one after another, throughout the day, holding them delicately between her fingers. And, after more than twelve-and-a-half hours of discussion, I realized it was the longest single interview I had ever conducted.

All geisha have an arts specialty—the *shamisen* stringed instrument, for example, or the small *taiko* drum. Miss Iwasaki's was dance. Sometimes, getting up to go to the kitchen to fetch more tea, she would do a little dance step on the way. When I asked her she said that she didn't even realize she was doing it. No cup or glass in front of me ever went empty during the entire twelve hours, and her refilling of them was so skillful and natural that I barely noticed it—or her husband slipping in and out of the room to help clear the dishes and bring in new ones. And at just the right moments, as I had been anticipating when to break the flow of conversation and ask, she inquired politely whether I might need to use the facilities. It was apparent how expert she had been when she was the top geisha of Gion.

Miss Iwasaki came from a wealthy, noble family in Kyoto, unlike the poor origins of the fictional Sayuri. I knew this from reading Iwasaki's own memoirs, *Geisha, A Life* (titled *Geisha of Gion* in British publication), which she wrote as a direct rebuttal to Golden's book.

We begin our discussion by sitting down to have tea, and she thinks I might like to see some pictures of her first, back when she was young and glamorous. She speaks in Japanese and has hired her own interpreter who knows and understands the Kyoto dialect used by geisha, which has its own set of exclusive vocabulary words, including calling geisha "*geiko.*" She speaks some English, and I had learned some Japanese. But she did not want to take any chance of being misunderstood. "This is from 1972," she says, pointing out a glamour shot from a magazine.

> I had a fever of thirty-nine degrees centigrade in this picture, that's why my face looks a little tired. Here I am putting on kimono. They promised they would not publish this part, because when a geiko-san is not completely dressed they don't publish the pictures. This is how they put on the kimono.

She points out friends, various hairstyles and hairpins, and what they signify: the various stages of a young girl's development, maturity, and availability. Even the length of a girl's eyebrows has meaning. Short eyebrows are for the young. Longer eyebrows demonstrate maturity. It's the opposite for sleeves. Apprentice geisha wear long sleeves that hang all the way down the length of their bodies; full geisha wear shorter ones.

"All of these costumes, I keep them even today. This house is small, so some are in the trunk room, some need restoration. This piece is an important cultural property," she says pointing out a kimono she is wearing in the photo.

> This is also a very important one, probably a national treasure, usually kept at Kotaji Temple. I have probably forty or fifty costumes, but I do not wear them, just keep them as cultural property. Also

the hair ornaments, I keep them. Some of them were made in the late Edo period. Maybe if I pass away, all the kimono and other hair ornaments can be donated to the museum. Right now I live here, but I used to have a house in Iwakura, a very large house covering 250 tsubo, that's quite large. By Japanese standards, 250 tsubo is huge, so I displayed my kimono there for people. If I give them to museum, they will keep them in storage, and only show them for special exhibits. So I am wondering if there's another way to show my kimono to the public.

Miss Iwasaki has a daughter named Koko who is a university student in Buddhist history.

She's a girl but she looks like a boy, so we call her Kosuke. She expresses her intention to keep her mother's costumes, and hair ornaments, as well as her family's Buddhist altar. She has been studying Noh [theater] and practicing Noh performance. When she was little . . . she refused to practice Japanese dancing. I wondered why she wouldn't do the same thing I did. I'm very glad she takes old traditional things to pass on as very, very important.

I mention that no geisha in these photographs or any I have seen look anything like the old-style Japanese woodblock prints of women with overly elongated faces and a certain masculinity of appearance. Had the ideals of beauty changed over the years for geisha? It is the influence of Kabuki theatre where men played the roles, she tells me. Western people might get mistaken impressions of geisha because of this certain artistic style, but no real women look like that. And very often, the women depicted in those prints are *oiran,* or prostitutes, not geisha or apprentices. Yet another example of misunderstanding in the West, she says.

"Have you read my book?" When I cite a few of her biographical facts from memory to prove that I have, she becomes more at ease and invites me to stay for lunch. At the table over our individual bowls of noodles there is another test—a common dish of fried dumplings set in the middle. It is offered to me, the guest, first. It is rude in Japan to stick chopsticks that have been in one's mouth into a communal dish (although not in China), so I turn my chopsticks around and take the dumpling with the unused ends. Miss Iwasaki smiles broadly, nods approvingly, and comments on my fine manners for a foreigner. How did I learn such a thing? she marvels. Thus, I am invited to the sitting room after lunch for tea.

She explains to me how Gion, the most prestigious geisha district, is divided into parts. There is Gion Kobu, or High Gion, of which she is a member, and in which Golden's novel is set. But there are also Gion Otsubu, the "pleasure quarter," and Gion Higashi (East Gion). There, the geisha are of a lower class, perhaps willing to indulge in sex for money. But never in High Gion. "We are very proud that we come from Gion Kobu," she says.

"That's where the confusion comes from, these other geisha districts." What she meant was Golden's confusion. I ask her about the lawsuit against Golden, and she tells me she is prevented by a settlement agreement from discussing its outcome. "But when he came here, I explained and explained and explained for over two weeks. I almost lost my voice. I thought he could understand," she says. "I explained so much about our life and our world, and yet it became like a confusion. That is why I really feel regret. His words are a fiction."

It was true. Golden's words were fiction. They were *intended* to be fiction. I pointed this out to Miss Iwasaki. No matter, she replies, the problem is the misrepresentation of the geisha world. Mistakes even I had noticed included petty details such as having geisha hang a kimono when, in fact, kimono were kept in drawers. She tells me she is not at liberty to talk about others because of the lawsuit settlement. But I take from our discussions that the worst crime in her mind is confounding the practices of prostitutes or lower-class geisha with those of the geisha of High Gion—namely, that the Sayuri girl has her virginity auctioned off in a system of *mizuage* (pronounced MEE-zu-AH-ge). "In a sense, he opened a closed world to the public, and I should be appreciative toward him," she says. "But the Sayuri he presented is not agreeable, because it is not how a *geiko* [geisha] really is."

A real geisha from this quarter never would have auctioned her virginity, she asserts. Miss Iwasaki herself did not, and nobody she knew or knew of did either. But Dalby and Downer had both recorded discussions with older geisha who reported the ritual deflowering of young girls back in the old days, an act which a patron pays the geisha house a large sum to perform. Dalby reported that the practice, in the area she studied in nearby Pontochō, had stopped before World War II. Downer was less specific about the area of Gion she had researched. Perhaps this could have happened in "lower" quarters, Miss Iwasaki says. Who knows what those low women get up to. But never in Gion Kobu.

Mizuage has another meaning as well, Miss Iwasaki states; fishermen speak of it to talk of the quantity of their daily catch. A day's cash register receipts are a *mizuage*. So when she had spoken of her *mizuage* with Golden, she says, she meant that her monthly earnings, the payments by customers to the geisha house in exchange for her presence at parties, were the highest of any geisha in Gion. When she said her *mizuage* was the highest in Gion, it simply meant that she had the most number of requests for her presence, not that a customer had paid for her virginity, she says. "Also, a real geisha from this quarter would never have slept with men she didn't care for, particularly when she had such relentless feelings for someone else," she says. She is speaking of Sayuri's consent to have sex with a patron she did not really like while at the same time she loved The Chairman alone. If you wanted to reduce the geisha world to crass financial transactions, she says, why not consider all marriage a type of ritual *mizuage* as well? After all, the tradition in Japan is that the husband's family buys a gift for the family of the bride. It is an exchange of money, she says tartly. Why not consider *that* the selling of a virgin? "Plus, right now my husband is supporting me. He is my patron in a way. All of the housewives of the world are in the same situation if we look at it from a different angle," she says.

As a reader of the book, I found Sayuri's emotion toward The Chairman is child-like, not developed at all. Also, Sayuri would not go and stay in the United States even though she has kept relations with The Chairman. So I thought that ending was a little bit strange, unfinished.

Jin joins the conversation:

No, she wouldn't go to America. A successful person in Japan would go to America only to enjoy it, but not to take up a new position. Japan may be a small country, but if a person is successful here, they would not uproot and go to a new job elsewhere. That is not Japanese people's attitude.

We discuss whether any geisha, or even any women, she had known had a single undying love for their entire lives. She had worked with hundreds of geisha over the years before she had retired at age twenty-nine, married Jin, and had her daughter. "Never!" she exclaims. Women usually are far better at acting in their own self-interests and seizing opportunities as they come. They are eminently more practical. "There was another man who loved her [Sayuri]," she says. "If I were in her position, I would have gone for him instead of The Chairman." Later, Miss Iwasaki will tell me of her first love, before Jin, but not yet. And because I have read her memoirs, I already know. "That handkerchief that The Chairman gave to Sayuri, maybe Mr. Golden got that idea from what I told him. Some people gave me handkerchiefs, and I kept them. So from that kind of talk, he made it up."

"Oh, she has hundreds," Jin says. "Beautiful embroidery, from China, near Macau or something like that."

"I still keep some. I have never counted. I would receive it, use it at least once in order to pay respect, then clean it and give it to somebody else. Only the ones I really like I keep."

WE TURN TO DISCUSSING the Western images of geisha, as submissive, docile, and gentle and whether, to be a successful geisha, a woman had to have a submissive nature. "That kind of impression is true, of continually serving the guests. However, it is our job, not our nature," she says. "As geiko (geisha), serving the guests is part of our job. If it weren't part of our job, we wouldn't be that gentle, that obedient, that considerate." She likens it to being a waitress or a flight attendant. They are service professions, too, she says, but nobody thinks waitresses have a submissive nature.

Last year when I had a book tour through the United States, I thought American ladies are much more conservative than we are. They are always considering their husbands and children. Wives are very obedient. They always look at their husband's faces, looking for direction what they should do. It may be the custom to do so, I don't know, but they always ask the opinion of the husband. It made me think that Japanese ladies are not that way. Japanese ladies may not speak straight at that moment, not express their thoughts on the spot, but later on they will criticize this and that. So maybe that's why people think Japanese ladies are quiet and obedient.

I mention that a Japanese friend had told me that it takes two or three years to get know the real mind of a Japanese woman, because she is concealing her true thoughts. "If a person can understand Japanese ladies well in two years, that's quite quick. It may take longer," Miss Iwasaki says.

Jin adds:

You know the expression *kata tenka*? It means the house is the housewives' kingdom, and in that way the house and the family members are peaceful and things will go smoothly. I think that's the best way, to keep *kata tenka* at home, and housewives and ladies will act on the outside like her husband is the ruler of the kingdom. When you look at the history of Japanese Samurai families or big merchants' families, usually at home the mother or wife is the king of the house. However, outside she is always very obedient to her husband, and always treats him as if he were a king, so that everybody will pay respect to him. I'm already over fifty years old, so I may have a more traditional way of thinking. I'm not sure about people twenty years old. Things are changing. But I think that's the way to have a peaceful and happy life for everybody in the family.

"I fully agree with him," Miss Iwasaki says. "That's the best way."

I wonder whether her agreement has to do with my presence, an act for an outsider, as Jin has just said. I ask them.

"We have two kings here," Jin concedes, smiling at having been caught out.

"Traditionally," Miss Iwasaki continues, "Japanese women were strong, psychologically and mentally very strong. Because they were strong mentally and psychologically that's why they could become gentle and act obedient."

Jin takes the opportunity to lament the state of Japanese youth. "These days young Japanese girls look tough; however, we call it *karaibadi,* meaning vacant inside. She has nothing inside, no inner strength, to support her psychologically."

MISS IWASAKI RETURNS to the subject of why westerners misunderstand geisha. She criticizes Dalby and Downer, though not by name, but says

> [S]ome of them were here for about three months or so and stayed in one of the establishments in Kyoto and just looked and experienced being a geisha, and they wrote a thesis or book about it as if they learned everything and knew everything. But in three months they cannot learn everything, they cannot know everything. For us it takes about ten years to learn this world. For example, they write about costumes and kimonos, but we wonder what age kimonos are they writing about? When they talk about how to wear kimono, there is a trend or fashion, depending on the period. The hairstyle as well. So when they talk about kimono from the Edo period, that is not appropriate now. And from the starting point, they have the wrong impression about geisha, that geisha is equal to prostitute. I'm sorry, but what these people wrote is wrong.

Based on reading those books, I had found that they both pointed out over and over that geisha were women trained in the arts, were keepers of Japanese tradition, and most definitely were not prostitutes, whose bodies were not for sale. Both took great care in making that distinction, noting the powerful lobbies in Japan dedicated to correcting any lingering misperceptions from the Occupation years. But upon re-reading them after my discussion with Miss Iwasaki, I realized that they both mention the auction of virginity of young geisha, the *mizuage.* That is what is common to all three books, including Golden's, and that is what has upset her.

"For those who are going to carry on the geisha tradition as a profession, we need to clarify at this point that the geisha are different from prostitutes," she says. I tell her that I don't think it needs clarifying. She insists that, because foreigners keep writing about auctioning of virginity and having sex with male patrons, it does. Surely it is what sells books back in the West, she says, but it is grossly inaccurate.

Miss Iwasaki directs my attention to more photographs taken of her in the old days.

This was taken when I was twenty-one. Do I look twenty-one? We were much more mature in those days. It's because we had a lot of training, going through a lot of lessons, and we attended events and parties every day, each one different, each guest different. So from going to the parties and meeting the different guests, we build up our mentality, our inner strength. Sometimes when we walked through the town, people would stop us and speak ill of us directly. All of these things strengthen us. Even when people stop us and pose nasty questions directly to us, we can never get angry, because inside, deep in my heart I am very strong. Maybe they're jealous, because only a few people can have this life or experience of working in [the geisha world.] We have elegant, gorgeous costumes, so they're kind of jealous. People have all different sides. That's their nature.

I ask whether these jealous people are wives, and Miss Iwasaki responds:

In the top houses in Japan, usually all the family members come to visit and experience parties; therefore, housewives don't have that impression, because they are among the guests. And sometimes we send the guest back home and thank the wife very much for sending him to our place. The housewives don't have any jealousy. In Japan we had a tradition of feudal lord having a [concubine], or in big merchant family, and the wife will take care of all the family affairs, and the second will take care of part of his business. So their roles are completely different. And the wife lives with her husband in the big house, and the second, even though she is a partner in the business, lives in the smaller house. So the jealously may not be from the wife but from the second woman.

Perhaps, she means, it is geisha who are more susceptible to jealousy.

She asks her husband to go get several of her kimono, her red maiko collars embroidered in gold, and a few ornaments. She spreads them one after another on the floor to show me, explaining the seasons for which each are worn and the hair ornaments accompanying them. It takes hours before she is ready to part with them again, folding them, expertly and carefully, back into their boxes wrapped in white paper and tied with white ribbon for her husband to take back upstairs. He stays there to leave us to talk.

"The whole idea is perfection," she says. "That's why we need so much training. We can't charge guests to look at imperfection. It has to be perfect." She continues

My parents are very religious. My father is from Shinto family, but both my parents believed in Buddha. The people at Iwasaki [geisha house, from which she takes her name] are also very religious. My husband often paints kind of religious paintings, too. That's why I practice Buddhism, sitting in front of the Buddhist altar. My husband says we have to treat everything with utmost care even the cup and saucer and the lamp, because everything has value, has its spirit in it. I believe myself that everything has spirit

First thing in the morning, I take water and change water for the flowers dedicated to the Shinto altar and Buddhist altar. That was a habit and custom ever since I joined the [geisha house], and therefore it became a part of my life. Without doing this, I cannot even drink a cup of tea for myself. When we have big ceremonies, such as for deceased family members, we pray together. But usually people just find a time suitable for themselves and we just sit in front of the altar and make a prayer. The Japanese Buddhist sutra is a book folded like an accordion. Sometimes I read that. Every day I sit and pray for peace and happiness. I do it for forty minutes every day. I was talking with an American the other day, about how when we listen to the speeches of President Bush, he always mentions God. But in Japan, no prime minister ever mentions God. In the Shinto religion there are millions of deities. It is difficult to call one of them the number one. If we do, the other will get mad!

Miss Iwasaki tells me she gets up between 6 AM and 7 AM, walks the dog, washes her face and hands, and begins changing the water for the household Shinto shrine. She makes café au lait for herself and tea for the Shinto deities. Then she spends her days working on her latest books and handling correspondence. "I really love to watch sports on TV," she says. "Each year when the Wimbledon tennis match, or the U.S. Open Golf, starts, I become short on sleep. During the Olympic Games, I don't sleep at all." Miss Iwasaki has been known to yell at the television.

Her husband goes off to play tennis, and by now it is dark and dinnertime. I make moves to pack up and go, but she insists I stay and orders sushi delivery. She has yet to tell me about what is wrong with the geisha world today, why it has been declining.

The academy where we have our lessons, they offer only training in the performing arts. They cannot teach how to calculate, how to do arithmetic. They cannot give a diploma. In my case, I really enjoyed doing hairstyles for other people, but even if I wanted to become a beautician, or anything else, like a police woman or something like that, I cannot apply because I do not have a high school diploma.

Miss Iwasaki had joined her geisha house, as many women used to do, while still a girl.

So I told them, we should provide a high school diploma. Otherwise the girls will have no confidence when they are becoming independent. Also, it is easy for us to stay in the lukewarm water of tradition. That was the system of *karayuki* [geisha houses], starting in 1872, so it is a little bit obsolete. Even if we like English and want to study it, we do not have any opportunity to do that. We don't know how to oppose or debate back, even if our world is explained to us in the wrong way.

Under child labor laws, girls are supposed to be seventeen before entering apprenticeship in the geisha world, but they used to enter at age eleven or twelve and become apprentices at age fourteen or fifteen, becoming full-fledged geisha at eighteen. If the geisha houses want to continue to attract high-quality girls from high-quality families, and not allow the profession to devolve into the low impressions that some westerners already have, Miss Iwasaki says, they're going to have to start offering more education and training.

We discuss the Japanese royal family, and Miss Iwasaki tells me she is on a first-name basis with some of the royals. She reminisces about old times with them, parties and such. It is a shame what they have done to that poor diplomat girl who married the Crown Prince, she says, muzzling her and keeping her shut in to produce an heir. She is Japan's Princess Diana, a beautiful and talented commoner who married into the Chrysanthemum Throne, but not allowed to have a public face at all. I tell her that the intermediary who had arranged my meeting with her also had requested that I meet the princess, and was told by the Imperial Household that she had "lost her voice" and would not be able to meet me no matter the date. It was unlikely, Miss Iwasaki agrees, to have been due to a physical condition.

As the hour draws late and exhaustion clouds both our faces, she invites me to come back. "Maybe one day is not enough," she says. There is more to say, and so many more memories she had not yet related. My cassette recorder's batteries were drained, and I had used up my tapes hours before. My hand was cramped with fatigue. As I leave, she clasps me to her breast and exclaims how she would have loved to have had me for a daughter.

Before I leave Kyoto, I go to a photo studio to have myself made up as a geisha, to try to experience what a geisha must endure every day. A makeup artist paints my face white, my eyebrows black, and my lips bright red. I choose a kimono, an *obi* belt, and sandals, and a costumer dresses me, binding my torso with ties, collars, and padding. It takes about an hour until I am the picture of traditional Japanese femininity. The thong-toed shoes, worn with a thin white sock with a slit between the toes, are impossibly uncomfortable. My head throbs from the tight hair ties pulling at my temples and the heavy weight of the big black wig they have placed on top of my head. I feel as though I

The author as geisha, 2003

can barely breathe or hardly move. Walking down the seven or eight concrete steps, where I am to have my photo taken outside, takes agonizing minutes. I cannot wait to get out of this costume. I cannot imagine having to put it on every day and maintain agility as well as a smile. All the other customers at the studio are Japanese, unable to contain their giggles at being dressed in a way that is almost as foreign to them as it is to me.

No wonder Miss Universe Japan had decided to forgo wearing a traditional kimono, I realized. Every year for forty-nine years, the Miss Universe contestants from Japan have walked out on stage bound in kimono and taking little tiny steps. The June 2003 Miss Universe Japan contestant, Miyako Miyazaki, decided to make a bolder impression on the judges. She dressed as a ninja—Japan's celebrated stealth warriors—backing out onto the stage hooded; then she tossed off her hood, swung around, and slashed at the judges with a sword. When I met her in Tokyo, she acted out the movements for me and explained her decision. Taking tiny steps in a kimono did not represent her strong disposition, Miyako said. She is athletic and wanted to use her body to make more of an impression.

People outside Japan don't understand how nice a kimono it is, or how expensive the fabric. For them, it is just kimono. It is a beautiful, gentle image. I'm not saying the traditional image is wrong. But little by little, I hope that people overseas will realize that there are different aspects to Japanese women. I like wearing kimono. It's difficult to do. But basically I wanted to demonstrate different aspects of womanhood, showing more movement, the parts which are more powerful, not just women being beautiful, but that there is strength and toughness inside.

Miyako must have made an impression on the judges. She came in fourth.

THE GEISHA WORLD in Tokyo is less constrained by tradition than in Kyoto. Tokyo geisha rarely underwent years of training, which meant they could reach a higher level of formal education than those in Kyoto. Chitose, age twenty, had studied secretarial skills at a two-year junior college before becoming a geisha in Tokyo, and was considered full-fledged six months after she joined.

I met her in Asakusa, which, while not the most prestigious geisha community in Tokyo (Shimbashi claims the title), is more accessible to outsiders. There are only fifty-four registered geisha in Asakusa and many are no longer active, according to the Asakusa Union Secretary General. By comparison, about 300 geisha worked in nearby Akasaka in the 1960s.[2]

I wanted to see Chitose's early afternoon drum lesson. Typically, a group of geisha hired to entertain at a function will play traditional Japanese music, and most choose an instrument to specialize in or, like Miss Iwasaki, learn to dance and sing. In the old days, many geisha knew how to play most instruments and could jump in to any ensemble in whatever role needed. Chitose came to the Union building for her appointment, and I followed her up the stairs to a tatami mat-covered music room. She wore a white and indigo print *yukata* (casual cotton robe) and a large *obi* around her waist. She had a large beauty mark above her upper lip. Her hair was dyed light brown, tied in a knot at the back of her head. When she is in her full geisha regalia, she later told me, she wears a wig.

She knelt on the mat, her arms perfectly straight in front of her, her wrists pointed downward, and with two wooden dowels she hit the small, raised drum following along on sheets of music and keeping time along with her middle-aged male instructor. "Haaaa-yaaaaoh," he called out, playing along with her on the *shamisen*, and she would sweep her arm across her body before returning it to the drum skin. I had to change position three or four times during Chitose's lesson so that my legs wouldn't fall asleep. She never moved her legs for the entire hour.

Afterward, I have a discussion over tea with Chitose, joined by Yachiyoko, who is still working as a geisha at age sixty-six. When working, she also covers her short hair, which is gray, with a wig. And in white makeup, she says, she doesn't look her age. These are the youngest and oldest working geisha in Asakusa. Yachiyoko is keen to dispel what she thinks are foreigners' misimpressions about geisha, and it seems this discussion is designed as a lesson for Chitose, too. Yachiyoko says:

> Some Westerners read books which must give them misguided information, but after they see us, they realize. For example, some people have an image of a geisha as girls from poor backgrounds being sold into the entertainment business. Nowadays, there's not so much that dark image. Those who like art and culture and who come from good backgrounds are geisha.
>
> Apart from dancing and entertainment, people sometimes think that geisha trick men. The biggest misunderstanding is that geisha are prostitutes. When geisha is written in characters, it means "person of the arts." We sell dance and our art, but we never sell our bodies. We are not prostitutes. Being a geisha is still the ideal of femininity for some people. The world of geisha is different because there are certain attributes, certain things we can do, that only geisha can do. It's fine that our world is quite special. It is not necessary for other women in Japan to take on our special attributes. That is why people come to us. If every woman in Japan was the same, there would be nothing special about us.

But when a geisha is not working, she becomes a Japanese woman not so different from anyone else. What we do at work may be regarded as an ideal, but it is part of the profession.

Without makeup and formal kimono, Yachiyoko is right: she looks like a regular woman in her sixties not so different from any other. But she had spent a lifetime mastering dance. As she shifts her legs to a new position on the tatami mats and apologizes for her bad knees, her movement is just barely perceptible above the low table where we are sitting. I can only manage a sloppy imitation flopping mine from side to side each time they start to tingle.

Why Yachiyoko had become a geisha was easy to understand. Her father had died when she was six. Her house burned in the fire bombings of World War II, and she couldn't go to school. Her mother "had to go away to earn a living," she said. Yachiyoko joined a geisha house when she was thirteen. Chitose's reasons were less immediately obvious. The daughter of a salaryman and a Japanese housewife, she was attracted by the glamorous appearance of geisha and wanted to be like them. "My parents' reactions were not so positive at first. But I had already made the decision, so they didn't put up a strong opposition," Chitose says. "I don't feel that I have rejected traditional family life. Of course it may be possible to get married and have children in the future," she says. "For me, being a geisha is just something I can do for a while, before that next stage of my life."

It is typical for Japanese parents to not wholeheartedly support their daughters' decisions to become geisha. Historically, it could mean giving up on conventional marriage and family life—as Yachiyoko did—and instead having children outside of the formal bounds of marriage. The geisha tradition did not prohibit marriage but, like most women in Japan, geisha were pressured to quit their jobs either at marriage or upon motherhood. Also, the period immediately after World War II, when "geesha girls" became a catch-all phrase for Japanese girls earning money from sex with U.S. troops during the Allied Occupation, also sullied the reputation of these traditional "arts people" among the Japanese public.

Yachiyoko and Chitose had both tried to read *Memoirs of a Geisha* in Japanese but neither had finished it. "I stopped because I found it unpleasant and disagreeable," Yachiyoko says. "I didn't like the way Sayuri was represented. I found it unpleasant that people would read that and think geisha are like that." In fact, the Japanese translation of the book was considered poor and, on top of that, the story itself was not appealing. The book sold poorly in Japan. Chitose had read Miss Iwasaki's book, however, and liked it.

I try to ask Yachiyoko, as politely as possible, whether she had experienced the *mizuage*. She tells me no, that her first sexual experiences were with a man she loved, a man of her choosing, who fathered her child. She met him when she was nineteen, and he was in his forties. They never married; he was technically married to someone else, though separated, she says. In-home divorce was common in those days, maintained for appearances' sake. It made no difference to Yachiyoko. She did not have to keep house for a man; she had the freedom to keep working as she pleased.

"It's really a totally different world being a geisha," Yachiyoko says.

Outside this world people are talking about how depressed the economy is, but in here you just hear the sounds of *shamisen,* the tea ceremony, things like that. You can say it's luxurious, just dancing, not to be troubled by the outside world. Once you get used to this world, it may be hard to leave it. If I had it to do over again, I wouldn't have chosen a different profession. I like this work very much. It's wonderful. You can get dressed up in nice kimono all the time, and also I love the dancing. I think I have been able to live quite freely, according to how I wanted.

Being geisha, we are in a profession of selling dreams. It is the most wonderful profession you can have.

I realize as we talk that Yachiyoko has had a lifetime of appealing to men, entertaining them, and holding them in her thrall. So, as a single woman, I decide to draw on her advice. What, I ask her, is the geisha's secret to it all, to finding Mr. Right and keeping him enraptured forever?

I hope for an answer that will reveal all the secret insights of the geisha world, a key unlocking powerful knowledge that will have any man I desired falling at my feet forever.

"You just haven't met the right one yet, dear," she says, adopting a tone more grandmotherly than geisha-like. "Relationships are about compatibility. You just have to wait for one who really suits you." As if any more proof were needed that geisha are just regular women after all.

The Other Side of Miss Saigon

KILL YOURSELF? Why would you kill yourself?" the Vietnamese woman responds, puzzled by my question and shaking her head. Her name is Nguyen Thi Hoa. She is sixty-five years old, and she wants to make sure she has heard me correctly. We hold our discussion on a rainy April night with the help of her Amerasian daughter and son-in-law in the upstairs loft of their Saigon home. No, it's a ridiculous idea, she thinks. Suicide doesn't solve problems, it just creates more. How would you make sure that your children are taken care of if you are dead? "When something bad happens to you, you just have to accept it," she says. "According to many of us Vietnamese women, after undergoing many hardships of the past, we feel satisfied. We think back beautifully about them, with nice memory in our hearts, and we feel happy to have had the experiences that made us stronger."

I had come to Vietnam to find a Miss Hoa, or someone like her, a woman who had had a love affair with an American soldier during the Vietnam War, had borne his child, and had stayed behind while he went back to the United States and married someone else. The story of Miss Hoa is nearly identical to the plot of the musical *Miss Saigon*, with a few exceptions—the child's gender, Miss Hoa's occupation, and the suicidal ending, of course. The musical was one of the most popular ever on Broadway, running for more than ten years and grossing more than $1.3 billion in worldwide ticket sales before closing in January 2001.

The story, based on Puccini's opera *Madame Butterfly,* was based on a play adapted from a magazine short story that was, itself, adapted in a sort of half-truth from an 1887 French novel set in Japan. By the time of its rewrite as *Miss Saigon,* by yet two more Frenchmen, and its London premiere in 1989, the story line had changed at least four times, the scenes growing more and more dramatic, and the woman growing more and more dependent, helpless, and victimized by fate. By its

Miss Saigon incarnation, it had become the tragic tale of an American soldier in Vietnam who has a love affair with a Vietnamese woman named Kim who turned to prostitution to support herself after her parents were killed in the war. After one night with her, he returns to the States on the last helicopter out of Saigon unable to take her with him, and then marries an American woman back home. In the dramatic ending, the American couple returns to Asia and meets Kim. She offers them her son, the product of her one-night union with the soldier, and then kills herself.

Miss Hoa had never heard the story of *Miss Saigon*. As I explain it to her, noting that it was a fictionalized story adapted from Japan, she suddenly understands. "Oh, well, maybe that's what a Japanese woman would do. A Vietnamese woman would never do that," she says. "Vietnamese women are very brave and hardworking, very tolerant." The Kim character in *Miss Saigon,* full of despair and desperation, didn't sound Vietnamese at all.

Instead, Miss Hoa's story, like that of so many women in Vietnam after the war, is one of perpetual stamina and unceasing resourcefulness. As she told it to me, I admired her courage and wondered how our perceptions of Vietnamese women in the West might be affected if the story of her life could be a triumphant stage success instead. "If I could turn back the clock, I wouldn't change what happened," she says. "I have no regrets. I am a happy, easy-going person."

I had found Miss Hoa through her daughter, a famous pop singer in Saigon named Phuong Thao. She is one of the only Amerasian celebrities in the country, and has been called the Mariah Carey of Vietnam. She and her John Denver-like husband Ngoc Le perform together as a kind of folksy duo, singing soft rock family-oriented songs that are wholesome enough to escape Communist government censorship. (They have, of course, written many other songs that they hope the government will allow them to record someday.)

It took several intermediaries and a week of phone calls from my Saigon hotel room to track down an Amerasian and a mother who had stayed behind in Vietnam. Occasionally you see a few on the streets of Saigon, people of mixed race now in their thirties or forties: a man whizzing past on a motorbike, his skin dark brown and his hair a curly afro, but his eyes most definitely Asian, or a woman in the market with a heavy walk and a pinkish tint to her freckled cheeks. Most, though, took advantage of a special resettlement program in the 1980s that enabled them to immigrate to the United States and start new lives there. Their total numbers have not been tallied, but they number in the tens of thousands.

Thao had been interviewed before, in 2000, by a crew from the ABC-TV News show 20/20. The crew filmed the story of Thao's reunion with her father, James Yoder of rural Virginia, after Thomas A. Bass, the author of a book about Amerasian children, *Vietnamerica,* had helped Thao locate him. But no one had ever interviewed her mother; Miss Hoa had declined to speak to 20/20.

When I called a cell phone number for Phuong Thao, I reached her and her husband on the golf course. They were out of town until the following day, and agreed to meet me at the landmark Caravelle Hotel in downtown Saigon. Formally, the city was renamed Ho Chi Minh City in 1975, but everybody calls it Saigon. Over Vietnamese iced coffees sweetened with thick condensed milk, Thao gazed out across the plaza, past the National Theater where she has performed, to the Graham Greene-memorialized Continental Hotel on the opposite side, and explained that she knew only a little of her history. Clearly she was the product of an East-West union, with her fleshy facial features and a physique more stout than that of a typical Vietnamese woman. Her mother was growing older and had never revealed the story of her romance with Mr. Yoder or the circumstances of her own birth. "I never asked her growing up, and she never told me," Thao said.

All Thao knew is what her father, whom she met for the first time in 1996 at age twenty-eight, had told her—that he and her mother had been good friends, and that they had a one-night stand. Those conversations took place in front of his American wife, and Thao knew she wasn't getting the whole story. Her mother wouldn't talk about it either, always changing the subject if it ever came up. When I said that I wanted to hear her mother's story, Thao readily agreed to arrange it. I should come over that night, she said. If she could listen in on our conversation, she thought, finally she would learn her own history.

IT BEGINS TO RAIN as my taxi drives through the dark rainy streets of outer Saigon and finally reaches the gate of the modest home. Despite the singing duo's fame, the house looks like all the others on the block, two-story concrete, with a small concrete courtyard out front, a dog, and a razor-wire-topped iron gate to keep out intruders. Phuong Thao's and Ngoc Le's mothers both live here, as do their two daughters, ages six and three. The children had started singing careers, too, and had become an integral part of the couple's stage act. The elder one runs up to me and starts speaking flawless, American-accented English. She learns English at school, she says.

We pass through the sparse living room where Le's elderly mother is sleeping and mount the stairs to their music studio. It is the only room of the house that has air-conditioning, and they think that I, as a foreigner, will be most comfortable here. There are tens of thousands of music fans in Vietnam who would give anything to be seated in this music studio between the famous singing duo, I think.

Miss Hoa soon joins us, fresh from a bath, wearing simple house clothes and a jade bracelet she has slipped over her wrist. Her hair is cut short and worn straight, the silvery top overwhelming the darker black hair at her temples. She has full lips and an impish grin. She sits tall and dignified in the chair her son-in-law has set out for her. Miss Hoa sprinkles a few words of English into her speech as we make our introductions. She used to speak well, she says, but she has had forty years to forget it all. She needs her son-in-law and daughter to help translate. "Today I find out her secrets," Thao giggles excitedly.

It was 1964, mid-year, when the American soldier came to Vietnam, Miss Hoa starts explaining, to Sa Dec, a small city eighty miles up the Mekong River not far from the Cambodian border, where the French colonial writer Marguerite Duras, the author of *The Lover,* spent her childhood. (John Kerry also paused in Sa Dec while piloting his Swiftboat, according to his autobiographical account.) Miss Hoa was working as a secretary, an office typist, for the 25th Division of the Army of the Republic of Vietnam (ARVN). Yoder showed up as a military adviser. She was twenty-six. He was the same age. In the evenings, he would conduct English lessons in the office for Miss Hoa and a few others. He was kind-hearted, a bit handsome but not overly so, and he was skinny, she recalls.

Miss Hoa was transferred to another unit in 1965, to a location sixty miles away, and left Yoder behind. Although there had been no romance between them when they worked together, he started writing her letters. "Reading the letters, I thought he loved me," she says.

> I liked him, too. But our letters didn't go so far as to talk about love. He went to America for one month and when he came back, he brought me perfume. I remember the brand. It was called, "Intimate." He came to my house to visit me and brought me the perfume. At that time, it was not easy for a Vietnamese woman to be with an American man. I was a little bit shy, so I just let things develop at their own pace. I was happy about his visit, but nothing happened then. He told me that when he came through the airport, customs stopped him about the perfume and he had answered, "Why can't I bring some perfume for my girlfriend?"

Miss Hoa was surprised to hear Yoder use the word "girlfriend." They had never been intimate. The name of the perfume, however, seemed to signal a desire to be, Miss Hoa thought.

> One time he asked me, "Do you have a boyfriend?" I said, "I have many boy friends." But I meant male friends from school. I didn't understand, and he had to explain it to me. Another time when Yoder went out on an operation he told me not to go on operations myself because it was dangerous. He said that if I ever got injured he would take care of me, hold me like this.

She cradles her arms as Yoder had done forty years before.

At last, when Yoder was scheduled to return to the States in June of 1967, Miss Hoa had been working in Cu Chi, the area twenty miles northwest of Saigon where the Viet Cong famously had built miles of underground tunnel networks to use to stage surprise attacks on American forces. Yoder wrote Miss Hoa another letter saying he was going to be in Saigon before shipping out. It was a long, wistful letter, full of memories of them standing on a bridge together, with a moon shining in the sky above them. It was very poetic for a soldier, Miss Hoa thought. She had written some poetry herself in those years, about the beauty of her country and, once, about an American soldier going home to visit his mother, as Yoder had done. They were published in a local newspaper. Yoder's final letter asked Miss Hoa to meet him in Cholon, the Chinese quarter in south Saigon where American soldiers lived in massive apartment blocks during the war. It gave the address of a bar, a date to meet him, and a time. She put on her best *ao dai,* the traditional high-necked, side-slit Vietnamese tunic worn over white slacks, and took the bus into the city. When she showed up at the bar to meet Yoder, he was in civilian clothes.

"I just thought we would see each other and have fun, as always, that I would talk with him. I didn't know anything would happen," she recalls. After all, in their three years of acquaintance, nothing more than "Intimate" perfume and a few romantic letters had been exchanged between them, despite the feelings they had for each other. "We met at the bar, and then we went to a hospital to visit a friend of mine, a Vietnamese colleague with a broken leg. After that, we had dinner together at a restaurant in a hotel. I didn't drink. He drank a lot." Returning to Cu Chi late at night would have been difficult for a young, unescorted woman; buses had ceased running for the night. So Yoder had rented a hotel room with separate beds, one for each of them, and they retired there— separately. But, during the night, Yoder got up and came over to Miss Hoa's bed. "I refused him the first time," she says. "Then the second time, I gave up."

The next day he went to the airport. I went home. I felt happy. I loved him, but I could not keep him back. He gave me his address in America, but I lost it. After that, I found out I was pregnant. I felt confused. I thought he might come back. But even if he did come back, it was difficult for a Vietnamese girl to get married to an American man like that. So I thought it was best to keep silent. I found out later that after three months he came back to Vietnam and applied to work again in Sa Dec, but his boss had refused the request. He wanted to be near me. But he didn't come to my house to find me. Until now I don't know why. My family was still there, even though I was away, so if he really wanted to find me, he could have gone to Sa Dec to ask them. I guess at that time an American soldier wouldn't dare to go to a Vietnamese woman's house like that. I found out later he was somewhere in Vietnam when Thao was born.

He is a very careful man. He is a Baptist, very strict. So maybe he felt embarrassed because he did something with me when he was drunk. I was happy about what happened with us, but maybe he was unhappy. I know that he liked me even more than I liked him. Once he told me a story about his sister getting pregnant before marriage and said good people don't do that. When his mother found out [twenty-eight years later] that he had a child in Vietnam, she wouldn't talk to him, wouldn't talk about it, at first. But when Thao went to America to visit, before she died, she gave Thao a family heirloom, a gold cross. The fact that her son had a daughter in Vietnam was terrible to her, so maybe it was terrible to him, too.

After the writer of *Vietnamerica* had found Yoder on Thao's behalf, it took him three years to return to Vietnam to meet her. Yoder had married an American woman, Ilene, and adopted her four children (from a previous marriage). He retired from the military in 1978, raised goats on a small farm in rural Virginia, and worked as a guard at a nearby state prison.

"That whole time, during all those years, I wondered if he was alive or not," Miss Hoa says. "I still hoped that someday I would find him, but it was a very futile hope. Still, I always had the feeling I would meet him again someday."

Miss Hoa decided the best thing to do would be to get on with her life, not to pine away waiting for an American soldier who might or might not—and didn't—come back to find her and their child. In late 1967, while she was pregnant with Thao, she became acquainted with a Vietnamese soldier.

I liked him very much. Every night he walked me back to my room. He knew I was pregnant with an American baby, but he did not care. We never formally married. There was still a war, so he would just come and stay for a while, and then go off to the war again.

Miss Hoa and the Vietnamese soldier had a son together. "But his family would never accept me, because of Thao. He was the first son in his family, so his marriage should set an example." He was reassigned to another, distant province and, because it became more difficult to travel on the roads, he came back less often. Then he married somebody else.

> He didn't tell me anything about it. I had a dream he had gotten married to a tall friend of mine in Sa Dec. In the dream, he came to me and gave me money, but I was so angry I threw it away. After the dream, with tears in my eyes, I sat down and wrote him a letter asking if it was true, my dream. He didn't answer me. That meant it was true.

So she took their son, who was then about three or four years old, on a long journey to the front to find him. She went to his office at the base camp. He was having a meeting in another office, she was told, so she sat down to wait for him. Their son started playing around on his father's desk, and then Miss Hoa found the wedding registration card there.

> I was shocked. The pain was very deep inside. I called him on the phone right then [during his meeting] and asked, "So is it true you got married to someone else?" He didn't answer. So I just hung up the phone. He was a kind man and he didn't want to hurt me. He came back to his office and told me the truth, that his family arranged the marriage and forced him to get married to the woman they chose for him. We stayed together that night. The next morning he took me to the bus station.

"When I was pregnant with Thao, he had told his family it was his child. But after she was born, we couldn't hide it. He wanted to be my hero," she says. The soldier, named Song, is listed as Thao's father on her birth certificate. Thao and her half-brother were raised by Miss Hoa's parents in Sa Dec while she was assigned to various military locations for the duration of the war. "We agreed not to tell my family that he married somebody else, so that he could still come and visit his

Nguyen Thi Hoa and and her daughter Thao

son. But, after the Liberation in 1975, everybody found out everything. He had to go to reeducation camp in the North."

Miss Hoa returned to Sa Dec to help raise her seven-year-old daughter and five-year-old son. Because it was dangerous to have been associated with Americans, and Miss Hoa had not only worked with them
professionally but had fraternized with one, she needed to distance
herself. She took all her letters and pictures from Yoder, and any belongings she had concerning America, and burned them as the Communists took control of South Vietnam.

> I was very poor after that. I had to take care of two children. I had to
> sell whatever I could get. Thao sold cakes around town. Also sugar,
> corn, cigarettes, croissants, anything we could get. I grew rice,
> caught fish, and sold that. I took meat out of coconuts and dried it
> to sell for coconut oil. I made candies. Thao could sing, and people
> gave her food. I didn't think about going to America. Only rich
> people could afford to take a boat and leave Vietnam.

Thao, who has been sitting quietly until now, wide-eyed at finally
hearing her mother's side of the story, starts adding in the parts she
was old enough to remember. "At school I began singing, and then in

the national group. My mother got a job there. She took care of clothes, their belongings, and we got money from that to survive. We didn't have a house. We lived in the place where the group practiced."

But Thao always had a hard time at school. As an Amerasian, children taunted her with jeers of "Bad mother, bad baby!" Later, even boyfriends would look down on her because of her mixed race and treat her badly, too. One beat her, calling her "half breed." "Because I was teased so much, I have a tendency to withdraw, to close in, to be thinking much more," she says. "When you tolerate a lot you become a little stubborn. For a long time, I never cried as a child. For a long time, I tried to hide my tears. Now I cry a lot to make up for it."

In the 1980s, the U.S. government sponsored the program to resettle Amerasians in the States. Miss Hoa and her son were eligible under the plan, too. She took Thao, who was twelve, to Saigon to sign up. But the papers got lost the first time, and they were notified a long while later that they had to reapply. But, by then, Thao had changed her mind about wanting to go. Her singing career had begun. She was talented, and she was on the fast track. She didn't want to have to start all over again from the bottom in a foreign country.

"I wanted Thao to go to America," Miss Hoa says. "It was difficult to survive all those years on our own." Clearly this was a painful memory for both mother and daughter, something that had driven a wedge between them. Miss Hoa had thought about Yoder a lot during that period of poverty, and she entertained the small hope that, if she went to America, she might be able to find him.

Several other men had tried to court Miss Hoa, but she refused them all. She wanted to concentrate on raising her children.

I never want to get married again, or go back to either of those two men. I still think men are good. But it seems that only men who got married to other women have loved me in my life. I saw a fortune teller and he said, "Don't be sad. No more men will come to trouble you."

After Song got out of reeducation camp he could find no work. Such men, the former soldiers of the losing Army of the Republic of Vietnam, frequently found themselves demoralized and unemployed.

While in Vietnam, I met several children of such men; they said that their fathers had spent most of their childhoods lying around the home—most likely a sign of depression—while their mothers worked to support the family and took charge of all family decisions.

Song fled Vietnam, becoming one of the thousands of boatpeople to seek rickety and dangerous passage abroad in the 1980s. Miss Hoa found out later that he had come to say goodbye to her and their son, but they had moved and he couldn't find them. For two decades, Miss Hoa had no news of him at all. But, by coincidence, the same year that Thao found her father, her half-brother found his, living in Australia. "I still loved Song for a long time, but he was very weak-minded. He just gets drunk all day, lying down. He only called me one time to say hello. He told me that he was a coward because of what happened," she says.

"I think that Yoder still loves me. When his wife is not in the room, I feel that," Miss Hoa says; but she quickly grows concerned that she has told me this. Yoder has maintained—for his wife's benefit, Miss Hoa believes—that they had just been friends who made a one-night mistake. He told 20/20 that their meeting in Saigon on the night before he shipped out had been by chance, not, as Miss Hoa says, arranged by his romantic, poetic love letter. And that is what Thao had believed until now, having only heard that brief explanation from her father.

Because Miss Hoa had been stationed outside of Saigon and only rarely visited the city during the war, her version is the one more likely to be true. Thao appears dazed now by all this new information. "My mother never told me anything about my father. So I just had a big question," she says to me in English, in front of her mother. Miss Hoa understands without her having to translate.

"I told you your Daddy worked here, and that you look like him," Miss Hoa responds, and then turns to me. "It was useless to tell her, because it wouldn't have changed anything."

Later, I reflect on why Miss Hoa has chosen to tell me, to speak so freely with a stranger. Perhaps it was because of daughter's celebrity in Vietnam, that she was flattered to be the focus of attention for a change. Perhaps it was because she sees the end of her life looming closer and, with Yoder's version the only one that had been told until now, she wanted to set the record straight. Perhaps it was simply because her daughter had asked her to tell me, and her decision to do so allowed me to be a bridge that Miss Hoa had been unable to cross with her daughter on her own for all of Thao's thirty-six years. I hoped that after my departure, Miss Hoa would recall even more details of her love affair, and would choose to share them with her daughter.

I HAVE TRAVELED ALL OVER THE WORLD, and I think Vietnamese women are the strongest in the world," Miss Mai, a social science researcher in Saigon told me. "Without the women, we could not have won the war." Because I met her through informal channels without making a formal request for an interview through the still-Communist Vietnamese government, I cannot give her full name without risking trouble for us both. Miss Mai served in a senior Army position herself, as an officer educated in Chinese, Russian, and English, fighting on the side of North Vietnam. She knows the stories of other women fighters because she helped an American researcher collect 4,000 of them for the book *Vietnamese Women at War*.

Vietnam has successfully fought—and won—against China, France, the United States, and Cambodia's Khmer Rouge in four major wars in the last century. So there is likely something to the assertion that the strength of Vietnam's women was a factor. Women acted not only as officers like Miss Mai, but as porters, messengers, medics, suicide bombers, intelligence gatherers—and, significantly, as militia forces trained in the use of anti-aircraft guns, and as combat troops, enduring at times the same harsh conditions as Vietnamese men. Historical precedent for women taking up arms helped serve as their inspiration. Women in the West had as a war-time role model Florence Nightingale, who as a nurse acted as rear support for the men in battle. But women in Vietnam had the Trung sisters. They were more like Joans of Arc.

During the occupation of Nam Viet (land of the Southern Viet people) by the Chinese in 40 AD, Lady Trung Trac, avenging the murder of her dissident husband by a Chinese commander, led the first major Vietnamese insurrection against China. She mustered her sister and a posse of other nobles, including twelve women—one of whom reportedly gave birth in the middle of battle and then continued to fight

with the infant strapped to her back. They won. Lady Trung then became queen of an independent state that stretched from Hue (central
Vietnam) into today's southern China. But the Chinese forces re-
grouped and invaded again two years later, causing the Trung sisters
to commit suicide by drowning themselves in a river.[1] A temple in
Hanoi honors them, and they are lauded as the country's first national-
ists in museums around Vietnam. In 248 AD, Lady Trieu An (or Trieu
Thi Trinh) led another struggle against China. The story is that she
had breasts three feet long, which she threw over her shoulders and
tied down as she led the men into battle.[2]

Vietnamese women's traditions of struggle continued. In 1952, a
sixteen-year-old girl, Vo Thi Sau, was executed by the French colonial
government for having killed two French soldiers. She later was held
up as a martyr. Another 980,000 Vietnamese women joined the insurrection against the French colonials to oust them in 1954.[3]

The Chinese had introduced Confucianism to Vietnam through
conquest, however, and that forced women into lesser roles. Vietnamese women of the North learned the Confucian "three obediences"
for women—to one's father, one's husband, and then, when they died,
to one's son. Confucian precepts dictated they have a pure heart, be
virgins at marriage, remain faithful to their husbands even after his
death, and follow the "four virtues" of hard work, appropriate speech,
proper physical appearance, and proper behavior. When Vietnam became independent again—in 1428 after yet another battle to throw
out the Chinese—the king who ascended to the throne in 1460 allowed women to possess property, share inheritance, and leave their
husbands under certain conditions.[4]

Still, after so many centuries of Chinese rule, the status of women
remained below what it had been when the Trung sisters were alive.
So women who ultimately joined the fight on the side of the North
during the Vietnam War (or the American War, as it is known in Vietnam), also were propelled by the slogan of the Indochinese Communist Party that promised equality for women. "Women are half the
people," Ho Chi Minh had declared. "If women are not free, then the
people are not free."[5] Additionally, the vice and corruption of Saigon,
which swelled with prostitutes serving GIs during the Vietnam War,
added moral power to their cause.[6]

Has it been a success? In some ways, yes; in many ways, no. The status of women, who were feeling the pinch of poverty as Miss Hoa did in the post-war years, did not change much in reality and in many cases got worse. Women have been promoted to some positions of power under Communism—including the titular position of vice president, and head of a food-processing monopoly—but not to the highest ranks. I interviewed one of the most senior of these women in Hanoi, Pham Chi Lan, for *BusinessWeek* magazine in 1999, and again for *Fortune* in 2004. She was executive vice president of the Vietnam Chamber of Commerce and Industry and still, even as an elderly woman, serves as an advisor to the Prime Minister on economic affairs. She is impressive, speaking fluently in the language of economics and finance, rattling off from memory numbers on state-owned enterprises and other economic data.

Miss Mai, who is now in her fifties, says that Confucian tradition has proved stronger than Communist ideals of women's equality, and that has been a disappointment to Vietnamese women who took up the revolutionary struggle in the first place. What has changed is that more women work in offices alongside men, rather than mostly out in the rice fields alongside them as they used to. "A lot of the time the women are smarter than the men, and more capable than the men," she says. But they get paid less and don't get promoted as often. Then again, she thinks, having seen for herself the working environments for women in China, Russia, France, and the United States on various trips overseas, maybe that's not too different from anywhere else.

Miss Mai invited me to meet the students at the freelance English class she teaches at night in an aqua-painted classroom in central Saigon. Seated at their desks when I entered were a dozen men and women, ranging in age from fifteen to forty-three. One was a waiter, another an office worker, another handled lubricants in a machine shop, a fourth was a construction worker, but most were university students taking additional English classes in their spare evenings. All were here with the goal of getting ahead through learning English. I asked them about men's and women's roles in Vietnamese society. I didn't realize that I would spark a shouting match that brought them to the edge of their English-language abilities.

"Women should take care of family," one of the young men said.

"Men are very selfish!" a young woman shouted back at him.

"This is the twenty-first century," insisted another woman. "Maybe before women didn't have the same status as men, but now times have changed."

At that, all the other young Vietnamese women in the room broke into applause.

CHANGING TIMES ARE NOT SO EASY to see in another country affected by the Vietnam War, Cambodia. I lived there for three years as a news correspondent in the 1990s, and found the status of Khmer women to be perhaps the lowest in the region. When I first arrived, Cambodia was still Communist, its government under the tutelage of the Vietnamese who installed it after they invaded to oust the Khmer Rouge in 1979. Cambodia gradually changed to a capitalist economy while I lived there and held elections under United Nations supervision in 1993. But the status of women remained low by the standards of its neighbors in Southeast Asia.

Cambodian women, as well as a lot of men, still don't have basic healthcare and education—two prerequisites to increasing their position in society. Only 29 percent[7] of women are fully literate (compared to 92.8 percent in Thailand), while 48 percent of Cambodian men are. Additionally, the more educated a woman is, the less marriageable she is considered to be. Grandmothers admonish that if girls are taught to read, they'll just write to boyfriends and cause trouble.

Nine out of ten women work as farmers, and two-thirds of them are able only to feed themselves and their families with their labor, not earn any income. Nearly one in ten children dies in infancy in Cambodia (95 deaths per 1,000 births, nearly triple the rate of 34 per 1,000 in the rest of Southeast Asia; in Japan it's 3.5 per 1,000; in the United States 7 per 1,000).[8] Of 169,000 Cambodian civil service jobs, a strikingly low 8 percent are held by women; not one of Cambodia's ambassadorial posts is held by a woman. But Thailand, Laos, the Philippines, Malaysia, Singapore, and Indonesia all have women ambassadors, and the Philippines' civil service is 54 percent women.

Cambodian girls grow up learning the *Chapp Srey* (Rules for Women) that teach them to speak quietly, walk slowly, and restrain their behavior. That's not unusual in Southeast Asian cultures, but some of the proverbs Cambodian children hear are: "A letter cannot be bigger than its envelope," the envelope, of course, being the man; and "Men are like gold, women are like cloth. If you drop them in the mud, the men will wipe clean." That's an admonition for girls not to have sex before marriage or they will be stained forever.

Many men, however, freely engage in sex before and outside of marriage with prostitutes, while women are expected to stay at home as "good mothers" whose sexuality typically ends with the birth of the first child. A Cambodian male friend told me that 95 percent of the men he knew in the capital, Phnom Penh, visit prostitutes to learn about sex before they get married, and many keep up the practice after that. "Do you like to eat crab?" a senior Cambodian government official once asked me, by way of explanation, when I encountered him with a prostitute instead of his beautiful and charming wife, whom I also knew. I said yes. "But do you like to eat crab every day?" he added.

In Thailand—where girls learn that women are "the hind legs of the elephant"—they grow up with the same admonitions to speak softly and walk quietly. But decades of economic growth and the benefits of widespread education have created a middle class in Thailand, and the women of the middle class and even below don't necessarily stand for their husbands straying outside marriage. "Lorena Bobbitting"—the phenomena of an enraged wife who cuts off her husband's penis—is so frequent that Thai newspapers report such stories only as briefs. I counted nearly a dozen cases in the three years that I read the Thai press daily.

In Cambodia, on the other hand, women frequently say that they recognize the right of a man to beat his wife. "The rights of men are stronger than the rights of women; this is tradition," said a twenty-nine-year-old Cambodian garment factory worker, Chean Theng, who shares a room with three other workers, including her elder sister, in an industrial zone outside of Phnom Penh. I sought out the women to talk about their lives and jobs one Saturday afternoon, and went to their cramped rented rooms where the women cook rice and a few vegetables using a communal hotplate and roll out mats on the floor when it's time to sleep. "Men in this generation, sometimes they have up to five women," she said. "There are so many women in this society, so men have a lot to choose from." That's true: because of decades of war in Cambodia, more than 52 percent of the population is female. Theng then told me she was divorced and sewing clothes to support her child after her husband abandoned her. "It's not a bad idea to have the man be the decision maker of the family," added Ech Saorun, her forty-seven-year-old colleague.

The tragedy is that it wasn't always like this for Cambodian women. They have a long history of sexual independence and power. Queen Indra Devi, the wife of King Jayavarman VII (1181–1219), was the dean of the university in the Khmer Empire, when the grand Kingdom of Angkor stretched from southern Vietnam through Thailand and up into modern-day Laos and Burma. In 1296, a Chinese emissary to the Kingdom of Angkor reported back to Beijing that Khmer women there were "highly sexed" in comparison with Chinese women, whose feet were bound in the time. "A woman will abandon her husband if he grows cold," the emissary wrote, "and if he goes far away she may stay faithful for a few nights, but soon she is sure to ask, 'How can I sleep alone? I am made of flesh and blood!'"

Not only that, but evidence of the power of women in governance remains in the Khmer language. The words for government officials— village chief, district chief, head of household, etc.—start with the feminine word *me* (pronounced "may"), which is akin to "fem" in English. *Me srok* (district) = District chief; *Me phoum* (village) = Village chief; *Me phreah* (house) = head of the household.

"So what happened to women?" wonders Sambo Tey, a Cambodian woman trying to improve their lot through education in her role at project coordinator at UNESCO (the United Nations Educational, Scientific and Cultural Organization). "Did we just forget ourselves and our power?"

It might be easy to blame the Khmer Rouge, who turned the country upside down and killed 1.7 million Cambodians in one of the horrific genocides of the twentieth century. But, actually, the Khmer Rouge, as devout Communists, put female cadres—usually their wives who were also devout revolutionaries—in senior positions. Tey is a survivor of the Khmer Rouge. She lost fourteen relatives including her father, who was killed at the notorious Tuol Sleng prison and torture center, and mother, who died from illness and hardship, during that dreadful 1975–79 period in Cambodia's history.

Tey thinks that the reason women lost their power may have something to do with the French, who brought in Vietnamese administrators with their Confucian traditions to rule Cambodia and imposed nineteenth-century French laws that curbed women's sexuality. Then, a cycle of indebtedness, which led to impoverished peasants and support for the Khmer Rouge, worsened women's status. Now, as Cambodia still struggles to climb out of poverty, Tey and others are trying to ensure that girls first get an education so that, by the next generation, women will have a better shot. "We are trying to make this '*Me*' come back," she says. For now, the steps are small: One of the major battles currently raging between the sexes in Cambodia is whether a husband has a right to sell the family cow or any other property without getting the signature of his wife. By law he doesn't, but that doesn't mean he adheres to it.

"Advocacy for women's rights here is all well and good, but if they are not ready, it creates confusion and problems in the family. Men still assume their superiority and an inferior role for women," Tey says. "As a woman, I don't know what happened to us, but the fight now between men and women here is very strong. The men say, 'I am the man, you are the woman.' It's still very deep in their heart.' I have confidence that education will help women compete." And, perhaps, allow them to get a little closer to the proud status Khmer women had 800 years ago.

Glamour of the Skies,

Sorority of Service

LET'S GET ONE THING STRAIGHT, we don't have matching bras and panties. I mean, who *does* have matching bras and panties? Maybe for special occasions or something, but routinely when you are doing ten-hour turnarounds to Bangkok? No way.

Vera sat back in her chair, a lounger in the lobby bar at the Conrad Hotel in Hong Kong where she and her fellow flight attendant for Cathay Pacific Airlines, Angela, had agreed to meet me. Both Malaysian women who had been flying for years—Vera for twenty-five and Angela for thirteen—they were in town together after weeks of separate flight schedules around the world, and were taking advantage of their rare overlap to have lunch in Pacific Place, a mall of luxury shops anchored by three high-end hotels.

I wanted to discuss the mystique of "Cathay Girls," the career choice that had turned them into glamorous objects of desire, envy, and sexual fantasy. Even women like Vera, who are in their forties, are still known as "Cathay Girls," a term coined when the airline was founded by two pilots—one American and the other Australian—in Shanghai in 1946. Cathay Pacific moved to Hong Kong after the Communist takeover of China a few years later and, for the five decades since, the airline's women in cherry-red uniforms have held an exalted place in regional lore—even though the uniforms were re-designed in 1999 and only juniors still wear red.

When Singapore International Airlines launched in 1972, its service and image had to compete with Hong Kong's iconic "Cathay Girls," so its marketing campaigns featured a tight-sarong-clad "Singapore Girl"—who projected exotic Oriental mystique and caring, comfortable service that still puts the airline at the top of traveler surveys year after year. Singapore Airlines' advertisements for direct

FOR THE FIRST TIME EVER,
FLY NON-STOP FROM NEW YORK TO SINGAPORE.

Singapore Airlines ad, 2004

flights from Newark or Los Angeles to Singapore still feature the girl. She gestures invitingly toward the dusk-drawn city just as the realm of the evening appears to be getting underway, promising, in the words of an investment banker I know who saw the ad, "a non-stop flight to the land of exoticism, pampered with eighteen hours of fore-play by these beautiful stewardesses."

Cathay's ads focus on airline performance. But, even today, "Cathay Girls" remain legendary for their ability to turn heads, and for contin-uing to evoke an era in aviation history when the word "stewardess" was associated with glamour, admiration, and desirability—not polit-ical incorrectness. An American Vietnam War veteran who returned to Saigon, after thirty-two years, via a Cathay Pacific flight, posted a travelogue online in which he called the attendants "uniformly skinny, uniformly stunning" in comparison with American flight attendants and concluded: "Feminism—hell, '70s-style Women's Lib—hasn't come to the Asian Airways (well, all one of them that I've ridden)."

In the early 1990s, the most sought-after notches on the bedposts of many young American, British, European, or Australian investment bankers or merchant trainees that I met in Hong Kong were "The Cathay Ten." That is, the ten nationalities of women recruited in those days to fly with Cathay.[1] Hong Kong is a small city, relatively, and Cathay requires its flight attendants to speak fluent English as well as a second language of a country to which Cathay flies. So the airline has long recruited bilingual, educated women from the highest social and economic rungs all over Asia—Malaysia, Japan, Korea, Thailand, the Philippines, India, among others.

Seeking out and successfully bedding a stewardess from each of the ten countries earned a man high-fives and whooping approbation from his peers. This was an era when Hong Kong represented the land of opportunity for young foreign males. College graduates could show up in Asia with no work experience, soon start managing $100 million dollars, travel every weekend to some exotic locale, and bed some of the most beautiful women in the world, all by age twenty-three. The English writer Simon Winchester, author of *The Professor and the Madman, The Map that Changed the World, Krakatoa* and other books, got himself blacklisted from Cathay Pacific flights for his 1992 essay accompanying a picture book, *Hong Kong: Here Be Dragons,* which stated baldly:

The Westerners, perhaps smooth young cadets from Swire's and Jardine's or Inchape, are pink-faced, fresh-scrubbed, and ever eager for the sensual pleasures of the East. Seemingly rolled out and snipped off in six-foot lengths of pinstripe, they take their Cathay Pacific stewardesses (known in the local argot as *LBFMs,* little brown fucking machines) to the discotheques and bars scattered around the territory. If the relationship progresses, then it is weekends in Phuket or Puerto Azul. And if the parental instruction, "Do what you like in the East, but on no account bring it back home" is ignored, then there could well be a wedding (though Swire's once forbade its cadets to marry local girls, and among some British firms' senior echelons, it is still considered rather bad form), with all the attendant delights and complications such a union invariably brings.[2]

I sat with Winchester at a luncheon celebrating the handover of Hong Kong to China in 1997, where he bragged about his blacklisting as one would of earning a medal in battle. The ban is legendary in Hong Kong, but not a bookstore in the city carries the book, which contains all manner of other imperious insults; to find it I had to go digging in a remote university library.

Having been confronted for years by these enduring images of the women of Cathay, I realized I had never heard the women's point of view. What did they think about being characterized in such ways, of being objects of such desire and derision? What were they really like, in ways that both fulfilled and defied the mystique? So I sought out a half dozen Cathay flight attendants; three were single, two were married to men from their home countries, and one had married one of her passengers—an American who approached her on a flight. Each had unique experiences, of course, but they were united in the common experience of having been approached dozens—if not hundreds—of times by Western male passengers (and, less frequently, Asian ones) seeking their phone numbers. It happened almost once a flight. Even those wearing wedding rings occasionally would be asked, "Are you an M.B.A.?" Married But Available. All had learned from their more experienced colleagues to deflect propositions by responding, sweetly, to the most persistent men, "Give me your card and I'll call you," which then put the power in their own hands. They rarely kept any cards, usually tossing them into the trash while still on board—particularly if the man wasn't flying first or business class. The flight attendants also, uniformly, felt tarnished by the actions of a few of the more wild girls among them. In high school, boys easily distinguished the reputations of one or two "easy" girls from the rest. Why couldn't they with the women flying Cathay?

Perhaps there is something in the association of service—the dedicated, in-cabin service in which these beautiful women have been highly trained—with sexual availability. I know from personal experience that flight attendants on major Asian carriers offer far more services than those on Western airlines. But I also know—having once witnessed a China Southern Airlines flight attendant clomp heavily past me through the aisle in flat shoes and rear-kick a lavatory door closed—that it's not just exoticism.

There is a gracefulness of demeanor that adds to the perception of service. Both "Singapore Girls" in their long-skirted sarongs and "Cathay Girls" in their smart suits, wearing mini-heels and gliding through the aisles like runway models, jump to help passengers with their bags, where Western flight attendants refuse. The Asian women are taught never to say, "We don't have any more," but instead, "I'm sorry, I'll go check for you in another class" and then to return with the most similar alternative on the plane if they can't provide the item. They answer call buttons immediately. They crouch down to eye level of their passengers when they are taking a request—in the case of Singapore Girls, bending forward to reveal cleavage as they do so. They make sure passengers are comfortable with pillows, blankets, drink refills, and any other needs. The airlines are consciously fostering an image of sexuality and servility—of Asian Mystique—and it not only sells, it reinforces it.

Perhaps a woman who is quick to service the needs of a comfortably reclining male passenger easily could be imagined serving his other needs as well. As my investment banker friend who has flown dozens of long-haul flights on Cathay Pacific and Singapore Airlines, put it, "Flying in any class, but especially First, where these women come and make your bed and tuck you in, with all that cleavage in your face, is quite extraordinary. If you want to get any work done, fly British Airways."

RECALLING WINCHESTER'S REFERRAL to her and her colleagues as LBFMs brings a sneer to Vera's lip. "He wrote some not-very-nice things about our cabin crew," she says understatedly, taking a sip of her iced tea to counter the bitterness and noting that she and her colleagues were happy to see him banned from Cathay forever.

Both Vera and Angela find their mystique amusing and enjoy the opportunities they have to travel, meet interesting people, and have the disposable income to buy whatever fashions or designer items they like from everywhere in the world. It *is* glamorous, they say. But it is also troubling to them at times. They note that the small minority of their colleagues—the party girls—who become overexcited by the newfound freedom of being away from home, particularly if they were raised in strict traditional or conservative homes, give the rest of them a bad name. "You know, we don't really like to tell people we are flight attendants," says Angela. "Like when we go to a party, and people ask what we do, we don't want to say. People will think we are easy." Two other "Cathay Girls," from the Philippines, told me of being cursed as "flying prostitutes" by a taxi driver unaware the women could understand Chinese, but also of being admired for their fashionable appearances and held up as models of wealthy, successful career women every time they go home.

Even women who don't run around find they don't know how to handle their sudden exoticism, the sudden attention from Western men. In their own cultures, traditionally a man who puts his arm around you, opens doors for you, buys you gifts, and wants to kiss you in public must really have strong feelings for you—feelings that back home would lead to marriage (although this is changing for the young generation growing up watching MTV). "Ladies First" can be an intoxicating experience for an Asian woman who has arrived in Hong Kong at age twenty, away from home for the first time, without friends, moral guides, or mentors.

Angela admits being the victim of this intoxication and the confusion that amorous attention caused in her early years of flying. She didn't know how to handle it at first, and men took advantage. It pains her to think she may have been just a bedpost notch in the Cathay Ten. Angela says,

> When we first come to Hong Kong we are gullible and naïve. You don't know anybody here, you are away from family. Then you meet someone and you think, "Oh, he really likes me." But you find out later it was not really that way. He's just using you to sleep with you. We are *very* gullible when we first arrive. Our parents never taught us intimate things, so we're not aware how to behave. Asian women don't know how to say "No" very well. You need to learn fast how to protect yourself.

She recalls a Frenchman she dated, who, it became clear, kept taking her out to show her off as a conquest to his friends. At group dinners at a Chinese dinner table, various dishes would be placed in the center, and the man would lean over and whisper into her ear, "'I like mushrooms, can you serve me a mushroom?' and 'How about a piece of chicken? Can you choose a piece of chicken for me?' And, 'Oh, now my teacup is empty can you pour me some tea?'" Angela recalls. "He just wanted me to serve him in front of the other people there, to show everyone that I was serving him." To Angela, who was raised with the custom in her Chinese-Malaysian family that the person who is hosting you does the serving, this was rude and offensive. If the Frenchman had invited her to dinner, he was the host. "I did it a few times when we went to dinners, but after a while I just refused. I said, 'No, forget it. When we go out, it is polite for you to serve me. I expect you to serve the food for me.' Of course in the home that's one thing. I would serve him meals, but in public, serving him like that, forget it!"

VERA IS GETTING READY TO RETIRE from Cathay service, she says. She wants, finally, to get married, to turn this transient life into a treasured memory of the past and settle down. So when an American on one of her flights from Los Angeles to Hong Kong told her not long before I met her, point-blank and with no pretenses, "I am coming to Asia to look for a wife," she was willing to consider the idea. After all, she was looking for a husband, too.

This man was from California, and he owned real estate in Las Vegas. He spent his time between there and San Diego. His first marriage, to an American flight attendant, had ended in divorce. He had heard good things about Asian women, he said. He had been to Thailand and Japan, places he thought were paradise for men. Now in his fifties, he thought an Asian—perhaps an Asian flight attendant— would be a better choice for his second wife than another American. He and Vera exchanged email addresses. They saw each other a few times. Negotiations began. Vera says,

We got very serious about it. We got to the stage of talking about marriage, and I said I expected to have domestic help, just someone coming in once a week to clean house or something like that. He said, "Well, if you loved me you would clean the house yourself." I said, "Well, if you want to marry me, you ought to have a maid." This guy expected that an Asian woman would clean for him, cook for him, give him good sex, everything like that. He was not interested in my real self.

"You know, they have these Philippine mail-order brides. Maybe they get the impression from that. They expect to put all Asians in this package," Vera says. "This guy told me he expects women to dress in sexy lingerie, in matching bra and underwear!" As she had said before, women who fly Cathay don't wear matching lingerie any more frequently than any other women do. Do you have matching lingerie on? she asked me. I had to admit that, at that moment, I did not. And, like her, I usually didn't—unless, as she said, it was a special occasion. "It's all so weird," Vera says. "When you show them your true self, they don't understand that."

"Or they don't want to understand that," Angela interjects. She has had similar experiences, not with an American man coming to Asia to look for an Asian wife, but with Western men who, like the Frenchman, refused to see her for who she really was, who wanted to glamorize her and treat her as an object of fantasy and conquest. How much of this was because she was a glamorous flight attendant evoking a previous era of aviation, and how much of it was because she was a Malaysian-Chinese she could not tell. But she did feel that Caucasian men often treated her in an exoticized, sexualized way. Often, Asian men on her flights were just rude.

"We are humans. We have feelings. We want to have good conversation, and everything else," Vera says. "Anyway, I sent him [the American wife-hunter] an email recently saying that I am going to marry someone else soon. I just got engaged actually. He wrote back that he's thinking about going to Japan now to look for a wife."

Vera kept mum about the details because she didn't want to jinx things. Being a flight attendant on Cathay had been an incredible opportunity for her. She was grateful that her gifts and her beauty had provided her financial independence, a glamorous existence, and the opportunity to see the world. Now, she couldn't wait to get married and settle down.

Although Vera was not yet at Cathay's maximum retirement age, she has flown for far more years than women previously had flown, and she is grandfathered in under an earlier set of benefits. Hong Kong's Equal Employment Opportunity law, passed in 1996, means flight attendants can keep flying until age fifty-five. Before that, women were eligible to retire with full benefits—indeed, were pressured to do so—by age forty or forty-five. Vera still can take advantage of the younger retirement age if she chooses. (Singapore Airlines' flight attendants fly for a maximum allowable twenty-five years, the same number Vera has logged, but typically fly for only ten years before being offered ground-staff positions.[3])

Before EEO laws, women who were already married, or who had children, could not join Cathay. Those who had children within five years of being hired would have to leave service. (It was the same way in the United States until 1967 when laws were passed banning dismissal at marriage or upon pregnancy.) Most airlines around the world still have strict rules about how flight attendants must look and carry themselves. They still have weight limitations proportional to height, and assign too-heavy flight attendants to work the ticket counter or transfer desk until they lose enough weight to look good in uniform again. "Cathay Girls," when traveling standby to go home and visit their families or to go on vacation, cannot wear flip-flops, flimsy blouses, shirts with political statements, mini-skirts, or blue jeans. Their hair and nails must be well-groomed at all times. And there is a certain look they must have to be hired in the first place. Beyond height requirements, weight limitations, and language ability common to every international airline, "Cathay Girls" are required to have certain facial characteristics. Flight attendants have told me that mixed-race Asian women who appear "too white"—with pink-toned skin and round eyes—have been rejected when they applied for jobs. The women must convey a look of exotic "Asian-ness" to be accepted into Cathay's crew.

Parveen, the flight attendant who had married one of her passengers, has the look. Light-skinned and almond-eyed, she is a Parsee (or Parsi), an ethnic group of Zoroastrians (the oldest monotheistic religion in the world, which influenced Judaism and Christianity with its theology of heaven and hell). The Parsee people originated in ancient Persia, but, persecuted by Muslims 1,000 years ago, they dispersed around the world. Often compared with the Jews, the Parsees number only about 100,000 people in diaspora communities in India, Canada, Afghanistan, Pakistan, London, Hong Kong, and elsewhere. Some also remained in modern-day Iran. Parveen was born in one of the largest of these diaspora communities, in Mumbai (Bombay), where Parsees have largely adopted Hindu customs.

Parveen is a friend of Vera's, and we met for dinner one night on one of Hong Kong's outlying islands called Lantau, where she lives in a luxury townhouse with her American husband, Stephen. A large community of working professionals who commute by hover-ferry to Hong Kong lives on Lantau, and the island functions as an affluent suburb with its own beach, open-air shopping mall, schools, and housing developments. Hong Kong's new airport is also on Lantau, making it convenient for Parveen to get to work. In fact, most Cathay flight attendants live on the island now.

Before 1998, when Hong Kong's Kai Tak Airport was centrally located in Kowloon, the flight attendants mostly lived nearby, in an apartment block housing 3,000 of them. The young Western bankers and merchants who pursued the women called it "The Chicken Coop." In Chinese, "chicken" is a slang word for prostitute. Getting laid there, they said, was "as easy as shooting fish in a barrel." The center for flight attendant nightlife was nearby, too, in bars such as Amoeba near the Peninsula Hotel, and J.J.'s disco in the Grand Hyatt just across the harbor on the Hong Kong side. With the relocation to Lantau, the flight attendant clientele and the men chasing them at those nightspots dried up; they eventually closed. The "Cathay Girls" nightlife scene—and their mystique among the bedpost-notching merchants and bankers of Hong Kong—has cooled somewhat, too.

"I'm very stubborn, and I don't like to be stereotyped," Parveen states, smiling as she says it. "I have a B.A. in psychology, and got certificates in psychotherapy, international travel and tourism, advertising management, and ad copywriting." Mostly, getting those degrees was just to get out of working in her mother's company. Her father owned leather factories. Her mother ran an advertising agency. Her family is wealthy, and Parveen grew up in a 3,000-square-foot house with servants and seven cars. Under British colonial rule, Parsees were favored for their height, light skin, and Anglicized ways, and given administrative roles. They tend not to eat the spicy food that Indians like. Parsees control the biggest industrial empire in India, the Tata group, as well as the largest privately owned conglomerate, Godrej.

"In India growing up, in the movies you always see the stereotypical Indian mother, very kind, staying at home, reading bedtime stories. My mom worked. She had her own advertising company; she was very strict, she was never at home," Parveen says. "She was also one of those stubborn people, always wanted to go out and do something." She arranged for Parveen to marry a fellow Parsee at age twenty-one. But the couple divorced after only a few months, when they realized they weren't right for each other.

Parveen's mother consented to her joining Cathay Pacific in 1990, only because she thought her daughter would come crying home. And plus, what could she do to stop her? "I stood up to my mother. I said, 'I'll give up everything and go and sleep in the road.' That was hard for me, because we were well-to-do," she says. "After that, my mother and I became best friends."

At first Parveen found the work difficult, not physically but psychologically. "Have you ever been called like this?" she says, raising her forearm from our dinner table and snapping her fingers three times.

"I cried after every flight. I cried for three months. I thought it was the worst job in the world," she continues. "Growing up, I had a bell, and I pushed it, and people appeared and asked, 'What do you want?' I had never picked up a dirty dish in my life, and here I was picking up 150 dirty plates in economy." The first thing she bought with her first paycheck was a big stuffed teddy bear to comfort her.

Passengers found the combination of her light skin and dark eyes exotic. In economy class, the tourists and first-time travelers would thrust their business cards at her, hoping for a night out and a one-night stand in their destination cities. But in business class and first class, men would try to chat her up a bit to gauge her receptivity before trying to hand her their cards, concerned about their egos, she says, and the fact that road warriors know they might see you again on the next flight. Parveen never kept any of the cards. She had a habit of going into the galley immediately after someone gave her one and throwing it away. She disposed of hundreds of them this way. "I was always fighting the stereotype of being easy to pick up," she says. Having Indian nationality made it worse. "It was the Indian girls who had a very 'social' reputation, let's call it that to be kind. And the Indonesians and Thais, they were like, 'Oooh, a white man is asking me out,'" Parveen says. "There were a lot of girls thinking it was an honor to be asked out by a white man, something to be proud of. And almost every Japanese crew was going out with either a (white) second officer or first officer, or some white passenger."

Parveen only rarely dated, never went out to clubs or discos, and instead spent her free time reading positive-thinking books or having dinner with two other Parsee badge-mates with whom she shared an apartment. Then, about six years into her flying career, she met her future husband.

He was sitting on the Upper Deck—the very first seat after the cockpit. I was the purser looking after them upstairs. We had a good crew so we were laughing a lot. I didn't speak to him except to serve him, you know, "Would you like tea or coffee?" or whatever. It was a JFK–Vancouver–Hong Kong flight. We [crew] got off in Vancouver. As we were preparing to get off, he comes up behind the curtain and pretends he is reading a magazine. You know, the stupid things men do, as if we don't know! He said, "I'd like to see you in Hong Kong." I just laughed. You know, typical passenger trying to pick me up. I'd learned how to avoid it: Tell them to give you their card and you'll call them. So he gave it to me. It was just the typical, "Okay fine, I'll call you." He said, "You're not going to call me, are you?" I said, "Oh yeah, yes, I'll call." I'm very bad at lying. So he said, "Do you promise?" That's what got me, the promise part. I always keep my promises. It took me about twenty or twenty-five days. You know, I don't drink, I don't go to bars. I hate the atmosphere. I didn't really want to go out.

Parveen decided to call her parents in India first. This man was not only *not* a Parsee, he was not even Indian. "I said, 'Is it okay if I go out with this passenger?' In case something happened, I didn't want them to tell me later that they didn't approve. I said, 'Tell me now.'" Her mother encouraged her, however. Knowing Parveen's dating history, her mother would rather see her daughter, who by then had reached the age of thirty-one, marry an American than nobody at all.

"When I phoned him, I said, 'This is Parveen.' I expected him to say, 'Who?' And then I would hang up. He said, 'Oh, I was just thinking about you, about why you didn't call me,'" she says. He, of course, wanted to see her as soon as possible.

We went to an Italian restaurant in Pacific Place, Grappa's. I went an hour early because I wasn't sure I would recognize him. I had done at least six or seven flights since then. The only thing I thought I might remember about him was his eyes, because he would look up and make eye contact and say, "Thanks," when I served him. He was connecting to me on a human level. When I saw him, I was like, "Okay, that's the one." So he asked if I would like a drink first. I'm thinking, "Okay, I don't like juice. I don't drink." I ordered sparkling water, and I go out so rarely, I didn't even know what kind they were telling me it was. After a couple hours we had dinner, and soon they started running the vacuum cleaner. I thought it was pretty rude. Then I looked at my watch, and it was one o'clock in the morning! We had been talking for five hours. I thought, as I went home and I was taking off my shoes at the entrance to my room, "Oh my god, I've been had. Nobody could be this nice."

But as it turned out, he was. He was very interested in her religious practices, too, which are now primarily Hindu. They have been married for seven years.

My husband is very interested in the culture. He does everything I want him to do. He likes going to the temple, on pilgrimages. Every morning he waits for me to put a red mark in his hair, a puja. It used to be for being victorious in battle [but now is a symbolic devotion]. If he has to leave early, I'll just get up, make some breakfast, and do it before he goes out the door.

Just because a man marries a "Cathay Girl," however, doesn't mean he gets full service treatment at home, even if she wanted to give it. Stephen, who is eighteen years older than Parveen and divorced from a British woman, tells Parveen that she is stronger and more stubborn than his first wife. Parveen says,

Maybe I should be the British one and she should be the Indian one. When I grew up watching Indian movies, it was always like "Your husband is God. Treat him like God." But treating Stephen that way, he would reject it. He would say, "Why give me the best piece all the time? I don't want the best piece all the time." You know, we're not giving the best piece out of force or because we're lowly, lowly women and these are men, but out of respect. You do it out of love. You want to give good things to someone you love.

Parveen does describe one of her badge-mates, however, a Korean who married a Western passenger and goes a bit too far. This Korean woman goes to bed in full make up, gets up in the middle of the night to take it off after her husband has fallen asleep, then sets her alarm to get up before him and put it on again so that when he wakes up, she will look beautiful for him, Parveen says. Apparently, she is afraid that, having chosen her at her fully made-up best, her husband will reject her if he sees her in her natural state. "The things some women think they have to do for a man," Parveen sighs. I notice then that she is not wearing any make-up, and her naturally kohl-rimmed eyes look absolutely stunning without it.

GERI AND MARICAR, the Filipina "Cathay Girls," married high school sweethearts from back home, and never even considered Western men. When we arranged to meet for lunch, they wanted to go get one of the only decent lunch salads you can find in Hong Kong, coincidentally, at Grappa's. I was beginning to think Pacific Place Mall was a de facto home-away-from-home for the Cathay Pacific crew. "I never thought of myself as exotic. For me, exotic means dark skin," Geri volunteers before we even place our orders. "Those Westerners always go for really, really dark girls. They think they're exotic looking."

Geri joined Cathay in 1989 at age twenty, and soon after married a man she had known since age thirteen. Maricar also married her one and only boyfriend soon after joining in 1995. While some of their badge-mates from training "went crazy enjoying the freedom" in Hong Kong, Geri says, these two kept far away from the men who gave them their business cards, also throwing them away before leaving the galley. They both had strong Catholic upbringings. "We're very square," says Geri. Both try to go to mass every Sunday, even if they are flying and find themselves in foreign cities.

Having their own glamorous careers, they find, gives them power with their husbands back home in Manila. "Both my grandfathers had mistresses and other separate families, and my grandmothers knew. We don't take that crap anymore," Geri says. "It was quite common in Manila. My mother left my father for the same reason. Our generation, I don't think we take it. A lot of women are working. In the past they were just staying home, cooking." Maricar, who also has a sister in the airline business and a father who is a pilot, agrees. "Times are changing. Men are more open to the idea that women can be their co-equals. They don't have to stay at home; they can have careers of their own." These women love *Sex and the City*. The show is seen widely in Asia, including in China, and is wildly popular with women of all ages. Maricar and Geri identify with the characters. "Especially Charlotte!" Geri says. So are these "Cathay Girls" feminists? "I just believe in some rights women have, but I'm not the extreme," says Maricar. "We're confused about feminism," Geri says, drinking the last of her post-salad espresso. "We want to be treated as equals, yet we want to be treated well, too."

THERE IS ANOTHER, FAR-LESS-GLAMOROUS and less-privileged world of Filipinas working in Hong Kong, a world far away from lunch salads and espressos and discussions of feminism and *Sex and the City*. It is the amahs, the Chinese word for maid, and the overwhelming majority—152,000 out of a total 223,000 amahs in Hong Kong[4]—comes from the Philippines. As domestic servants, they represent the most ubiquitous image of servility to foreigners. But, unlike the glamorous, high-profile women of Cathay, these women are a largely invisible part of the service industry, except in the homes of foreigners and wealthy Chinese where they work in silence except for the occasional "Yes, Mum" uttered in response to every request from their employers.

One day of the week—Sunday—is their one day of rest from cleaning apartments, cooking meals, and caring for the well-off children of Hong Kong. After mass in the Tagalog language at St. Joseph's Church—a bright blue concrete structure on the hill leading from the Mid-levels district where thousands of the amahs work to the Central business district around the harbor—they congregate in hundreds if not thousands of small groups in any free spaces they can find, spreading picnic blankets on the ground and sitting down wherever there are a few spare feet of concrete—in front of the Bank of China tower, at the Star Ferry Terminal, in enough public places that the Hong Kong government occasionally debates banning them but doesn't out of the realization that, finally freed for one day of the week from tiny maid's rooms in the apartments of their employers, they really have nowhere else to go.

They group themselves by communities of hometowns, ethnic groups, and language. The quiet, "Yes, Mum" utterances of the week become vivacious chatter. They swap stories, comparing the relative generosity or parsimony of their employers, as well as how much money they have been able to save up to send by wire transfer to husbands, children, and extended families back home. President Ferdinand Marcos set off the exodus in the early 1980s, mobilizing Filipinos to go abroad to earn hard currency and reduce destabilizing unemployment back home. Of the Philippines' 84 million population, 8 million people now work overseas in 186 countries.[5] Glamorous Cathay flight attendants like Geri and Maricar are a tiny minority of them; most of the rest of the Filipinas working abroad have built successful careers in ways more like Aida Montajes and her sisters.

It is on Christmas Eve, at the midnight mass at St. Joseph's, that I run into Aida's sisters, Marilou and Crispa. Thousands of Filipinas, arm-in-arm, hand-in-hand—spilling out onto Garden Road because St. Joseph's is packed from altar to vestibule, with standing room in the parking lot only—are just singing the last refrains of "Silent Night" under the festive icicle lights strung from the church and the tingling scent of incense. It is a warm night, requiring only a light jacket for those standing outside. When the priest ends with, "May God bless you forever and ever," the congregants shout back "Merry Christmas!" instead of a quiet "Amen," and a live band kicks up a rousing version of "Feliz Navidad" at 1:15 AM that sends the women dancing out of the pews and into the streets as they head home to celebrate the holiday.

The sense of community and kinship among these women is powerful. I had told the Montajes sisters I was planning to be there, and I guessed that being one of the only blondes in a crowd of raven-haired Filipinas has made it easier to spot me. I wanted to meet the sisters at Christmas time so they could tell me about their lives. Aida's employers were away for the holidays, and the women had an unusual amount of free time that I hoped would provide a glimpse into their world. But Aida had missed midnight mass. It turned out that her eighteen-month-old son, Anthony Joseph, or A.J., had suddenly needed minor surgery, and Aida needed to stay home with him. The next day, Christmas morning, I met her in her employers' kitchen, with a surprisingly cheerful A.J., a Band-Aid over the boo-boo from his incision, at her side.

The story of how Aida ended up a single mother is a sad one. After working in Hong Kong for ten years, Aida told her employers she wanted to leave to go marry a man from back home. She had known the man since they were eight, and they had kept in touch via letters over the years. At thirty-eight years old, Aida had saved some money and could not wait much longer if she wanted to have children. But the employers did not want her to leave. Instead, they offered to hire the husband as a driver and handyman and bring him to Hong Kong—even though they had already paid to send Aida to driving school to be able to chauffeur their two children, and even though they were also employing Aida's sister, Marilou. The employers did not really need three full-time domestic helpers, but they wanted to keep together what felt like a family. So Aida got married, got pregnant, and returned to her job in Hong Kong. Her husband followed a short time later. After being in Hong Kong for only two months, shortly before their baby was due, Aida's husband stepped out into the street in front of the apartment building and was struck by a bus and killed instantly. It was his first time living in a city where cars drive, like in its former colonial ruler England, on the left-hand side of the road. Aida had to bury her husband before having her baby. She isn't bitter. She feels sad sometimes, but she believes in the common saying of Filipinos, *Bahala na ang Diyos*. It means "God will take care of everything." "For me, this is just my destiny," she says.

The sisters let Aida speak for them, as she, now age forty, is the eldest among them and the chattiest. Marilou, always quiet except for the occasional "Yes, Mum," takes over preparing Christmas lunch with the help of Crispa, who works elsewhere but has come over for Christmas. They take chicken wings and braise them in soy sauce and brown vinegar on the stove to make *adobo,* which is as to Philippine cuisine as spaghetti is to Italian. They boil some *bok choy,* the cheapest green vegetable in the market, and cook some white rice. A couple of friends were coming over as well. By the time we sit down for lunch at midday around a tiny table in the maids' quarters where we balance our plates on our knees, there are seven of us, twelve chicken wings, and a small mound of vegetables. The employers' eight-place-setting dining table is just on the other side of the door. The sisters, happy to share what they have, insist on offering me their humble Christmas meal. I think it rude to refuse. I claim, guilt-ridden after a chicken wing and a teaspoon of vegetables, that I am full. Because of me, one of the women will only get to eat one wing.

BOUNCING A.J. AS SHE TALKS, Aida tells me she started working by age eleven on the southern Philippine island of Leyte, where she was born. Leyte was the scene of one of the most memorable battles of World War II between the Japanese and the Americans, and it is now one of the poorest provinces of the Philippines. The family has seven girls and four boys in all. They grew up in a bamboo, wood, and thatch house in a village of 1,000 people. After Aida started working, cleaning houses while staying with a cousin in the next province, she attended class only sporadically and never finished high school. Instead, she got a job in a furniture factory on the island of Cebu when she was sixteen, then in a students' canteen, and then, finally, housekeeping for a family in Manila. "In Cebu, my employer wanted to send me to school, but in my mind I wanted to help my family. I wanted to earn money," Aida says. Their parents were farmers. They grew rice, root crops, and vegetables. It was just for their daily consumption and sometimes if there was extra they could sell it, but the farm was not big enough to sell much. When Aida's older sister, Remy, who had gone to Manila first, left for Hong Kong to clean apartments there, she found a job for Aida in Hong Kong, too. "When my sister called me to come to Hong Kong, I didn't want to come. I didn't have ambition to work abroad," Aida says.

> I was doing some buying and selling business on the side, like T-shirts and blankets. I had a lot of customers and I was good at that. So when my sister called, I told her I'm not interested. I told her to call my cousin because my cousin really wanted to come to Hong Kong. She called me two times to ask me. She tried to get another sister, but that sister had stomach problems.
>
> She said, "But they're American!" Western employers are better than Chinese. They treat you better. But that Filipino family in Manila where I was working, we were like family with them; all of our seven sisters worked for them at one time or another. I changed my mind when my sister kept trying to get my other sister with stomach problems to come. I didn't want her to have to work. The American family from Hong Kong sent me the money to come, so I was lucky. I didn't have to pay an agency. That was in December 1990.

Agency fees are advertised to be in the neighborhood of a couple hundred dollars, but once the girls sign up, they are fleeced for extra costs, such as for a visa, passport photos, and plane tickets, and other "processing" fees of $1,000, $1,500, or more. That's a fortune in the Philippines. Those who have help from family members who have gone before them are lucky.

Aida was lucky in other ways, too. The government-set minimum wage for a full-time amah in Hong Kong at the time was $364 per month, but her American family paid her $494. In Manila she had been making $16. She sent any extra money she could, about $115 per month, back home. She wanted to help her mother, Angelita, who is in her seventies now, build a new house. Her father had passed away, and there was only one brother left at home to eke a living out of the farm. Thatch and wood did not hold up well during the typhoons and tropical storms that struck Leyte every year. When Aida was young, she remembers seeking shelter at neighbors' houses during storms. With the money she was sending home, her mother was starting to buy building materials. And just in time. A typhoon in 1992 "broke it to pieces," Aida says. Between the earnings of her and her elder sister, they managed to fund the $6,000 cost of a concrete house. Now during typhoon season, the neighbors come to the Montajes's house to seek shelter.

Aida also paid for her youngest brother to attend the Merchant Marine Academy so that he could find a job in shipping. He hasn't so far, but at least he has an education that Aida never had. Aida wanted to send Marilou, the youngest sister, to college as well, but she and Crispa decided to emulate Aida's success in Hong Kong. There was no guarantee of a job at home, even if they did seek higher education. "As long as our government won't change, there's no work in the Philippines. It's really hard to get a job there," Aida says. "Even if you have college graduation, if you don't have the right looks and connections, it's hard to get a job." All three sisters in Hong Kong alternately send money home now, the equivalent of about one month's pay each time, or $650. By Leyte standards, that makes the Montajes sisters wealthy.

Remy, the eldest sister who lured Aida to Hong Kong in the first place, was sponsored by her American family to go to the United States, to western Massachusetts. Before long, she got married, to a man from Virginia. "But they are divorced now. Now she's working two or three jobs at the same time, living in Virginia," says Aida. Whereas Remy used to have at least Sundays off, now she doesn't have any. "She was sending money to Philippines, too, but I told her not to anymore, because her life is so hard there. We can send money from here." The irony that a Filipina amah in Hong Kong seemed to be living a better life than her sister who now had an American passport was striking.[6] Millions of women in the Philippines grow up watching American TV shows, and many believe that marrying an American—or any Western man—is a ticket to a better life. Aida and her sisters, and, seemingly, the millions of Filipinas working abroad and sending money home to improve the lives of their families, have found that the ticket to a better life is themselves.

As we finish our conversation and I leave the women to finish their heartbreakingly modest meal, I open the refrigerator door to take out a bottle of water I had asked to keep chilled while we had our conversation. I can't help but be surprised that the refrigerator is stocked with several pounds of fresh jumbo shrimp, three or four whole fish, steaks, bunches of vegetables, and four batches of brownies. The employers, I knew, were away for weeks. I ask Aida about all the food. "Oh, we don't want to eat very much for lunch," she says, "that's our Christmas dinner."

Screwing, Getting Screwed,

and Getting Ahead

You look like you could use a sandwich," the large Canadian businessman says to a tall, skinny Filipina with stringy hair standing at the bar at the Café Havana in Manila. It sounds like a joke, but it is a pickup line. Not that one is needed. It is a rocking Friday night, and the young woman has told me that she is trying to find a foreign husband. We had cast glances around the bar together to see who looked promising. This man is 6' 5", with the look of a former high-school athlete going softly into his early forties. He isn't wearing a wedding ring. She considers him a good prospect.

He tries to explain, remarking that he weighs 220 lbs. and she must weigh next to nothing. She doesn't get it. She thinks he is offering her food. She says she isn't hungry. He starts talking about his shoe size. Big, apparently. "You know what they say . . ." he says.

"What?" the sandwich girl replies. It's unclear whether she simply can't hear him over the loud Buena Vista Social Club music from the seven-piece band a few feet away, can't understand him, or is asking him for the answer. Not like it matters.

"About big feet," he says. He high-fives his drinking buddies, the free hands not holding San Miguel beers slapping together, and they break up in hoots of laughter. The reference is lost on her. A big rich foreigner is a big rich foreigner, and anatomy has little relevance. She stands in silence after that, watching the band, occasionally casting a smiling glance at him to make sure he is still watching her. It is hard to keep his attention, and she is trying hard to appear not to be trying too hard. There are many girls here eager to capture the notice of these three Canadian men, only one of whom is wearing a wedding ring. Not that that matters either, but a man without a ring is a better place to start when looking for a husband. At least the tall girl has an advantage. Her height puts her a head above the other Filipinas at the bar, and the big guy seemingly likes that. She is taller than most Filipino men, too, which probably hasn't helped her marriage prospects so far. Maybe this time will be different.

When the band breaks between sets, canned Santana comes over the sound system. The Canadians think the music sucks. They like rock 'n' roll. They seem restless, commenting on the unattractiveness of the smaller, waif-like women dancing clumsily in front of them trying to catch their eyes, but the men are reluctant to leave without having scored for the evening. "They're dogs, man," one of them says. The large one decides to take the sandwich girl back to his hotel. She agrees. She doesn't negotiate for money. After all, she hopes to capture his heart. But more than likely, she expects that he will give her a little something, maybe the Philippine peso equivalent of US$30 to US$50, if she is lucky. Taxi money to get home, it's called, even though a taxi to the other side of town costs around US$5, and she probably would take public transport anyway. She is gambling that he will like her enough to make it last, to take her away from the poor economic conditions in which she grew up and in which her family still lives. If she loses, she still may get more in one night with him than an average unionized wage worker in Manila makes in a week, and more than her relatives in the countryside can make in a month. From her perspective, even if he is stingy, it is worth the gamble.

After they leave together, his buddies, who all played football and rugby together in high school, let me in on a secret. They have a bachelor party planned for him the weekend after next. He is getting married to a Canadian, and this is his next-to-last fling, or maybe his next-to-next-to-last, depending on next weekend's activities. So, the tall sandwich girl would not marry him after all. The best she can hope for from this transaction, then, is generosity.

A short time later, I feel a hand on the top of my head twisting my gaze to the opposite side of the bar. When I am released and allowed to look, I see one of the remaining Canadians, the one with the wedding ring, zipping up his fly. A young woman sitting on the bar rail in front of him wipes her mouth with the back of her hand, turns to me, and beams. I had heard of blow jobs at the bar before, at the Rose bar in Bangkok, and in the Wanchai red-light district of Hong Kong. An American had told me of seeing a Thai girl give head to a fellow financial analyst behind a strategically held raincoat while he was seated on a stool at Superstar one evening after work. The girl, when finished, turned and spit the man's seed of life into an artificial potted plant. Yet, this was the first time I had witnessed what was a seemingly not-uncommon event. These exchanges were usually just cash-and-blow, rather than being accompanied by hopes and dreams; unable to partake of it myself, I was unable to find out how much it cost.

> Power often contains a sexual element, but the Philippines is somehow special. . . . Offering head to whoever happens to be king of the mountain seems to have become second nature to many Filipinos. To be down there, between the legs of the Spanish friar or Uncle Sam, or Ferdinand Marcos, or whoever, has become the natural place to be. But screwing has another meaning as well: that of betrayal. Philippine history is also a story of betrayal; those who offer head so willingly usually end up being screwed in both senses of the word, the bitter and seemingly ever-recurring experience of a submissive people that expects too much in return.
> —Ian Buruma, *The Missionary and the Libertine*[1]

When I had read these words, it struck me as an odd portrayal of a people—screwing, submissive, and screwed. I had been to the Philippines several times before. I had interviewed a previous president, the Central Bank governor, several prominent business leaders, a female editor-in-chief, the second woman to be elected President of the Philippines, Gloria Macapagal Arroyo, back when she was a senator, and the Filipina "Cathay Girls" and amahs in Hong Kong. The Philippines has its problems, of course, economically, politically, and otherwise, but I hadn't gotten the impression that Buruma describes. Then again, I had not been examining issues of screwing and sexual power, only those of economics, politics, and business. So I went back to the Philippines to do so, not just in the case of men like the Canadian businessmen and thousands of others like them, but Filipinas as well.

THE CAFÉ HAVANA at the Greenbelt III shopping mall in Manila's business district, Makati, is packed on weekend nights. Although it is walking distance from the city's most expensive luxury hotels—the Shangri-la, Mandarin Oriental, Peninsula, and Oakwood—most of the foreign businessmen who end up at this bar, on the advice of their respective concierges, have taken a taxi. If it is their first time to Manila, they are surprised to see this level of wealth. They were thinking garbage dumps, shanties, traffic jams, and power outages. Instead they find an always-electrified mall with a Calvin Klein retail outlet, a Starbucks, and other high-end chain stores. No Gap, or even discount racks, just expensive displays in store windows. During the day, fashionable, manicured Manila-ites click around the mall in high heels, wearing sunglasses indoors and dangling trendy Gucci or Dior purses from their forearms.

At night, the goal here sometimes turns to finding another kind of fashion accessory: a rich foreign boyfriend, husband, or one-night stand. A Philippine friend of mine knew some female university students at the Café Havana one evening who moved their dinner table over to join a group of foreign businessmen and then left with them. For money. College is expensive, they reasoned. And they have to keep themselves in nice clothes and shoes—and able to go out to nice restaurants. Plus, if he's divorced, or getting divorced someday, there's a chance of a lifetime if it works out.

Having a wealthy white husband is a status symbol, a value perhaps dating from Spanish colonial rule when the mixed-race lighter skinned people, the *mestizos,* held the country's wealth and privilege. They still do. Privileged or underclass, rich or poor, it seems everybody in the Philippines—or at least at the Café Havana—is seeking better opportunities. Offering head so willingly doesn't always mean you get screwed. Sometimes it means getting ahead, too.

I HAVE MET WOMEN in various countries in Asia who have sex with men for money, but who aren't professional prostitutes. After all, if you date a man, they reason, he takes you out, buys you presents. This is the same thing, maybe a little bit more, in a quicker time frame. In

Japan, the term is *enjo kosai,* which translates literally into "a helping acquaintance," and primarily is practiced by teenage girls having sex with older Japanese men for money to buy expensive purses and clothes. Foreigners, however, are not part of it. That sex is Japanese-only. In Southeast Asia, this practice is evident not only at Café Havana, but at the Hard Rock Cafés all over the region. They are known pick-up spots. Asian women wanting to meet foreign men go there. Foreign men looking for sex go there, too. But sometimes the men—like the English machine parts salesman I met in the Hard Rock Café in Manila one night—just wander in and never know what hit them.

Peter is a straight-up, straight-laced, solidly middle-class kind of fellow from middle England, and I have changed his quite classically English name to another similar one lest I risk giving him away to his wife, to whom, by his account, he is happily married with two kids. Affable and not one to enjoy his own company more than that of others, he struck up a conversation with me at the bar after having been stood up, he told me, by a Filipino business partner.

The last time Peter had come to town, he said, the Filipino had insisted they conduct their meeting in the VIP room of a club where Filipino businessmen regularly do business. The walls were glass and the Filipino gave Peter the honored guest's view of the club's topless dancing (which is illegal in the Philippines). It was rather difficult to concentrate on giving the presentation, the Englishman recalled with characteristic understatement, and quite a bit different than the sales calls he was used to making back in England. He suggested they change seats. They did. But then he realized that the object of his sales pitch wasn't concentrating, either. The only solution was to order bed sheets, apparently readily available on the premises, and tape them over the glass until business was concluded. After they had reached a deal, the Filipino presented the Englishman with a "thank-you present" in the form of a young woman, and left the room. The woman disrobed and crawled on top of Peter as he sat in his chair. "Wham bam, thank you m'am, and that was the end of that," Peter said. I asked whether he was an enthusiastic recipient of this gift, since he had just told me about his wife and happy family back home.

"Well, I'm a man, aren't I?" he answered. "All in a day's business in Manila."

It was not long before the bar filled up. A famous Philippine actor was on stage launching his debut pop album, and at least a couple hundred young female enthusiasts had paid a 400 peso (US$7.27) entry charge, which includes two free drinks, to cram into the room to see him. One of these enthusiasts, who introduced herself as Cherry, took the empty stool to my right. She wore a tight, white low-cut shirt and ordered a glass of red wine. Peter reached over me and said hello.

Cherry's breast-length hair was dyed a cinnamon blonde, and she had a considerable overbite that caused her lips to pucker attractively when she closed her mouth. She said she was alone. This was unusual for a Filipina, to be drinking alone at a bar, unless she was a pro working the pickup scene. But then she said she was from out of town, from the other side of the Laguna de Bay, southeast of Manila. She had come to the capital to apply for a work visa for Sweden. Her younger sister had married a Swede she met while working as a waitress in a Swedish restaurant in Manila. Cherry wanted to go to Sweden, too, to work in a restaurant in Stockholm. She tried working as a waitress in her hometown, but was earning only 400 pesos a month. That was as much as it cost her to get into the Hard Rock. Like many Filipina workers overseas, she intended to leave her seven-year-old son—from a failed marriage to a Filipino—with his grandparents when she left.

"Oh my goodness, I get up four o'clock in morning to go to Sweden Embassy. Oh my goodness," she said, sounding a bit like Suzie Wong who used the same expression with somewhat less frequency than Cherry in the 1960 movie starring Nancy Kwan and William Holden. I wondered if this was intentional, if she had ever seen *The World of Suzie Wong*. I thought of the opening scene, where Holden's character meets Suzie Wong on the Star Ferry in Hong Kong and she tricks him into believing she is a virgin rather than a prostitute with a child, which he later discovers is her true identity. Like Suzie Wong, Cherry was impossible to gauge from initial impressions.

She launched into her ordeal of waiting in lines and the all-day paperwork that one must endure when applying to work in a foreign country, and said she had to go back in early in the morning. She liked Swedish people, she said. Americans, too. "Oh, I don't like English," she declared when Peter volunteered his nationality. The salesman didn't know how to react, but he took it in stride. Cherry turned to me to say that she used to have an English boyfriend but she decided not to "go with him." I wasn't sure whether this meant permanently or temporarily and what "going with someone" would involve. "He shorter than me!" she exclaimed. I couldn't tell from her position on the barstool, but I noticed later that Cherry is about 5' 2" in heels. It seemed that her anti-English bias had more to do with the height of the one Englishman she had met, and that she was waiting until our bar companion stood up to pass judgment on the second one. She liked Swedish guys because they are tall, she said, and added that she had a boyfriend in Stockholm from when she visited her sister for Christmas. "But maybe he go with other girls now, I don't know, oh my goodness," she said as if there eventually would be hundreds more to choose from. She was worried now, though. The Swedish consular officer who conducted her interview asked her if she wanted to marry a Swedish man. She had said yes. Now, Cherry worried, they might reject her. She needed more letters from the sponsoring restaurant and more financial guarantees from her sister.

Then she pointed out the large "yobs" sitting at the end of the bar drinking beer—a couple of intimidating large men with big necks, moustaches, and gold chains. They looked like linebackers. "They are American," Cherry said. "No good, very stupid. I go with them yesterday. They say, 'You want to fuck? You want fucking?' I say, 'Hey, fuck you.' They really stupid."

I continued to wonder what her verb "go with them" meant. I wondered if she was confusing stupid with just plain rude. This was a woman who defied easy classification. In just a half-hour or so of talking she had indicated that she was an out-of-towner, an ex-waitress, a would-be emigrant, a divorcee, and a mother. It seemed like she might be a bar girl, too, but it was difficult to ascertain whether she was a pro. In some ways she acted like one, in other ways she did not. The only clear category that seemed to suit her was "party girl."

When the conversation turned to where to have fun in Manila if you're not interested in the movie-star-turned-crooner on the Hard Rock Café stage, she volunteered to take me and the salesman to the sliver of a red-light district called Burgos Street. It is about two blocks long with bars along both sides, the remnant of what used to be Manila's thriving red-light districts. Our first stop is Flamingo, a popular place at the entrance to the strip where the dancers on stage are wearing bikini tops and bottoms, the standard uniform of every go-go dancer in the Philippines, as well as numbered badges used to order them for sex in the back room. Occasionally, a girl who looks teenage comes to the front of the stage and wiggles more suggestively than the other girls who recede into the background. She seems to be the pride and prize of the bar. Probably, because she is dancing in the premier go-go bar on the entrance to the strip, within easy police crackdown, she must be legal age, but just barely.

The bar has some Asian businessmen, Koreans, and Japanese— some so old they seem to be nodding off—as well as white men. Cherry says she has been here before. The Englishman ducks out to take a phone call, which seems to be from his wife given the late hour in Manila and the early hour back in England. He is gone awhile. Cherry wants to dance and pulls me onto the small parquet dance floor in front of the stage. Some of the prostitutes who are considered too old or too unattractive to dance onstage, or who specialize in servicing lesbians, join us. They try making flirty eye contact with me, just in case I might want to ditch Cherry and hire one of them, or perhaps have a threesome. I remember what some lesbian prostitutes I'd encountered before had told me—that women usually aren't big, sweaty, and hairy like many white guys are. It's easier work. The DJ, seeing a sudden group of prostitutes on the dance floor, spins Madonna's classic *Like a Virgin*. I can't decide if it is funny or cruel, a gaggle of the least-desirable prostitutes in a go-go bar singing along with the lyrics: "*Yeah you made me feel/Shiny and new/Like a virgin.*"

When Peter returns we move on. Most of the strip's bars are similar, and air-conditioned to a chill—the better for accommodating businessmen in sports jackets as well as keeping nipples erect on stage. When I am ready to say goodnight, Peter and Cherry see me to a taxi and then wander off together in search of more drinks. The comic irony of having danced with prostitutes to *Like a Virgin* resonates with me all the way back to my hotel.

A FEW NIGHTS LATER, I arrange to meet the Englishman at the Café Havana, and as we are chatting there at the bar, catching up on how his last two days' business has fared, Cherry walks past us in high heels and a tight metallic-tinted dress with a plunging neckline. She is braless and her nipples are outlined through the nylon. It's difficult to tell whether she is ignoring us or doesn't see us, but it doesn't seem to be a coincidence that she is here. When the Englishman grabs her arm, she shrieks with happy surprise. "Oh, I think I'm drunk already, oh my goodness," she says, apologizing for not seeing us and falling onto my lap as she greets me. As Peter leans to kiss her on the cheek, he puts his hand around her waist in an intimate way.

She recounts to us her alcohol intake over the last several hours, a vodka shot and then another tequila shot and then a glass of red wine and then another tequila shot, at a Swedish bar where she had gone after her long day again at the Swedish Embassy. Cherry has a way of tediously detailing the events of her days. She is still waiting for faxes to come from Stockholm, still worried she is going to be rejected because of the honesty of her responses. The Englishman offers to buy drinks and she orders red wine. Considering that Cherry can barely stand, I suggest a glass of water. I am curious about their intimacy. When the Englishman goes to use the bathroom, she confesses readily. "I want to be honest with you," she slurs. "I spend night with him." He had served her tea at his hotel room sitting table before undressing her, she tells me. She was touched. I ask if Peter gave her money.

"Fifty dollars first night, again second night. Not too bad, right?" Considering her paltry US$7.27 monthly intake as a waitress, US$100 in two nights wasn't a bad haul. And there was one more night to go. I ask what she thinks of Peter. "It's not love, I don't love him, he don't love me," she says. "It's just like that." She has no long-term designs, she says. She is twenty-eight, a mother, with hopes for a taller, younger husband, and a job in Scandinavia. He is forty-one, married with kids, and leaving for England the following day. "He's too old," she declares. "But he is good man. He knows what woman needs when her boyfriend is far away," she says, "and what man needs when the wife is far away." It sounds like she is parroting something Peter had told her. She assures me they used a condom. As he returns, she puts her hand over her mouth to shut herself up and giggles.

Cherry had no moral dilemmas, and her admission made me recall an obscure study I had found in a Manila women's library titled "Sex and the Single Filipina."[2] It was published in 1982, long before Filipinas were growing up watching MTV or any other of the factors people point to as reasons for change in their societies. It concluded that teenage Filipinas "ignore traditional cultural norms concerning premarital sex, and usually without guilt," but that "to the superficial observer, the young Filipina is extremely sexually conservative." Almost all the girls in the study had been raised in strict Roman Catholic homes, but nearly 80 percent had experienced cunnilingus and fellatio before age twenty-one; 94 percent had experienced manual genital stimulation by boyfriends; 72 percent had had premarital intercourse by the age of twenty-one.

Like in Japan, this was yet another example of the gap between outward appearances and the reality. After all, cultural norms in the Philippines, including Catholicism, were imposed by Spanish colonialists. Clearly they did not wipe out attitudes toward sexuality, they just drove them under the surface. "The discrepancy between traditional norms on premarital sex and the actual behavior of the young, educated Filipina is dramatic," it said. The study noted that in 1967, "psychotherapists detected more regret among [Philippine] women who were virgins at marriage for not having experienced premarital coitus than among those women who did experience it," and that 85 percent felt no anxiety, guilt, or feeling of "loss" of their virginity the first time they had sex. The only anxieties among the remaining 15 percent had to do with what might happen if their fathers found out.

This finding also seemed to contradict a theory I frequently heard from Western men in Asia: that because women raised in Buddhist cultures did not have the same concept of sin as in Christian cultures, they therefore had fewer hang-ups and guilt about sex than Western women did. I had always been skeptical of this assertion. (A female Japanese psychiatrist, Dr. Reiko Kayama, who interviewed several hundred young Japanese women and had written several books, had told me: "I don't agree that Japanese women think sex outside of marriage is okay. It is split about fifty-fifty, the same as other societies. We may not have Christianity, but we do have ethics and morals as determined by the society. There may not be 'guilt,' as from sin, but a negative feeling from violation of societal values.") This Philippine study seemed to prove that Catholicism's strictures weren't the only factors in creating sexual mores. Filipina girls raised in strict Catholic homes had all kinds of sexual experiences as teenagers, and did not feel guilty about them.

CHERRY, STILL DRUNK, WANTS TO DANCE and pulls the Englishman to his feet. He tries to oblige but stumbles around, and she is unable to move quickly enough to keep her exposed toes out of the way of his sturdy English shoes. She decides we should go back to Burgos Street, to see the midnight cabaret show at Jools. It is the largest and classiest of the Burgos bars. Here, the women are professional line dancers with an advanced repertoire of high kicks, splits, sashays, wriggles, and elaborate costume changes. If the Moulin Rouge ever needed extras, this would be a fabulous place to recruit them. As we enter, the dancers are in black negligees, twisting around poles on stage to a slow refrain from Nazareth before the rapid stage act begins: *"Love is like a flame/It burns you when it's hot/Love hurts."*

The dancers make about 1,000 pesos (US$18.18) a week for several hours of this strenuous, choreographed, and highly practiced performance. I find out because Peter, also curious and ever-affable, has gotten up to ask them for me. Cherry, in three nights with the Englishman, will make perhaps US$150. One of the girls on stage is clearly more buxom than the rest, and she draws Peter's lusty attention. He can't keep his eyes off her. "That one just have baby," Cherry announces. "She have milk." Cherry is just guessing, but she is probably right. Peter looks disappointed by this fantasy-puncturing realism and returns his attention to Cherry.

Cherry winks at me as I get up to leave them there together, the Englishman getting worked up by the dancing and she planning her next, lucrative move. I wish her luck in getting everything she hopes for. Not that she needs it. She's doing a pretty good job on her own.

Angeles City, Philippines

Having seen the definition-defying world that exists between prostitution, love, and an immigrant's visa in Manila, I decide to see the real Philippine underworld of Angeles City, home to the U.S. military's former Clark Air Base, about a two-and-a-half hour drive north of Manila.

The main road into town could be any medium-sized strip of commercial development in the United States, with a Shell station, a Dunkin' Donuts, and a Western Union. There's a McDonald's and a Goodyear Tire Center. The American brands are all there. The only noticeable difference is the roads: They are filled with Toyota sedans, Fords, and other conspicuous evidence of the Philippines' emergent middle and upper-middle classes. But the traffic is reduced to stop-and-start by the working class's means of transportation, the jeepney, which pulls over on call to pick up and drop off passengers. Essentially it is a jeep, its chassis elongated to fit two benches in back, like a covered pickup truck on steroids, all shiny aluminum and chrome, some brightly painted in Grateful Dead swirls, with stairs at the back to allow passengers on and off. From my air-conditioned car I can look over and see into these open-air transports, hot, dusty, and fume-filled for those inside. There is a young woman, her face made up and her shirt cut low, on her way to work, probably, as a bar girl. There are an estimated 400,000 prostitutes in the Philippines.[3] It is easy to spot them on public transportation in the late afternoons and early evenings.

I had once read a description of these U.S. military base areas, quoted from a 1984 *Playboy* article by the novelist P. F. Kluge. He described the town surrounding what used to be the largest U.S. military installation in Asia, the U.S. Navy base at Subic Bay.

And now, here you are, and it looks like a Mexican town, something the Wild Bunch might ride into, everything facing a main street, with jeepney after jeepney of sailors tumbling out, the smell of barbecue mixing with diesel fumes, cute, lively, incredibly foul-mouthed girls saying hello and asking what ship you're from and offering head, and the jukeboxes from a dozen bars playing all at once and the song you notice is Julio and Willie doing, "To all the Girls I've Loved Before," and you climb to King Daryl's, where dozens of girls await just you, and you take a chair right at the edge of the balcony, with a King Shit view of the street, and you have a beer in one hand and a pork-satay stick in the other, and a woman between your legs, which are propped up against the railing and you know you have come to a magical place, all right, a special magic for a nineteen-year-old Navy kid, the magic of a place where anything is possible. And cheap.[4]

The U.S. military bases in the Philippines closed in 1992, however; there is no more King Shit view in the town Kluge described, called Olongapao City. It is hardly worth going there, they say, ever since the mayor, Kate Gordon, ordered all the bars in the red-light district closed. The old Subic Naval Base, the former home of the Seventh Fleet where those nineteen-year-old Navy kids once resided, is now a freeport industrial zone with office buildings, Asian electronics manufacturers, and the regional air hub for Federal Express. There are websites run by Americans who used to be based there with names of frequented bars, photos of "The Girls of Olongapao" as far back as the 1940s, and mundane postings such as "They are keeping up with cutting the grass and the place continues to look good."

So, if you want to see the visible sex legacy left behind by the U.S. bases, you must go twenty-five miles inland from Subic to Angeles City, specifically Fields Avenue, the old sex strip outside the still-towering gates of the old Clark Air Base. Kate Gordon wasn't the only mayor in the Philippines fed up with red-light districts. There used to be a thriving one in Manila, too, in the historic area known as Malate. The mayor there, Alfredo Lim, ordered all those bars closed in the 1990s. With the exception of the small and somewhat tame Burgos Street where Cherry and Peter and I went, and another seedy strip for cheap prostitutes servicing local Filipino men in Manila, the sex industry of the Philippines is concentrated in Angeles City.

It is a Saturday night, but there is no atmosphere of fun or frivolity on Fields Avenue. The special kind of magic for the nineteen-year-old Navy kid is still possible, and still cheap. But the consumers of it now are nothing like the clientele of King Daryl's. It has been a long time since most of them were nineteen. Calling the barely two-lane street an avenue is being generous. There is a casino, even a church, places to grab a fast-food meal, and, further down the strip, dozens of bars with names like Pick-up Disco and Massage Palace designed to pique the interests of the prurient. A sign on one reads, "Wanted Sexy Dancers, up to 200 pesos top commission PLUS." That's US$3.64. Presumably the PLUS, which is circled, is whatever the girl is able to negotiate for sex on top of that.

THE STREET IS DOTTED with wandering foreign men, the older ones gaunt and with white hair, the younger ones paunchy. Their pale skin, suddenly exposed in T-shirts in the tropical climate, and white hair, if they have much left, makes them resemble ghosts as they wander the streets from bar to bar. Few are in groups or with anyone at all. The isolation of being checked out from life is a solitary experience, a cold despair, and they project an abject loneliness, an unspoken admission of failure: a failed marriage, failed relationship, failed expectations never fulfilled. Probably none of these men imagined he would end up here in life, alone, among the sex clubs and prostitutes. They seem anesthetized, in search of tender rejuvenating skin, hoping that human contact may somehow restore their sensation, vitality, and youth. What they can buy here, unlike with prostitutes in their own countries, is affection and a sense of feeling attractive again.

I AM WANDERING MYSELF, looking for an opening, an opportunity to slip into this world where I can observe without participating. Amid the strip of enclosed lounges is a corner café, open to the street, with a round bar in the center. Voodoo Bar, it is called. It hardly looks bewitching, but it does seem more inviting than the nightclubs with blackened glass doors, and signs under the neon lights out front saying "No Unescorted Ladies." I don't know if that means me or just Filipinas, but I don't want to try. I decide on the Voodoo Bar.

A few older men are perched against the open-air railing, scanning the street, waiting to be propositioned, or to spot a new, soft, fresh target offering rejuvenation, or at least sensation. A woman is sitting at the bar alone, the only woman there besides me. She, too, is scanning. She is a prostitute, I can tell by the way the front panel of her dress doesn't quite reach back to her underarms, leaving the sides of her breasts exposed as she leans over the bar to sip her drink from a straw.

"Where are you from?" she calls out, smiling, after observing me for a moment to see whether I seem to be waiting for someone or sitting alone. I invite her to move next to me. As she gets up from her barstool, the square-panel dress, held up by spaghetti straps over her shoulders, falls forward and threatens to expose her nipples. It reveals the faded remains of a flower tattoo on her right breast that was either badly done or badly removed. She grasps the straps with strong tugs to pull them up again.

Her breasts are ample, and so is the rest of her body. Her midsection falls out over the sides of her dress where the fabric ends at her hips. Her name is Berlinda. She is twenty-three, from the large island in the southern Philippines, Mindanao. This is the island where Muslim separatists have been agitating, violently, to separate from the Philippines and form an independent country. Berlinda isn't Muslim. Catholic, she says.

As we chat, Berlinda eyes the movements over my shoulder from time to time. When she realizes I have caught her at it, she admits she is watching for someone, an American—very handsome—that she had met the night before. "He say he like me, supposed to come back." But so far he hadn't. Berlinda's life, I surmise, is probably filled with broken promises and dashed expectations to the point of numbness. She shrugs off her disappointment. I ask why she doesn't try any of those old guys perched at the railing. "Too stuck up. Boring also," she declares. Perhaps she had already tried. They are a somewhat motley lot. One, by the way he is dressed in out-of-fashion but once-well-made clothing, seems to be an old-age pensioner from Europe. Another could be North American, with floodwater khakis, dark socks and sandals, and a gut hanging over his belt. None is younger than fifty. All—maybe a dozen—are drinking alone. Not much potential there, it seems, beyond quick sex and a haggle over the price. And surely Berlinda doesn't want to be seen talking to another man, or leaving with one, if her prize from the night before should happen to turn up. She is right to give them a wide berth.

"You want to hear my life story?" she asks when I tell her I am a writer. She doesn't mind that I want to take her picture and possibly publish it, and she poses for several photos. Every working woman like Berlinda has a story, and almost every one is eager to tell it to a sympathetic ear. Maybe it is because they hope to evoke sympathy and money. Maybe they are simply grateful for someone interested in what's inside their hearts for a change, rather than inside their clothes. Likely, because many of the women working in Angeles City have their own sad tales of poverty, failed relationships, or abuse, they can't find much consolation in each other. To a foreigner, these tales are sad, tragic, horrible. To a fellow Filipina prostitute they seem normal.

"It's a sad story. You will cry." As she speaks, her eyes start to moisten and she wipes them with a practiced swipe of her index fingers. "But I am strong. Really strong," she says. "I believe in God. She never give more to me than I can handle."

The feminine pronoun surprises me. Declarations of belief are common in a country where 85 percent of the population is Roman Catholic. "What religion are you?" is a question foreign visitors get right after "Where are you from?" But the macho, Spanish-descended patriarchal version of the religion that Berlinda would have been raised in would hardly countenance a reference to God in the female. Because Asian languages commonly use the same, neutral pronoun for both "he" and "she," I decide this could simply be more grammatical error than feminist declaration. I refrain from interrupting her.

Berlinda is right; she does have a sad story. She was raped while in her second year of high school and became pregnant. Abortion is illegal in the Philippines, so she had to drop out to have the baby, at age seventeen. Her daughter is now five. She eagerly pulls out her wallet with a photo of an adorable girl, her hair in pigtails. She is proud, and turns to the bartender to show him the photo, too.

Berlinda used to have an older sister, but "violence-torn" is one of the descriptions commonly used for her hometown in news reports, and her sister was a victim. "She die. Shot with shotgun," Berlinda says. Her sister had been working as a security guard. As she describes her, her eyes start to moisten again, and again she makes her practiced sweep with her index fingers to wipe away her tears. "She was prettier than me. Whiter skin," she says. Now the family is just her, her mother, and her daughter. Mother is old, unable to work. And father? "No." Berlinda shakes her head, refusing to say more.

It is becoming clear why Berlinda has chosen this line of work. What do you do when you have two other lives—a baby and a mother—depending on you? You come to Angeles City. If you're lucky, you find a rich husband to take you, all of you, to a foreign country. If you are less lucky, he will take just you and you can send money home. So far, Berlinda hasn't been lucky at all. "But I am very strong," she says again. "God never give more than I can handle."

Berlinda, 2004

I ask why she doesn't work in a factory or a store. "Not finish high school!" she says, as if I am quite dense. Education levels are high in the Philippines. Adult literacy is 95 percent, among the highest in Asia. And you need connections and references to get a job, even to be a housecleaner. Berlinda, I realize, is at nearly the lowest rung of status and education in the Philippines, virtually unemployable in any profession requiring any skill.

She wants to know about me, about my family. I tell her I have a brother, younger. He is a monk. She doesn't understand. "In a monastery," I say. "Like a priest."

"Oh, I think your brother be handsome," she says, imagining my light hair and pale skin in male form. She brightens and turns coquettish as her right spaghetti strap again falls dangerously off her shoulder. "If he meet me before, he not be priest!"

Suddenly, Berlinda wants to change venues. Perhaps the American she hopes to find is elsewhere. I pay the bill, and we dash off. It is common for women to walk arm-in-arm in the Philippines, and so we do, she in four-inch heels and a flimsy dress, me in jeans and comfortable sandals, attracting more than a few glances from the ghostly old white guys who stare as we walk down the street. She is taller and heavier, an unusual twist on the typical large white man/small Asian woman couple I had grown used to seeing, and so—for that reason alone—we are an unusual pair.

Berlinda, it seems, has realized that my white face can help her get into the clubs where she is normally restricted. Suddenly, I have turned from sympathetic ear to entry ticket. She pulls me along surprisingly quickly for someone in such shoes, and finally comes to a stop in front of the Blue Nile. It is one of the big nightclubs on the end of the strip, its sign lit neon blue beneath a stone pharaoh's head at the door. Young women beckoning outside in gold lamé act as titillation for male passersby. The "Blue Nile Executive Hotel," conveniently across the street, is decorated in the same tacky Egyptian decor. "No unescorted ladies," the sign on the club reads. The aim is to keep out the freelancers like Berlinda who might want to compete (at a lower price) with the girls on offer from the bar inside. We walk in, and nobody stops us. We are escorting each other.

People seem to know her and some say hello. "I used to work here. Dancer," she explains, shouting over the music. "But other girls jealous of me, so I no work here now." It's one possible reason, I think, but Berlinda looks to be about fifteen to twenty pounds heavier than the scrawny girls dancing on the stage in their gold lamé bikinis, numbers pinned to their tops or bottoms so that men from the audience can order them easily. Berlinda looks older, too. The dancers all appear to be nineteen or twenty, and some younger than that. I understand why the industry and those who patronize them have always called them "girls" rather than women. Women, frankly, seems to be a word they might grow into when they are no longer this nubile and this young, but older, sexier, and more experienced. Like Berlinda. Full-breasted, lusty, and prone to holding back tears, she is a woman for sure.

It costs 1,000 pesos (US$18), paid to the bar, to take one of the girls to a back room or to the hotel across the street for short-time sex, Berlinda tells me. Then the bar pays the girl half of that, 500 pesos (US$9) commission. All the girls dancing in bikinis on stage in the high-end bars on this strip cost the same, and many lower-end bars, like the one with a sign advertising "Wanted Sexy Dancers," are cheaper. While dancing is what it's called, in actuality it is more like pacing. With about twenty or thirty girls on the stage at one time, there isn't much room for wild moves or showing off. The music thumping through the sound system at the Blue Nile is Eminem, Beyoncé, the usual hip hop and R&B—music that most young Filipinas, with a fondness for sappy love songs, hate. Some girls try to make sexy, half-hearted gyrations. But most just bop and shuffle, smile as seductively as they can, and try to catch a customer's eye so he will order their number from a passing waiter. Unlike in Thailand, no one is topless; it's illegal.

Berlinda tells me that 500 pesos for sex is what she made when she was dancing, too. "Sometimes they pay more if they like you, but up to them, like tip." I don't have the heart to ask her how much she, older, slightly overweight, and freelance, charges now. Most likely, it is whatever her customer will give her. Sometimes that might be a lot, and sometimes not very much. I wonder whether Berlinda also has to pay off a mama-san or pimp in exchange for being left alone to operate on the strip. But again, it seems rude to ask, and I don't think she'll tell me anyway.

Berlinda seems to believe in the fantasy—that someday this seedy strip will cough up a white knight to take her away and provide for her and her family. Whatever she has to do in the meantime to get by is a meaningless charade, not her real life or her true identity. If Berlinda can still get someone to pay 500 pesos, it ends up cheaper for the guy because he doesn't have to pay the bar fine. Plus, he would get the benefit of her years of experience. But most of the men patronizing this realm don't want experience. They want youth—rejuvenating, innocent, and naïve. At twenty-three, Berlinda is sadly over the hill compared to the skinny youthful flesh being offered.

Berlinda pulls me by the hand through the room, the strobe-lit stage on one end and the bar on the other, and cushy lounge chairs in between filled with men—most of them at least thirty years older than the dancers and all of them white—watching the stage. We are looking for the handsome American from the night before. Not here, apparently.

"Let's go," she says, and soon we are darting in and out of similar clubs along the strip, the only difference being the themed décor and the colors of the bikinis the girls wear on stage. To one after another we go. Not there either.

As she leads me hand-in-hand into the Cheetah's Lounge, we run into someone *I* know. I am surprised. The left-behind sex strip in the middle of the Philippines is the last place I expect to see an old acquaintance. But he is an old Asia hand who has been knocking around the region since the Vietnam War days. I guess I shouldn't be surprised. He is on vacation, he explains, alone. He invites Berlinda and me to join him for a drink.

The Cheetah's Lounge is somewhat different from the hard-core sex palaces a little further down the strip. The girls are packed onto the stage wearing their numbers here too, of course. But this bar has something of a perhaps unintentional, comical edge. The girls are in cheetah-print bikinis, with a kind of fringe over the pubis to resemble a costume out of *Tarzan* or the *Jungle Book*. The waitresses are in short-shorts of the same material, cut high enough in back so that their butt cheeks peek out the bottom. As one bends over to pour some drinks, I think, "Wilma Flintstone, rated R." I can't fathom why a distinguished old Asia hand would want to vacation here. The Philippines has lots to offer a tourist, but very little of it is in Angeles City. This place is miles from the beach, and there is nothing to do nearby but perhaps play a round of golf in 90-plus-degree heat. How much paid, anonymous sex would one want on holiday anyway? After a couple hours of watching scantily-clad girls pace around on stage, doesn't it get a little dull? Perhaps he just appreciates the comedy of the surroundings.

Berlinda, still holding my hand, cozies up next to me to overhear as he and I catch up on our news, and I try to explain what *I* am doing in such a place. He seems intrigued at the thought that Berlinda and I could be lesbians, and peppers me with leading questions. I am tempted to make up a story, but, being devoutly heterosexual and wanting to keep the truth as my reputation, I don't. Ah yes, I think, if I were a guy, social etiquette would call for us to be comparing boastful notes on last night's pussy. Berlinda seems intrigued by him. Here, at last, is a handsome white knight American worth bothering with. He looks rich, and if I am talking with him, maybe he could be good-hearted, too. She flashes a brilliant smile and joins the conversation, her long, dark, wavy hair cascading over my lap as she leans across.

"What?" says my old acquaintance.

"She said she thinks you're handsome," I say loudly. I'm not sure why I am acting as their go-between. Berlinda speaks English pretty well, and I hadn't had problems understanding her.

Berlinda tries again, moving her hand from my knee to his as she engages him in flirtatious pleasantry. With her other hand she keeps tugging the falling spaghetti straps from her misbehaving dress.

"Sorry, what?" he says. Perhaps he is too distracted by the dress and the breasts it keeps threatening to expose. Or perhaps the music is just too loud.

"She says she wants you to call her," I shout.

"It's really hard to understand her accent," he says. Nonetheless, she takes out her cell phone and he dutifully writes down her number. (Cell phones are cheap and ubiquitous in the Philippines, and even poor prostitutes have them.) I wonder what will happen between them when I go back to Manila.

Compared to other bars, the music at the Cheetah's Lounge is more tempered, too. As the three of us sit arm in arm on the faux-animal-print settee, a song that all the dancers know and like comes on, finally, and they begin swaying and singing aloud at the tops of their voices, their knees bending as they strain to the lyrics: "... *May you find that love that won't leave you/May you find it by the end of the day/You won't be lost, hurt, tired or lonely/Something beautiful will come your way* ..."

The song seems apropos, somehow, for young women facing the certainty that the loves they find here *will* leave them by the end of the day, and possibility that they will end up hurt, tired, and lonely, their souls lost along the way. I steal a glance at Berlinda, and she, too, is singing aloud, her eyes again turning wet before the characteristic swipe of her index fingers takes her tears away. When the song is over, she grasps my hand again, pulls me to my feet, and—with goodbyes and promises to call from my old acquaintance—she continues us on our mission.

Out on the street it has started to rain lightly. Our original handsome American—the focus of our quest—is still nowhere to be found, and we have been looking for him for some time now. Berlinda seems disappointed at the thought that (it being well after 10 PM) it is too late. He probably has engaged someone else for the evening. Men always have been a disappointment to her. When I ask if she had ever had a Filipino boyfriend she looks as if I had slapped her. "They rape me! Why I do anything with them?"

She'd like a nice American husband she says, but her most serious brush with one was nearly as painful, and her eyes start to moisten again as the story comes spilling out.

> I was married before to U.S. Air Force guy from Guam. He want me to go with him there but when I try to get papers, I find out marriage is FAKE! So I tell him come back, get me, because it is easy for him to travel and I cannot. But he don't come. He never come back. He just screw around with me, go with other girl. He phone me, he say, "Come without daughter just you only." So I say, "Fuck you!"

Berlinda is angry now, almost causing a scene in the street as we walk. "I like American husband, but not fucking guy like that one! I don't want my heart broke again. Any guy for me, he take my daughter, too."

I am not sure what to say. How does one respond to a woman's grief over a litany of rapists, assholes, and ghostly consumers of her body? I wish I could calm her, to tell her not to be angry—but, hell, who wouldn't be?

Suddenly, there is a strange smile on Berlinda's face as she looks over my shoulder and motions me to turn around. The man approaching is the youngest foreigner I have seen so far in Angeles City. Suddenly, Berlinda switches character and turns on her charms. "Richard!" she shouts, running up in the middle of the street and giving him a delighted squeeze.

"My ex-boyfriend," she declares excitedly. We are near the Champagne Bar, and we decide to go inside for a drink. "He was my boyfriend before," Berlinda whispers as Richard leads us to a table. "But he's a butterfly, go with lots of girls."

Richard appears to be in his thirties, what you might call a strapping lad, from the north of England. He is a somewhat monosyllabic fellow, or perhaps it is just shyness around women. He confirms that he works in the Philippines. "Sort of," he says. Doing *what*, he won't say. He likes it here, he says. He doesn't talk much; it seems to strain him. I imagine that bar girls are probably less-demanding conversationalists, and that he isn't used to questions. Perhaps he's a dropout—like the other ghostly men of Fields Avenue, but twenty years too early. Or a scraping-by businessman. Or a spy. Lots of spies work in the Philippines, as the Muslim insurgency in the south is developing links to al-Qaeda. Angeles City is the old heart of the Philippines' military installations, even though the U.S. military is gone. And Richard does have a rugged-protector sort of demeanor that one imagines in a secret agent man. I will never find out. The following week, walking down Khao San Road in Bangkok, I will pass him. I will turn around and call his name. He won't hear, or won't want to. Maybe Richard is not his real name. Or maybe it won't be him, instead just one of thousands of young white men trying to disappear in Asia.

The Champagne Bar is a small, narrow railcar of a place, with a stage running all along one side, mirrors along the other, and room for only one row of tables in between. I tell Richard how much I like Berlinda, and I throw in that I think she is beautiful. "Yah, she used to be," he agrees. I cringe and hope Berlinda didn't overhear. She looks down and adjusts her straps again. Whether her self-consciousness is due to the dress or to Richard, I can't know. We are seated at the foot of the stage, where yet another multitude of girls in rainbow-hued bikinis is swaying above us to the music. I begin to think there must be a monopoly issuer of go-go bar bikinis, all exactly the same but for the color.

As Berlinda and Richard chat, I meet our waitress. Elaine is from a large, poor family in the neighboring province, Tarlac, and she has a cheerful but plain, "girl-next-door, who you would trust to feed your dog" kind of look. She wears a long-sleeved, peach-colored uniform. It has a high neck, but cuts off just below the pelvis and, other than legs, it shows little skin compared to the bikini-clad girls on the stage. Because Elaine's skirt is so short, however, her white underwear is visible when she sits down.

Elaine and her fellow waitresses make 75 pesos (US$1.36) a day for showing up for work and urging customers to buy drinks, and they can be "bar fined," she says. As is the case for every girl working in the bar, customers can offer the bar 1,000 pesos for her—that's what Elaine pays in rent per month to share a room with three other girls—of which she will get to keep 500 pesos (US$9) in exchange for sex. It hasn't happened yet in the two months she has worked at Champagne, she says, looking down at her flat chest, obscured by heavy fabric, as if by way of explanation. But she is open to the possibility if somebody who isn't too fat or ugly wants to have sex with her. After all, she says, she is doing this job to make as much money as possible. And 500 pesos is a week's pay. Plus, there's the possibility of a tip if the customer likes her and is generous, she can say no if she doesn't like the look of him. She had a Filipino boyfriend before so she is not a virgin. "I only had sex one time, though," she confides. At twenty-six, she is older than Berlinda, but is years younger in life experience.

"What about that guy? Would you go with him," I ask her, gesturing toward an enormous white man with fat rolls both above and below his belt and a white beard covering the bulge underneath his chin. He seems to suffer from the type of obesity that has its origins in genetics rather than diet. It is difficult for him to sit on a chair without the bulk of his midsection burgeoning off the seat, and it is only because both legs are planted wide apart on the floor in front of him that is he upright.

"He comes here a lot. We call him Santa Claus and say, 'Hey Santa, what are you doing here so early?' No, I wouldn't go. But he likes to go with somebody else anyway." Elaine points to a stocky woman with a certain toughness about her. The woman is in jeans and a black T-shirt, seemingly the type who would be at home at a heavy metal concert or on the back of a Harley. The music blasting in the bar is Joan Jett's "I Love Rock and Roll," and soon the biker girl is putting on a little dance show in front of the man, making eye contact while gyrating in front of his open, obese legs and mouthing the lyrics: *Can I take you home where we can be alone?*"

He appears amused in a way that, surely, comes more easily and often to high school football captains and the sharp-dressed GQ-Esquires of the world than to the morbidly obese. The biker babe's attention has allowed him to feel, if only for a while, like an attractive man. I wonder if there is something allegorical in the forlorn, obese white man purchasing the affections and flesh of a young Asian woman in order to experience fleeting desirability. But then imagining the logistics of a sexual consummation causes me quickly to banish the thought. Surely she can handle him, I decide, as long as she remains on top. Maybe even if she doesn't.

I TURN BACK TO BERLINDA and Richard to see another woman approach their side of the table, a dancer from the stage who has just removed her number. It seems Richard has purchased her. She joins us for a drink.

The girl is small, young, sultry, and dark, with big almond eyes, a broad nose, and pouty red lips, which she covers with her hand when she speaks. When she tells me where she comes from (she also is from Tarlac), I realize why she seems so demure. Her right front tooth is missing. No matter, she tries not to speak much anyway. Like Richard. Perfect for him. Soon they will go to a back room for sex. I look to Berlinda for explanation. "We're just friends now," she protests, and says she doesn't care. But it seems she does. Finally, Berlinda's misbehaving dress has so annoyed her that she stands up and declares that she will be right back. She is going to go change.

As Richard and the toothless girl nuzzle wordlessly, Elaine and I keep talking shop. Some bar girls, including Berlinda, are embarrassed by the subject of money, but Elaine seems to enjoy quantifying things. She seems like the kind of person who could end up running this bar someday. She explains that, apart from the possibility of a man taking her out for the "bar fine" and her daily wage, there is one other way for her to make money—if someone buys her a drink. For every 125 peso (US$2.73) "ladies drink" that someone buys her, she gets to keep 50 pesos (US$0.90) commission. I offer to buy her a drink.

"Really?!?!" she exclaims. Apparently, I am the first to ever do so. It seems perfectly reasonable to me. Here I am, taking up her time and sharing her secrets. The prospect of increasing her daily take-home pay by nearly 67 percent makes her jubilant.

She jumps off the seat and runs to the bar, perhaps afraid I might change my mind if she dallies. While she is gone, word spreads. Suddenly my status in the bar has changed: the white guy I initially had walked in with had purchased a dancer, the prostitute we came with was gone, too, and here I was buying a ladies' drink for a plain, never-bought-out waitress with more business sense than sex appeal. This prompts the bar dyke to head straight for me. Many bars employ at least one stocky, spiky-haired woman for foreign lesbians. At such moments, it becomes clear that in Asia's infamous red-light districts all tastes can be accommodated. I chat with the woman briefly and determine that she is from Mindanao, like Berlinda. Just then Berlinda returns, and I note that they both are from the same island. They confer for a moment and conclude that their respective hometowns are far away—meaning that they are likely from entirely different ethnic groups, too. Mindanao has about a dozen ethnicities, and tour operators there commonly offer trips to see "tribal people." Displaced and, as an ethnic minority, most likely out-statused, the bar dyke cedes her ground and leaves.

Berlinda's clothing change has transformed her into someone suddenly bright and cheerful. She is wearing tight, low-rise jeans and a cropped black T-shirt that, while imprinted with a faded "Versace Jeans Couture," is so threadbare that it allows the white bra that she has put on to show through. The shirt also allows her ample midriff room to swell just a bit over her thick-belted waistline. I admire her comfort with her body. She starts dancing between the tables. "Come, I teach you," she says, pulling me up beside her. She shimmies like a belly dancer with the ferocity of a paint mixer. There is no way I can move that fast, I think, even to get out of the way of speeding traffic. Elaine joins us, and she can shimmy, too.

As Richard and his toothless dancer sit close together watching us, Berlinda decides it is time to leave. I reach to pay the bill for Elaine's drink, which looks vaguely like a White Russian or a Bailey's. I ask what it is. "Chocolate milk," she says, grinning like a kid. Berlinda grabs my hand before I can move to pay for my beer and her pineapple juice. At 43 pesos each (US$0.78), they are absurdly cheap anyway. "Richard can pay," she says, dragging me out of the bar and declaring that we now need to find more men to buy us drinks. Between her ex-boyfriend and my old acquaintance, we had made out well on the last two rounds.

"I am so glad I met you," she purrs, clinging to my arm as though I am the substitute for her lost sister. "You are so nice."

"You are, too," I say.

"Not always," she replies tartly. "Depends on how I feel."

As she smiles impishly, I notice the moistness of her eyes again, and the practiced swipe of her index fingers. She is cheerful now, but her eyes are still watering. I start to wonder if Berlinda is afflicted not by a propensity for sadness but by an eye condition.

Soon we are at the last bar of the night. It is a disco with a raised center stage in the round. There is a 50-peso cover charge and, of course, I pay. I buy drinks, too. They are playing the usual Eminem, Nelly, and Mary J. Blige songs, *Without Me, Hot in Here,* and *Family Affair,* the bar anthems of 2003–2004. Berlinda insists that I dance with her. She shimmies and wipes her teary eyes with her index fingers. Definitely a condition.

It seems that we have come to the bar where a locally popular band plays after midnight, and where girls who haven't found customers for the night end up for a drink and companionship before heading home alone. There are a few old white men looking for one last try as well but, by now, most have gone to bed with their pick of the evening. As the band sets up on the center stage, Berlinda senses I am starting to think about my departure. I note the late hour and tease her about whether she should get some sleep to be able to get up in time for church in the morning.

"Even I don't go to church, I have God in my heart," she says. Berlinda prays a lot, it seems. It's logical. Having a profession that puts you in emotional and sometimes physical danger must surely prompt the desire for divine protection.

"Can you do favor for me?" Berlinda asks. "Can I borrow 200 pesos? I pay you back."

"But I don't know when I will come back here," I reply. Just at that moment I sense that I have misunderstood Berlinda's question. I immediately regret it.

"Okay, 100 pesos?" she pleads.

We sit in silence as the band begins its first set. Part of me feels hurt that our new friendship has been reduced to a financial transaction. Or perhaps that was the intent all along; but if that is the case, it is an absurdly small amount to ask for. She wants less than US$4— US$3.63 to be exact, about the price of a coffee at Starbucks, but almost three days' pay for girlie bar waitresses. We both know she wouldn't pay me back.

I think about it for a moment. I have taken up Berlinda's entire evening, preventing her from finding a customer who could have paid her more than double her request. It is simple, really. I have money, she doesn't. Why wouldn't a friend share what she has? I open my wallet and hand her first the 100 pesos and then another 100. I consider giving her more, but I don't want to hurt her feelings by being patronizing. She asked for 200, I would give her 200. We watch in silence as the band plays another song.

After awhile, it is clear that there is no more to say. I turn to give her a hug and a kiss on the cheek. I wish her luck. "Call me," she instructs, holding her fist to her ear in mock-telephone style in a futile attempt to restore girlfriendly relations. We both know that the camaraderie we had has been ruined by money. It is worth it to her, as it is unlikely that I will ever return. There will be no other means to keep in contact. Berlinda doesn't have email. She doesn't know how to use a computer—I know because I had asked her if she ever considered signing up to be a mail-order bride. She answered that she would like to, but that you have to know how to email.

I hope that the white knight she desires will come for her soon.

A FEW DAYS LATER I am standing outside the Quiapo (pronounced Key-AH-po) church in Manila. The church is formally named the *Basilika ng Nazareno* (Basilica of the Nazarene) because it holds a life-sized ebony statue of the sacred image that was first brought to Manila by the Spanish in 1767. It is barely nightfall, and the two towers flanking the Baroque façade of the church are bathed in creamy yellow light, and gnats and bugs whizzing and circling in the glare.

The plaza in front is teeming and festive. And this is an ordinary weekday, not even the weekly devotional day that draws thousands of people making offerings to the Black Nazarene. Market sellers are doing a brisk trade in mangos, dried fish, and boiled *balut* eggs (inside is a baby chick that had been just about to hatch) for eight pesos (US$0.14).

Among the vendors, actually lined up along the periphery with the stalls selling religious beads and candles, are the herbalists. As I stand in front of one of their carts observing the stacks of what look like enormous basil leaves, dried roots, various plants, and bottles of medicinal oils, I think of Berlinda. In a country like the Philippines, where the teachings of the Catholic Church hold enormous sway over politics and keep abortion illegal, perhaps thousands of women like her—who have been raped or who don't want to have their lives disrupted by having babies—have stood exactly where I am standing now, in front of these carts.

One of the concoctions, a dark liquid in a glass bottle, is marked *Pampa Regla*. It is a "period regulator," returning menstrual flow to women who have lost it through pregnancy or other causes. But that's just the mild stuff, considered somewhat unreliable anyway. I am interested in the hard stuff.

"Do you have Cytotec?" I ask the grey-haired woman selling the herbs. She is surprised and looks at me quizzically.

"How do you know about Cytotec?" she asks.

I tell her that a friend told me. Actually, it is common knowledge among Filipinos that, if you want to abort a baby, you go to Quiapo Church, find the herbalists, ask for Cytotec. It is not designed to be an abortion drug. Manufactured by G.D. Searle & Co., it is prescribed to treat and prevent stomach ulcers. But if you search for Cytotec on the Internet, the first item that comes up is a warning from the U.S. Food and Drug Administration: "ADMINISTRATION TO WOMEN WHO ARE PREGNANT CAN CAUSE ABORTION." Lest that sound like an endorsement, it continues with a frightening fact: "UTERINE RUPTURE HAS BEEN REPORTED WHEN CYTOTEC WAS ADMINISTERED IN PREGNANT WOMEN TO INDUCE LABOR OR INDUCE ABORTION BEYOND THE EIGHTH WEEK OF PREGNANCY."

Because no one knows exactly how much to take, hundreds and perhaps thousands of Philippine women every year end up in hospitals hemorrhaging of ruptured uteruses because of the drug. A feminist I know who writes a column for the *Philippine Daily Inquirer,* Rina Jiminez-David, has spoken to doctors about the fact that an estimated 400,000 Filipinas a year have illegal abortions, and of those, around 500 or so die, many from Cytotec-induced uterine rupture. "Doctors tell me that if a woman comes in with complications, they let her bleed for a while, just to teach her a lesson," she had told me, adding that some die as a result. "There's a whole attitude that is punitive and judgmental against these women."

The herbalist I am speaking to now takes a good look at me and decides I could be Cytotec material. I can see her mental calculations: No obvious health problems, possibly pregnant but not too pregnant. In the pre-Spanish Philippines, such women, called Babaylan, held enormous power in their communities. They were sexual women who cured people. The Spanish denounced them as witches and persecuted them. Now their modern-day equivalents merely sell herbs from carts in front of Qiapo Church. She takes a careful look around to make sure no one is watching and unzips a pouch around her waist. The sheet of pills she produces has an aluminum backing printed, Cytotec, 20mg. There are three left. "You only need one," she says. Cherry had told me, in one of our discussions at the bar, about a friend who was so desperate not to have a baby that she took six. She barely lived.

"One hundred twenty pesos," the herbalist says.

Probably this is a foreigner's price, and she would sell it to a Filipina for less. But still, even without attempting to bargain, US$2.18 for an over-the-counter abortion seems cheap. No wonder it is popular. I beg off and tell the herbalist I was just investigating the price and availability.

I wonder whether, for US$2.18—a little more than half of the amount I gave Berlinda at the bar—her life could have been different. Without a baby she could have finished high school, married as most Philippine women do, and likely found a job using her mind or hands instead of her body. That is not to say Berlinda would have wanted an abortion even if it were an option. She is a Catholic. Catholic beliefs oppose abortion. But it isn't clear how closely she would have adhered to them as a young, vulnerable rape victim. The one time during the evening with her when I tried to broach the subject of whether she had wanted the child, she refused to let her mind or her heart go there. How could she? What happened in the past is the past. She loves her daughter now, and making a living to provide for her is all that matters.

As I start to leave, I pause briefly at the large Mercury Drug at the edge of the square. It strikes me that, in contrast to the *Pampa Regla* on clear display for sale nearby, there are no condoms visibly for sale here. There hadn't been any at the small market I passed on the strip on Fields Avenue either. Rina, the columnist, had told me that condoms are available somewhere under a back counter if you ask for them, but that not too many people—and especially not women—are comfortable asking.

Supermarkets and 7-Elevens, which are plentiful in Philippine cities, don't sell condoms at all. The reason is because a group called "Couples for Christ" organized a boycott in 2002, after 7-Eleven positioned condoms—like it does in every other Asian country where it operates—on the counter next to the cash register. That promotes promiscuity, the group argued, and "Couples for Christ" sent schoolchildren from Catholic schools out to promote a boycott instead. The result was so devastating for 7-Eleven that the company decided not to sell condoms at all. Supermarkets joined in the decision. As a result, finding condoms in the Philippines is no easy task.

The pill is legal and, as in the United States, it requires a doctor's prescription. Unlike in the United States, however, because the Philippines is a heavily Roman Catholic country and the church bans artificial contraceptives, social pressures actively discourage women from taking them.

A professional woman I know in Manila was aghast one day in 2003, when the female president of the Philippines publicly blamed mood swings on having used artificial contraception when she was younger. "For all you know, I became ill-tempered because I took birth control pills," President Arroyo had barked testily.[5] She was half joking but, rising as she does to attend 8 AM mass every day, she has made clear her opposition to anything but strict church teachings and the Church-approved, less-effective rhythm method. Lest the public think she is priggish, however, she has stated publicly, as well, that she and her husband have an active sex life.

Arroyo gets low marks among feminists because of her anti-artificial-contraception stance and her positions on issues that affect women in general. The burgeoning population is a huge social problem in the Philippines. The unemployment rate was 11.4 percent in 2004, and the population of 84 million people was growing 2.4 percent a year—the highest rate in Southeast Asia. The Philippines also has the highest land density in the region. There are simply not enough jobs or enough land for everyone born in the country: there are 300 people per square kilometer in the Philippines but only 80 people per square kilometer in Malaysia, and 130 in both Indonesia and Thailand. Those numbers correspond with relative wealth per person as well; 70 percent of Filipinos live below the poverty line.

No matter—Arroyo has stated that if Filipinos keep having babies at this unsustainable growth rate, they can just export them to jobs overseas as health care workers or domestic workers.[6] It is true that the 8 million workers already abroad send home billions of dollars and keep the economy afloat—US$7.6 billion in 2003. Every day, however, 2,000 Filipinos, including many of the best-educated minds, leave the country and their families behind and don't return for years, if ever.

Many who leave are uneducated domestic helpers and entertainers, but also included are the country's best doctors, nurses, engineers, and transport specialists. In the Philippines, a doctor earns around US$400 a month. In the United States, nurses alone can make ten times that amount, US$4,000 a month,[7] and U.S. quotas allow 50,000 foreign nurses to enter every year. For so many Filipinas, going abroad as workers or as wives is the only means to get ahead. It is a mentality instilled by their mothers and by the influence of TV.

José Rizal, the Philippines' famous novelist and social critic, blames Philippine women for perpetuating the colonial mentality, for giving children "the message that foreign is high-tech, foreign is powerful, foreign is desirable and good. They exhort their children to get good grades in school so they can go abroad to earn dollars," he writes. "They have allowed themselves to become the conveyor belt of colonialism and the many problems it has spawned."[8]

Rizal's solution, laid out in the Rosales saga—four novels dealing with Philippine history is the path taken by his novels' heroine, Ermita, a prostitute born from the rape of her *mestizo* mother by a foreign conqueror. Ermita had screwed her way to the top, achieving the prized goal of a rich American husband. But she returns to the Philippines and to her real childhood love: a Filipino man. By rejecting prostitution and her foreign husband and returning home, she finds pride and dignity, and her Filipina identity.[9]

SUCH A SOLUTION is nowhere in evidence as I visit the Café Havana again on my last night in Manila. As usual, the Filipinas are working the foreign businessmen at the bar. Some are professionals like Berlinda, and others, like Cherry and the sandwich girl, are something in between. All want love and a ticket abroad but will settle for money if that's the best offer of the night. I notice an Australian, a lugubrious man close to sixty or maybe older, wearing a wedding ring. He is alone. He is trying to chat up a twenty-three year old, trying to get her to come back to his hotel for a drink, with or without the girlfriend she has with her.

The girl is cute and sweet. She tells me she already has a boyfriend in America, much younger than this fellow. Probably richer, too. If there were a better prospect in sight, then she might trade up—but not for an old, married Australian. She tells him she doesn't want to leave. This creates an opening for a slightly haggard pro, a woman seemingly in her forties who, from her exposed, stretch-marked midriff, it seems has had at least one child if not more. She is brazen and crass. She tries stroking the Australian—asking where he is from, if he wants a date. He tries to get rid of her. When she identifies me as a friendly place of refuge, she comes over to regroup before trying him again. Her fleshy stomach presses into my forearm as she makes physical contact, leaning in close on my lap. It is not unpleasant, but then I am not her target as the Australian man is. She tries him once again.

At around one o'clock in the morning I turn to leave, ending my glimpse into this complex world of screwing and sexual power—of guiltless sexual freedoms versus Catholic and social mores; of the unavailability of condoms and social obstacles to the pill; of the illegality of abortions but the incidence of 400,000 of them every year; of a female president who denounces the pill but condones an active sex life. It seems paradoxical and confusing, these choices and the lack of them for a Filipina, these contrasts of Eastern culture and Western religion. I leave with more questions than I had when I arrived.

THE AUSTRALIAN FOLLOWS ME OUT and invites me for a drink. Having been spurned by the twenty-three year old and then spurning the aggressive prostitute in turn, this man is trying a last pathetic attempt at Manila companionship. I decline, and ask why he wasn't interested in the woman coming on to him. "Bleeeeeeeeeh!" he exclaims, giving an exaggerated shudder and walking off alone into the night. Sometimes, I gather, even desperate white men know when the tables are turned, and when to avoid both screwing and getting screwed.

Who's Playing Whom

IN ASIA, the East-West cultural divide, gender divisions, as well as economic disparity make it hard to figure out who is playing whom in the games of sex and power between Western men and Asian women. Misimpressions, stereotypes, and cultural misunderstandings color the perspectives of both sides, and the spaces where the perspectives meet are blurred. I have observed this on a small scale in interactions in more than a dozen major cities in Asia. But in a few places it is so glaringly pervasive, it merits chronicling. We have seen some dimensions in Manila. Okinawa, Japan; Bangkok and Pattaya, Thailand; and Jakarta, Indonesia add more complexity.

Okinawa, Japan

At the Globe & Anchor club at Camp Butler, Okinawa, the haze of testosterone is so dense you can almost smell it. It is the scent of power, raw strength, and libido, of several hundred men solo on a Saturday night—men at the peak of their reproductive capacity. There are thirty-seven U.S. military bases with more than 25,000 American troops on Okinawa, Japan's version of Hawaii at the southern end of the Japanese islands. On a Saturday night, Camp Butler is ground zero for the social life of the island's 15,500 Marines (most of them between eighteen and twenty-two years old). The Marines from the other bases come here if they don't go into Okinawa City, the capital Naha, or the bar and red-light district called "The Gate" along a street outside Gate 2 of Kadena Air Base. They are on the prowl.

But these Marines are not only hunters, they are also prey.

The Japanese women here use connections to get through the gates. Someone with a base ID, coordinating with cell phones, meets them and signs them in. The Japanese woman who escorted me in wanted me to see what really goes on. She is married to an African-American herself, so she is not passing any judgment, she said, but some of these girls are really out of control in trying to hook up with an American guy. Japanese women even come to Okinawa on vacation from Tokyo just to have sex with them, she said, much as it was in vogue for them to go to Hawaii and have sex with American surfer dudes ten years ago,[1] and to Bali and Thailand to have sex with local men there today. These stories about American soldiers raping girls in Japan, she said, well, you ought to see what goes on at the Globe & Anchor, see what *the women* are doing.

Of course, there is no excuse—anywhere, anytime, ever—for rape. When a girl says, "No," it means stop. Full stop. This woman's point, however, was that painting Japanese women as the passive, innocent victims of aggressive American soldiers does them a disservice. It's not only the American men who are the aggressors in Okinawa, she said; somebody ought to write about that!

The girls she is talking about are known as *ame-jo,* "American-(loving) girls," and their large subset, *koku-jo,* "black-(loving) girls." These are girls who sit under tanning lights or decline to sit—as most Asians prefer—in the shade at the beach. They cornrow their hair like Snoop Dogg or kink it like Beyoncé; get surgical implants in their buttocks and breasts; learn dance moves by watching MTV; and wear the skimpy hip-hop fashions that they see in specialty magazines dedicated just to them. Some are big girls, heavy-set, and even tomboys, who find that Japanese men—who generally prefer baby-doll cute as their sexual aesthetic—aren't attracted to them, and vice versa.

Hip-hop groupies have something of a cult status in Japan. These girls got bling—or at least think they do. I gawked at one who brushed past me and plunged into the realm of the hip-hop room in high heels. Her hair, dyed Mariah Carey honey brown, was pulled high into a pony tail, and she wore rose-tint sunglasses, a skimpy halter, and the shortest white short-shorts I had ever seen, so high they ended at the middle of her well-tanned buttocks and exposed their lower ends as she walked. She might well have been less provocative if wearing nothing at all. I asked the bouncers, one of them a big guy from New York City wearing a large gold chain and pendant over his T-shirt, if they thought her efforts had been a success. "She *think* she a

"Koku-jo"
(black-loving girls)
images from *Luire*
magazine, Tokyo,
April 2003

ten," one said with the yawning disinterest of someone who had seen it all. "Back home she be a six."

They're not the only *ame-jo* here, however, just the most numerous, darting in and out of the hip-hop room, the biggest in the three-dance-floor club where amps the size of postal trucks pound with the pulsing beat of Ja Rule, Nelly, Jay Z, and Mary J. Blige.

The Marines in the hip-hop room, mostly men but a few tables of women as well, are mostly black. In the other rooms, the Marines segregate themselves by music and race as well: there's a Latin room playing salsa, samba, and meringue, where the men are mostly of Hispanic origin.

And there's a third room where they blast good ol' down-home rock 'n' roll. This one is the least popular with Japanese girl groupies. Somehow, word has gotten around that if you hook up with a white guy you meet in there and end up married, he'll take you to some rural trailer park somewhere in the South where you have to live in poverty.

The Latin room is hip, however, in the groupie hierarchy. The guys at least live in big cities back in America, New York, maybe, or Miami,

or L.A., and the music is cool and sexy. The girls here, of course, are trying to look Latina—large hoop earrings, hair slicked back and knotted like tango dancers, and swishy skirts to salsa in, as opposed to the shorts and hip-hugging pants of the hip-hop room. I meet one girl named Emiko, twenty-six, who has a Cuban-American boyfriend. On this particular night he is away on rotation, so Emiko has come with her fellow students from her international tourism courses at the university to salsa and enjoy the music. "Don't take this the wrong way," she says in perfectly colloquial English, "but a lot of the white guys don't have rhythm. I need a guy with rhythm." She plans to marry her boyfriend, she says, but neither set of parents approves of this relationship, even though the couple is living together off-base.

Emiko is Okinawan, an ethnic minority in Japan. Okinawans have wider eyes and tend to be shorter, darker, and broader than the Japanese, as they are ethnically related to the indigenous people of Taiwan.[2] Traditionally, women held higher status here than they did in the rest of Samurai-ruled Japan. Okinawa was part of China until 1872, and is as close geographically to China and Taiwan (300 miles) as it is to Tokyo. White-clad priestesses still conduct Okinawan religious ceremonies. The culture and cuisine have Chinese influence, and the language is as different from Japanese as Italian is from French, sharing cognates but not mutually intelligible.

Traditionally, Okinawans lived together before marriage—sometimes as early as age thirteen—at the girl's family home, and they legalized the marriage and moved out only upon the birth of a child. Before then, the couple could separate at any time. Today, Okinawa has a higher rate of divorce, birth, and single motherhood than does the rest of Japan.

Many older Okinawans maintain an avid dislike of the military—20 percent of Okinawa's civilian population was killed, many by Japanese atrocities, during the infamous World War II battle. Many also view the crowding of so many U.S. bases into such a relatively small island as an act of racism by the "superior" Japanese imposing its defense burden on a minority people. That's why Emiko's family doesn't want her marrying military. She hopes to persuade them otherwise, however; it has taken time to train this boyfriend of hers, and she doesn't feel like starting over: "At first he thought I would do certain things, like walk three steps behind him, but I didn't act like that. We are equals in the relationship now, but it took one year to teach him that. Now he listens to me." But Emiko was already experiencing the type of tension I had heard about from other Japanese-American couples. She wants to keep going out on Saturday nights. That's why she hooked up with an American in the first place. It's fun. She likes to dance. Her boyfriend, however, wants to stay home and settle down.

It is harder to talk with the *koku-jo* girls in the hip-hop room. It is louder. The girls have attitude, perched in poses at the edge of the dance floor waiting for their black knights to sweep them off their feet. They don't want to ruin the affect by acting all friendly, especially when, in their experience, foreign women don't act friendly toward them. The pumping music is J. Lo's *"Even if you were broke, my love don't cost a thing . . ."*

ONLY BECAUSE MY ESCORT IS MARRIED to an African-American herself can I penetrate this barrier somewhat. Not with the hottest of the scantily-clad hot chicks here to be pursued and bedded, but with a sweet young thing called Chika. She is twenty-seven and she could be a light-skinned black woman, except that she says she is a full-blooded Okinawan. Her hair is permed into wavelets, and she wears a zippered sweat jacket over her revealing halter and hip-huggers. She knows my escort, and so she agrees to talk with me.

Next to the hip-hop room is a restaurant decorated like a '50s-style diner serving cheap hamburgers, Cokes, and milkshakes, where the young men who want to take a girl away from the throbbing dance floor and negotiate what comes next can find some quiet while proving that they are not cheapskates who'll just invite a girl out to the parking lot. That's where we go.

Chika is big and somewhat buxom, so she didn't need breast or buttocks implants, but she says a lot of her friends have them. She likes to try out her English, which is halting but is improving with her frequent trips to the Globe & Anchor.

> I try to have conversations with guys, but they just ask the same questions, like "How old are you?" and "Do you have a boyfriend?" or "Do you like black guys?" Off-base there are too many other girls, from Tokyo, so that's why we come here. There are more men here.

She means that the Tokyo girls are more sophisticated, out for sex; Okinawan girls have a bit of an inferiority complex in competing with them. Plus, unlike Tokyo girls, they live here and want to meet boyfriend-material and ultimately husband-material guys. They're not on sex vacations. The Marines, however, usually don't know the difference.

> Meeting a guy at a club, it's not good. We know that. But we don't really have any other opportunity to meet them. Some of the American girls don't like us, so we can't talk to them. They're mean to us. I try to talk to them, but they just ignore me. We're competition.

Chika used to have an American boyfriend, but she is single now. She wouldn't mind another one. The hip-hop world is exciting, and Okinawa, where she has lived her whole life, is otherwise just a dull tropical island with a few war museums and beach resorts. "American men seem so sweet. They know how to treat a woman. Japanese guys don't know how to talk about their feelings. But American guys do. They say, 'I love you,' things like that." Plus, my escort informs me, Japanese girls think black guys are better in bed than Japanese men. That's a big part of what drives this scene.

Technically, there is no difference in the Japanese language between the words "like" and "love," both of which translate as *suki*. That has a lot of Japanese declaring their love prematurely to an American when they really only meant to say, "I like you," and Japanese girls thinking their American beau loves them when he really only meant to point to the word "like" in the dictionary. Japanese guys typically don't use the word until they're ready to marry a girl, and often not even then.

But in Chika's mind, even though it's good that American men talk about their feelings, they throw their words around too easily and just use them to get what they can. "They're just enjoying Okinawan women while they're here. They're just trying to use us. They want to know if we have a car, so we can take them out to shops or take them around. I had one boyfriend say, 'I love you. I'll call you.' But after a few weeks he didn't call anymore. Now I don't know where he is." This is puzzling to Chika. How can a guy who loves you not call you anymore? American guys' feelings, even though they share them more readily, must not mean very much.

When I had met with Suzuyo Takazato, a member of the local City Assembly who keeps a close eye on these "institutionalized international relations," as she called them, in her work as an activist trying to reduce U.S. military presence in Okinawa, she told me Chika's experience was common. "If you interview Japanese women here, they all say they want to meet American boys. It's normal. They see American movies and want to meet someone who looks like a movie star. People say, 'Since the Americans are there, why don't we use them, learn English from them?'" she said.

"Japanese women say American men are very sweet, very gentle, very good at sharing their feelings. It is true in a way. But they want free sex, free meals. Using words doesn't cost money. When they meet Okinawan girls, they say, 'You have lovely eyes, lovely smile.' That is not familiar to Japanese women," she continued. "Japanese men don't think this is a way of showing affection. So we can't calculate whether this is true love or not."

Next I meet Yukari, a twenty-one year old with cornrow hair extensions. She does them herself every couple of days, she says, then takes them out to wash her hair and then braid it again. "I'm a tomboy," she says, explaining her presence and penchant for hip-hop style. "Japanese guys don't like me. I'm not really here to pick up anybody, just to have fun. But if somebody talks to me, I'll consider it." Judging by the hundreds of men in the room getting worked up into sexual competition with every pint of beer and scantily clad, passing *koku-jo*, somebody talking to Yukari at some point during this evening is a sure bet.

From the Marines' point of view, this is a dangerous game. "A lotta guys really love this," explains an enlisted man named Jamal—who has fixed on the only blonde in the room, me, as the evening's most interesting possibility. "These Japanese girls, they go home with you, and they don't ask you later, 'Where you been? Who you been out with?' But you gotta be careful. They're trying to get pregnant so you'll take 'em to America." Every good Marine, he says, carries his own condoms.

A few days later, I get more of the American perspective on what happens after club closing time from a white, twenty-three-year-old army sergeant from Alaska. He has been a bouncer at Shooters, a hip-hop club on "The Gate" at Kadena Air Base, for a while now and has been stationed on Okinawa for several years. The area roared during the Vietnam War with men passing through on their way to and from combat. Though The Gate is much tamer now, it still has prostitutes and live sex shows, as well as the Japanese *ame-jo* girls. Obviously the *ame-jo* are the men's first choice, as their company is free and they sometimes have cars. "I've seen it all," the young sergeant begins.

Mostly at The Gate, these guys are all Marines, a few Army. The Air Force guys are strange; they never come out. There's a lot of guys just out of high school, eighteen, nineteen. Guys are sluts. They'll sleep with anything that moves. In the barracks, there are these guys, you hear them with the Japanese girls. The girls just kind of lay there and take it, all kind of subservient-like, screaming and making squeaking sounds like about how "big" it is, like it hurts so bad because it's so big. The Japanese guys, I've seen a lot of Japanese porno videos, and the guys are really small. But in *anime* [animation], they've got these big "tree trunks" coming out of their laps and the girls have these huge tits, and they're making 'em scream in pain because they're so big, and that's what these girls are acting out with American guys, this fantasy, like they're supposed to scream like that. So the rest of the day you hear these guys elbowing each other, like, "I made her scream all night," so it's like an ego thing, domination and all that.

But these Japanese women, a lot of them, they're over thirty, they've been around for a while. They know exactly what they're looking for. A lot of them are just looking to have sex, whereas a lot of the Americans, they're young kids. And they're like, "Why don't you call me? What are you up to?" wanting a serious relationship and all that. But Japanese women don't call you. They make you want to call them, be with them, with this whole subservient act. It's really manipulation, because they're really trying to get the guys to marry them. I'm not into that submissive-manipulative thing. I grew up with strong women, my mother and my sister. In my house growing up, you want some food, you make it yourself. I can't be with someone who doesn't speak English. For me, it's fifty-fifty equals. A friend of mine was like, "I lost my English-Japanese dictionary. How am I going to talk to my girlfriend?" Just to talk, they're like every five seconds looking in the dictionary. The girls are trying to get the guys to marry them so they can come to America. I don't blame them. It's kind of boring for them over here.

The Filipina girls here, too. Same thing. There over here on six-month visas working in the clubs and they've got six months to find an American husband. The mama-sans down the street at Moonlight try to grab the guys as they go by, get them to come in and pay $20 a drink. These single guys they've got money, so they do it. To go home with a Filipina girl from there is $150. If you want to date them, you have to do it on the side, but you know that every

Friday-Saturday night they're back at the club going home with somebody else. The ones who get married and go to the States end up trying to bring their whole family over, parents, brothers, sisters, cousins. Then once she's got a green card, she'll divorce you. You're just a ticket! The minute you marry them, they stop this whole subservient thing, and they're like a total bitch. A lot of guys are like, "Whoa, what happened!?!"

You know why these girls like the black guys? Because they see all these music videos and all think these guys all have a million dollars. And if they don't have a million dollars, they're going to have a million dollars when they go home and make their rap video.

I get more of the Japanese women's perspective on all this from the abandoned mothers at Annette Eddie-Callagain's law office. She is an African-American lawyer in Okinawa trying to track down American deadbeat dads, both white and black, who father children here. If they're still in the military, she tries to get their C.O.s to get them to fess up. But most have left active duty, making it harder to track them and attach their incomes for child support. "Women come in, they're crying, the kids are crying, she's about to get evicted, the baby needs diapers, milk, and he's gone," Annette says.

A lot of them are dictionary relationships. I say "dictionary relationships" because they need a dictionary to communicate. A lot of those are doomed from the beginning. It's hard enough in relationships, and in these there's no communication. There are a lot of cultural problems. In Japanese relationships, once a baby is born, all her attention goes to the baby. The baby sleeps with the mother. If you're a Japanese man, you understand what's going on. An American man doesn't understand what's going on. He'll say, "All she talks about is money." I say, you don't need a divorce, you need to understand what's going on culturally. He says, "I feel like I'm just a wallet. She's just asking me for money." All the attention goes to the child, so he goes out, he's drifting away; she doesn't know why he's turned his back on her. Neither of them understands the cultural difference. Then he goes back to the States, and he's gone.

Junko is one of these women. She met her husband when she was a twenty-nine-year-old English teacher; he was a thirty-one-year-old sergeant from Florida. "I didn't necessarily want to meet an American. I didn't have any interest in American guys. I was just a little stressed and lonely at that time," she says. "The way he treated me was so different from how Japanese men treat women, roses, flowers, chocolate, cards, music tapes. I just kind of fell for him. He spoke only a few phrases of Japanese. He thought I was cute."

She keeps her sons, ages five and eight, occupied with toy trucks as we talk.

> Everything was going fine. Then I got pregnant. I was submissive. I didn't pressure him, didn't argue. It was convenient for him. I put up with stuff. We got married the day before I had the baby. I didn't really want to marry him. He was a little bit strange. I got married for the baby. He was Dr. Jekyll and Mr. Hyde. He changed. But I didn't want to be a single mother. I was tricked, that I was treated well at first, now that I think about it. I had a college education and he didn't, junior college only, and I was more stable financially. . . .

Junko followed her husband to Florida when he left active duty. He got a job as an auto mechanic, and she ended up living in worse economic circumstances than she was used to. His mother treated her badly. He kept a girlie magazine that had published pictures of his naked sister under their bed.

"He started beating me, strangling me. He would lie to the police and say it was my fault. I didn't complain until the end, and then I started throwing things at him." She ended up at a women's shelter in Miami before fleeing to Japan with her elder son, pregnant with her second. "I called him from the shelter. He said, 'It's not my baby.' He stopped taking calls." She has been trying, with Annette's help, to collect child support. "In an international marriage, you have a wall of language between you," Junko says. "He would assume I didn't know anything and didn't know any better because I couldn't speak English well, and then use that to his benefit."

It is hard not to see the paradox here, the contrast with the story of Madame Butterfly, abandoned and pining away for her American military man, Lieutenant Pinkerton, to come back to her and help raise their child.

A Madame Butterfly, it seems, doesn't commit suicide—she keeps the kids and sues for child support.

Bangkok, Thailand

"I want nice guy, good heart, big dick, lots money, buy me everything," a twenty-one-year-old Bangkok bar girl named Mo tells me.

Wow. That could be a motto for an awful lot of women in the world, I think.

Mo is wearing a shirt that reads, "I am free, I am fabulous, I love Sexy girl." She comes from Isan, a poor province in northeast Thailand, where many of the bar girls working in Bangkok sex bars come from. She is employed at the Pharaoh Bar on Soi Nana, the most accessible and open of Bangkok's three notorious red-light districts catering to Western men. The others are Patpong, where foreign tourists freely walk into the ping-pong-ball and "smoke-cigarette-in-the-pussy" shows as yet another stop on their Thailand tourism itineraries; and Soi Cowboy, a seedier strip, where the humiliation of naked women onstage seems more extreme and most appreciated by a grizzled clientele. I once saw a bar girl there pour beer down her completely naked body and rub it over her breasts and into her pubic hair. Because I may have been the only one in the bar watching her eyes instead of her body, I could see her dismay and disgrace. In another bar game, men can enjoy the Alpha-Male power of purchasing a bucket of ping-pong balls and throwing them through the bar to watch the Thai girls scurry and crawl on the floor to collect them. Each girl who grabs a ping-pong ball collects 50 baht from the bar (US$1.20).

Of course, there is also a Bangkok sex world I am not describing, primarily catering to Thai men, where women, many trafficked from Burma, Cambodia, Laos, China, and Nepal, are kept in locked rooms and forced to have repetitive sex with many customers for little money. I have talked with trafficked women before, and their lives are brutal, horrifying, and shortened by disease. But they are not the women typically encountered by foreign men, who are willing to pay more for not only sex but for the mystique and the possibilities of love and companionship that accompany it here; thus, the base, mystique-less world common to prostitution everywhere is outside my scope.

The scene at Soi Nana appears the least exploitative, generally speaking. The hedonism of GIs on R&R from the Vietnam War endures here—evoked by anthems by the Rolling Stones, The Doors, and Neil Young that never fade away but instead pump perpetually through the acoustic systems of bar after bar. Here is where foreign men come for drinks under the neon, to seek continually replenished potential "Brown Sugars," or for a chance to find an island in their arms/country in their eyes. They pick a "Cinnamon Girl" to go running together, chasing the moonlight: *I could be happy the rest of my life/With a Cinnamon Girl.*"

Neil Young's aspirations work both ways. "I want somebody to take care of me really good," says Mo, "with lots of money to have everything that I want." I ask her what everything she wants is. She ponders barely a moment, then rattles off a list, counting on her fingers. "I want house. Want land. Buy car. Open Internet shop. Restaurant," she says. "And gold shop. But really I want to open a bar." In other words, Mo wants power, to be the boss here in her own world. Dark-skinned and treated as underclass in Thailand's strict class hierarchy, she wants to reverse her status. Working at the Pharaoh Bar is the best way she knows how to do that. Like most Thai bar girls I have met over the years, and unlike those in other countries of Asia, she does not want to leave Thailand. She simply wants to be on the top of the heap in her own society, for a change. If a foreigner wants to marry her, he can come here. That would up her societal prestige, too. Thailand has a nice life, she says. She tells me she makes about US$700 per month, about five times the average monthly household wage in Thailand,[3] and sends roughly US$200 home to her family every month.

I ask her why not work in a factory or a bank. "This is my choice," she says. "I cannot work in an office. It's really boring. I like meeting lots of people, having fun. I choose this." Other lines of work, even for those with college degrees, don't pay nearly as well, either. An electrical engineer in Thailand makes a starting salary of $465/mo.; a junior accountant $244. With Mo's education level of high school, her only choice of office work might be as a receptionist in the service sector, for example, making just US$121/mo.[4]

I can tell already from our brief conversation that Mo is skilled in a quality called *aw jai*. It is a term Thai men use for women who act outwardly soft and pleasing but who ultimately ending up dominating the men. The Chinese have a similar term, *sa jiao*. Neither of these terms has an English equivalent; the closest approximation might be Southern Belle, Scarlet O'Hara-style.

Mo's first choice in sugar daddies is American, she says. She had one of those once, from California. He paid the bar—where she started working during school breaks at age sixteen—50,000 baht (US$1,163) for her virginity five years ago, she says. The bar kept 20 percent, but Mo got to keep US$930. She liked the precedent that set and is proud of it. "He was the first guy for me, but not the last guy!" Barring a rich American, she'll settle for a German. A Japanese would be fine, too; they have money. As we have seen in statistics cited earlier, increasing numbers of German and Japanese tourists are taking wives from Thailand back home with them.

Mo says that she always uses condoms. They are provided by the bar as part of Thailand's massive, government-funded AIDS-awareness campaigns that have scored enormous successes over the past decade in reducing HIV transmission rates among sex workers.

When Mo's American went back to the States, she wrote letters to him saying she missed him. Writing letters is a major source of income for bar girls in Thailand. Often, women get several hundred dollars in extra income every month from naïve men who go back home thinking they are saving their "girlfriends" from having to work as prostitutes, helping out their poor or accident-prone families, or, as in one case I knew of, paying for orthodontia. If a guy ever comes back to town, there's a quick juggling act of borrowed apartments, sick parents, and contrived lives to make him think that he's the woman's one-and-only true love—until the man goes back home again and the girl goes back to work at the bar. "I always say I miss him," Mo tells me. But does she really? "Maybe," she says coyly. "I just try to make him miss me!"

The differences in perceptions between bar girls and foreign men are fascinating. I once read an account of an American man in his forties who came to Thailand to find a nice old-fashioned girl after striking out with women back home.[5] "Cliff" approaches a beautiful, twenty-year-old Thai in a supermarket. She tells him she works as a bar cashier. He asks her out, takes her to the beach, and teaches her to swim as she clings to him in the waves. She laughs the whole day. (Thais have a smile for every emotion, the saying goes.)

Cliff falls in love. He takes her to dinner; she doesn't know how to read the English menu, so he orders her a big steak-and-potato dinner. He teaches her to use a knife and fork (Thais usually eat with spoons), and marvels with pride at how she enjoys it. She smiles the whole time. When she is due at work, she wants him to pay the bar fine so she doesn't have to go. He thinks work is good, that women should have careers, and insists that she go, believing she is just a cashier. They live together this way for several months.

"I was getting happier and happier my dreams were coming true with a dream girl in a tropical paradise," Cliff said. "She appreciated everything I did because she has had such a poor life until now living with me. I was happier than I have ever been. I made her happy and I felt like a man for doing it." Some nights, she doesn't come home, telling him she goes to stay with her girlfriends because she misses them. He is understanding. But, one night he shows up at the bar and finds his girlfriend in the arms of a man who has paid the bar fine to buy her out that night. Cliff's world comes crashing down.

Here is the woman's side:

I go supermarket, see old man no hair. I drop money. I wait. Man wi no hair take money, give me. Man ha eyes smiling me. Good heart, I tink. . . . Cliff wan go beach. Me no like beach. Sun too much. Hot too much. Friend give me bikini she wear Go-Go bar. No like. Me shy. Thai men look me. Me no like. Go swim. Me afraid, no like. Cliff take arm, pull me in watta. Swim no like. Boring. Beach no like. Wan go room. Go dinna afte beach. Food no like. Cannot eat.

How eat? No spoon! Restaran no like. . . . Cliff say me, no pay bar!
Say me work! Me stay with Cliff, Cliff no pay. Cliff stingy man.

Her version of his arrival at the bar goes, "Handsome young [for-
eign] boy, he pay drink, pay bar, no stingy. We go dance togeda.
Stingy Cliff come! Me say young boy only friend. Stingy Cliff angry
too much. Young boy customer teeth go." Stingy Cliff, it seems, had
head-butted the young man's teeth out. The book's German inter-
viewers conclude, after conducting a number of such discussions and
experiencing such relationships themselves, that "Thai women are
clever and great actresses. They are strong. They endure. These attributes make them very good at what they do to and with foreign men."[6]

IF MO DOESN'T MEET the sugar daddy of her dreams—"I won't
find my soul mate in Soi Nana!" she says—she has another out. She
can always go home and get married. Back home she will be a rich
girl, valued for marriage because of the money she has earned in the
big city. "But I'm selfish," she says. "I don't want to have to take care
of Thai guy." There is debate among academics as to whether prostitution is socially acceptable in Thai society, or whether it labels women
who do it with a social stigma. Anthropologist Niels Mulder in *Inside
Thai Society* writes:

> Prostitutes cash in on the ambiguous cultural values of prestige,
> power and money. There is nothing wrong in prostituting oneself
> when it results in money or powerful protection. As long as a
> woman cares for her relatives and recompenses her parents with
> gifts and money, she can still see—and present herself—as a good
> person."[7]

But ask upper-class Thais and they'll turn up their noses at that
thought. Many a bar girl, accompanying a foreigner to a swishy
Bangkok affair, has been treated like dirt by the other Thais present,
her status revealed by her use of a base vocabulary word, her manner of
dress, or a mannerism imperceptible to foreigners but glaringly obvious to class-conscious Thais. No matter how much money she makes,

she will still be treated as underclass by the members of Thai society who already have the money and power. Technically, prostitution *is* illegal in Thailand.

I encountered these attitudes myself sitting on a shaded bench on a Sunday afternoon, near a soiled beach in Pattaya, ninety miles southeast of Bangkok. Pattaya has perhaps the largest and most notorious concentration of foreign-catering prostitutes in Asia—an estimated 4,000 per square mile.[8]

The French writer Michel Houellebecq, in *Platform,* calls Pattaya a "cesspit, the ultimate sewer where the sundry waste of western neurosis winds up." Sex strips sprung up in this beach town to service the nearby American military base at U-Tapao, which also was at its zenith at the height of the Vietnam War. Now, however, the clientele primarily is thousands of Europeans and Russians, who are seeking cheaper alternatives to the sex trade in Bangkok in bars that play house music and Euro rock such as Rammstein's anti-marriage song, *"Du, Du Hast, Du Hast Mich."* Translation: "You, You Hate, You Hate Me," or "You, You Have, You Have Me"—the meaning left deliberately ambiguous by the dual meanings of *hast.* I was in a Go-Go bar that played the song after a German (a regular, so the workers knew his nationality) had ordered a bucket of ping-pong balls so he could send the bar girls scurrying to pick them up, and when I looked up the lyrics later I realized it was one of the most tellingly ironic moments I had seen. The German, however, was thrilled, viewing it as a reward for his patronage.

Sharing the bench with me on this lovely afternoon in the soiled surroundings was a twenty-six-year-old factory worker who makes 160 Thai baht (US$3.72) per day assembling electronics. She had come on her Sunday off, taking the bus by herself, to see what the notorious Pattaya was all about, and planned to take the bus home again at 4 PM. We watched couple after couple stroll by on the paved sidewalk along the beach—enormous white men, many old with bulging bellies, hand-in-hand with seemingly tiny Thai girls who otherwise find it culturally uncomfortable to hold hands like that.

These prostitutes earn about 500 baht (US$11.63) for short-time sex after the patrons have paid the additional bar fine of 500 baht. What a girl negotiates with a client if he buys her out of the bar as a

Pattaya, Thailand, 2004

"girlfriend" for days or weeks is up to her; but, not wanting to ruin his illusions by asking for cash, frequently she will ask for 18K gold jewelry which she can return to the gold shop, minus a 10-percent service charge, after the man goes home. (On Soi Nana, where Mo works, short-time sex costs 2,000 baht (US$46.50), whole-night sex 3,000 baht (US$70).)

Most of these women, I learned in my nighttime explorations of the bar scene, have kids back home, failed marriages, or bad Thai boyfriends. They hoped to get a leg up again by entering this trade, perhaps for a short time, or longer if it continued to prove lucrative. The factory worker on the bench next to me had experienced misfortune, too: Her husband had been killed in an accident and she was raising their seven-year-old son. Her choice for doing that, however, was working at the electronics factory. The fact that these women can make in just one hour more than triple her salary for eight hours of work doesn't sway her decision in the least. "Pattaya bad," she declares in halting English after watching all this. "Thai lady bad. Foreign man bad. Bad together!"

BACK IN BANGKOK, I want to find out from Mo whether the big-foreign-guy / small-Thai-woman, or old-foreign-guy / young-Thai-woman disparities make a difference to the women on the receiving end. Not really, according to Mo. Other bar girls had told me they even like a bit of a belly on a man—a *poompui*—which in Thai society is an indication of prosperity, and which also makes a man appear Buddha-like. Mo also supports the consensus I heard that older guys

Mo and Gai at
Pharaoh Bar,
Bangkok, 2004

are better than younger guys. One reason is that they're more serious than young guys who flit around and have lots of girlfriends. "Old guys take care of you and have good hearts," she says, "but not too young, not too old is best."

"Sometimes guys who look really shaggy pay a lot of money, so we don't know who is rich and who is poor," volunteers Mo's "big sister" at the Pharaoh Bar, Gai, who is forty. Once Gai was married for a year to a Sino-Thai man. After that she started working as a cashier in a bar, but soon found it didn't pay enough (US$233/mo.). Going with foreign men paid more. Now she is involved with a Norwegian oil worker who travels often to Bangkok and who she says plans to set up her and her son in a new house. He sends her money every month, ostensibly to keep her out of prostitution. To her it means she can be choosier about the customers she sleeps with. "He asked me to go to his country, but I don't want to, so he got a three-month assignment to come here," she says. She is from Bangkok. She doesn't want to leave. It's almost an ideal situation if it works out. She and her son get a nice place to live, he comes for a few months at a time, and the rest of her time is her own. "I don't want to get married again," she says. "We like our lives here. We are not victims. This is our choice."

The Girl in Red

The basement bar of the Grand Hyatt-Erawan Hotel in Bangkok, called Spasso, has a reputation among foreign men as the best place to meet high-end Thai prostitutes. These are no Pattaya girls or Patpong girls, or even Soi Nana girls. They're not from poor provinces, they're not bored with their lives, and they don't want to marry anybody here. What they want is money. This is the highest of high-end, open prostitution in Asia. I had been here before when I lived in the region, and a manager once told me that only certain, select girls are allowed in. On a typical evening the scene looks like this:

Standing at the bar is a young woman with skin so dark she is probably from Laos. Also giving her away as non-Thai is her jewelry, a thick silver necklace. Thais generally prefer gold. She is intimidating, not looking at anyone, and not smiling. It is early, and the best prospects of the night have yet to arrive. When a foreign man, dressed in a Polo shirt and seemingly in his mid-twenties, makes a move, she turns away. Too young, too naïve, and possibly not rich enough for this scene. The women here determine who talks to them and who doesn't.

Outside the bar's glass window, a man is hesitating to come in. He peers inside through his round, owlish glasses. Probably he is a hotel guest. The young woman can tell because it is more than ninety-five degrees Fahrenheit outside and the man is wearing a wrinkled grey wool sweater to fend off the air-conditioning. It chokes tightly around his shirt collar and gives him the look of a disheveled scientist. He is alone, and uncertain whether to cross this threshold, but finally he decides to plunge into this Bangkok experience. He passes by the intimidating Lao, who quickly evaluates him by his clothes and watch. He passes her test. She decides to catch his eye and smile broadly; her teeth, I see for the first time, are the same bright white as her tight V-neck sleeveless Tee. Having watched dozens of bar pickups and talked with many bar girls over the years, I sense her conclusion without even asking her: He might be a possibility if nothing better comes in.

Suddenly she has competition. A girl-next-door-cute young woman in a tight red V-neck shirt and blue jeans prances over on heels, nods to the ice queen Lao, and slaps her handbag on the bar right next to the man in the grey sweater who has sat down and now is studying the drinks menu. She startles him. Studying the menu is good, she thinks. It means he is from out of town, probably has an expense account. She turns to talk with her friend in a blue denim halter and matching skirt.

These girls are pros from Koh Samui, the one in denim tells me, the island vacation spot off Thailand's East Coast that has become more built up and more popular with Western sex tourists in recent years. Having graduated from that scene—and able to afford fashionable clothes, sleek cell phones, and well-trimmed hairstyles—they are at Spasso, screened in by the management. I don't ask her if that means they pay for the privilege, or whether the bar merely wants to keep up its reputation for high-end women. I doubt she would tell me anyway. Their act, unlike that of the intimidating Lao, is to appear like two girlfriends out for a drink, having fun.

The girl in denim also tells me that the grey sweater man is from Spain. At this moment, he is visibly torn between approaching the ice queen Lao and talking with the friendly girl in red at his side. So the girl in red needs to make him want her. She turns to chat with a heavy-set older man with a salt-and-pepper beard eating a personal-sized pizza alone at the corner of the bar. Perhaps he's a better prospect anyway. She turns her back to the sweater man, leaving him sitting uncomfortably with the fruity cocktail he has ordered. But after a few moments and just before it is too late, she turns to him again. Then back to the bearded man. Back, forth. Chit, chat. Which one will pay more? Playing on jealousy, she has made the sweater man forget all about her Lao rival. Her friend, who appears to be about ten years older, attracts the attention of neither man. She will have to wait until later, until more alcohol is consumed.

Finally, the sweater man moves to ask for the bill and the girl in red makes her move. She stands on her tiptoes and whispers into his ear, most likely one of the lines bar girls use over and over again. "You're so sexy. You're so handsome. I like you. I want to go with you. You're not like the other men here. You're special. I want to sleep with (or have sex with, or fuck, depending on her judgment of which word choice will be most effective) you." It is what he wants to hear, a beautiful young Thai woman just out with her friend at this hotel lobby bar, has chosen him! What luck! Bangkok *is* a magical place! He looks elated and flattered. She leans over and whispers in his ear again. This time it is her price.

These women do not settle for "taxi money" or whatever the man feels like slipping into their purses in the morning. This is a transaction, cash-only, up-front, short-time, so that she can be back at the bar again in an hour or two. Probably, she has guessed that a man like this might pay a lot for a Bangkok experience. Probably, she has said US$200. Or maybe 10,000 Thai baht (US$233). Or maybe more. The sweater man suddenly balks. He looks embarrassed, descends from his barstool, says good night to her, and leaves quickly, without even a second glance at the ice queen Lao. Not that she would have looked back at him now anyway.

The girl in red returns to the bearded man. He knows what this is about. They chit chat, negotiate. There is back and forth, likely price haggling, before he pays his bill and makes a trip to the bathroom. She has whispered her last price into his ear, and he has told her he will think about it. When he returns from the bathroom her eyes are glued on him for a signal. Will he accept? He nods, then motions to her to meet him out front. She grabs her purse, wishes good luck to her friend, and scores for the evening.

Jakarta, Indonesia

The Virgin of Tanamur

The Tanamur disco in Jakarta is a well-known spot among foreigners and upper-class Indonesians. I am here because I had read about it, in a novel by an American man, as a Western male fantasy palace, a ground zero of desire and base bodily function without accountability, affection, or concern:

. . . where girls outnumbered male customers 10 to 1. A host of girls, Jujus and Titis ranging in color from toffee brown to a balsa wood beige. Regardless of skin tone, Bryn was dismissive of them, referring to them all as LBFMs—Little Brown Fucking Machines. They were rent girls, Bryn told [Laney], to be taken home and banged silly.[9]

I wondered what kind of humanity there was in seeking sex partners that one would regard as "Little Brown Fucking Machines" to be "banged silly." Even if most of the women working at Tanamur wouldn't make suitable life partners for the type of rich, privileged white Anglo-Saxons that the passage describes, it seemed to be a distortion of the circumstances and the hopes, dreams, and desires that put these young women on the receiving end of such categorizations, unable to counter them. I decided to go find out.

While the club's heyday was in decadent pre-1998, Suharto-era Indonesia, at the time of my visit Tanamur is still the most infamous club in the country, riding on its reputation as "the oldest disco in Southeast Asia," "one of the sleaziest spots on the planet," and, for Indonesian women, "a great place to pick up [foreign] men."[10] I met about a dozen young women hoping to do that, find foreign men of means, who would care for them and provide for them—and hopefully even love them—not cast them with racist invective. Like women I had met in the Philippines, Okinawa, Thailand, and elsewhere, the women here wanted escape from the economic circumstances that drove them to this work. I couldn't imagine that pre-1998 "Jujus" and "Titis" were all that different. This was the same kind of crowd, only different faces.

Real, live, very human Meri is twenty-six and is from Madura, an overcrowded island that had its own kingdom separate from Java until the eighteenth century. Among Indonesians, Madurese women have a reputation for almost mythical sexual ability. But Meri is half Sumatran, half Javanese, and is Madurese only by geography, not ethnicity. She has an overbite, her left front tooth so prominent that she has difficulty drawing her upper lip completely over it. The overall effect is becoming, even cute. She tells me that some of the girls here, her friends, are prostitutes, including a young woman named Jee who wishes she spoke English better so she could join our conversation. They are friendly and sweet. They have gathered around us, cooing about my light hair and white skin, giggling, and urging us to dance. But instead of dancing, which she has to do every night to make customers feel at ease on the dance floor, Meri feels like talking about her life.

Her job, and that of the other young women here at this relatively early hour for a club, is to show up by 9 PM, Wednesday through Saturday, so that when customers start arriving after ten o'clock, or more like closer to midnight or later, the disco doesn't seem empty. The girls gather on the dance floor or around the banisters before the men arrive, sharing camaraderie and stories of their days. They are supposed to stay until at least 3 AM, urging customers to dance and generally keeping things festive. What they do after that is up to them.

Based on the bar women I had met elsewhere, I expect Meri to tell me that she sometimes goes home with customers for extra money and a chance at love.

I am surprised when she tells me she is a virgin.

I believe her. Indonesia, the largest Muslim-majority country on earth with 220 million people, has more conservative sexual mores than other countries in Asia. Only 23 percent of Indonesian women surveyed by *Femina,* one of the most popular women's magazines, thought premarital sex was okay; 69 percent did not. But, as is the case everywhere, espoused beliefs and actual practices are not always the same. *Femina*'s teen magazine offshoot, *Gadis,* or "*Girl*" found that half of its teen readers are sexually active, and that they do it in cars because there are too many people at home. "We were surprised about that," *Gadis*'s editor, Didin Ambardini, had told me. "Indonesia is a traditional country, but there is [casual] sex here, drugs, too.

Meri has been telling me about her former boyfriend, from London. She met him in this club. He broke up with her after seven months when she wouldn't have sex with him. Now he is marrying someone else, another Indonesian. He broke her heart. It is one of those fresh breakups that seems to penetrate the core of her, causing her to second-guess her decisions, her thoughts, everything she said and did while with him. "No man want me," she says with a sigh of self-pity. "Maybe I'm stupid," she laments, for not playing it right, for not knowing how to play men.

She is clearly troubled by the recurring thought that if she had had sex with him then he might have stayed with her, possibly even married her. But she is religious—she follows Muslim practice and prays five times a day—and she wants to be a virgin on her wedding night. "I do more than kissing," she volunteers. But no sex. "If the first night with your husband there is no blood, he know. So you cannot." She doesn't ruminate on the fact that there is a double standard for men. Life is just like that, she says. That's how it is.

Meri doesn't sleep much. Like a lot of the women working here, except for the few hardcore pros who need no other means of income, Meri works a day job. She sells insurance. "Marketing!" she says brightly. Life, auto, home. She sounds like a commercial when she speaks about it. She prefers the sales job to the disco job, but it doesn't pay enough to quit Tanamur entirely. Because the club is only open four nights a week, and only busy for two, she works both jobs. At the club, she says, she constantly fends off offers. "Men say, 'You have nice body, come on, come to my hotel.'" She manages to evade them, but sometimes they are so persistent she feels compelled to respond, "'Give me your room number, I come after.'" She doesn't go, of course. Once, a Chinese Singaporean offered her US$200 for sex. That's almost half of the average Indonesian per capita GDP, in other words, a relative fortune. Still, she didn't go. She probably could have figured out how to game him, to get some money for some of the sexual acts she is prepared to do, without going all the way. But she doesn't know how to play this game, and she doesn't want to learn.

"I cannot," she says, her thoughts turning dark. "I afraid of sin. I have a God."

MERI AND I DECIDE TO GO SHOPPING TOGETHER the following day. She arrives at my hotel carrying a trendy purse, a Discman, and a case full of CDs: Celine Dion, and a few Indonesian singers I don't know. She is listening to Beyoncé. The song "Naughty Girl" is escaping from the earphones, and she keeps offering them to me to listen. It's a catchy song, heading up the pop charts that week, *Tonight, I'll be your naughty girl . . . I know you want my body.* It seems Meri would like

Jakarta Undercover comic,
October 2003

me to think that she is cool, not some stick-in-the-mud virgin Muslim girl.

The trendy mall where we go is a long ride in the taxi. When we arrive, our first stop is a bookstore. Meri cheerfully peruses the cookbooks and fashion magazines. I find a copy of *Jakarta Undercover*. The book has been a best-seller in Indonesia since it came out in 2002, spawning a sequel and even a comic-book version. Written by an Indonesian journalist, it purports to reveal the real goings-on of Jakarta nightlife. Indonesians claim to be shocked, but enjoy being voyeurs enough to buy hundreds of thousands of copies. The chapter titles indicate the contents: Nude Ladies Nite VIP Casino; Chicken Nite Private Party; Ladies Escort No Hand Service; Orgy Order Massage Ladies; Sex Sandwich Sashimi Girls; Triple X Salon-Salon Eksekutif; Sex Drive Thru.[11] The comic-book version is fairly explicit and almost always sold out. There's supposed to be an English version. Meri asks the store clerk, and finds that it is not yet available.

I ask Meri what in it shocks her most. She gives an answer I had heard from other Indonesian friends: that men rent outfitted Pajero jeeps—with cushions, mini-bar, TV, and stereo—pick up bar girls, have sex while being driven around in Jakarta's notorious traffic, and then return the cars three hours later. It does confirm the findings of the women's magazines, that there are lots of girls out there having sex in cars, even if they think it's immoral.

But what shocks me most is the way the book shows sex as so freely available—often quite literally free. The men, both foreign and Indonesian, enjoy sexual services in salons, casinos, Japanese restaurants, clubs, discos, cars, and bars, on page after page, complete with sound effects such as "Srruppp" and "waaahh." The men are the organizers, the girls, often naked, are the service providers. There are no condoms, no second thoughts, and no responsibilities.

The girls in the book don't get many lines, except for occasionally introducing themselves, offering a choice of services, and uttering short phrases such as "Have fun, yaaa!" "Awesome body," "Good evening, can I join the party?" and "Come to mama . . ." It seems this representation of women is no surprise to Indonesians. When I ask a well-known Indonesian feminist about it later, she says simply, "Well, what do you expect in Indonesia?"

Meri and I go have lunch. She tells me she has a college degree in accounting and that she had worked for three years doing ledger sheets for a small company in Jakarta before the impact of the Asian Financial Crisis hit hard in 1998. After that, she went to Singapore for a year to work as a waitress. When she came back, the only job she could find at first was at Tanamur. No matter the condition of the Indonesian economy, foreigners would still go out and clubs would still need girls. At least it was a job; official unemployment figures were around 15 percent.[12]

We walk around the mall again, ogling diamonds in a jewelry store display and deciding that the cute French-brand tops in another store are too expensive. In a shoe store, Meri caresses a pair of $20 stiletto heels with fake rhinestones rimming the ankle strap. She sits down for a free hair analysis at a store selling botanical products. It is a magnifying camera transmitting to a TV screen and they run it through her long, dark locks trying to sell her their special shampoo. She doesn't buy.

We decide to leave. It is a long way back in the taxi. In the backseat, the sunlight lands on her forearm and I notice some scars. Cigarette burns. She has at least four that I can see. It's a hazard of the job, she explains, when you're working in a club and people are waving their cigarettes around. I wondered if the author of the book I had read had been one of them. I wished I could introduce him to this young woman. No LBFM, this is Meri, a bar girl, broken-hearted virgin, trained accountant, and insurance policy saleswoman, who prays five times a day to Allah, and just wants a nice husband who loves her. Yes, there are players among the young, beautiful women at Tanamur on a Saturday night. But there are lots of non-players, virgins like Meri, too.

We pass through the rich neighborhood of Pondok Indah, past large mansions of the wealthy. Indah means "beautiful," she tells me. Pondok means, ironically, "hut." She remarks that the houses look like castles. It causes me to think of a saying I once heard, that inside every American girl is a princess dying to get out. Correction: "inside *every* girl."

The Rich Girl of Tiga Puluh

Tiga Puluh. It is a bar in the basement of Jakarta's Le Meridian Hotel. It means "thirty" in Indonesian, and this is the source of a joke among the expatriate community: that thirty is the average age difference between the foreign men who go there and the Indonesian women they pick up. When I arrive I realize it is no joke; it appears to be true. The white male clientele is older, white-haired if they have much hair at all. The women are in their twenties or early thirties. Here, most are professional prostitutes, called *ayam* in Indonesian slang. It means "chicken."

Again, this kind of prostitution is not a straight transactional arrangement. A man simply meets a woman and invites her to leave with him. If he is clueless about the scene or new to town, she'll invite him. Usually, no money is discussed. If he is still clueless the next morning, she'll spring it on him then. Daniel Ziv, a long-time Jakarta resident and the author of the book *Jakarta Inside Out,* had told me:

> There is an implicit understanding that the man is going to pay for sex, because the expat obviously has money and the Indonesian woman is in need of money or has less of it. That it's not discussed beforehand allows the woman to feel she is not a prostitute, and the man to feel he's not paying for sex.
>
> The next morning it's disguised as "taxi money." If the relationship continues, he feels he's got a nice Indonesian woman friend who shows him around, and she gets a sugar daddy. The economic disparity is obvious. I can't imagine that a fat, sweaty fifty-seven-year-old oil man thinks [a young beautiful Indonesian woman] is attracted to him because he's so good looking and such great company.

This happens in Thailand and the Philippines, too. But Jakarta is different, Dan insisted, because the expat men engaging in it usually don't have marriage in the backs of their minds. In the Philippines, even poor women speak English well and there is more cross-cultural familiarity because of the long-term American involvement and history of mail-order brides. Marriages between bar girls and westerners are common enough to keep the girls gambling, like playing the lottery, that they'll be the lucky ones next. It happens in Thailand, too. In Indonesia, the cultural factors of Islam and a lesser degree of Western contact historically act against marriage expectations. "These guys are all about taking these girls home and paying them twenty bucks, but marrying them is something different," Dan told me.

> Thailand has always been a stereotype, that it's where you go to get a beautiful Asian wife, in part because it's so anonymous. If you're a fifty-seven-year-old guy going to Pattaya, you can get lost in the crowd, everyone else is doing it. There's no shame in it. Jakarta doesn't really have that dynamic. These things are noticed more easily here.

I wondered why Indonesian women put up with that. Dan thought it had to do with self worth—a lack of it among Indonesian women.

"In Indonesia, there is a sense that *any* white guy is better than an Indonesian. You walk into a shopping mall and you're the grand prize. The women eye you, they flirt. They're sexual, they're intriguing, and they're intrigued," he said. "Jakarta has always been a very sexually open and promiscuous place. The promiscuity here shocks me."

Dan had sent me to other pickup scenes such as Block M, a neighborhood where Jakarta's expatriate oil men and chemical engineers crowd the Sportsman's and D's Place. I found these bars flush with Brits, Aussies, Kiwis and Americans downing beers and putting their arms around waitresses dressed like Suzy Wongs in slit skirts.

A nearby disco, the Lintas Melawai, is known as the last, late-night resort of the desperate expatriate. It doesn't get revved up until after 1 AM, and any man who hasn't found a bed partner for the night elsewhere can surely find one here among the older-but-still-lovely women who have yet to find their Prince Charmings but are still hanging on to the hope. The night I went, I was surprised to find myself a welcome sight for several *ayam*. "I go home with you? I'm A/B," a petite, soft-spoken Javanese of thirty-six asked me. I told her I was not, and asked if she didn't prefer men. She did, in theory. She still hoped to get married and have children, but she was over the hill by Indonesian standards and nearly there by expat ones. So why me? She gestured to a large, overweight, mustachioed foreigner, Australian and seemingly in his late fifties, who otherwise might end up as her night's work. "You are better," she stated flatly in her cooing voice. I could see her point.

BACK AT TIGA PULUH, there is a band playing R&B and hip-hop. The lead singers are African-American, male and female, as is the bass guitarist. The bar is full of white guys checking out the evening's possibilities. I exchange smiles with a few *ayam*, wanting to talk to some but not wanting to ruin their prospective transactions. It's best to let them pick you, I had found, to keep the conversations from being monosyllabic. Their motives range from outright pickup as at the last-desperation bar, to simply wanting to practice their English, wanting to improve their status in the bar by looking like they're on a girl's night out with a foreign friend, or wanting to keep themselves in reserve for someone they're expecting later.

When a Chinese-looking woman comes over, taps me on the arm, declares it boring to drink alone, and invites me to sit with her at the bar ringing the stage, I suspect the reason is none of the above. I notice a slight British accent. Her name is Ria. I tell her I am writing a book. "Well, you've met the right person," she declares.

We start talking about the *ayam*. I feel funny using the term, but Ria does so easily and I decide maybe it's not as impolite as I think. She doesn't look like an *ayam*. She is wearing an expensive gold necklace. She has a long-sleeved knit cardigan sweater buttoned to a V-neck. She doesn't wear a bra, but her torso has more fabric on it than most *ayam* here. To be sure, I ask her.

"NO! Of course not!" she says indignantly. Then she offers to buy me a beer, to supplement the one I already have, and pulls a US$100 bill out of her wallet to pay for it. This may be for my benefit or an accident, but it seems to improve her status at the bar. She waves it around to get the bartender's attention and then tucks it back in with an "Oh, sorry," after a few people around us have taken notice. Then she pulls out a 100,000 Indonesian rupiah note instead. It's only worth US$11.75, but it's not a common bill. ATM machines in Jakarta spit out rupiah in denominations of R50,000. If you're carrying R100,000 notes, then you have another source of cash.

Ria has established that she has money. Still, an Indonesian woman alone in a pickup bar drinking among the *ayam* knows she needs an explanation for her presence—as opposed to a foreign woman who could be staying at the hotel and simply not have known better. "I met that guy the other night," she says, gesturing to the male lead singer on stage. "He told me to come see his band."

"He said I had a nice body. But anyway, I'm fat! So he's bullshit. I've got a belly and a fat ass and no chest." Ria is slightly hefty by usual Indonesian standards, but I wouldn't call her fat. More like a healthy size ten. A man more used to American proportions would certainly be interested. The singer keeps making eye contact with her from the stage. But, as soon as he does, she turns away with a haughty toss of her head.

"I think he's ugly anyway," she declares. Actually, he is handsome by American standards, but he is dark. In Indonesian culture, as in most of Asia, dark skin is associated with peasantry and poverty. The rich elite are white from staying indoors, the poor are dark from working outside in the fields—no matter whether it's true. Therefore, dark is ugly, and white guys are the most handsome of all. Ria doesn't acknowledge this when I point it out. She soon finishes off two more beers, which she has ordered by demanding that the bartender scrape off the foam before serving them to her. I compliment her purse. It is marked Ming, a designer brand sold in high-end Asian department stores. "Oh, it's a cheap one, not expensive, 1.2 million only," she says. "Rupiah, of course!" She laughs. It is more than US$140.

Ria was born in Jakarta, she says, and educated at boarding school in the U.K. She is not a Muslim. She is ethnic Chinese. Her father was a timber tycoon, a Christian, who made his money in Borneo cutting logs and turning them into furniture. The Japanese pay top dollar for teak and other hardwoods. He made a lot of money. But both of her parents have passed away and her brothers run the family business. Ria works there sometimes, when she feels like it. Even if she doesn't, she has all the money she needs. She is twenty-four, going on forty.

When she was twenty-one, she was living in Europe with a German boyfriend, but her mother fell ill with leukemia and Ria had to come home. The German came with her, and they lived together for awhile in Jakarta. But then he wanted to go home. Her mother was dying. Ria let him go.

After that there was a Japanese boyfriend, and now there's a Saudi. He does marketing for the Saudi national airline, and had wanted her to be a flight attendant so they could travel together. But she'd have to live in Saudi Arabia. She doesn't want to, not because of how women are treated there—although she says it is better than what outsiders think—but because Saudi Arabia doesn't allow alcohol. "I am not ready for that," she says, taking a long sip of her foamless beer. She likes him, she says, but is not thinking about getting married now. Someday she expects to get married and have children, but in the meantime she just wants to have fun, to play.

She feels warm in her sweater and hand-fans herself, lifting her chin haughtily and rapidly flicking her limp wrist. "I'm so hot!" she declares. Flick, flick, flick. She does this a lot. If she weren't being serious it would almost be self parody.

An Arab man, drawn by my light hair, approaches us. He says he is from Yemen. He's a goofball; he had been waving his arms at us from the other end of the bar, and then, when I swiveled my chair to move him out of my line of sight, he kept up the game, moving to any place in the bar I set my gaze.

"Let's play with him," Ria orders me. "Male ego, you know! I like to get them to the edge. Just play with them. Then just when they can't take it anymore, leave 'em. Ha!"

This is a game that seems dangerous and not particularly fun. You never know how strange men in *ayam* bars are going to react. She tries to engage him but he wants to talk to me. I ask him politely to go away. Ria is disappointed in me. "Oh come on, *really*!" she says. Clearly, I don't know how to have fun. I don't know how to play men. She thinks I need another drink to loosen up and buys me another beer—a small one, I insist. She orders a large for herself. No foam.

When Ria gets up to use the bathroom, an *ayam* steps on Ria's chair to propel herself up onto the bar. She starts to dance. It is for the benefit of a European in his late fifties; he gazes up at her as she swivels her hips and squats suggestively in repeated vertical figure eights. Ria returns clearly annoyed. She waits for the young woman to realize she wants to reclaim her seat. When the dancing *ayam* keeps it up, Ria taps her on her bare, mini-skirted leg and points sternly to the floor. The European tries to intervene. Ria scolds them both until they leave in a huff. "I mean, come on. *Really*!" she snarls, reclaiming her seat.

There is more attempted eye contact by the R&B singer. Ria leads him on a bit, playing her game by seductively returning his gaze, then turns to me and declares he is ugly all over again. As the band prepares to play its last number, she borrows my pen and grabs my coaster. "I'm going to CJ's," she writes on the back. When the singer again looks to her chair, she has disappeared around the back of the stage waiting for the opportunity to deliver it to him. I motion to the singer that she is standing there. But he never gets the coaster; instead the bass player takes it and pockets it. I am not sure if the interception is a protection move. Ria is too drunk to realize.

Soon we are in the back of a taxi headed to CJ's. It is another club, at the five-star Hotel Mulia. It is after 2 AM, and I ask Ria what time she has to work in the morning. "Well I don't *have* to work," she says. I wonder whether she works at all.

When we reach CJ's, an exodus of club-goers waiting for taxis outside indicates it has closed as well, but the hotel is filled with men wearing yellow blazers milling about. Ria has her arm around my shoulders in a tight embrace as we ascend the stairs. She is in four-inch heels and would still be taller than I am if she were barefoot. The men in yellow blazers are staring at us. "Golkar!" Ria stage-whispers into my ear.

Golkar is the political party of former dictator Suharto, who was ousted in 1998 after thirty-two years in power. His party is still around, however, and, it turns out, is holding a convention here to choose which candidate to field in July 2004 elections.

"I hate them," she says. I am not sure whether she means politicians in general or Golkar in particular. When Indonesia was ruled by Suharto and his Golkar party, the ethnic Chinese community of eight million had to carry special ID cards; they were not permitted to hold certain government jobs. Even the celebration of the Chinese New Year was banned. But the Chinese community still managed to do well, controlling about 70 percent of private economic activity. When Suharto was forced to step down after violent street protests in May 1998, the mobs turned their rage over economic instability on the ethnic Chinese, burning and looting their houses and killing up to 1,200 people. The police and military were either powerless to stop the pogroms or didn't want to. Ria's family had already fled, some to Singapore, others to Australia. Successive Indonesian governments have since tried to lure back the ethnic Chinese and their money. Ria and her family came back.

Ria decides we need to get something to eat. It is 2:30 in the morning. When we reach the spacious coffee shop, most of the seats are filled by the Golkar delegates. They fix their eyes on us as we seek out an empty table.

"What?" Ria demands harshly and haughtily at one of the staring Golkars, then translates her question into Indonesian. "Apa?" He has not taken his eyes off her since she walked in, and rather than dissuade him, this only encourages him.

"Well, why don't you just come sit here then if you're going to be staring and listening?" she says loudly. He doesn't understand either the English or the sarcasm, but he does take it as an invitation. As he joins us, Ria suddenly switches from annoyed to coquettish. "Let's just play with him," she says to me. It seems I am going to get to see her in action—to see her game of winding men up and then dumping them when they get to the point of frustration.

Ria orders a tuna salad sandwich for us to share and then begins comparing her skin tone to his—she is much lighter, she concludes, even with the suntan she got from lying at the swimming pool in Malaysia, where she went to see her Saudi boyfriend the previous week. She pulls her sweater off her shoulder to show him her tan lines. She sticks to English because he has limited ability in the language and it gives her the upper hand. Her lighter skin, she has made clear, accords her the higher status between them, too. He should be panting to be with a woman like her. Clearly, he already is.

He says he is from Kalimantan, the island of Borneo, and a Dayak. They are among the most famous of Indonesia's roughly 300 ethnic groups for one reason: they were headhunters. These days the Dayak people are Christian, though still stereotyped as savages, cannibals, and sorcerers by fellow Indonesians. When ethnic clashes in Indonesia make international news every few years, it is usually because Dayaks are killing the majority-Muslim Madurese, who settled in Borneo because Madura was too crowded—by cutting off their heads. This Dayak man says his father wore feathers and his mother had elongated earlobes characteristic of the native inhabitants of the Borneo rainforests. Ria sniffs and tries to convince him she is Korean by saying a few words in the language. He insists she must be Filipina. She doesn't let on she is Indonesian, perhaps because it would be socially awkward for a descendant of wealthy ethnic Chinese traders who made a fortune off the Borneo rainforests to have anything to do with a descendant of Borneo headhunters.

"I am so hot," she declares, leaning back on her chair and hand-fanning herself. Flick, flick, flick.

We ask him who Golkar has elected as its presidential candidate at the convention this evening. "Wiranto," he says.

"Who's Wiranto?" Ria coos, batting her eyelashes at him.

"Wiranto?! He's a war criminal!" I exclaim. "*Militer*," I say in Indonesian to let him know I know the rap on the guy. As if he would care what I think. Ria smacks me under the table and lets out a "shhhhhhhhh." Apparently, she also knows that General Wiranto is the former head of the Indonesian military indicted by a UN tribunal for crimes against humanity; gangs backed by troops he commanded killed about 1,400 people during the separation of East Timor from Indonesia in 1999. Ria, I had forgotten, is just playing. My candor is disrupting her game.

He starts to stroke her arm. I decide to play my own mischief and ask him in Indonesian how many wives he has. Legally, a Muslim man may have more than one in Indonesia. "No," he grunts in English for Ria's benefit, believing she doesn't speak Indonesian. "Don't have wife."

I find this hard to believe. An unmarried Indonesian man in his fifties would be a liar, a widower, or, least likely, a divorcee. The Dayak traditionally live in a longhouse, which is akin to a large, one-story apartment building. Extended families are communities. The living spaces of sometimes an entire village are connected by a communal verandah. Widowers and divorcees don't stay single, especially ones of such high stature that they are sent to Jakarta for a political convention.

He makes a grab for Ria's breast. Ria pulls back, grabs my arm, and declares that we are a couple. "We're lesbians," she says emphatically. I am not sure whether she means it to deter him or encourage him, but it's unlikely he understands anyway. Probably, this man has understood from Ria not that she's rejecting him, but that we are planning to come up to his room together. He eagerly calls for the bill, signs for our shared tuna sandwich, and propels us to the exit.

Ria keeps up the act till we get to the lobby; he is trying to put his arm around her, she is maneuvering and ducking. Halfway to the elevator she leaves him there, grabs my hand, and makes a bolt for the front door. It is one of those moments when the oddity of it all suddenly hits you, and you wonder what on earth you are doing, running through the lobby of a Jakarta luxury hotel at 3.30 in the morning, hand-in-hand with an ethnic Chinese woman, fleeing an ex-headhunting tribesman-conventioneer who has bought you a tuna sandwich and expects you to have sex with him. He doesn't pursue us, and just stands perplexed for a moment. He had thought things were going so well, that his trip to Jakarta was about to be a resounding success.

I don't ask Ria for explanation. I know this is the enactment of the game she had told me she likes to play. What puzzles me is that she thinks this is fun. I am just trying to keep a sense of humor. As we wait for taxis, she feels the need to explain anyway.

"HE'S GOVERNMENT!" she says. "Even though I am Indonesian, I hate this fucking government. Even though I was born here, I hate it. *Really*! I don't give a shit."

Now I am surprised more than puzzled, but considering that Ria had had three beers to my every one, maybe such an outburst isn't all that surprising. "Fuck," she reiterates, "I don't give a shit." We both say goodbye, get into separate taxis, and go home.

A FEW NIGHTS LATER, my last night in Jakarta, I text message Ria on her mobile phone. We had planned to meet again, but there had been a torrential rainstorm flooding the streets. "Bad weather! R U out somewhere?" I write. She replies right away: "fucking shit, yeah. i tried so hard 2 get a taxi. haven't get it til now. still trying. if i get it, i'll go 2 '30' bar. Wht about u?"

She means Tiga Puluh, the place we had first met. When I arrive she has been standing near the entrance waiting for me, and motions that we should find seats. When we do, there is a stage light directly in our eyes. Ria takes out her sunglasses and puts them on. I compliment them for looking chic. "Six hundred thousand only," she says (nearly US$71). "Not expensive."

This time, I offer to buy Ria a drink. "Oh come on. *Really*!" Again she whips out the US$100 bill, again attracting the status-affirming attention of others at the bar. I don't insist. But I notice that for every small beer that I order, she orders a large one, no foam, and drinks it twice as fast. The same R&B singer is onstage. Ria stares at him seductively and he makes eye contact. The bass player says hello, too. I wonder if he had thought Ria's note was meant for him. "I am so hot," Ria declares, leaning back in her chair and fanning herself with her hand. Flick, flick, flick.

The band works through its same repertoire, some *ayam* get on the bar to dance again, white guys case the room to determine which young exotic object of desire they will invite to their beds and thank with "taxi money" in the morning. Again, much alcohol is consumed. Everything is exactly the same as when I was here a few days before, only some of the faces are different. Later, the R&B singer comes to talk with us. He is curious about Ria's blatant interest. He is an American Muslim convert, he says, from Philadelphia, who moved to Indonesia more than ten years before. I assume he must have a wife here; or had. Was he really interested in Ria or just flattered? But Ria snubs him and walks off. She has no need of men. She was just playing.

It occurs to me that if I come back to Jakarta in five years or ten, to this club or to one that may have taken its place, the scene will be exactly the same, repeating in perpetuity. I wonder, somewhat worriedly, if Ria will still be drinking at the bar—beer, no foam—and waiting for a chance to play.

China Doll, Dragon Lady

The Party has decided not to admit you at this time and to continue your development," Polly snapped at the student applicant seated before her and a half-dozen of her fellow Chinese Communist Party student cadres in a university classroom used, by day, to teach classical Chinese literature. Her tone was sharp, authoritative, a 180-degree change from that of the bubbly college student with a pony tail who had chosen "Polly" as her English name—which was the way I had known her until this moment. Now, speaking Chinese, she was transformed. This incongruity of outward strength and inner softness, of outward softness and inner strength, the projection of girlishness versus power—the dual images of China Doll and Dragon Lady—this is what I had come to China to explore. Polly seemed to be the perfect example.

"What do you think about that?" she barked at the student, who was starting to squirm uncomfortably. "Can you tell us any reason why our judgment has been in error and we should reconsider you at this time?"

The applicant's face turned ashen as she struggled for a response. She already had endured two years of trying—unsuccessfully—to be admitted as a Communist Party member. Now, as a fourth year, a college senior, who soon would graduate from this university in the province of Guangdong in southern China, there would be no more chances. Those applicants unable to join the Party during their final year of university would find it more difficult to do so after entering the career world.

In actuality, the admission committee's goal was to catch these potential new members off-guard, to see if the prospect of rejection would cause true disappointment, so as to gauge their sincere desire to join the Party's ranks. So this student and seven others whose applications were being considered, were summoned one evening to an "emergency meeting, attendance required," at 9 PM. Polly and the other members of the committee had text-messaged the applicants on their cell phones, giving them twenty minutes' notice to assemble at the second-floor classroom of Building No. 3. Modern members of the Communist Party, it seems, must be willing to drop whatever they are doing—and must carry mobile phones.

Polly had gotten special permission from the Party to allow my presence, in my capacity as a teacher at the university that semester, and I, too, was summoned with twenty minutes' notice. I had been dining in downtown Guangzhou, the provincial capital formerly known as Canton, with fellow foreign teachers, and I had to drop my chopsticks and race back to campus to make it. "Just go straight to the back. Don't talk to anyone," Polly directed me when I arrived nearly out of breath. Polly and the Party's campus leader told me that, to their knowledge, I was the only foreigner ever allowed to witness a closed Communist Party meeting.

One by one, the candidates were told to come in from the hallway, close the door, and take a seat facing the classroom desks. After each had stammered a pleading response as to why the Party should reconsider and allow him or her to be admitted, each candidate was asked to perform a self-criticism, a long-time Communist practice that historically has been a feature of purges and inquisitions.

"What are your failings?" Polly demanded. "How will these hurt the Party if we are to admit you?"

The second candidate, also female, grew visibly angry under this line of questioning and retorted in a way that made the Party cadres question her humility. "She wanted the Party to come to her, rather than her come to the Party," Polly later told me the admissions committee's conclusion had been. The third candidate, a lanky young man wearing a basketball team jacket, couldn't think of any failings either, but when pressed by Polly's drill questions, he thought up a few ways to improve, primarily in the area of his study skills, which he said were lacking. I could tell from the sidelong glances that the student cadres gave one another after these applicants' responses that they did not always approve of the answers.

Out of the eight candidates summoned to defend their applications to the Party that night, only two were successful. The student Party cadres selected the basketball player and one other young woman who proved to have sufficient humility and a "pure mind" to join the Party—that is, good intentions in desiring membership, not just wanting to list it on their resumes or use it as a way to get a good government job after graduation. That didn't mean they'd made it yet, however.

The chosen two would be invited to submit seven documents for their formal applications: a recommendation letter from this committee; a biographical history; a list of their failings and potential areas for development; their goals for joining the Party; how the Party could benefit from their membership; photocopies of any certificates or awards they had received so far; and a demonstration of their knowledge of Party precepts such as the "Three Represents"[1] of former President Jiang Zemin. The applications could still be rejected by the higher-up Party cadres at the provincial level.

This admissions committee was just doing a screening test, doing its best to keep membership limited to a select few. The admission rate I had just witnessed—two out of eight candidates—was typical. The Party wanted only those with true vocation. Just 10 to 20 percent of students on campus are allowed to join the Party, and those chosen are a privileged elite. Polly is so smart and so accomplished that the Party accepted her in her second year. It wasn't her idea to join at first; a teacher pulled her aside and suggested she apply, and after attending a few meetings she decided that she was a believer. She liked the idea of Communist utopia, where people live together communally by giving according to their abilities and taking only according to their needs. Even if it was not attainable in her lifetime, Polly believed, it was an ideal goal toward which humanity should strive.

Every year, since her first semester as a freshman, Polly had won a half-tuition, Class 1 scholarship, worth 2,000 yuan (US$241), for her "high morality," "high academic achievement," and "top physical fitness." Apart from the top grades, students must be leaders recognized by fellow students and teachers, and must place at the top of their classes in physical fitness.(Polly was a campus badminton champ.) Only about 300 of the 9,400 undergrads on campus earn Class 1 status. When I asked Polly what it meant to have "high morality," she joked that everybody always asks to borrow money from her, thinking she is a pushover. They don't always pay her back, either. In a sense,

CHINA DOLL, DRAGON LADY   337

this appealed to her Communist sense of idealism, giving according to her abilities to those who need it. But she wasn't so sure about the real need. One borrower, for example, wanted to buy a Discman.

It struck me that, if she were from the American Midwest instead of Sichuan province in the middle of China, Polly would have been a cheerleader, valedictorian, student council president, community center volunteer, Candy Striper, and, probably, Homecoming Queen. She wasn't beautiful in a beauty-pageant sense, but she had an adorable enthusiasm that lit up her face, a kind of ebullience that caused you to hardly notice that her skin was sometimes blemished from the air pollution of Guangzhou (almost everyone's was), and that living in a dormitory—six girls to a room and several dozen to one bathroom—made it sometimes difficult to wash her hair. When she spoke, she answered questions with such a cheerful, emphatic "yes" that her pony tail would bob along with her head. And that's why I was taken aback to see her in action at the Party meeting, directing intimidating questions at the applicants and making them squirm in their seats.

Why some of the smartest, highest achievers on campus wanted to join the Communist Party in the first place was a mystery to me at the beginning. As China's government has maintained its strict control over government and political life, it has been loosening its controls over the economy for the past decade and shifting from a state-run economy to a capitalist one. Thus, joining the Communist Party—which has stated that it intends to someday hold multi-party democratic elections nationwide—would not seem to be the wave of the future for bright young recruits. The cynics say that young people join only to get ahead, that joining the Party provides networking opportunities and a means to obtain and advance in government-related public sector jobs. It really is the only club in town, and to get ahead in certain sectors, you have to be a member. But in a metropolis like Guangzhou, with more than ten million people a two-and-a-half-hour train ride from Hong Kong, most college graduates end up in the private sector anyway, joining the expanding offices of Procter & Gamble, the most sought-after recruiter on my campus, PricewaterhouseCoopers, Ernst & Young, and other multinational companies.

Rather, their decisions to join the Party have to do with a desire to better the society and themselves. China has few means of social activism—no Girl Scouts or Boy Scouts (or Guides, as they are known in Britain); no church groups delivering meals to shut-ins; no Candy Stripers volunteering at hospitals; no campus environmental or political action groups—outside of the Party structure. Meeting Polly had caused me to think about my own history of involvement in societal causes. I had been a Girl Scout, and a member of my church Youth Group spending a couple weeks of high school summers building houses for the Appalachian poor. In college in Washington, DC, I had volunteered in a church-run soup kitchen, and protested apartheid outside of the South African Embassy. But community groups and public protests will get you arrested in China.

For those with the drive to better their society, to make the community a better place to live, the legally sanctioned place to do so is within the Communist Party structure. Polly, I knew, got up every Sunday morning to teach 7 AM English classes (for free) to mid-level government bureaucrats in a classroom of a nearby primary school. One Saturday morning, when I called her cell phone for help from my non-English-speaking tailor shop, where my lack of proficiency in sewing vocabulary in Chinese had caused more misunderstanding than resolution, Polly shouted into the phone as the sounds of whizzing cars nearly overwhelmed her voice, "I CAN'T HEAR YOU! WE ARE CLEANING THE ROAD!"

When not volunteering as a street cleaner, Polly was constantly busy painting signs for campus events, meeting with fellow students after just about every class in order to organize student contests and competitions, and always so late to the cafeteria at mealtimes that there was little food left by then. Fortunately she didn't eat much. Every Friday night at 7 PM, she called her parents in Sichuan province—a thirty-nine-hour train ride away, which she traveled at the beginning and end of every semester and at Chinese New Year break, and sometimes had to sit on her suitcase in the aisles or between cars because of overcrowding. "I joined the Party because I feel a strong spirit, a feeling inside, for self-development and for advancement of society," she had told me on the first day we met, when she had been a volunteer showing around the new teachers. "A lot of the time young people today just care about themselves."

The self-betterment goal is also part of a larger trend in China. Self-help sections of bookstores are so popular that on weeknights and weekends, they are packed with people thumbing through already-well-thumbed copies of Dale Carnegie classics and Spencer Johnson's *Who Moved My Cheese,* translated into Chinese. The leader of the students' Party unit at my campus, who had chosen the English name Rock, gave that as his primary reason when I asked him. "Knowing what others think of you will help you to know your weaknesses and improve them," he said. His decision to join was not without internal conflict, however. He was the first person in his family to apply, and while his parents were proud, he said, his grandmother to this day cannot walk properly because of being "struggled against" during the Cultural Revolution of 1966–76. It was a ten-year period of turmoil in China's history in which students like Polly and Rock were encouraged to become Red Guards, to rise up and struggle against authority. Red Guards were incited to beat their teachers and government officials and denounce their own parents as a way of combating elitism and re-instilling revolutionary fervor. More than three million people were persecuted or purged, and many thousands died. Today, the Party officially acknowledges that "mistakes" were made in this period.

Even Polly has had moments of internal struggle along with her zeal. One evening, over dinner at a Sichuan restaurant with a fellow female Communist, she told me the story of her mother and a brother eleven years younger than she is. With a few exceptions, it is illegal in China to have more than one child, but her parents really wanted to have a second. Traditionally, boys were more valued in Confucian society, carrying on the family name as well as being responsible for the parents' care in old age. The preference continues today, such that for every 100 girls born in China, there are 117 boys.[2] So, when their first child was born a girl, Polly's parents wanted to try again. Polly was five when her mother became pregnant. She remembers her mother's belly swelling until she was at seven months, and then having the authorities come to her house to drag her mother away and forcibly abort the child. Her mother became very depressed after that.

China is the only country in the world where suicide rates are higher for women than men—54 percent of those committing it are women, a rate five times higher than most other countries,[3] and suicide accounts for 30 percent of women's deaths from non-natural causes.[4] Polly and her family grew worried about her mother. But before long, she became pregnant again; and again, the authorities came, dragged Polly's mother, screaming and kicking, off to the hospital, and forcibly aborted her fetus.

When Polly was eleven, her mother became pregnant for the fourth time. This time, her mother did not wait for the police to come take her away; early in her pregnancy, she fled to a relative's home in another city to have the baby there. When she returned home with a newborn child, officials came to the house and demanded a fine of 10,000 yuan (US$1,205)—a small fortune in their remote Sichuan town. It turns out that Polly's parents had saved their money for years waiting for this day. When the fine collectors came, they were ready with the cash.

This doesn't happen everywhere, and the law is applied unevenly in China. Sometimes officials look the other way and don't intervene at all. Sometimes they come to collect the fine upon learning of the pregnancy, rather than forcing a woman to abort. Polly's mother encountered enforcement of the law at its most extreme. When I expressed shock at how her poor mother must have felt at being dragged off at seven-months pregnant and forced to abort a baby she wanted, Polly was quick to defend the government's One-Child policy. China has too many people, she said. We need to have such laws. Our discussion obviously had troubled her overnight because the next day she sent me an email to explain further. "Please don't consider it too terrible," she wrote, "because our country has too large a population. There is no other way for us except the One-Child Policy. All the Chinese people can fully understand our government's dilemma, although they cannot always obey the rules."

More than ten years after her mother's struggle to give birth, however, Polly was considering not having children at all. There are lots of things she wants to accomplish in life, she said, and maybe you have to give those up if you get married and have a baby. Even though she has a boyfriend in a far-away province—who at first I thought might be an invention for the benefit of Rock, who mooned over Polly whenever they were together—she intends not to get married until at least age thirty. The Chinese word for "wife" is made from the combination of the characters "woman" and "broom." To write the Chinese word for "good," you must combine the characters "woman" and "baby." For Polly, this seemed a subliminal reinforcement of the value: She wondered aloud whether a decision not to have children might make her a "bad person." Chinese women believe it is their duty to society to bear a child, preferably a son. She had been taught that from an early age, and her own mother's agony and trauma just to do so had been her example of womanhood since she was five years old. Then, again, there were lots of people like her mother who had second children in violation of the law, so for the sake of society she could afford not to.

Polly had brought her resume and job applications cover letter to dinner that evening, and she asked me to go over them and fix her mistakes. She wanted to have a career first and decide what to do about her personal life later. "I am an optimistic, active and congenial girl," she had written. "Full of confidence, I have great character to challenge creative jobs. Because of my education and practices in university, I form good ability in organization and coordination and foster my team spirit as well as problem-solving skills." I suggested that she remove "Communist Party student cadre" from her resume, explaining to her that the multinational corporations to which she was applying did not necessarily value Communist ideals. She decided to leave it in her cover letter, but remove the words "Communist Party" and leave only "student cadre" on her résumé. A sharp recruiter who valued leadership abilities would spot it, and perhaps someone who did not might miss its meaning.

Upon graduation, Communist-adherent Polly was recruited to work as a number cruncher in a capitalist American accounting firm, an irony she did not entirely grasp. For this next stage in her life, she asked me to help her choose a more suitable English name, something more adult-sounding and mature. When I chose one for her, she was thrilled, and she switched it that very day. Suddenly, Communist girl Polly had become the realist professional woman "Pauline."

I understood her internal conflicts and desires because of a number of discussions I had had with a Chinese professional woman who worked in finance in Shanghai. She and I had met while living on the same floor of graduate housing in England, where she was getting her

M.B.A. I will call her Mei Li, although that is not her real name. Unlike many Chinese, including Polly/Pauline and Rock, who introduce themselves to foreigners with sometimes strange English names,[5] Mei Li had introduced herself to me using her Chinese name. When I first met her, she wore her hair long and unstyled, had round bookish wire-rimmed glasses, never wore makeup, and, like Polly, seemed to be a sweet young overachiever who had graduated at the top of her class, from the Yale of Chinese universities, Fudan. As grad students together, she taught me to sing "The East is Red," China's famous revolutionary song lauding Mao Zedong, learned by schoolchildren of her generation all over China.

When we met up again in Hong Kong a few years later, she was transformed. She had become a sophisticated investment banker, with tailored suits, contact lenses, a stylish haircut, and bright lipstick. But at work, even though she held an M.B.A. from a prestigious university and had spent two summers as an associate at London bank, she was enmeshed in the drudgery of menial tasks. Her bosses gave her typing, but American men five years her junior and with far less experience were sent out to client meetings. It was frustrating, and she couldn't help but feel that her American and Chinese male bosses viewed her more as an office girl than a career professional. She wasn't a good typist, and told her boss so. Her ability was in numbers. No matter; the boss thought Chinese girls should type.

Mei Li's personal life was a challenge, too. Over dinner in 1997, we discussed the quest to find a husband. When her parents in Shanghai—practicing with their friends and acquaintances the tradition of matchmaking—tried to interest her in potential suitors, Mei Li found the men to be unsophisticated and unsuitable candidates. They had never traveled. They were so provincial. In Hong Kong, the white men she dated posed their own set of challenges in the form of expectations of what a Chinese woman should be like. Mei Li, by her own accounts, was a bad housekeeper and could not cook. She found that she disappointed the white men who rode the elevator up to her high-rise Hong Kong flat by inviting them to find themselves a drink in her messy kitchen, if in fact she had anything to drink at all. She went in there only rarely, since she never cooked at home. "Men always expect that I'm going to serve them because I am Chinese," she complained on a 1999 visit to New York, where she had come to do a bank training program. Were she a Western woman, she felt, surely these men wouldn't expect such things of her.

Eventually, through the large community of Shanghainese living in Hong Kong, Mei Li found a partner. "We got married for very practical reasons," she explained when we met for tea at Shanghai's Portman Hotel in 2004. She looked not only sophisticated now, but elegant, too, with her milk-chocolate colored cashmere shawl, hair upswept into a bun, and large gold earrings. There was something different about her now, too. Was it marriage and the maturity of age? I asked. Yes, she said, and the fact that she was three-months pregnant. "We are very complementary," she said of her husband.

> He is very smart and logical, very even-tempered and rational. I am very short-tempered. His parents were high school teachers, and when they heard about me they were quite unhappy. I was two years older and from a higher-status family, and not so pretty in their opinion, because of my cheekbones.

I had always thought Mei Li's high cheekbones were the most striking aspect of her face, but she told me they are bad luck in China. As she explained, she wrote the Chinese characters for cheekbone, *quan gu,* into my notebook. The first word, *quan,* is a homonym for "power," in Chinese. Thus a wife with high cheekbones, it is believed, will dominate her husband. "I had consulted a fortune-teller before, and he had told me I would have to marry someone with a high bridge or a big nose to compensate," she said. "So I had been thinking that I would have to marry a foreigner." White people in China are known by the derisive nickname, *da bizi,* "big nose." I had known some men living in China who had taken to responding *xiao guanzi,* "little pipe," whenever they heard the insult. This was only wise, they told me, if the guy was shorter than you and likely incapable of beating you up.

In Mei Li's family, her father was a senior government official and her mother was a telecom engineer, and because she was an only child, her parents had raised her with the same expectations for high academic achievement and professional advancement they would have put on a son. She says,

They never said that explicitly, but they always told me to concentrate on my schoolwork and not focus on boys or anything distracting. Plus there were hardships in those days so we didn't have makeup or feminine clothes, so you didn't really feel any different from being a boy. I learned to do makeup by going into department stores in Hong Kong, where they put stuff on you and then you buy it. I'm not very good at it still. I had to work at learning it all, just had to set about learning how to attract a man. I just decided I was going to set about it like a project. I always went out for dinner with different people and joined new groups so that I would meet different people.

When she met her husband, it was at a group dinner in Hong Kong. "Actually we didn't pay attention to each other. I thought he was too young, so I didn't take him seriously," she said. Eventually, however, they began to talk at events organized by mutual friends, and they started dating. "I thought he would be suitable," she said. The two married and Mei Li quit her unsatisfying investment banking job in Hong Kong. She moved back home to Shanghai to start her own business.

Mei Li was not really one to be overly enthusiastic about having children either. "I think it's troublesome," she sighed.

There is pressure to have a baby. I feel that I must complete this mission, so that I can do other things once I have done my duty. When you are in your thirties, some kind of hormone something in your body starts to affect your thinking, that you probably need to do something else in life than just a career. I still want to be a career woman, but also I want to contribute to society. Having a child will also help develop the society. Today in China people respect wealth instead of knowledge or responsibility. So people like myself who have been able to get a good education and set some kind of example, we have to show that there's another way of living, not just a materialistic one, but being responsible. It's hard to convince people in their twenties of that now.

Plus, she added, "having a man's baby is a good way to keep him." Shanghainese men had a reputation in China for being more faithful to their wives than those in, say, Guangzhou. And Mei Li's husband was as cosmopolitan, well-educated, and well traveled as she. But still, one never could be too careful.

"I hope it's a girl," she said as the waitress came with our bill. I expressed surprise at her departure from the norm, but it made sense as she explained it. "If it's a boy, you have to have all the expectations of high achievement. What if they don't do well? You blame yourself. If it's a girl, you don't have all that. In fact, you hope she's not so smart so that she will settle with someone easily." Mei Li planned to take three months off from her work when her baby was born, and then return to the world of high finance.

As we prepared to go, I asked Mei Li about her domestic life, recalling that she had told me she was never a good housekeeper. She smiled.

Well, they say that Shanghainese men treat women as more equal partners compared to men in other parts of China. Traditionally they would do the shopping and the cooking, and the women would do the childcare. My husband's father does this, the grocery shopping, the cooking, and also he mops the floor. But these days, the standard of living is very high in Shanghai. You can afford to hire help, a driver, etcetera. You don't have to do everything yourself.

With that, she offered to have her car and driver take me back to my hotel.

BECAUSE MAO HAD DECLARED that "Women hold up half the sky," women in post-revolutionary China were urged to join the workforce and take up equal roles with men in society. After the Communist victory in 1949, the number of women in the industrial labor force rose from 600,000 to more than 50 million in the 1990s.[6] Since then, more than 80 percent of working-age urban women in China have held jobs outside the home. This is not to say that women in China have achieved parity with men in the workplace. Yet, in comparison with women professionals in other parts of Asia, women in China frequently have had more opportunities for professional advancement—more like those for women in Europe and the United States. The women of the urban elite may have had bound feet for 900 years of China's past, but today they run factories, universities, shops, and businesses.

"Women in China don't like to just be housewives," said Sharron Xu, who is the General Manager of Research and Development at the Shanghai International Group (formerly Shanghai International Trust and Investment Corp., or SITICO) which operates investment banking, trade finance, and insurance businesses. Sharron is one of the most senior businesswomen in Shanghai, and a known figure on Wall Street from when she used to head the investment banking division putting together international bond offerings. I went to her office one afternoon to talk about her exemplary career, and we sat in a conference room overlooking The Bund, the famous stretch of riverfront dotted with the magnificent buildings dating from Shanghai's colonial era.

When Sharron was first starting out in the early 1980s, she said, she would drop off her daughter at "boarding kindergarten" on Monday mornings and pick her up on Friday afternoons. This is typical of the way urban working mothers solve their childcare dilemmas; some schools accept for weekly boarding children as young as age two and a half. Parents can visit during the week if they wish, but they are permitted to leave the children until the weekend. When Sharron took advantage of this system, she was working full-time at the Bank of China and spending evenings trying to get her B.A. To be promoted at work, she had to make up for her education, lost during the Cultural Revolution, when millions of urbanites were dispatched to the countryside to take up manual labor in the name of revolution.

When Sharron was seventeen, she got sent to the extreme north, to Heilongjiang Province, near Russia's Siberia, to drive a tractor on a wheat farm. She could not return to Shanghai until 1978, when she was twenty-four. "I lost a lot of time," she said, "the best years." It took five years of night school for her to earn her B.A.

"It's not easy to be a working mother in China," she said. "You have to balance your job and your family." The system of boarding schools leaves women free to work, and that makes it easier than for working mothers in other countries, she said. "Maybe for Western people they think this is not good, but this is a good system of education in

Shanghai," she said. Her husband, also Shanghainese, teaches at Jiao-tong University, and he always has been supportive of her career and her decisions. "It may be easier for women in the southern part of China. There's more respect for women's independence here," Sharron said. "In the northern part of China, they have a more man-centered ideology. They call it *dananzi zhuyi*."

Even in Shanghai, however, a survey of 1,000 graduates from ten local universities, conducted by the Shanghai Women's Federation, found that 56 percent of female graduates felt discriminated against during their job search; once they landed jobs, males received an average income of 2,706 yuan (US$326) per month, and females 2,441 yuan (US$294).[7]

But Hu Shuli, the female editor-in-chief of China's most respected weekly business magazine—*Caijing*, based in Beijing—scoffs at the idea that men are the only ones responsible for this. She is evidence of how far women can advance in northern China, at the epicenter of power, and she thinks women could achieve even more if they didn't hold themselves back.

Shuli is one of the most sharp-tongued, quick-minded women I have met, never keeping an opinion to herself unless she deems it a strategic advantage to win her point later. Even in English, her second language, she has a tendency to speak quickly and finish others' sentences for them, grasping the thought before the speaker can even articulate it. I went to see her one day at her modest apartment on the third floor of a dingy government-subsidized apartment block in Beijing.

We spent the morning discussing freedom of the press, or rather the lack of it, in China. Shuli has gone farther than anyone in China in pushing boundaries without being shut down by government censors, but her magazine has been sued for "libel" by a company whose fraudulent accounting books were exposed in an article. The company was inflating its earnings through falsified revenue, and it became the first publicly traded company ever to be de-listed (although, technically, its listing was taken over by another company), thanks to her investigative reporters, whom she pushed until they nailed the story. In the controlled environment in which the press operates in China, however, *Caijing* still had to pay a large fine for libeling the company's reputation.

After our lunch together, Shuli summoned her driver to take us to her office. Riding in the back seat of her blue sedan as we sped along Chang'an Avenue in Beijing, past Tiananmen Square and the gates of The Forbidden City where a woman Empress had been in power 100 years before, it struck me that if there were more women like Shuli in China, they undoubtedly would be running the country.

"Women in China have no glass ceiling, but they take for granted their equal status under liberation, and they don't want a high position," she said, pausing between sentences to order her male driver to switch lanes in the heavy traffic. "They still think men should take higher positions than them, so they give it up. Now, to show higher status in China, they want to marry a rich husband and not have to work. These women take for granted the position that women have achieved in China."

Our discussion made me recall the old Chinese proverb that held that the most attractive women are uneducated, unsuccessful, and untalented: *Nuzi wu cai bian shi de.* "A woman without talent is pure virtue (beauty)." Shuli thinks it is nonsense. Most families need two incomes these days.

But I knew one of these women who did not want to aspire to the top. She was the assistant dean at the university where I was teaching; and, she later told me, her aspiration was not to rise within the university administration. What Emma wanted instead was a happy marriage and a family. Just as soon as she finished her Ph.D., she said, she was going to get married, quit the administration part of her job, and simply stick to teaching. No more promotions. Her priority was going to be family. Emma had seen so many marriages torn apart by the demands of academia, where teachers are expected to be the "moral compasses" of students, and to give out their cell phone numbers and take students calls (about even non-academic questions) late into the evening and on weekends. Emma's first marriage had suffered from her striving. She did not want it to happen a second time.

When Emma first came to greet me at the train station upon my arrival in Guangzhou, we surprised each other. We both had expected someone taller and older, and perhaps a bit more visibly experience-worn. She was sweet and soft-spoken, wearing one of the pretty, feminine dresses that she wore to the department every day. She thinks pants make her look short.

When Emma offered to lend me some plates and utensils during my stay and led me up to her apartment to collect them, I saw that she had two giant stuffed teddy bears in her bedroom. Her first questions to me were whether I shared a passion for the sappy, romantic movies she loved—*Runaway Bride, Pretty Woman, Four Weddings and a Funeral,* etc.—and whether I loved watching *Sex and the City* as much as she did. When I told her my New York apartment was near the café and park where Meg Ryan and Tom Hanks meet in *You've Got Mail,* she nearly fainted with envy. Her favorite fruit is the pomegranate because it looks like it's filled with little colorful diamonds. She once dragged me on a seemingly endless walk through the smog and heavy traffic of Guangzhou to show me her favorite dress shop where everything was too frilly for my taste.

But beneath Emma's girlish exterior, I came to learn, is the persistence of a bulldog. Frequently, she looked like a girl bursting with a secret, and when she had that look, I knew she was going to ask something of me. Resistance would be futile, for a refusal would keep her coming back for days with more demanding alternatives, nicely and sweetly, of course, until I finally realized that her first request was indeed the best of all possible alternatives. Everyone in her circles in Guangzhou, it turned out, already knew this. They all take Emma's calls.

Even with this ability to wield power and influence, however, Emma didn't want to rise through university ranks. When she was approached by the Communist Party to join, and even urged to do so by her bosses as a good career move, she refused. With her late hours in the office and her free time guiding students' moral compasses, she is busy enough already.

And in her every free moment, between classes, on the way to meetings, in a taxi, waiting in the food line at the cafeteria, she text messages back and forth with her boyfriend on her cell phone. He is a practitioner of traditional medicine and reflexology. He writes *Wo ai ni,* "I love you," to Emma—an expression of sentiment atypical for Chinese men—and calls her his "wife," even though they are not formally married, in the manner of very serious couples. Because I saw Emma so frequently keying on her Nokia, I asked her about him.

"We met online," Emma explained. "Have you seen *Tokyo Love Story?*" I hadn't, and disappointed her yet again with my disinterest in sentimentalism. She had seen all dozen or however many episodes.

> I ordered the television series *Tokyo Love Story* from Bertelsmann on-line, and there was a place on the website to leave messages. I saw one from a man saying he wanted a girlfriend, age twenty-five, just like the heroine in *Tokyo Love Story*. I sent him an email saying, "I don't want to be your girlfriend because anyway I am over twenty-five, but she is my heroine, too, so I think we have something in common."
>
> She is a very romantic person, very optimistic. I sent it and forgot about it. Two weeks later I got a response from him, and then he telephoned me. After the phone call, he told me that he thought I was his ideal woman. That was four months ago. So a month later, for his birthday, he flew to Guangzhou to meet me. I was so disappointed when I first saw him. He is twenty-nine, and I am thirty-four. He looked so young, so immature.

Emma pulled out a picture of a young man with a boyish face, square jaw, and a square-cut hairline to show me. "I thought, 'How could I rely on someone who is so immature?' So I had my friends meet him and scheduled many events with my friends while he was here."

> At first he said he thought I needed to find someone of my same ed-ucation level, so he failed that first test. Here, if you are a woman and have a Master's degree, it's quite a lot. And I am planning to start my Ph.D. next year. So my aunt met him. She pointed out all my faults. She said, "My niece is not such a good housecleaner, and she is very career oriented. You had better think about that if you want to have a serious relationship with her." But he still did, so he passed that test.
>
> So then I had a tea party with five girlfriends. They were all go-ing to ask him questions, but then they decided against it, so they

just tried to talk about things with him in roundabout ways. He passed that test. Then I had a classmate's sister come up all the way from Zhuhai and we had lunch. She had told my classmate fourteen years ago that my husband was not trustworthy. She knew that by reading his face. In China, we have not only palm reading but face-reading, too. She could see something in his face, in his eyes, that he was not trustworthy. So she told my classmate that. But my class-mate never told me. When I told her finally that I was divorcing, she said, "I told my sister that fourteen years ago, but she never told you." So I wanted her to meet him. She said he had a good face. So he passed that test.

My husband left a year and a half ago. He had an affair when I left to go abroad to do my Master's degree. We had gotten married in February, and I left in September. He refused to visit me. He had the affair while I was away. He is the kind of man who can't stand to have a wife in a higher position than he is. He is also a lecturer at the university. People would say jokingly to him, after I got pro-moted, "Oh, you have a leader at home." But actually, I was very submissive to him at home, always cooking and doing the cleaning. In China, men don't like if their wives are more educated or have a higher position than they do.

Emma and her husband had started dating while they were fresh-men in college. They both were offered teaching positions in the de-partments they graduated from.

Our friends said that he married me because it was the conclusion of a nine-year relationship rather than the start of a lifetime. I asked him why he married me then if he really didn't want to be with me for the rest of his life. He said, "Why do you think marriage should last a lifetime?" When I came back after my semester away, he was staying out all night a lot of the time. He told me it was work. I wanted to believe it. I spent many sleepless nights waiting for him to come home. I never knew when he would come and go. I devel-oped insomnia. So finally one day I called his department head and asked, "Do you require your lecturers to put in so much overtime?" He said, "Yes, we require some overtime, but not overnight, not like that. Perhaps you are the last person to know what is going on." It was really a terrible time. In a small campus like this people gossip, and everybody knew everything except me. He never told me anything. If he had told me, I could have accepted it, but he moved out without even telling me the reason.

He is still together with her, but they moved off campus. Sometimes I bump into him. And her office is on the first floor of my building. My office is on the second floor. But now when I see her, because I have a boyfriend now, I feel confident. So I have been through a lot in these past few years.

Emma and her boyfriend were waiting to get married because she was planning to go abroad again to work on her Ph.D. "I don't want to make the same mistake as last time," she said. "Also it is too new, and I want to see what happens with him over time. He told me that he has never married yet because he has been waiting for someone like me all this time."

The infidelity problem Emma describes—and to which Mei Li had alluded—is a growing one for women around the region. Asian women frequently told it me it was the most serious problem they faced in their marriages. A number of the cultures of Asia have century-old traditions of polygamy—not only in China, but in countries whose original people migrated from China—Korea, Vietnam, and Thailand. On top of that, some Southeast Asian cultures legally allow polygamy because of Islam or indigenous practice—Indonesia, Malaysia, and Brunei. The Philippines was polygamous before the Spanish colonialists arrived. And in Japan, traditionally the husband sought sensual pleasures outside the home, rather than with his "virtuous" wife who then became "mother" in his eyes as soon as children were born. Monogamy was never a traditional value in most East Asian cultures.

Still, for a long time, poverty helped keep men at home. Quite simply, the majority of men in pre-industrialized Asia were too poor to support more than one woman. Only the rich could afford it. Additionally, Communism outlawed polygamy as a feudal practice in Vietnam and China. But now, with the growing economic prosperity of the past three decades, Asian men increasingly have found it prestige-enhancing among their peers to take a mistress or "minor wife." It demonstrates wealth and virility, two important aspects of East Asian masculinity. In Malaysia and Indonesia, men made more prosperous by economic development have more means to consider polygamy as a lifestyle choice—perfectly legally.

In downtown Guangzhou, I regularly passed an apartment block said to be where second wives were "kept" by visiting businessmen from Hong Kong. And just across the border from Hong Kong, in Shenzhen, there is a well-documented "mistress village" for Chinese wives of Hong Kong men. Sometimes they are merely women denied the right to live in Hong Kong because they are mainland Chinese. Frequently, however, the men have "first" wives in Hong Kong as well.

All this doesn't mean the first wives are passively going along with this return to "tradition." There is a growing embrace of feminism throughout the region to combat it. Islamic feminists in Indonesia boycott establishments owned by known polygamists. As discussed previously, in Thailand women "Lorena-Bobbitt" straying husbands with frightening regularity, and wives throwing acid in their husbands' mistresses' faces to disfigure them has been a rising phenomenon. Reading the Hong Kong newspapers one day, I stumbled on a brief article that began, "The number of men being beaten by their wives in Hong Kong has reportedly quadrupled in the past four years as women refuse to accept their husbands keeping mistresses."

I had met a group of Chinese women dedicated to confronting not just infidelity but larger issues of sexism in Chinese tradition. We went to see a stage performance of *The Vagina Monologues* in Chinese one evening in Guangzhou—the only performance in China before the government banned it. A Chinese sexologist, Li Yinhe, at the Chinese Academy of Social Scientists in Beijing had told me that Chinese women were lacking awareness of their sexuality: 26 percent have never experienced orgasm during sex, compared to about 10 percent in the United States and Britain. She also told me Chinese people have sex comparatively less often than other nationalities: about 100 to 110 times per year, compared to more than 150 times per year in France.

The performance of *The Vagina Monologues* was part of a growing sexual awakening among Chinese women. One of the women accompanying me was the writer Zhang Nian, who was part of this group of women who had declared opposition to monogamy as a standard only applying for Chinese women. The blogger Mou Zimei, whose website chronicling her sex life with many partners was shut down by the Chinese government, was another. The group, about a dozen women in all, met in bars in Guangzhou to discuss their liberation from the constraints of tradition. Nian told me she would never marry, and that she insisted her boyfriend marry someone else instead of her. He did so. But the two remain lovers, and Nian has other regular sex partners as well.

> I saw my friends getting married and it was like a window being shut, with their husbands and children becoming their whole universe. I told him, "I don't want a marriage contract to be a contract on my body." He couldn't understand this. But if you want to sleep with someone you should be able to. It is human nature not to have limited sexual partners. Men feel free to do so. There should be equality.

We discussed China's traditions and the best-selling book *Shanghai Baby,* written by Nian's friend Wei Hui, which portrayed Chinese men as emasculated and the sexual ideal as a dominating white man. It was banned in China for its blatant sex, but counterfeit copies had been widely read. "She lost hope in Chinese men," Nian explained. "A lot of men criticize Wei Hui because it challenges them. I believe there's a Wei Hui in every Chinese woman's heart." As we sat through the performance, and *The Vagina Monologues*'s scenes progressed into the segment where audience participation is encouraged in making "sounds of sex," Nian joined the couple hundred Chinese women in the auditorium in building their squeals into a collective shriek of orgasm. "Yin dao" she wrote in my notebook. It means vagina in Chinese.

WHEN EMMA VISITED the States almost a year later, I took her to the Café Lalo, where Meg Ryan had sat with her rose waiting for Tom Hanks. She had started her Ph.D., she told me, and she and her boyfriend were still crazy about each other even after her semester abroad. They planned to marry when she finished, in two more years.

She wanted her picture taken against the Café's wall, and later sent me a copy with a note written on the back, "*Xiang xin zhen ai he qi ji*—to the belief in true love and magic feelings."

I took her to Macy's, the shoppers Mecca she had heard about. She bought eye cream to get a free Estée Lauder gift pack. Then she wanted to see the top of the Empire State Building, even though it was a rainy day. It wasn't the view of New York that interested her so much as a pilgrimage to the final setting of *Sleepless in Seattle*. When she got home to China, she wrote this email account of her last ten minutes in America before leaving for the airport.

Emma at Café Lalo,
New York, 2004

I rushed to a bookstore opposite to my hotel. I knew my luggage was too heavy with dozens of books, but I still did not want to lose my last chance of buying books in America. At the sight of the book *Sex and the City* (the original collection of column writings), I suddenly remember this is the must item I promised to take back to my colleagues and single female friends in their thirties. I immediately purchased the book, but was a bit hesitating whether I should spend $23 on another book entitled *Woman Power, the Companion to the Proper Care and Feeding of Husbands*. The big subtitle on the book jacket reads "Transform Your Man, Your Marriage, Your Life." On second thought, the book may be a good investment if it can really bring happy marriage as promised.

She bought it.

There was another aspect of this China Doll/Dragon Lady dichotomy for Asian women which I wanted to explore, that of Martial Arts Mistress and Dominatrix, the steely cold projection of strength and power portrayed by Asian villainesses of the screen. In China, women routinely practice morning tai chi in public parks. It is tame exercise—part stretching, part balance, and part concentration. But, apart from professional athletes training for professionally organized *wu shu* martial arts competitions, it is difficult to find regular women in China who practice martial arts. The discipline seemed to be better preserved outside mainland China, where the middle classes had the luxury of nighttime leisure activities.

I decided to look in the ethnic Chinese communities of Southeast Asia, which are striving to maintain their cultural and Confucian traditions untouched by Communism's cultural eradications. Singapore, for example, has a large community of adherents to Chinese martial arts traditions, including kung fu and its branch *wing chun*—which Bruce Lee demonstrated in *Enter the Dragon,* the first American-produced martial arts movie, in 1973.

The fascinating aspect of *wing chun,* other than the fact that it gave westerners their first mass on-screen exposure to martial arts, is its origin. Legend has it that a Buddhist Abbess at the famous Shaolin monastery in central China taught Shaolin's kung fu techniques to a young woman named Miss Yim so that she could fend off the unwanted advances of a local bully back during the Qing Dynasty (1662–1722). She trained day and night, then challenged the man to a fight and beat him up. Miss Yim then married somebody else, and passed on her fighting techniques to her husband, who passed them to others. The tradition then developed with improvements by subsequent generations of students who mastered the techniques and added their own, so that when adherents of kung fu challenged the adherents of *wing chun,* those who had mastered *wing chun* won.

So I went to the Wing Chun Kuen Training Center in Singapore to meet some of the women there who are maintaining the tradition: Teresa Oh, who is a forty-one-year-old former police officer turned guard at Changi women's prison; Jamie Tan, a twenty-eight-year-old banker who also does tai chi and yoga; and Celeste Pang—the youngest and most girlish of the three—who works in corporate communications. These women train three to four nights a week, punching a bag filled with metal balls and boxing with a wooden "horse" by banging their forearms against its protruding wooden dowels. Everything they did looked painful—and indeed was, I discovered when they invited me to try it—but they all had turned to *wing chun* for mental discipline and fitness reasons. It was more or less the same as joining a health club, except this was a Chinese tradition, and it was developed by a woman. Wing chun had another added benefit, a silent feeling of power that came from having the ability to kill anyone with one blow—not that the women would need that ability in ultra-safe Singapore. But still, they said, it was not only the ability but knowing they had the discipline to control it—to use fatal force only when there is no other option to subdue one's attacker—that made them feel empowered.

I asked them what they thought of the way martial arts women are portrayed on screen and how that compares with their lives. Again, the issue of strength and weakness, toughness and girlishness, was central to the discussion.

> TERESA: Hollywood is Hollywood. When I see Lucy Liu, I just think "Oh, American-Chinese." They're different. We are raised more conservative here.
>
> JAMIE: I don't mind that image of being strong and steely. You can't be so emotional when you're doing martial arts. It shows that a person is strong.
>
> CELESTE: But it doesn't have to be so obvious. People are always shocked when I say I do martial arts, and more shocked when I say I do training three times a week.

Rather, these women made a point of saying that they're just real women. Celeste likes to dress up and wear makeup, and she cries over sad parts of movies. She calls herself a "positive and friendly" person. Jamie likes cartoon characters such as "South Paw" the dog, and Japanese *anime*, particularly a story about androids with the ability to feel. Teresa picks up stray kittens, and now has three. Her first was Whiskers, who weighs eight kilograms (eighteen pounds) and looks like Batman. She found him when he was the size of her hand, near the subway on her way home from work. "It would have been trampled by all the people going to the MRT," she said. "It was just meowing looking for its mother. I decided to keep it."

These inconsistencies—between picking up stray kittens, wearing makeup, and crying over sad parts of movies, and being able to kill a

Celeste Pang, Jamie Tan,
and Teresa Oh,
Singapore, 2004

person with a single blow—seemed to be the aspects that rarely came through in the kick-ass screen portrayals.

Next, at the Singapore Karate Association I found Cindy Tan, a forty-four-year-old fourth-level black belt in karate, a martial art which originated in Okinawa. Other than being a karate instructor, she describes herself as "just a normal housewife at home. I still dress up, dress sexy for dinner and certain occasions. I wear earrings. When I see a sad show on TV, I cry. We are still females, we are still girls. We have very emotional feelings. We are still sensitive." There's really only one major difference between martial arts women and others, she said. "You have to be careful when you discipline the kids or you can really hurt them."

I was not able to meet the professional female *wu shu* athletes of China,[8] so it took going to Japan to meet a woman who pursued martial arts as a full-time career. I flew to the southern island of Kyushu to

meet her—two-time Olympic judo gold medalist, Ryoko Tamura. She
is Japan's version of Mary Lou Retton, and her nickname is "Yawara-
chan." *Yawara* means "soft" or "tender," a word usually used to describe a pillow or a bed, or used in the context of cooking, and *chan* is
a diminutive, like *-ita* in Spanish or *-ette* in French. Ryoko is tiny for a
judo champion, and at 4'7" she frequently is far shorter than her opponents. But she is a tenacious competitor. She won the judo World
Championships an unprecedented six times straight, and took gold at
the Sydney Olympics in 2000 and again in Athens in 2004.

At the time that I met Ryoko, she was twenty-eight and engaged to
a star Japanese baseball player. (Six months after our meeting, she
married him and changed her name to Ryoko Tani.) She brought
along her fellow judo champ, Harumi Nakahashi, to our discussion at
a coffee shop near her training center in the city of Kumamoto. Ryoko
and her friend ordered cheesecake. The both spoke of taking on a role,
like acting, upon putting on the white cotton judo uniform, or *gi,* and
stepping onto the mat.

Ryoko got the idea to take up judo while accompanying her mother
to pick up her brother at judo practice. "I saw a girl throwing someone
and thought it was really cool," she said. "I wanted to be strong and
throw someone, too."

A long time ago, Japan had a male-dominated society, but since I
was born, I have felt that men and women are treated equally as long
as one tries one's best. Especially in judo, it is a very active, very aggressive sport. I have practiced among men ever since I was little. So
I have never been conscious of being a woman when I practice with
them. People told me that once I put on a *gi,* I should have a man's
mind, I should be like a man. When not wearing a *gi,* you're a
woman. In order to win, there are so many things I have had to learn
from men's strength, such as being very tough, not giving in easily.

I believe that strength or unbending nature, and that of a beautiful heart, are the same in both men and women. However, judo
started as a men's sport. Then European women started doing judo
and, ten years later, judo for women started in Japan. When I was
little, the image of it being a men's sport was strong. So I practiced

with boys as my opponents. Through that experience, I wanted to be as strong as a man. Now there's a beauty to judo, and this is something that only women judo athletes can enjoy, that when you are in *gi* you can be strong, you can be tough. But once you take off your *gi,* you can be a woman and you can enjoy shopping, dressing up, putting on makeup and you can really cherish that aspect of being female.

I was rather late in age when I started caring about my hair or wearing makeup. I was too busy with judo and didn't really have time. Putting on makeup and going shopping are fun and I didn't know there were such fun things before. Now I know how fun it is and am really enjoying them. This is something my mother always told me, to remember that I am a girl, even though I am playing judo among boys. Tying my bangs with a ribbon on my forehead was something she started to remind me of that. So I have always done it.

Kyushu, or Fukuoka [city] where I am from, has a particularly male-dominated conservatism. There's a saying that women should walk three steps behind a man, or something like that, according to the traditional Japanese value. I was raised in a family where the father was the center of the family and a very strict disciplinarian. But my mother supported my father and she was very kind, very gentle. I want to be like my mother.

Because of her judo success, Ryoko's father decided to get a chiropractor's license to tend to her sports injuries. I asked whether this meant he was the one walking three steps behind her. "Now that you mention it, yes! He is very happy about it, though. He keeps supporting me from behind." Because Ryoko's pending nuptials were in the news, I asked what the role reversal meant for her marriage.

"I am sure I will support my man after marriage," she said.

But at the same time, I believe that my future husband will support me with a very open mind and big heart. I'm saying this because probably after marriage I will continue with judo. I would like our married relationship to be something that brings out our potential in each other and from each other. If that is possible that would be wonderful. That is the kind of relationship I would like to have. Sometimes I may walk three steps behind him and support him. But sometimes, other times, I may lead him, and he may walk three steps behind me and support me. That's my ideal.

At this, Ryoko's friend joined in. "When I visit Ryoko's family, I am impressed with how much her mother supports her father. In my house, my mother expresses opinions. She is very much like an American type of woman. My father gets yelled at!" Harumi said. "So I really respect Ryoko's mother. She really handles her father. She has so many wiles!"

I asked Ryoko which parent she considers the family boss.

My mother. I found out my father cannot do anything by himself. My mother cooks meals, cleans, and does the laundry for us. Without mother, my father doesn't know where things are or what to do. My mother is the leader, showing which way to go. Father deals with things with one method. But mother can come up with different methods, different approaches to things, not only for me but for my father. So she is very open.

Compared to some time ago, this man-dominated society aspect is fading out. In the workplace and society, men and women are standing more on equal levels, I feel. I am aware that, as judo was a man's sport to begin with, my contribution to women becoming equal is that the popularity of women's judo has surpassed that of men. It used to be that just the men's team won gold medals. Now I proved that even Japanese women can get the gold if we try very hard. This is something I have convinced myself, that if you try very hard, your dream will come true, and even women can do it.

Power Women

Don't turn around," my backseat companion ordered in her posh, Oxford-accented English as we sped through the streets of Rangoon in a white Toyota Corolla. Our pursuers were agents from the five branches of internal security and intelligence of Burma's military regime, she said, and if I showed them my face they would take my picture for the files they kept on people considered dangerous enemies of the state.

My companion was Aung San Suu Kyi, the Burmese opposition leader who had been elected by a popular landslide in 1990 but who had never been allowed to take power. Instead, Burma's generals had kept her mostly under house arrest since then, and I was taking advantage of a rare break in her confinement to meet her. I had disguised myself in sunglasses and a baseball cap to reach our early morning rendezvous point at the home of an intermediary, Suu Kyi picked me up and ordered her driver to race us back to her compound on University Avenue.

Because Suu Kyi (pronounced Soo Chee) is followed everywhere, agents of the regime suspected something was up and were waiting to take a photo of whoever arrived. They did not get a clean shot of my face, and they would pursue me the rest of the day—until I was deported on the 4:30 PM flight to Bangkok because of this clandestine meeting. They finally got a clear picture as I mounted the plane's stairway from the tarmac.

As we entered the gates of her compound and Suu Kyi invited me into her home, I could understand her magnetism and popularity among the people of Burma. If there is a definition of gracefulness walking, she is it. We talked for several hours over a long, leisurely lunch of rice and fish. We discussed economic sanctions against her country, which she wanted maintained to keep pressure on the regime. She preferred that the world continue to call her country "Burma," she said, after the majority Burman people who live there—not "Myan-mar," the name adopted by the military generals in 1989 (*Myan* means fast, *mar* means strong.) She asked for news about the outside world, as she was almost completely cut off from world events. We also dis-cussed why she had not been able to ascend to her rightful place lead-ing the nation. The male generals in power do not want to cede power—to anyone, but especially not to a woman.

Suu Kyi represents the type of Asian female political leader to have reached global prominence, daughters or wives of former male leaders who inherited the mantle of political power from men. Suu Kyi is the daughter of nationalist hero Aung San, who was assassinated after ne-gotiating independence from colonial ruler Britain in 1947, when Suu Kyi was two years old. Because of this acceptance of women inheriting power, Asians elected the world's *first* female head of government, and they have elected more prominent women leaders than any other re-gion of the world.

In 1960, when the U.S. populace was enamored of a playboy presi-dent and his ever-faithful wife, the island nation of Sri Lanka elected the world's first female prime minister, Sirimavo Bandaranaike, the widow of Sri Lanka's assassinated leader. Not until 1979, when Britain's Margaret Thatcher was elected, was there a second. Ban-daranaike later passed that power to her daughter, Chandrika Ku-maratunga, whose own politician husband also was assassinated. Significantly, Bandaranaike endorsed her daughter as her successor over her son, who, she said, was too disorganized to run a country.

One reason for this transference of power from husband to wife or father to daughter involves Hindu tradition—which, for the purposes of this discussion, has some influence in the politics of Burma, In-donesia, and other parts of Indianized Southeast Asia. Hindu girls are *paraya dhan,* or "somebody else's wealth." When women marry they take on the caste and status of their husbands—and that can also translate into his political power after his death. But it is not the only reason, particularly in the Christian-majority Philippines, where it likely has to do with women being respected as "mothers." Politically that has translated to blessed caretakers of the nation, full of duty and devotion. Piety plays a role, and women who aspire to power are seen at Catholic mass every Sunday if not every day. Other cultural factors in each country matter as well. But whatever the complexities behind the reasons, the potency of this power inherited man to woman is one that no man-to-man political succession in Asia has been able to match thus far. This is an important aspect of the power structure in Asia that few Westerners understand. And frequently, the power of female political leaders in Asia is either minimized or denigrated by stereotypes.

The list of nearly a dozen Asian women inheriting the mantle of power from husbands or fathers includes Corazon Aquino of the Philippines, whose husband Benigno was ordered assassinated by Ferdinand Marcos, and current President Gloria Macapagal Arroyo, who is the daughter of the pre-Marcos Philippine President Diosdado Macapagal. It also includes Megawati Sukarnoputri of Indonesia. Derided by most who meet her as not particularly bright, being the daughter of her late father Sukarno (who ruled Indonesia from 1945 to 1967) was the only qualification she needed for the presidency. Dubbed the "Queen of Silence" by Indonesians who grew dismayed with her inability to rule, however, she was not reelected to a second term in 2004.

Increasingly, however, there is a new kind of woman winning public office in Asia—who through her own education and experience is being valued as a political leader in her own right. In discussions with a dozen female assembly members, mayors, governors, cabinet secretaries, civil service officers, and parliamentarians in Asia, I found that, after the wives and daughters of elected men have lowered the barriers to public office, these women without titles or political inheritances are starting to break through them.

Women also are helped by gender quotas starting to be adopted in a number of countries. In Indonesia, for example, a 2003 election law directs political parties to "give consideration" to fielding women as thirty percent of their candidates. Ironically, President Megawati spoke out against affirmative action for women, and feminists blasted her lack of concern for women's issues. The quota law is believed responsible for increasing the number of women elected to Parliament from 44 of 500 seats (8.8 percent) in 1999, to 65 of 550 seats (11.8 percent) in April 2004.

"Who is called to fulfill this commitment? Those who have been involved in the community, activists like me," Latifah Iskandar, who was elected to Indonesia's Parliament from Yogjakarta, told me. She had long been involved in women's Islamic causes in her city and is a successful businesswoman, owning shops that sell Islamic clothing for women. Even though I am a woman and we met in her home, she covered her head in proper Islamic fashion. Like all of the Islamic women activists and feminists I met in Indonesia and Malaysia, she viewed her headscarf not as a symbol of oppression as westerners sometimes think, but as a symbol of nationalism and of freedom, allowing her to go anywhere and do anything she pleased. (It provides the added benefit of never having to worry about a bad hair day, other women have told me. College students felt that their parents trusted them more if they wore the headscarf, and they also felt immune from crime wearing it as well. As a result, 50 percent of Indonesian female college students now wear it, a drastic increase from just ten years ago.)

"I promote the basic Islamic understanding of the equality of men and women. I have been struggling for the empowerment of women from a marginal level for a long time," Rep. Iskandar told me. "Now I will have an opportunity to make a difference in a more strategic way, from the center of power, to change the system." She received the largest number of votes in her district, garnering 35 percent, but she wouldn't have been a candidate if it weren't for the quota.

IT WOULD TAKE ANOTHER ENTIRE BOOK to do justice to their stories, to show how so many women have struggled to build their political awareness from the ground up. But one woman who is emblematic of them is Reiko Nakajima, the mayor of Haki, Japan. Hers is a town of 9,000 people in farm country near some hot springs outside of Fukuoka in southern Japan. It is the domain of the *Kyushu danji*—men who, influenced by Korean immigration and, living closer to South Korea than to Tokyo, adhere more closely to macho Confucian traditions than to the comparative liberalism of the nation's capital.

Mayor Nakajima had arranged to meet me at the Haki Farm Station, a combined rest stop and farmers' market that sells coffee, organic produce, and fresh-baked bread. It was created and built under her mayoral tenure, primarily employs women, and gives the town's farmers (women also comprise the majority of farmers) an outlet to sell their produce locally. The mayor is late, unusual in Japan, and she comes rushing in all apologies. We get coffee and sit at a window table looking out over a field of pansies.

"I am forty-eight years old and I am a farmer," she begins. She grows shitake mushrooms, gingko nuts, and rice. Her husband is a civil servant, but he comes from a farming family. When Reiko married him, she moved onto the family farm—with four generations of her husband's family under the same roof. "Walking three steps behind your husband, so to speak, is still prevalent especially in the agricultural areas here. That's why I ran for Mayor." Originally she came from a similar town about forty miles away.

I was a daughter of an agricultural family, so I worked under my parents from very early in the morning until very late at night. I was very busy even before my marriage. It was very repetitive work. When I was young, I passed the exam to become a civil servant of Fukuoka Prefecture and started to work at a nursery school. When I left to get married, my father said, "Why feel regretful? You are a woman! No matter what job you get, you won't have a career anyway. Only men have to worry about that." So I had a lot of experience in women being second-class citizens. My parents recommended I marry a man from Haki, who was arranged by introduction. I didn't want to. I was anxious. My father said, "You are too young. You have no experience to find a man. You have to trust my judgment." In those days, the best years for women getting married were twenty-three to twenty-five. I didn't know much about him. It was just *que sera, sera*. Our fourth meeting was on our wedding day. Not many young people marry like this anymore. In my time, people had to accept marriage through a matchmaker.

"As the bride of a farmer, we have to do a lot of work: cook, work in the fields, keep our obligation to the community and to relatives, and take responsibility for childrearing. Women are considered to be in a support position. Our jobs are not valued highly." Reiko and her husband had two children. When their first child was a daughter, she felt pressured to have a son the second time around.

> I realized that child-raising for boys and girls is totally different. If the husband is the only son, he is treated as the treasure of the family. I married that kind of man. My husband was very important to family members. I was treated in a different way. I thought I was losing social awareness because I was cut off from others. I thought after my children were grown, it would be too late because there's a huge gap between me and the rest of the community. I thought I would lose my humanity.

Reiko also found that gender disparities in farm work were cause for dissatisfaction among women. Reiko is a sturdy, able-bodied woman, but she found herself allocated only menial, repetitive farm tasks. "In agriculture you have to be a hard laborer. But when it comes to the most important part of the job, it's always done by men. It's not a woman's job," she says.

> When I asked why the important tasks are only allocated to men, I was told it's too difficult for women to do. But they didn't let a woman try, so how could they know? For example, pruning trees is done by men. So men cut the branches and women's job is to collect and burn them. It's nonsense to divide the work like that. If you study how, women can do it. If we did nothing, we would be doing that into the next century. Women were not being used according to their ability.

Reiko worked out in the fields, and started wondering about it all, about the status of women. Perhaps it was time for a change, she thought, so her daughter wouldn't have the same destiny. She began sitting on an agricultural advisory committee for Fukuoka Prefecture, where she learned that 60 percent of local farmers were women. The committee traveled to Australia and New Zealand in 1993 as part of a government-sponsored agricultural inspection team.

I found out about the lifestyles of women farmers in New Zealand and Australia. Japanese women work hard but they never learn or pay attention to societal affairs. We didn't even know about the WTO [World Trade Organization]. I thought, we have to empower ourselves to learn about these other agricultural areas, and broaden our view. Our situation is brought about by ignorance. We have to change it.

So, in 1994, Reiko formed a study group of some women she knew. She invited a few farm women at first, then the owners of the nearby hot spring hotels, who were mostly women. They invited a few shop owners, and they knew some retired women who used to be office workers. Reiko named it the "Ms. Association," and she told the members they were going to "change the landscape" of their lives. Eventually the group swelled to about forty women.

"I never imagined I would become the Joan of Arc of agricultural women. I just wanted to lead a small movement in an agricultural county. I just wanted to change my own life," she says.

I watched what my mother did for her whole life, and I didn't want to be like her. There was only one option for my mother's generation. I thought that if I had the same life as my mother, there is no human rights in that. There's no progress if we just continue what the previous generation has done. I had a chance to do something. I wanted to enjoy my life and wanted to have a life worth living. I knew my daughter is at more of a disadvantage than my son. I talked with people about this and said, "Let's stop this in our generation so that the next generation won't suffer."

At first I struggled with my family. I knew our perspective was quite limited. I wanted to broaden it to community and societal problems. In the very beginning we studied about agriculture itself. Eventually we began to study gender discrimination. For example, always in retail, the wife keeps the shop, but the plans are decided by men, and executed by the women. This is a problem we had in every part of society. Then the next step was to discuss what we can do to change it.

The women of the local hot springs decided to improve the reputation of their resorts, which had become known as areas of prostitution. They kicked out prostitutes operating in their spas, and they put social pressure on others who didn't. They embarked on a beautifying campaign to put flowerpots along the streets. They encouraged Reiko to run for one of twenty-four seats in the town assembly in 1995. No woman had ever run before. "At first my husband and parents were opposed. He said he would divorce me, but he didn't. Many people said, 'No woman can do this job.' But I was so determined. I thought that if I back away from everything I had achieved so far, I would be lost."

The town was shocked when Reiko received 581 votes, the highest number of any candidate in the race.

> Still there was a lot of criticism of me. They said it was only women who supported me. So for four years I was forced to accept a lot of menial jobs at the Assembly. They looked at me with very cold eyes, not very sympathetically. In the beginning, many men said, "You're a woman, shut up," or "You're a woman, you have no say in this." I had to prove that I am an able person. I wanted to achieve something that could not be achieved by male Assembly members. Every time we had a meeting, I challenged the mayor, and I had meetings with women to explain the town budget to them. I thought local women should be familiar with Town Hall, because the objective of politics is to improve our daily lives.

Reiko ran for Assembly again in 1999 and nearly doubled her votes to 987—again the highest number. The candidate garnering the fewest number of votes to earn a seat got 280. "Many men had said, 'You just got votes because people are curious about you, and you'll lose the second time. So I was elected the second time. But I was still not elected chair of the Assembly. They made me a committee chairperson instead." Reiko then ran for mayor in 2002. She became Mayor Nakajima, the fifth woman elected mayor in all of Japan's roughly 3,200 municipalities. Now she is the boss of all the stalwart men in the Assembly. Her old Assembly seat was won by another woman.

"Still there is strong criticism against me," she says.

They say, "Maybe you can be a good Assembly member, but not a good mayor." I am the first woman mayor in all of Kyushu, so there's a lot of interest in me. That means I have to do something extraordinary. My intention is to change the top-down decision-making process to the bottom-up. It doesn't matter whether man or woman . . . we have to put emphasis on people.

Mayor Nakajima's husband has come around to the idea of his wife running his hometown and has stopped threatening divorce. "I forced him to withdraw that remark! I told him to wait until after the election and then he could divorce me," she said jokingly. "No, no, we have a good relationship. Many men hate the idea that their wife is stronger. Three steps behind is expected. But he realized there was nothing he could do to change my decision. Now he takes my laundry to the shop and shines my shoes. In return I make breakfast for him."

She appointed women to head the Board of Education and the Social Welfare Council. She extended the hours of the town day care to 7:30 AM to 7 PM, Monday through Saturday. It used to be open 8 AM–5 PM weekdays and until noon on Saturdays. She also extended the span of ages of children accepted there, to include from newborn to age six. This lets working mothers return to work full time after their children are born—and that means Mayor Nakajima can encourage women not to leave civil service once they marry and have children, as women tend to do in Japan. The women currently working at Town Hall have not been serving in their positions long enough and do not yet have seniority, so Mayor Nakajima has not yet been able to appoint any of them as managers or division directors. Any woman who would have had seniority by now has left. If the current crop of mid-level women can just last another ten years, which they can now do more easily with extended day care, then the changes the mayor will have put into place will last long after she is out of office—through those women in senior government positions.

"Gradually we have been able to change the whole county," Mayor Nakajima says.

In the past, women weren't able to go out to meetings or participate in meetings, not only in Haki but elsewhere in Japan. When you have strong intention to change, you can. But a lot of women just accept the ideas given to them by men, and are reluctant to change. We don't want to go ahead of men, but for each woman to participate and be evaluated fairly in society. We had to empower ourselves. It's a very thick barrier in front of us regarding women as second-class citizens, but steadily there are signs of change. I'm confident our society is changing.

On the way out to the parking lot, the Mayor stopped to greet several people she knew, posing for a picture in front of the pansy field under a sky that was threatening with rain. Before leaving Haki, I took a drive through the former red-light district/hot springs area. It had become G-rated and teeming with flowerpots due to the efforts of her women's group, resembling a Disney-like ideal of a quaint, narrow Japanese street. There was not a prostitute or neon light in sight.

At the time that Mayor Nakajima was serving her second term in the Assembly, something remarkable happened in the next Prefecture over. The residents of Kumamoto Prefecture, population 1.8 million, elected a woman as governor.

Yoshiko Shiotani was one of only three women among the forty-seven governors in Japan.[1] She invited me to dinner at the top of the Kumamoto Castle Hotel. When she arrived I was surprised at how tiny she was. She was nearly seventy but her hair was dyed jet black, and she

Reiko Nakajima, Mayor of Haki, Japan, 2003

was wearing a light-pink frilly collared suit and pearls. Her image was of delicacy, quite the opposite of the sturdy Mayor Nakajima. Her strength, it turned out, lay in the changes she had been bringing to the government. She had been lieutenant governor first, taking over her boss' job in a landslide special election after he died in office in 2000.

I had been driven to the hotel by Junichi Tanizaki, the director of the prefectural Office of Gender Equality, and had asked him about having a woman boss. "When she was first inaugurated, I was a little startled," he said.

> My concern cleared up in a couple of days when she said she was sticking to [ongoing government] policies. She brings the views of a woman and housewife because of her previous positions [as a trained social worker and head of government social services], and I really respect that. These are areas in which a male governor may not be strong. And also she has a very strong spiritual strength.

Governor Shiotani is a convert to Lutheranism. As we sat down to dinner with two members of her staff and my translator, I could see through the window behind her the enormous three-tiered phallic projection of the reconstructed Kumamoto Castle, originally built in 1607 and which, according to guidebooks, is one of the greatest castles of feudal Japan. "Kumamoto is a rather conservative area and the traditional values here are the domination of men over women," Governor Shiotani started out.

> A lot of men think, "What can women do?" Older men think all women will be obedient to them. I am not that type, so for some men it may be surprising to them. As a woman governor, it is hard to break such prejudice. As soon as I became governor, I began promoting a gender-equal society. I changed the law in the prefecture so that women do not have to change their names at marriage, which is the law elsewhere in Japan. People criticized me for that. The national law still hasn't changed yet, but many other prefectures now are following suit. I'm not a feminist or doing this for the sake of women's lib. It's just that for women, human rights should be respected equally.

Like the mayor of Haki, the governor of Kumamoto has been trying to promote women in civil service positions. Women rarely go into finance, personnel, or land acquisition; Governor Shiotani has changed that. She requires that all government committees be made up of 30 percent women—in line with recommendations from the Gender Equality Office in Tokyo, acting on United Nations-recommended quotas—or she won't approve their recommendations. She also had sent women "on loan" to positions in the national government that previously have gone to men. "I am asked, 'What will you do if those women fail?' I reply, 'You don't ask me what I will do if the men fail.' It's not women failing or men failing, it's Mr. So-and-So or Miss So-and-So failing."

Deep inside at the gut level, the women of Kyushu are strong. The domination of men over women has been the tradition here, so when women have the opportunity to express themselves, they grab it and seize it. The women in this area have always harbored a strong desire to change this male domination tradition, so maybe that's why they elected me.

Men in my office now come to work saying, "I iron my own clothes." "I do the dishes at home." My husband always does the laundry. That generation of men does not usually do things like that. Other people don't believe me when I tell them.

"My husband when he is asked to do lectures, he said, 'I clean house, I do laundry, I cook.' But my children say he is lying. He cooks, but he just stir fries some meat, that's all. He calls it cooking" she said, jokingly.

When I asked her about her role models, she mentioned Albert Schweitzer and a few Japanese men, but not a single Japanese woman. Frankly, there had never been any women like her—until she and two other women were elected in 2000. Together, the "Three Arrows," as they call themselves, have urged the prime minister to change national policy on issues of health care and domestic violence. The three made national news by presenting their demands, jointly, to the prime minister, who responded by starting to recite an old Japanese expression: "When three women get together . . . they become very noisy."

Except he didn't finish his sentence, Governor Shiotani did. "They become very committed!" she interjected.

When I later met with another of the "Three Arrows," Governor Fusae Ohta of Osaka, who was the first of the three to be elected when her predecessor resigned in a sexual harassment scandal, she told me she expected half of Japan's governors to be women by 2050. Ohta also had served as a lieutenant governor, in a neighboring prefecture. "A senior woman colleague once told me that women need to work as hard as a dog, with the brain of a man, but act like a lady. I think in the future we will work with the brains of women," she said. "Women leaders are good for society because they don't have the obligatory connections men have, and they can work for the society instead of special interests. People are starting to recognize that."

The "Dragon Lady" of Hong Kong

If China had allowed an election to be held in Hong Kong in 1997 instead of hand-picking a man to lead, it most likely would have been won by Anson Chan. She was chief secretary, the top-ranking civil servant and Hong Kong's highest-ranking woman, from 1993 until her resignation in 2001. In other words, she ran the day-to-day operations of the 190,000-employee government, even though Britain had a governor until the 1997 "handover" and China installed a "chief executive" after that.

Chan is a tall, regal woman, the daughter of well-to-do refugees from Communism who fled from Shanghai to Hong Kong in 1948, when she was eight years old. She speaks in a somewhat-imperious, British-accented tone. On occasion she has been dubbed "Dragon Lady," in the Hong Kong press, in the long-standing practice of casting powerful Chinese women in such light. The comparison is accentuated because of the year of her birth, a Year of the Dragon in the Chinese astrological calendar.

She invited me over for tea which she served me herself in flowered bone china teacups and, as we sat on her prim settee, she discussed her struggle to rise through the ranks to become the highest-ranking woman in Hong Kong's history. She also told me the real reasons behind her resignation, but I had to agree not to publish them. Officially, Chan resigned for personal reasons, "to spend more time with my husband."

"I never in my wildest dreams thought that I would become Chief Secretary," she said. Mrs. Chan was only the second woman to join Britain's administrative service.

> I remember very well our own fight for equality of pay and fringe benefits within the Hong Kong government. Because when I joined the HK government in 1962, women were still paid 75 percent of a man's pay for doing the same work. The government gave us this reason for not giving us fringe benefits, that it's the man's responsibility to provide a roof over your head, educate your children, etcetera, so you don't need it. And in the early days in my career, I have to say fortunately not very many of my male colleagues, but a few, used to take the view that, "Oh, you're not really taking your work seriously. You're only there to earn pin money, you know." That was their attitude.

To fight discrimination, Chan and some colleagues set up a trade union that, through long, slow, persistent struggles, achieved pay parity for women in government service by 1975 and benefits parity by 1982. Benefits amounted to up to 66 percent of take-home pay, so they were worth the continued seven years of fighting. "I've never felt that the best way forward was to take very extreme action, like taking to the streets, burning your bra and whatnot," she said.

> A lot of Chinese men have very, very traditional conventional views about the proper role for a woman, which is in the home, in the kitchen, looking after your children, your husband. But my own husband, I suppose because he has been brought up in the Western way, I have to say he has never demonstrated that sort of tendency. But I used to come across male friends who used to say to me, you know, "Why are you working so hard? Why do you think this career is so important?" as if to say, "You ought to be content just being a housewife and a mother." But I sometimes feel—I know

people talk about how there is greater liberalization and whatnot in Western advanced countries—but I sometimes find that some Western males can be even more conventional and old fashioned than Asian males, particularly in the financial field.

Early on in her career, particularly in the days leading up to drafting the annual budget when Mrs. Chan worked in the Treasury, there were long stretches when she would work until 11 PM or midnight.

And you do suffer from guilty pangs: you're not giving enough time to your husband, you're not giving enough time to your children. But I've tried consciously to balance that side of my life with my career, and I hope my children don't feel that they have ever been neglected in the course of growing up.

All of her bosses were men, of course, both British and Chinese. "Only one or two were sexually discriminate," she said.

There was one boss, British, who used to comment on the length of my dress. Yes! Oh, yes! "Too long, too short." But I just sort of shrugged it off. In fact, I remember distinctly one day I was in his office and he asked me to turn around so that he could see my skirt, or whatever, from behind. But that was one of the very, very few instances, if you like, that smacked of sexual overtones. Yes, I did it! Because you were too frightened not to. But I just put that down to experience. I think he said something like, "Not bad," or something like that.

I used to get terribly upset when I was passed over for promotion in the early days of my career. But after a while, for your own inner peace, you have to learn to be philosophical about these sorts of things. So if promotion comes, well then good. If promotion doesn't come, you mustn't allow it to affect your performance. You just go on doing what you think you should be doing.

I asked her about her public image, about being described from time to time as "Dragon Lady" by the Hong Kong press.

I think, subconsciously, it comes back to this question of stereo-types. You must know that certain attributes in a male are not quite so acceptable in a female. It's spoken of in very disparaging terms, like, if you're being too aggressive. I remember one of the descriptions that was used in a rather derogatory sense against me was that I was too emotional, whatever that means. I don't think I was too emotional. If by emotional you mean I feel passionately about certain things and I'll speak out, then, yes, I am emotional. I think that is a very good quality to have. Somehow men, some men, find it extremely unattractive to have a woman who is aggres-sive. But aggressiveness is considered to be a very good quality in men.

[As a woman,] everything you do, the way you talk, the way you walk, the way you dress, the way you look, projects either a favor-able image of the government or an unfavorable one. So you have a duty. But to achieve equality you don't have to give up your femi-ninity.

To Preserve Your Femininity or to Fight Like a Man: Two Views from Korea

Mrs. Chan's assertion is a matter currently being debated by women in power in South Korea. Women are starting to break into public life, despite Korea's reputation as the most conservative, Confucian-influ-enced culture in Asia—a country where women quit their jobs after marriage with even higher frequency than in Japan, and where there are fewer elected women than in any other OECD country (just 5.9 percent of lawmakers, compared to 7.3 percent in Japan and 13.6 per-cent in the United States).

One of the women breaking the barrier is Kang Gum Sil, the first woman to be appointed to a cabinet minister position in South Korea. She told me that if she hadn't maintained her feminine traits—speak-ing softly, acting flexibly, and being nice and polite—she never would have reached the level of justice minister (the equivalent of U.S. attor-ney general).

I later met a prominent feminist and writer in Seoul who was angry with Minister Kang for not acting tough enough and setting a public example for other Korean women on how to fight to get ahead in a man's world. But Minister Kang had told me that it is precisely her refusal to give up her feminine traits that has made her a role model. Schoolgirls write essays about her being their hero, she said. But even more importantly, Minister Kang has been mentioned as a possible future presidential candidate. She is wildly popular. "Maintaining femininity is no longer seen as a disadvantage, but as an advantage," she told me. She was wearing a bright pink linen blazer over a mauve dress, a pink-faced watch with a pink leather band, a pink necklace and matching earrings, and a purple bracelet. She was even more femininely dressed than Governor Shiotani in Japan. "Simply put, I am just being myself in everyday life," she said.

> I have been a judge for fifteen years. The legal sector is very male-oriented, very hierarchical. Instead of adjusting to the vertical hierarchy, I maintained my position. I did not change my attire, my fashion tastes, to suit the Ministry of Justice, and I maintain my personal demeanor as I did before, regardless of my position at the Ministry.

By doing this, she said, men don't feel threatened on their own terms. Sometimes her male subordinates get out of line and she is forced to take more aggressive action, but for the most part, she says, it works better to be nice and polite. She cited statistics that women now make up 50 percent of incoming law students, as well as medical students. The number of women prosecutors in her department is also about equal to that of men, she said. New government policies require that 30 percent of new hires in the government and police force be women. "So in the near future," she said, "there will be more progress and this will lead to almost equality." The word "almost," I thought, was revealing.

BUT THERE ARE OTHERS IN KOREA who think women need to project toughness instead, to achieve full equality. Fight injustice, stand up for your rights, and challenge the men who are holding you back is what the most senior female police superintendent, Kim Kang Ja, who dressed in all black for our discussion, thinks. If she hadn't done that, she believes, she never would have reached her position. "I have a lot of force in my small body," Superintendent Kim told me when I visited her office at police headquarters in Seoul.

It's a reality that women have to put more effort than men and be better than the men. Based on my experience, I tried twice as hard and was twice as good as men. For women, if you don't work hard enough or don't work efficiently, [men] look down on you. But if you do well, they get jealous, they unseat you, knock you down. The kind of women who act submissive and say "Yes," to men, those kinds of women can have more advantages than those who challenge men. The bosses will like her more and she'll get ahead. But for me, I cannot bear inequality of the sexes. I consider our male-oriented society an insult. I can't bear the thought of being treated unequally.

Her solution has been to fight back hard.

When Superintendent Kim joined the force in the 1970s, female police officers weren't promoted. They were allowed on the force only to type and process paperwork. To be admitted, women had to line up in shorts and sleeveless T-shirts and be judged.

If she was pretty, they passed her. If she wasn't, or had a scar, they dismissed her. Men just had normal physical examinations. So I went to the national women's rights committee and told them that such a thing happened at job interviews for being a police officer, and they complained to the police, so that doesn't happen anymore.

You couldn't get promoted without taking a training program, and women were not allowed to take it. So I fought it, and I was the first woman to undergo the course. I wanted to show that women were capable of doing what men do. So I went out and started to catch criminals. People were surprised that a woman could also do what was thought to be a man's job. In the 1980s, women officers were exempt from overnights and emergency duty. So men would say "Why don't women work at night? They don't work hard. Why do we have them here?" So I came in and worked all night as an example. At first they wouldn't let me, so I just came in and stayed up on the night shift with the guy already there. Since then, all female officers in the city started doing night shifts, too. When it spread all over the country, women officers complained that I made their work load heavier and harder. But they were just accepting inferior status before.

Superintendent Kim said she never takes holidays and works even on Sundays until 10 PM. "Being a police officer fits my character. When I walk down the street and see the insects of our society eating the leaves, I can't just walk past it. I have to do something."

In 1995 Superintendent Kim was denied promotion again, "because I am a mere, meek woman," she said. So she decided to do something a man could not do. She knew that the street corner police boxes were at their weakest in the middle of the night, when the assigned officers would be dozing. So she started working from 3 AM to 6 AM—before her regular work shift—patrolling the streets from police box to police box and making sure the men weren't sleeping on the job. "I did it for three years, every day, except Sundays. And at the same time I was assigned to work the day shift. So I was working all day, plus those three hours. That would be unthinkable for a man. A man couldn't do it." When Superintendent Kim alerted the media to her mission, it put pressure on the police commissioner to promote her. Instead he assigned a man to follow her around, to catch whenever she might slip up in order to compile a record of mistakes to fire her.

But one day [the commissioner] personally came up to me and complimented my work. Because I had worked so hard, the security in my area was spotless. Everything was perfect. After that, people began to think that women could be good at police work, so they put other women into those jobs. Then I was put in charge of three police bureaus, and became the highest ranking police woman in the country.

Recently, Superintendent Kim has been advocating that the police take crimes against women and children—namely domestic violence, rape, and the abuse of prostitutes—more seriously. Typically in Korea, a man who beats his wife is let go with an admonition not to keep disturbing the neighbors. A prostitute is regarded as a "dirty woman," Superintendent Kim said, and police rarely do anything to curb abuses against them. Media exposés have uncovered prostitutes who were kept locked in inhumane conditions, with cockroaches everywhere, and who were starved to keep them thin.

So, in 2002, Superintendent Kim created a squad of female officers to handle such crimes. "It's a sad reality that the male police did not do anything," she said. Her squad staged surprise raids and started carrying out inspections of brothel areas in conjunction with U.S. military police. The 8th U.S. Army awarded her unit a plaque after she succeeded in cleaning up Seoul's notorious red-light areas, including one called Miari, Texas—a seedy warren of sliding glass-fronted brothels lit with candy-pink fluorescent strip lights, where girls sit showcased on straw mats inside waiting to be chosen by the men walking by.

Now, her female officers circulate in such red-light districts and distribute stickers and handheld compact mirrors with a hotline number—written in English, Korean, and Russian—for reporting abuse. So far, police have rescued more than seventy prostitutes who'd called the number. "The pimps don't like the attention, but the prostitutes are more confident and conscious of their human rights," she said. Male police officers—including about 100 who used to take payoffs to look the other way—were angry, too. Superintendent Kim had seriously clipped their incomes with her cleanup campaign.

> My colleagues say I have a bad character because I am not afraid of the effects of my actions on my fellow police. I try to ignore them, but I hear it. People hate me because I am not a traditional Korean woman. The Korean woman's spirit is modest and shy, but I am not. I stick out, I brag, I am not shy. I want people to see me just as myself with no prejudice, no bias.

THE BATTLES OF SUPERINTENDENT KIM, as well as the rise to power of Minister Kang, are evidence of the changes occurring in Korean society. Turning on the television during my first trip to Seoul, I saw a Korean nun giving a sermon. When I changed the channel, I saw a Korean woman slapping a man in the face. I had just come from the government's Ministry of Gender Equality, where the assistant minister Kim Young Ok had told me of progress—along the lines of what Minister Kang also described—of more girls enrolled at universities, more women attaining higher office, and more women entrepreneurs branching out on their own.

When I met Korea's most successful businesswoman, Kim Sung Joo, founder and CEO of Sungjoo International, she told of that struggle.

> My first mission was that I just wanted to prove women can do as good a job as men. I wanted to prove women's strength and advance their "soft power." Men use more muscles, a macho way of working. To succeed without drinking, without bribing and without engaging in corruption like that, that became my second mission.

She accomplished both, racking up $100 million in annual sales before the Asian Financial Crisis in 1997, and managing to survive since then when a lot companies went bankrupt. "With our clean hands policy we became one of the biggest duty-free operations in Korea, with one-sixth of the market," she said.

> As women, we care for the society. Who else can fight against corruption? If someone like me can't do it, there's no hope for the society. All these women who are highly educated quit their jobs when they get married, what a waste. It's like a sin for the society. I say to women, you're waiting for men to crack the system for you? I say no way. Working and participating in public affairs is not a right, it's a duty. When we prove ourselves, society will change for us.

When two women reporters pushed to be allowed to cover the war in Iraq, their Korean news organizations sent them. One was Insun Kang, the Washington correspondent for the *Chosun Ilbo* daily newspaper, a forty-year-old mother who keeps in daily contact with her husband and daughter back in Seoul, and was embedded with U.S. troops in 2003. "In front of the fear of death, no one is brave, no man, no woman," she told me when I met her in her Washington, DC, office. "Knowing that freed me. Isn't it great that all human beings are equal in that situation?"

I thought back to what Assistant Minister Kim had told me about those kinds of realizations just starting to take hold in Korean society. "Ten years from now, there will be quite astonishing improvements for women in Korea," she had said. "We reinvent ourselves every day."

On the Campaign Trail with a Philippine Sweetheart

Efren Reyes reached out his hand to help pull me up onto the presidential campaign truck packed with movie stars. In the Philippines, Reyes is the equivalent of, say, Harvey Keitel or Willem Dafoe, an actor with an edge and offbeat looks who often plays the bad guy. Sitting on benches on the flat-bed truck are the likes of Robert DeNiro, Bruce Willis, and Clint Eastwood. Even the Philippines' own Brad Pitt is here. It is because one of the most famous movie stars in the Philippines, Fernando Poe, is running for president. And with him on the truck is the "Sweetheart of the Country," his running mate, Loren Legarda. I ask her if she really is a sweetheart.

"No, I'm tough," she answers bluntly. Sometimes a political slogan is *just* a political slogan.

Loren is wearing her trademark blue jeans and white button-down shirt with her first name embroidered in script over her heart and in big block letters on the back. She tells me she has dozens of shirts and several pairs of jeans, and after a day on the campaign trail she takes off the dirty, sweaty ones and puts on a clean version of the same outfit for dinner. She keeps her long hair in a ponytail and is not wearing any jewelry. She advises me to take off mine lest the enthusiastic supporters surrounding the truck jump up and grab it. Loren once had an earring ripped out that way and her earlobe bears the scar. She has open scratches and cuts on her hands and forearms from where people have been reaching out to her on the campaign trail. They won't heal until the campaign is over.

The Philippines loves Loren. She was the youngest woman ever elected to the Senate, at age thirty-eight, and she gained prominence as she rose to Senate Majority Leader in her six years in office. She resigned from the Senate to run for the vice-presidency. The reason she was running with Poe instead of being invited onto the ticket of incumbent[2] President Gloria Arroyo, she said, is because then there would be a double-woman slate running for the highest elected offices in the country.

The percentage of women holding elected office in the Philippines is high compared to that of the rest of Asia—and even higher than in the United States. Of the Philippine Congress, 17.2 percent are women (of the U.S. Congress, 13.6 percent are women); of seventy-four provincial governors in the Philippines, fourteen are women (18.9 percent); in the United States there were six women out of fifty governors in 2004, and only fifteen women had ever been elected to the office since 1925. But that doesn't mean it's easy. "It's still difficult to be a woman politician in the Philippines," Loren tells me. "You cannot expect fair treatment all the time. Men expect that you are the weaker sex."

Our truck, one of several in a campaign caravan, starts on a long, three-hour journey through the blazing sun. It is infernally hot, and the movie stars, Loren, me, and several staff members working cell phones and clipboards to set up the next campaign stop take turns sharing the shade under a tarp tied to poles on the four corners of the flatbed. There is Gatorade in the coolers under the benches.

Loren and Poe wave to the crowds thronging the truck, keeping one arm high in the air until it drains of blood and switching to the other. What they have in common is that neither has a political pedigree. Neither comes from one of the land-holding ruling clans that dominate Philippine politics. The Aquino-Cojuangco clan, for example, has produced one president (Corazon), three senators, several congressmen, and a mayor. A lot of common Filipinos like the idea of a screen hero instead. "F–P–J!" they chant as the truck passes. "F–P–J!" Those are Poe's initials. Occasionally the masses emit calls of "Lor-EN, Lor-EN, Lor-EN!" Even though they are campaigning in the territory of yet another presidential candidate, Ping Lacson, the reception is warm and the crowd is thrilled. It is hard to know whether the enthusiasm is for the candidates themselves, or generated by the sight of their movie-star heroes all passing through the small towns simultaneously.

It is a bit like a Mardi Gras parade. Poe and Loren throw out rolled-up T-shirts, candies with their names on the wrappers, and bandanas. They send the crowds scrambling to catch them. Because young able men always seem to grab the spoils, the candidates and movie-star helpers aim the goodies at women and children, sometimes bonking them on the head with an unexpected flying T-shirt.

When our procession is over and thousands of Filipinos en route have been encouraged to vote the FPJ-Loren ticket, Poe heads off to another rally in the capital. We climb into Loren's Isuzu SUV to speed off to the next stop. From the backseat, Loren works her political circuit, her staff placing the calls, handing her the phone, and then logging the calls: Someone is donating a printer; someone named Father Noli wants to celebrate mass with her on the eve of the elections; does the mayor at the location she plans to visit in the morning know she will be there? The conversations are rushed and chaotic. She chews out her underlings from time to time.

Our next stop is a country club with a luscious golf course. Loren jumps out of the car and greets the men standing there. "How am I doing in your district?" she asks. It is the provincial vice governor and his brother, a congressman. Their father has spent many years as governor. This is the Remulla family, the power brokers who control Cavite Province on the southern shores of Manila Bay, and this is an important meeting. Loren is seeking their endorsement. It is worth 1.2 million votes.

The Remullas provide a club townhouse for us to freshen up and invite us for dinner in an hour. "Males have a tendency to look at women like me, young, as new kid on the block. But the advantage of being a woman is that you can achieve what men cannot, through your charm," Loren tells me. Later, when I watch her work her magic on the patriarch and his powerful sons at dinner, I see what she means. In the townhouse as we relax in the meantime, Loren takes a shower and puts on a clean version of her jeans-and-white-shirt outfit. Her chief of staff turns on the TV. By coincidence, one of Loren's campaign commercials is on. It features a ten-year-old girl. "When I grow up, I want to be intelligent," she says. Then a scene flashes of Loren shaking hands and picking up babies. "I want to be able to answer all the questions," the girl says. There are more scenes of Loren glad-handing. It concludes with the girl again: "I wish I could vote." Loren's policies have aimed at women's rights, and in the Senate she sponsored anti-domestic violence bills, agricultural projects for women, and anti-trafficking laws. While the commercial is not directly about empowerment, the subliminal message of appealing to women is there.

Loren Legarda campaign poster

After dinner we all head for a campaign rally organized by the Remulla sons. "My opponent came here last week," Loren tells me on the way. "They didn't commit their support to him. Now they will publicly declare their support for me. This family is very important." Dinner, it seems, was a success. But as we jump out of the SUV, Loren is surprised at the size of the crowd, numbering only around 3,000 people. "Oh my god, this is a big rally to them? This is nothing," she complains. "You could drive caribou through this crowd." Still, Loren climbs onto the stage and works her charm. The Remulla brothers each hand Loren red roses. The crowd cheers for the "Sweetheart of the Country." Loren cites her record in the Senate, pledging to do even more if elected vice president. The crowd cheers. She promises to provide schools, jobs, and health care. The crowd cheers again. Then music starts and she and one of the Remulla brothers sing a duet. It wouldn't be a Philippine political rally without the candidates breaking into song.

There is a long, late-night drive back to Manila, and we arrive in the capital after 11 PM. All along the way, Loren works the phones again, trying to reach fellow politicians and get them to pledge the support of their constituencies. "I need your help and value your

Loren Legarda and Fernando Poe, 2004

friendship," she repeats into the cell phone several times in the course
of an hour. Loren has one more week of campaigning to go. I am about
to drop from just one day's worth. She had gotten up at 5 AM, and will
do the same tomorrow to make it to an 8 AM rally in another far, away
province. She will be lucky to get five hours' sleep.

When we reach her gated home, she shows me around. Her house is
beautiful, with gorgeous artwork on the walls and a lovely tropical
garden out back. But it is quiet. Her boys, fourteen and eleven, are already asleep. She says that her husband is still at the office, working
until midnight. As I turn to shut the enormous wooden front doors
behind me, I leave the Sweetheart of the Country, for the first time in
eighteen hours, completely alone.

"The world has come to know about Asian women leaders," she had
told me during the day. "We have a second woman president in the
Philippines. We have Megawati and Aung San Suu Kyi. Increasingly
there are women who are leaders in their own right." Loren is one of
them.

In the end, the Poe-Loren ticket lost the May 10, 2004, election.

President Gloria Marcapagal Arroyo was elected to serve for six years, beating the movie star Poe by a little more than a million votes. Loren's race was closer but still a loss. She received 14,218,709 votes to her opponent's 15,100,431.

But the Sweetheart of the Country is young and ambitious. Just wait until 2010.

Epilogue:

Demand Creates Supply

Go to the Time Warner Center on the southwest corner of Central Park in New York City, and walk up to the glass facade of the Mandarin Oriental Hotel. The doors are opened for you, timed to the precise moment you step through the threshold into the cool marble entryway, by an Asian man dressed in uniform who bows slightly as he welcomes you. Take the elevator to the 35th floor lobby, where the lighting is subdued and recessed, and pass the staff standing at attention at the check-in counter. Most of the staff is Asian,[1] as are the waitresses in the lobby bar—where the cushions are creamy satin and the service is more deferential than cheerful. Your server, dressed in a *cheongsam*-inspired slit skirt, will do her best to accommodate your every request, including checking the bar to find fresh mint for your iced tea, even though it is morning and the bar is not yet open.

The setting is meant to evoke luxury, as is the case at all luxury hotels. But what is special here is the care that the management takes to evoke the Asian Mystique and, quite literally, "the magic of the Orient," according to the hotel's promotional materials. This is not just service with a smile, but service with a bow as well. "Our luxury brand strives to delight our guests by providing service that is gracious and sincere and steeped in the values of the Orient," the materials state. "We are committed to exceeding [guests'] expectations by surprising them with our ability to anticipate and fulfill their wishes."

Rooms decorated in dark tropical hardwoods have satiny round throw pillows on the beds, paper-lantern-like lights illuminating the bedside, and Thai orchids on tables at the windows. Japanese prints hang on the walls. Copies of *China Chic* by Vivienne Tam grace the Chinese coffee tables of every suite. There is no single Asian cultural

Mandarin Oriental Hotel décor, New York, 2004

motif: Thai, Chinese, Japanese, and Indonesian are blended. Everywhere the décor is "Orientalized," based on the images of Asia developed through centuries of East-West contact—a Western aesthetic
with Asian characteristics. The Mandarin Oriental Hotel Group,
which began with a single hotel in 1963 in colonial Hong Kong, now
operates nineteen of these hotels, undoubtedly among the best world,
in London, Miami, San Francisco, and, of course, in the major business
hubs of Asia. Room rates are $280 to $595, depending on the city.

This adaptation of "Oriental" style for westerners is big business. It
draws millions of customers to home decorating stores such as Pier 1
Imports and Bombay Company; to Shanghai Tang clothing stores to
buy expensive silk jackets and gowns in styles that most Chinese
haven't worn in 100 years; to the proliferating Asian-design spas and
reflexology parlors; and to fusion restaurants such as Vong and its
many imitators.

Even within Asia, this style is in evidence at a number of establishments that rely on Western clientele. Restaurants such as Face, with
locations in Shanghai and Jakarta, Lemongrass in Bangkok, The Bon
Ton in Kuala Lumpur, The Mandarin in Saigon, Indochine in Hong

Kong, and dozens of others, lure expats with this similar type of Orientalized décor—luscious tropical plants, heavy teak or cane/rattan, ceiling fans, subdued yellow lighting, candles, and a heavy dose of colonialist nostalgia. The Metropole Hotel and the Press Club restaurant in Hanoi do as well, appealing to our colonial Graham Greene. The irony is that Oriental style is so successful that it has become hot with a certain set of fashionable, or wanna-be-fashionable, Asians, as well.

But, typically, ask an Asian to choose the restaurant and you will see an enormous contrast in the aesthetic. The Chinese in China, for example, generally don't mind florescent lighting, and in fact complain that these foreigners' restaurants are too dark to see the food. Quality of food is more important than the atmosphere. There is no need for tropical plants or hardwood. The Chinese prefer round tables conducive to groups, rather than square traditional Chinese ones seating only four. A simple white tablecloth over a round piece of plywood works just fine even in high-end Chinese restaurants. Luxury in China looks gaudy to Western eyes—red, pink, and gold, lit in white light, rather than hardwood brown, creamy silk, and ivory, lit in muted yellows. Chinese don't want colonial and old, they value bright and new.

And when Malays and Thais, for example, want an upscale restaurant, they tend to choose foreign cuisine and foreign décor—French or Italian, Chinese or Japanese—frequently at a luxury hotel. For cheap and convenient fare, outdoor food stalls and simple noodle shops with almost no recognizable décor at all are the most popular..

In other words, our version of "Oriental" style is not really Asian. It is Western—a reflected image of what westerners think Asia looks like. And it sells. Pier 1 Imports sold $1.87 billion worth of furnishings in fiscal year 2004, with net profits of $118 million. The Mandarin Oriental Hotel Group reported revenue of $541 million in 2003, and pre-tax profits of $28.6 million.

Singapore Airlines and Cathay Pacific are the most popular carriers in Asia, also playing on the Asian Mystique by fostering the images of servility and sexuality through the service of their flight attendants. These are the carriers operating out of the two international gateway cities of Asia—no flight on Singapore Airlines or Cathay is ever domestic. Every flight is international, relying primarily on businessmen traveling the region. If you fly domestically inside China, for example, on China Southern or China Eastern Airlines, or even domestically inside Indonesia, on Garuda Indonesia Airlines, you will see something different. These airlines rely on their own countries' nationals for their business, and you can sometimes find service just as surly as that of some American and European carriers.

There is nothing new about selling our images of the "Orient" back to us. San Francisco's Chinatown realized the potential of tourism as early as 1906, for example, as it struggled to rebuild from an earthquake and fire. By 1915, Chinatown had staged its first beauty pageant featuring girls with "looks that made China's beauties so fascinating," dressed in skintight *cheongsam* dresses, to lure white male tourists. The result was that, by the 1930s, Chinatown earned nearly one-fifth of the city's tourism dollars.[2]

By the Great Depression, tour guides had to work even harder to keep the dollars coming in. So they turned Chinatown into the "wicked Orient," spinning tales of a secret underground world of drugs, gambling halls, and prostitution, where Chinese and white girls alike were enslaved, according to Iris Chang's *The Chinese in America*. The Chinese built fake opium dens and leper colonies for white tourists—who were both horrified and thrilled to have their stereotypes confirmed. This coincided, of course, with the successes of the stories of evil Dr. Fu Manchu, a fictional character invented from a visit to London's Chinatown and from the imaginings about what went on in a world impenetrable to white people. The Chinese of San Francisco's Chinatown took those images and sold them to the willing. A businessman there opened a club called "Forbidden City" in the 1930s and hired hundreds of Chinese women to dance nude on stage—and established Asian women as an ethnic minority "talent" performing, as at The Cotton Club in New York, for a mostly Caucasian audience.[3]

In Los Angeles, teenagers in Chinatowns started pulling rickshaws for white sightseers, Chang writes. In New York during the same period, tour guides warned visitors to hold hands "for safety" as they walked down Mott Street, and paid Chinese residents to stage tension-filled dramas including knife fights between "opium crazed" men over a prostitute.[4] In reality, however, the Chinatown neighborhoods of the

1930s were becoming safer. But selling the images of violence, sex, and underworld mystery is what played to Western tourists.

Casting Asia as sexual and dangerous is what has drawn the eyes of the West to the East for centuries. The writer Ian Buruma's fascination with Asia, for example, came from a Japanese theater director selling those images to Western audiences. The play Buruma saw in Amsterdam as a young man in the 1970s, which first sparked his interest in Japan, "mixed Western and Japanese imagery in a way that made both West and East look bizarre and marvelous. His Japan was like a great, colorful souk, or like a costume party," Buruma writes. "He made Japan look sexy" in a stage version "of a sensual Orient that has attracted libertines and appalled missionaries for centuries."[5]

When western writers get to Asia, they are tempted, and encouraged by their editors, to write about a mystical, exotic world of difference that they imagined before their arrival, of images based in existing stereotypes and misperceptions. After all, that is what sells books and articles back home. I know because I, too, have been on the receiving end of editors' phone calls, asked to write stories from Asia that are different! Gripping! Exotic! Sex-drenched! I also have put pressure on myself to comply with expectations without being asked.

Several years ago, when I was Asia Editor at *BusinessWeek,* I was summoned to a meeting of top editors. We were planning a cover story on Coca-Cola's expansion in the region for our Asian Edition. The magazine cover photo we had chosen was of a young Chinese woman sucking suggestively on a straw protruding from a Coke can. "It's too come-hither," the only female assistant managing editor on staff at the time declared. She objected to the photo and had summoned us to ask for a new one. The Chinese girl was clearly sexual and objectified. The point of the image was not the beverage but how she was drinking it. The editor was right. As I was the only other woman in the room, all eyes turned to me. "It doesn't bother me so much," I said, dissolving into namby-pamby-ism. "I guess it sells magazines." I was so inured to such images that her objections hadn't occurred to me on my own, and even when they were pointed out, I resisted the change. *BusinessWeek* ran that cover. Plain vanilla reality can be too boring.

"Freeing Sex Slaves," and "Saving Angkor Wat," two of *The New York Times'* special reports on Asia in the first half of 2004, featured westerners to the rescue of poor Cambodia—in the form of prostitutes and crumbling historic monuments. *The New York Times* also writes many uplifting articles about the empowered women and splendid modern architecture of Asia, of course, but they don't merit entire special reports. The only other one featuring Asia in the same time period had to do with China's economy. But "Freeing Sex Slaves" remained prominent on the Asia-Pacific news page of the newspaper's website for the rest of the year and into 2005.

It's not just American media. London's *Financial Times* printed a wonderful tale of a visit to the region of a Chinese minority, the Mosuo, in central China. The Mosuo are one of the last surviving matriarchies of China, where women invite men into "trial relationships" to father children, who then become the responsibility of an extended household instead of two parents, the article said. The male reporter attempts to be an invitee, but is told that if he really is a serious contender for fathering a Mosuo child, he must demonstrate it by coming back another time to the remote locale 8,000 feet above sea level at the border of Yunnan and Sichuan provinces. The headline to draw readers to an article otherwise rivaling a *National Geographic* journey into an untrammeled realm? "My Date with the Free-loving Mountain Nymphs."

OFTEN, ASIAN WOMEN ARE AWARE of these Western perceptions of Asian Mystique and know how to play them to advantage. On one side, the professional prostitutes of Asia are masters of it. But even some of the most successful, upstanding businesswomen of Asia know the game, too. Hong Kong businesswoman Marjorie Yang, for example, who built a multi-million-dollar business in the garment trade through her Esquel Group, told me of sitting in the front row of her classroom at Harvard Business School and feigning that she would cry if the professor called on her. She realized the professor's perception of Asian women was of weakness, and she decided to play upon it. "You've got to use what you've got, right?" she said. Her sentiments are far from unusual.

Also, there are vested interests in preserving the image of Asian women as victims, such as those of the charity organizations that are simultaneously acting in the women's interests and issuing reports on their exploitation. It is true that Asia harbors terrible injustices, as does every region in the world. There would be no remedies for the wrongs, no help for poor exploited prostitutes and sex victims, without funding. Helping victims of exploitation is a just cause, of course; but there would be no funding for these causes without painting a picture of exploited victims. Sometimes the same parties who have an interest in helping them also have an interest in victim-hood as public image. It is worth millions of dollars in donations and public funds.

And then there are the blatant money-makers. Chinese-American writer Ming Tan, who wrote the book *How to Attract Asian Women,* is but one example. She ignited a firestorm when she tried to teach an evening course on pointers for men at The Learning Annex in New York in 2003. After outraged protests by the Asian-American community, the course was cancelled, but the book is available via Amazon.com.

Hucksterism to varying degrees plays out all over Asia, too. Rustic villages in northern Thailand thrive on the sole purpose of demonstrating hill-tribe life to Western tourists, complete with elephant rides and lots of souvenir beads for sale. In the Philippines and Indonesia as well, visitors can sign up for similar tours to see "native" people, crossing that fine line between tourism and consumerism of "Asian people."

And, of course, there are the bars of Bangkok, where the fantasies of the sexual, servile Asia play out every night on the stages of hundreds of bars like Super Pussy, where the exotic sexual Orient is for sale. Nowhere does the economic maxim hold truer than here—Demand always creates supply.

The stereotypes and perceptions held in Western culture as a result of all this imagery, commerce, interaction, and history make up the Asian Mystique. We are avid consumers, literally buying it as well as buying into it. So, to stretch the metaphor, *caveat emptor.* Beware. Be aware. Without awareness we risk continued vulnerability to the dangers of seeing through its distorted prisms. We miscalculate, we underestimate, we misjudge, we stereotype, we foster subconscious racism, and we misunderstand. Our relations and relationships—both business and personal—feel the impact. We slight others, and we slight ourselves. The true price of indulging this consumerism, of keeping up the demand, and of maintaining the Asian Mystique is far higher than we know.

Acknowledgments

I AM HEAVILY INDEBTED to the following finest, most supportive group of friends, chapter readers, and project advisors anyone could ever ask for. Their rich diversity of experiences contributed enormously to the formulation of my ideas and knowledge base: Robin Luckey, who provided a mailbox, a home away from home, and an unfailingly patient ear and eye for ideas and drafts at all stages of this endeavor; Joe Robison, my Google guru and support in technical and other ways; Priscilla and George Brandon; Anya Schiffrin; Jeanne Moore; Jessica Smith in Tokyo; John Bussey in Hong Kong; Ian Johnson in Berlin; Sandy Szakach; Kathy O'Connor; L. Brooks Entwistle; Robert Templer; Michael Thomas and Rohany Nayan; Amy Cortese; Beth Kwon; Susan Kwan; Sarah Jackson-Han; Scott Billings; Doug Sederberg; and Richard Hornik.

Those to whom I am grateful for helping set up interviews and introducing me to contacts, or who provided additional research help or a spare bed for the wandering traveler include: Karen Ma, Dick Christenson, Mark Davidson, Rebecca MacKinnon, Kumi Yokoe, Barry and Jan Petersen, Warren Soiffer, Naoko Hatayama, Michael You, and Izumi Koide in Tokyo; Zane Ritchie and Ayumi Nishina in Kyoto; Betty Hoffman in Okinawa; Masami Shinozaki in Fukuoka; Liu Ji-Ou in Shanghai; Mary Kay Magistad in Beijing; Chris Cromyn in Guangzhou, Mark L. Clifford, Tina and Michael DiCicco, and Frederik Balfour in Hong Kong; Ginny Chung in Seoul; Girlie Linao in Manila; Amy Kazmin and Matt Schafer in Bangkok; Zainal Abidin, Alita Assagaf, and the indefatigable Elma Harsan and Lidya K. Tandirerung in Yogjakarta; Sidney Jones and Daniel Ziv in Jakarta; and John McAuliff and Susan Hammond during my trip to Vietnam. Additional thanks go to Anna Shen, Julia Cosgrove, Geraldine Kunstadter—and to my father, Charles R. Prasso, and to my mother, Susan, *in memoriam*.

I am also grateful to the hundreds of people who expressed enthusiasm for this project, who patiently spent hours with me in interviews, many of whom were so much more generous with their time than any reasonable person could expect. Because I have been asked by many of them to keep their names confidential, I cannot thank them by name. I trust that they are aware of my gratitude for their enormous contributions.

Additionally, this book would not have been possible without a grant from the U.S.-Japan Foundation which sent me to Tokyo as a Media Fellow, and the help of Ruri Kawashima and Betty Borden at the Japan Society; my wonderful PublicAffairs editor Lisa Kaufman; and my ebullient agent Elaine Markson.

Notes

THE ASIAN MYSTIQUE

1. B. L. Putnam Weale, *Indiscreet Letters from Peking*, 246, from Diana Preston's *The Boxer Rebellion* (New York: Penguin Putnam, Inc., 1999), xxv–xxvi.

2. Ian Buruma, *The Missionary and the Libertine: Love and War in East and West* (New York: Vintage Books, Random House, 1996), xix–xx.

3. For more details see Joyce Wadler, *Liaison* (New York: Bantam, 1993).

4. David Henry Hwang, *M Butterfly* (New York: Plume, Penguin Books, 1986), 98–99.

5. Edward Said, *Orientalism* (New York: Vintage Books, Random House, 1978; 1994 ed.), 11.

MYSTERY, SEX, FEAR, AND DESIRE:
A BRIEF HISTORY

1. Sterling Seagrave, *Dragon Lady: The Life and Legend of the Last Empress of China* (New York: Random House, 1992), 18.

2. Seagrave, *Dragon Lady*, 10–11.

3. Diana Preston, *The Boxer Rebellion* (New York: Penguin Putnam, 1999), ix.

4. Seagrave, *Dragon Lady*, 15–16.

5. Seagrave, *Dragon Lady*, 14–15.

6. Preston, *The Boxer Rebellion*, 331–32.

7. Preston, *The Boxer Rebellion*, 332.

8. Dawn Jacobson, *Chinoiserie* (London: Phaidon Press, 1999), 12.

9. Manuel Komroff, ed., *The Travels of Marco Polo {The Venetian}* (New York: Liverlight Publishing Corp., 1926), 78.

10. Komroff, ed., *The Travels of Marco Polo*, 125–27.

11. Komroff, ed., *The Travels of Marco Polo*, 235.

12. Komroff, ed., *The Travels of Marco Polo*, 188–89.

13. Jonathan D. Spence, *Chan's Great Continent: China in Western Minds* (New York: Norton, 1998), 17–18.

14. Jacobson, *Chinoiserie*, 13.

15. Jacobson, *Chinoiserie*, 13.

16. Spence, *Chan's Great Continent*, 33–35.

17. Jaime B. Veneracion, "From Babaylan to Beata: A Study on the Religiosity of Filipino Women," *Review of Women's Studies* 3, no. 1 (Dec. 1992), 1–15.

18. Barbara Mahel, *The Situation of Filipino Women* (Manila: Guaranty Press Inc., 1988).

19. Giles Milton, *Samurai William: The Englishman Who Opened Japan* (New York: Farrar, Strauss & Giroux, 2002), 142.

20. Milton, *Samurai William*, 146–47.

21. Ian Buruma, *The Missionary and the Libertine: Love and War in East and West* (New York: Random House, 1996), 73.

22. Buruma, *The Missionary and the Libertine*, xvii.

23. Stanley Karnow, *Vietnam: A History* (New York: The Viking Press, 1983), 55.

24. Panivong Norindr, *Phantasmatic Indochina* (Durham and London: Duke University Press, 1996), 20.

25. Trea Wiltshire, *Encounters With China: Merchants, Missionaries and Mandarins* (Hong Kong: Forum Asia, 2003), 15.

26. Wiltshire, *Encounters With China*, 19.

27. Lesley Downer, *Women of the Pleasure Quarters* (New York: Broadway Books, 2001), 157.

28. Downer, *Women of the Pleasure Quarters*, 158–59.

29. Stella Dong, *Shanghai: The Rise and Fall of a Decadent City* (New York Harper Collins Publishers, 2000), 37.

30. Dong, *Shanghai*, 42.

31. W. Somerset Maugham, "The Outstation," in *Collected Short Stories Twentieth Century Classics* (New York: Penguin Books, 1995, 1921), 4:346.

32. Edward Said, *Orientalism*, 186, 188.

33. Said, *Orientalism,* 190. Nerval cited in Said, at 183.

34. Preston, *The Boxer Rebellion,* xxv–xxvi.

35. Preston cites E. Sellon, *The Ups and Downs of Life* (1867), quoted in D. Judd, *Empire* (London: Harper Collins, 1996), 179; and B.L. Putnam Weale, *Indiscreet Letters from Peking* (London: Hurst and Blackett, 1906), 246.

36. Preston, *The Boxer Rebellion*, xxv–xxvi.

37. Downer, *Women of the Pleasure Quarters*, 190, citing "Gaijin no Shit-suren" in Osaka Mainichi Shimbun, Mar. 3, 1903, quoted in Kosakai, *Morgan Oyuki: Ai ni iki, shin ni shisu*.

38. John Beecroft, *Kipling, A Selection of His Stories and Poems* (Garden City, NY: Doubleday & Co., 1892, 1956), 2: 444.

39. Stanley Karnow, *In Our Image: America's Empire in the Philippines* (New York: Random House, 1989), 67.

40. William Manchester, *American Caesar: Douglas MacArthur: 1880–1964* (Boston, Little, Brown, and Co., 1978), 17, 157.

41. Karnow, *In Our Image*, 269.

42. Karnow, *In Our Image*, 170.

43. John W. Dower, *Embracing Defeat: Japan in the Wake of World War II* (New York: W.W. Norton & Co., 1999), 80.

44. Dower, *Embracing Defeat*, 124–26.

45. Dower, *Embracing Defeat*, 127.

46. Dower, *Embracing Defeat*, 128–30.

47. Dower, *Embracing Defeat*, 130.

48. Liza Dalby, *Geisha* (Berkeley and Los Angeles: University of California Press, 1983), 182.

49. Lesley Downer, *Women of the Pleasure Quarters* (New York: Broadway Books, 2001), 206.

50. Dower, *Embracing Defeat*, 132–33.

51. Dower, *Embracing Defeat*, 138.

52. Caroline Chung Simpson, "Out of an Obscure Place: Japanese War Brides and Cultural Pluralism in the 1950s" in *differences: A Journal of Feminist Cultural Studies*, 10, no. 3 (1998), 234.

53. Simpson, "Out of an Obscure Place," 253, 259.

54. Philip Short, *Mao: A Life* (New York: Henry Holt, 1999), 2, quoting American writer Agnes Smedley, who considered Mao effete and overly intellectual. She did describe plain spoken down-to-earth Chinese men such as Chu De, who headed the Communist armed forces at the time, in more masculine terms. American communist Sidney Rittenberg echoes Smedley, recognizing Mao's "almost feminine mouth" when he sees him, 390.

55. "Probable Developments in China," ORE 45–49, Central Intelligence Agency, June 16, 1949, declassified for release Oct. 21, 2004.

56. Karnow, *Vietnam: A History*, 97.

57. Karnow, *Vietnam: A History*, 214–15.

58. Karnow, *Vietnam: A History*, 247.

59. Iris Chang, *The Chinese in America: A Narrative History* (New York: Viking Penguin, 2003), 26.

60. Chang, *The Chinese in America*, 46.

61. Stephen E. Ambrose, *Nothing Like It in the World: The Men who Built the Transcontinental Railroad 1863–1869* (New York: Simon & Schuster, 2000), 150.

62. Chang, *The Chinese in America*, 83.

63. Preston, *The Boxer Rebellion*, xxi.

64. Chang, *The Chinese in America*, 118.

65. Chang, *The Chinese in America*, 173–74.

66. Chang, *The Chinese in America*, 168.

67. Graham Russell Gao Hodges, *Anna May Wong: From Laundryman's Daughter to Hollywood Legend* (New York: Palgrave Macmillan, 2004), 82.

68. Hodges, *Anna May Wong*, 115.

69. Hodges, *Anna May Wong*, 79–80, 92.

HOLLYWOOD, BURBANK, AND
THE RESULTING IMAGININGS

1. Screen actress Anna May Wong had her own TV series for eleven episodes in the fall of 1951, *The Gallery of Madame Liu-Tsong*, in which she played a beautiful proprietress of art galleries who got involved in international intrigue. She also made a few guest appearances on other series. The Dumont Network that produced the show is defunct, and the episodes are believed lost.

2. *Cheers* in 1993 had 80.4 million viewers; *Seinfeld* drew 76.2 million in 1998; and *Friends* in 2004 was seen by 51.1 million, according to Nielsen Media Research.

3. Giles Milton, *Samurai William: The Englishman Who Opened Japan* (New York: Farrar, Straus & Giroux, 2004).

4. It was known in Hollywood at the time that the actor playing Anjin, Richard Chamberlain, was gay, and that James Clavell initially didn't want Chamberlain in the role. Instead, Clavell had pushed to have Sean Connery play Blackthorne, and then Roger Moore, but when both of them declined due to other commitments, he finally consented to Chamberlain.

5. This was not the practice in Japan at that time, although it did become common in the late 1800s after Japan's reopening. Instead, visiting foreign sailors enjoyed the company of prostitutes assigned to service Dutch traders

aboard their ships, according to *Samurai William: The Englishman Who Opened Japan*.

6. Kevin McCloskey, "Heartthrobs: Lucy Liu," http://www.prevue magazine.com (2002).

7. Eugene Franklin Wong, "The Early Years: Asians in the American Films Prior to World War II," in *Screening Asian Americans*, ed. Peter X. Feng (New Brunswick, NJ: Rutgers University Press, 2002), 57; Iris Chang, *The Chinese in America: A Narrative History* (New York: Viking Penguin, 2003), 207–08.

8. Graham Russell Gao Hodges, *Anna May Wong: From Laundryman's Daughter to Hollywood Legend* (New York: Palgrave Macmillan, 2004), 90.

9. Hodges, *Anna May Wong,* 123, 147.

10. Liam Lacey, "The Eyes of a Stranger," *The Globe and Mail* (Toronto), June 4, 2004, R7.

11. Reina Lewis, *Gendering Orientalism: Race, Femininity, and Representation* (New York: Routledge, 1996), 72.

12. Advertisement in *Vogue* (June 1, 1935: 44), cited in Sarah Berry, *Screen Style: Fashion and Femininity in 1930s Hollywood* (Minneapolis: University of Minnesota Press, 2000), 120.

13. Berry, *Screen Style,* 134–35 (citing *Vogue* advertisement of April 1, 1936: 109).

14. Berry, *Screen Style,* 135 (citing *Vogue* advertisement of July 1, 1936: 82).

15. By this time, stage productions set in Japan were all the rage, with hugely successful Gilbert and Sullivan's *The Mikado* having opened in 1885.

16. James A. Michener, *Sayonara* (New York: Ballantine Books, 1953), 105 (dialog taken from the novel).

17. Lesley Downer, *Women of the Pleasure Quarters* (New York: Broadway Books, 2001), 140–42.

18. Janet Maslin, "Seeing and Believing: A Movie's Power Over Attitudes and Action," *The New York Times*, Feb. 22, 2004, Week in Review, 5.

MATTERS OF MEN AND COUNTRY:
THE INCREDIBLE LIGHTNESS OF BEING PORTRAYED

1. Yul Brynner often claimed to be half Japanese and half Swiss, born Taidje Khan on the island of Sakhalin that is disputed by Russia and Japan. But in actuality he was born of Russian mother and a Swiss-Mongolian father named Boris Bryner in the city of Vladivostok in Far East Russia, making him of one-quarter Asian descent—though in his role as the King, with

his shirt open to reveal a hairless chest, he exemplified an exotic sexuality new to Hollywood and won an Oscar for Best Actor for the role.

2. Iris Chang, *The Chinese in America: A Narrative History* (New York: Viking Penguin, 2003), 207.

3. Chang, *The Chinese in America*, 207–08.

4. Manuel Komroff, ed., *The Travels of Marco Polo {The Venetian}* (New York: Liverlight Publishing Corp., 1926), 140.

5. Stella Dong, *Shanghai: The Rise and Fall of a Decadent City* (New York: Harper Collins, 2000), 141.

6. Stephen E. Ambrose, *Nothing Like It in the World: The Men Who Built the Transcontinental Railroad, 1863–1869* (New York: Simon & Schuster, 2001), 150–52.

7. Stephen L. Morgan, "Economic Growth and the Biological Standard of Living in China, 1880–1930," in *Economics and Human Biology*. 2, no. 2 (June 2004), 215.

8. Dong, *Shanghai*, 26.

9. "Adult Sex Toy Expo Touches Sensitive Area," *Shanghai Star*, *People's Daily Online*, Aug. 8, 2004, http://english.people.com.cn/.

10. Lesley Downer, *Women of the Pleasure Quarters* (New York: Broadway Books, 2001), 37–38.

11. Downer, *Women of the Pleasure Quarters*, 39.

12. Nicholas Bornoff, *The Pink Samurai: Love, Marriage & Sex in Contemporary Japan* (New York: Simon & Schuster, 1991), 425–27.

13. Bornoff, *The Pink Samurai*, 84–90.

14. Dong, *Shanghai*, 125.

15. Pico Iyer, *The Lady and the Monk: Four Seasons in Kyoto* (London: Vintage Books, 1991), 53–54.

16. Ian Buruma, *The Missionary and the Libertine: Love and War in East and West* (New York: Random House, 1996), 54.

17. Graham Russell Gao Hodges, *Anna May Wong: From Laundryman's Daughter to Hollywood Legend* (New York: Palgrave Macmillan, 2004), 80.

18. James Brooke, "Neighborhood of U.S. Base is Hot Real Estate in Korea," *The New York Times*, May 31, 2004.

"RACE-ISM," FETISH, AND FEVER

1. There were actually two signs, "No Dogs Allowed" and "Only for Foreigners," which amounted to the same thing, but the two have been com-

bined into the memory of one sign in legend, according to Stella Dong's *Shanghai: The Rise and Fall of a Decadent City* (New York: HarperCollins, 2000), 198.

2. Anna May Wong never married, saying she could not find a suitable husband in the conservative Chinese community; laws banning interracial marriage weren't lifted in California until Wong was forty-three. Lucy Liu was still single as of mid-2004, and she publicly noted the difficulty of meeting men after playing the types of roles she has had on screen.

3. Tomoyuki Tanaka, "Disparity in Asian/white Interracial Dating FAQ," Usenet, [soc.couples.intercultural] last-modified Mar. 1, 1995.

4. By comparison, 412 German women had East Asian husbands as of 2002. Tables do not show any statistical impact from the reunification of Germany. They do indicate a steady annual decrease in popularity of Philippine wives, from 1,105 in 1992 to 401 in 2002, coinciding with the rise in popularity of tourism to Thailand and subsequent increase in marriages to Thai women. "Eheschließungen nach der Staatsangehörigkeit der Ehepartner (Asien)," *Siehe Fachserie* 1, Reihe 1, 1992, Tabelle 8.11, S. 88–89.

5. Joan Walsh, "Asian Women, Caucasian Men: It's a Growing Trend in the Bay Area's New Multicultural World," *San Francisco Examiner*, Sunday supplement, Dec. 2, 1990.

6. Beth Kwon, "Me So Ornery," *Time Out New York*, no. 286, Mar. 15–22, 2001.

7. I have condensed two separate lists into one with consecutive numbering and made minor grammatical corrections to aid clarity.

8. I have cleaned up errors and misspellings and added capitalization only where the meaning might be unclear or hard to read.

9. Wanwadee Larsen, *Confessions of a Mail-Order Bride* (New York: HarperCollins, 1989), 3, 23–24.

TEN PEOPLE, TEN COLORS

1. The names of Yukie and her family members have been changed to conceal their identities.

2. This data is from 2000; women in managerial positions have increased from 9.9 percent in 1995. *Women in Japan Today* (Tokyo: Gender Equality Bureau, Cabinet Office, 2003), 21.

3. Institute for Research on Household Economics, http://www.kakeiken.or.jp/english/index.html.

4. Karen Ma, *The Modern Madame Butterfly* (Tokyo and Rutland, Vermont: Charles E. Tuttle Co. 1996), 167, 176.

5. The over-fifty, under-fifty divide in the mindset of Japanese men is great enough that sociologist Seiko Yamazaki, Associate Research Director at the Dentsu Institute for Human Studies, predicts an enormous impact on the Japanese corporate workforce in ten years, when those older men resisting change and keeping Japanese women out of management positions retire.

6. Taiki Morohashi, "Nihon no taishu zasshi ga egaku jenda to 'kazoku'" in *Media ga tsukru jenda*, Muramatsu Yasuko and Hilaria Gossmann, eds. (Tokyo: Shinyosha, 1998), 194–96.

7. The trend, called an "M-shaped curve" for the way that women's participation in the labor force looks on a graph—rising until the mid-twenties, then falling off during childbearing years—then rising again afterward, had been the case for Britain until the 1980s, but now is not duplicated in any other OECD reporting countries, according to the Tokyo Cabinet Office, Gender Equality Bureau.

8. Emiko Ochiai, *The Japanese Family System in Transition* (Tokyo: Yuhikaku Publishing Co., 1994), 11.

9. Among OECD countries, it is lower only in Korea, at 48.8 percent. "FY2002 Annual Report on the State of Formation of a Gender-Equal Society" (Tokyo: Cabinet Office, Gender Equality Bureau, June 2003).

10. Ma, *The Modern Madame Butterfly*, 199–225.

11. Kyodo, "Mori Takes Turn at Insulting Women," *The Japan Times*, July 2, 2003.

12. *The Japanese Family System in Transition*, 114, (reporting 28 percent of marriages arranged as of 1983, but no data since then).

13. Gary Schaefer, "Divorces Hit All Time High," *Associated Press*, Sept. 17, 2003. U.S. data is from 2003; Britain and E.U. data is from 2000.

14. *Steps Towards Gender Equality in Japan* (Tokyo: Gender Equality Bureau, Cabinet Office, 2002), 5.

THE REAL MEMOIRS OF GEISHA

1. Lesley Downer, *Women of the Pleasure Quarters* (New York: Broadway Books, 2001) 59. Even a public exhibit of Rodin's *The Kiss* proposed for the 1930s was cancelled due to public outrage over such a display—not over the naked bodies but of the kiss itself, Downer reports. The sculpture was not exhibited until after World War II.

2. Liza Dalby, *Geisha* (Berkeley and Los Angeles, California: University of California Press, 1983), 180. There is no comparable data for Asakusa.

THE OTHER SIDE OF MISS SAIGON

1. Stanley Karnow, *Vietnam: A History* (New York: Viking Press, 1983), 100; Sandra C. Taylor, *Vietnamese Women at War* (Lawrence, Kansas: The University Press of Kansas, 1999), 19.

2. Taylor, *Vietnamese Women at War*, 19.

3. Taylor, *Vietnamese Women at War*, 31.

4. Karnow, *Vietnam: A History*, 104–05.

5. Taylor, *Vietnamese Women at War*, 23.

6. Taylor, *Vietnamese Women at War*, 42.

7. This figure, from the U.N. Educational, Scientific, and Cultural Organization, is lower than the government-reported rate of 61.1 percent, because it includes semi-literacy.

8. Cambodian government data for 2000, compared with World Health Organization and U.S. Census data from the same year.

GLAMOUR OF THE SKIES, SORORITY OF SERVICE

1. Cathay later added Sri Lanka as its eleventh recruiting country, but there are too few Sri Lankans to change the "Cathay Ten" tally sheet. Currently, Cathay recruits only Hong Kong residents who speak English and either Mandarin or Cantonese.

2. Simon Winchester, *Hong Kong: Here Be Dragons*. Rick Browne and James Marshall, eds. (New York: Stewart, Tabori & Chang, Inc., 1992), 51.

3. Kannan Ramaswamy, *Singapore International Airlines: Preparing for Turbulence Ahead*, The Garvin School of International Management case study (Thunderbird Institute, 2004).

4. Some 66,000 amahs are from Indonesia, and smaller numbers come from Nepal, Thailand, and mainland China. Mary Ann Benitez, "Maid wage cut a political football," *The South China Morning Post*, Dec. 23, 2001.

5. Government statistics, compiled by the Center for Women's Resources, Quezon City, Philippines.

6. This is not necessarily typical, however. Many amahs who come to the United States or Europe with families they started working for in Hong

Kong find higher pay, bigger rooms to live in, and an opportunity for travel that they never had before.

SCREWING, GETTING SCREWED, AND GETTING AHEAD

1. Ian Buruma, *The Missionary and the Libertine: Love and War in East and West* (New York: Vintage Books, Random House, 1996), 141.

2. Alex Gilandes, "Sex and the Single Filipina," *The Omega Women* (Makati, Manila, Philippines: Philippine Education Co. Inc., 1982).

3. International Labor Organization estimate, cited in Dario Agnote, "Sex trade key part of S.E. Asian economies, study says," *Kyodo News*, Aug. 18, 1998. A second source, Gabriela, Statistics and the State of the Philippines, July 24, 1997, cited on www.catwinternational.org, estimates 300,000 prostitutes.

4. Quoted in Buruma, *The Missionary and the Libertine*,142.

5. "Arroyo admits taking birth control pills as a young mother," *DPA* (*Deutsche Presse-Agentur*), Mar., 12, 2003.

6. "Philippine leader said runaway population growth not too bad," *DPA* (*Deutsche Presse-Agentur*), Oct., 24, 2003.

7. Ellen Nakashima and Edward Cody, "Filipinos Take 'Going Places' Literally," *The Washington Post*, May 26, 2004, A15.

8. Albina Pecson Fernandez, "Rizal on Women and Children in the Struggle for Nationhood," in *Review of Women's Studies*, 2, no. 2 (1990–91), 10–33.

9. Buruma, *The Missionary and the Libertine*, 154.

WHO'S PLAYING WHOM

1. Karen Kelsky was a Ph.D. candidate in anthropology at the University of Hawaii (1992–93), and documented twenty to thirty beach boys on Waikiki Beach (white and black) who specialized in short-term sexual relationships with Japanese women tourists. So conspicuous was this behavior that the Waikiki Health Center in 1992 started an outreach program to give away free condoms to Japanese women on the beach. (For more on this, see Ma, *The Modern Madame Butterfly,* 66–71.) In recent years, Hawaii became less popular (and more expensive to the declining Japanese yen), so Japanese women shifted focus to men in Bali and Thailand. This has been well docu-

mented in the Japanese media, in articles with titles such as "Japanese women prefer Thais" (*Kyodo/agencies*, June 21, 2001), which noted that the number of Japanese females in their twenties visiting Thailand in 2000 totaled about 142,000, compared to only 89,000 Japanese male visitors in the same age group, up by nearly 8 percent from 1999, and that Japanese women say they go to "relax," "ease their stress," and "to have fun" with Thai men.

2. Anthropological data from William P. Lebra, *Okinawan Religion: Belief, Ritual, and Social Structure* (Honolulu: University of Hawaii Press, 1966).

3. 6,084 Baht (US$142), based on an average number of wage recipients per household of 1.8, a minimum wage of 130 Baht per day and an average of 26 working days per month, as calculated by the ASEAN Focus Group at Australian National University, September 2000.

4. Thailand Ministry of Labor figures, 2002.

5. Morgan Lake and Kristian Schirbel, *Love, $ex & Trust: Romantic Adventures in Thailand* (Phuket, Thailand: Meteve Phuket Co., Ltd., 2000), 48–62.

6. Lake and Schirbel, *Love, $ex and Trust*, 13.

7. Niels Mulder, *Inside Thai Society: Interpretations of Everyday Life* (Amsterdam: The Pepin Press, 1996), 71.

8. The largest red-light district in Southeast Asia, called Dolly, is in Surabaya, Indonesia, and caters mainly to the shipping trade—merchant mariners of Thai, Filipino, and other nationalities.

9. Karl Taro Greenfeld, *Standard Deviations: Growing Up and Coming Down in the New Asia* (Hong Kong: Chamelion Press, 2002), 139.

10. "Tanamur Finally Tamed," www.jakarta24.com, June 2004.

11. Moammar Emka and Nursalim Syah, *Jakarta Undercover* (Komik) (Jakarta: Gagas Media, 2003).

12. *CIA Factbook* (1999).

CHINA DOLL, DRAGON LADY

1. The theory declares that "the Party must always represent the requirements of the development of China's advanced productive forces, the orientation of the development of China's advanced culture, and the fundamental interests of the overwhelming majority of the people in China." This is generally interpreted to mean that the Party should represent previously excluded business people and the private sector.

2. Stephanie Hoo, "Official: China Aims to Balance Gender," *Associated Press*, July 15, 2004.

3. Elisabeth Rosenthal, "Suicides Reveal Bitter Roots of China's Rural Life," *New York Times*, Jan. 24, 1999.

4. About 280,000 Chinese commit suicide annually, 150,000 of them women: "Chinese Women's Organization Helps Reduce Suicide Among Women," *People's Daily*, Nov. 20, 2003; "Suicide: Fifth Biggest Cause of Death in China," *People's Daily Online,* Nov. 29, 2002.

5. I once had to talk a man named Kejin out of adopting the name "Kitchen," and suggested he call himself "Kevin" instead. Foreigners always find it shocking the first time they meet a "Hitler," which is not an uncommon choice of name.

6. Louise Williams, *Wives, Mistresses & Matriarchs* (London: Orion Books, 1998), 84.

7. "Sex bias exists in local job market," *People's Daily Online,* http://english.people.com.cn, Aug. 9, 2004.

8. My visa status did not allow me to make interview requests through formal channels.

POWER WOMEN

1. A fourth woman was inaugurated in the northern island of Hokkaido in May 2003.

2. Arroyo assumed the presidency in 2001 when President Joseph Estrada resigned in scandal; she was running for election for the first time. Presidents by law are limited to one six-year elected term.

EPILOGUE: DEMAND CREATES SUPPLY

1. When asked about proportion of Asian employees, the hotel responded that the preponderance of Asian staff members was just a coincidence. My subsequent visit did indicate the staff to be more ethnically mixed.

2. Iris Chang, *The Chinese in America: A Narrative History* (New York: Viking Penguin, 2003), 203–04.

3. Chang, *The Chinese in America*, 205.

4. Chang, *The Chinese in America*, 204.

5. Ian Buruma, *The Missionary and the Libertine: Love and War in East and West.* (New York: Vintage Books, Random House, 1996), xiii–xvi.

Selected Bibliography

The volume of books, articles, websites, television shows, theater produc-tions, films, music lyrics, poems, and historical material providing fodder for this topic is so immense that to list everything—including fifteen years worth of observations and discussions, plus a year and a half of intensive in-terviewing—that influenced my formation of ideas on this subject would take its own volume. For that reason, I have selected primarily those print and Web materials that I relied on repeatedly or used in a formative way throughout the book, and those which provided specific source material. That means—by necessity—leaving out the dozens of works of stage and screen (which are cited in the text along with the year), the museums and li-braries of several cities where I compiled material, numerous CDs or record albums, and interviews with hundreds of people in numerous countries of Asia and the West.

Agnote, Dario. "Sex trade key part of S.E. Asian economies, study says." *Ky-odo News*, August 18, 1998.

Ambrose, Stephen E. *Nothing Like It in the World: The Men Who Built the Transcontinental Railroad 1863–1869*. New York: Simon & Schuster, 2000.

Aquino, Gaudencio V. *Philippine Legends*. Mandaluyong City, Philippines: National Book Store, 1972.

Asian Women United of California, ed. *Making Waves: An Anthology of Writ-ings by and About Asian American Women*. Boston: Beacon Press, 1989.

Bamber, James. *Sex, Lies & Bar Girls: The ABC's of Bar Fines & Short Times*. Bangkok: Bangkok Book House, 2003.

Bass, Thomas A. *Vietnamerica: The War Comes Home*. New York: Soho Press, 1996.

Becker, Jasper. *The Chinese*. London: John Murray (Publishers) Inc., 2000.

Beecroft, John. *Kipling*. Vol. 1, 2, *A Selection of His Stories and Poems*. Garden City, NY: Doubleday & Co., 1956.

Benedict, Ruth. *The Chrysanthemum and the Sword: Patterns of Japanese Culture*. 1946. Reprint, Boston: Houghton Mifflin Co., 1989.

Benitez, Mary Ann. "Maid wage cut a political football." *South China Morning Post*, December 23, 2001.

Berry, Sarah. *Screen Style: Fashion and Femininity in 1930s Hollywood*. Minneapolis: University of Minnesota Press, 2000.

Blackburn, Susan. *Love, sex and power: Women in Southeast Asia*. Victoria: Monash University Press, 2001.

Bliss, Jennifer. *But, I Don't Give a Hoot! The Life and Times of Bernard Trink, Bangkok's "Nite Owl."* Bangkok: Post Books, 2000.

Bornoff, Nicholas. *The Pink Samurai: Love, Marriage & Sex in Contemporary Japan*. New York: Simon & Schuster, 1991.

Brooke, James. "Neighborhood of U.S. Base is Hot Real Estate in Korea." *New York Times*, May 31, 2004.

Buruma, Ian. *Inventing Japan, 1853–1964*. New York: Random House, 2003.

_____. *The Missionary and the Libertine: Love and War in East and West*. New York: Vintage Books, Random House, 1996.

Chandler, David P. *A History of Cambodia*. Boulder, San Francisco, Oxford: Westview Press, 1992.

Chang, Iris. *The Chinese in America: A Narrative History*. New York: Viking Penguin, 2003.

Chong, Denise. *The Girl in the Picture: The Story of Kim Phuc, the Photograph, and the Vietnam War*. London: Simon & Schuster UK, 2000.

Chrichton, Michael. *Rising Sun*. New York: Ballantine Books, Random House, 1992.

Clavell, James. *Gai-Jin*. New York: Bantam Doubleday Publishing Group, 1993.

_____. *Shogun*. New York: Dell Publishing Co., 1976.

_____. *Tai-Pan, a novel of Hong Kong*. New York: Dell Publishing Co., 1966.

Dalby, Liza. *Geisha*. Berkeley and Los Angeles: University of California Press, 1983.

Dales, Laura. "Feminist Identification and Identity in Kansai Women's Groups." PhD thesis, University of Western Australia.

Doi, Takeo. *The Anatomy of Dependence (Amae no Kôzô)*. Rev. ed. Tokyo, New York, London: Kodansha International, 1981.

Dong, Stella. *Shanghai: The Rise and Fall of a Decadent City*. New York: Harper Collins, 2000.

Dower, John W. *Embracing Defeat: Japan in the Wake of World War II*. New York: W.W. Norton & Co., 1999.

Downer, Lesley. *Madame Sakayakko: The Geisha Who Bewitched the West*. New York: Gotham Books, Penguin Putnam, 2003.

———. *Women of the Pleasure Quarters*. New York: Broadway Books, 2001.

Duiker, William J. *Ho Chi Minh*. New York: Hyperion, 2000.

Edwards, Louise. *Women in Asia: Tradition, Modernity, and Globalisation*. Ann Arbor: University of Michigan Press, 2000.

Eheschließungen nach der Staatsangehörigkeit der Ehepartner (Asien), Siehe Fachserie 1, Reihe 1, 1992, Tabelle 8.11, S. 88–89.

Emka, Moammar and Nursalim Syah. *Jakarta Undercover* (Komik). Jakarta: Gagas Media, 2003.

Ensler, Eve. *The Vagina Monologues*. New York: Villard Books, Random House, 1998, 2001.

Fadiman, Anne. *The Spirit Catches You and You Fall Down: A Hmong Child, Her American Doctors, and the Collision of Two Cultures*. New York: Farrar, Straus and Giroux, 1997.

Faludi, Susan. *Backlash: The Undeclared War Against American Women*. New York: Anchor Books, Bantam Doubleday Dell Publishing, 1991.

———. *Stiffed: The Betrayal of the American Man*. New York: William Morrow & Co., 1999.

Farrer, James. *Opening Up: Youth Sex Culture and Market Reform in Shanghai*. Chicago and London: The University of Chicago Press, 2002.

Feng, Peter X., ed. *Screening Asian Americans*. New Brunswick, NJ and London: Rutgers University Press, 2002.

Fernandez, Albina Pecson. "Rizal on Women and Children in the Struggle for Nationhood." *Review of Women's Studies*, I, no. 2 (1990–91). University of the Philippines, Dilman, Quezon City.

Gender Equality Bureau. *FY2002 Annual Report on the State of Formation of a Gender-Equal Society*. Tokyo: Cabinet Office, Gender Equality Bureau, June 2003.

Gilandes, Alex. "Sex and the Single Filipina." In *The Omega Women*. Makati, Manila, Philippines: Philippine Education Co. Inc., 1982.

Golden, Arthur. *Memoirs of a Geisha*. New York: Random House, Vintage Books, 1997.

Greene, Graham. *The Quiet American*. London: Penguin, 1973.

Greenfeld, Karl Taro. *Standard Deviations: Growing Up and Coming Down in the New Asia*. Hong Kong: Chamelion Press, 2002.

Hamilton-Paterson, James. *America's Boy: A Century of Colonialism in the Philippines*. New York: Henry Holt & Co., 1998.

Haw, Stephen G. *A Traveller's History of China*. London: The Windrush Press, 2002.

Hessler, Peter. *River Town: Two Years on the Yangtze*. New York: Harper Collins, 2001.

Hodges, Graham Russell. *Anna May Wong: From Laundryman's Daughter to Hollywood Legend*. New York: Palgrave Macmillan, 2004.

Holdsworth, May. *Adorning the Empress*. Hong Kong: ForumAsia Books, 2002.

Hoo, Stephanie. "Official: China Aims to Balance Gender." Associated Press, July 15, 2004.

Houellebecq, Michel. *Platform* (*Plateforme*). London: Vintage, Random House, 2002.

Hsi Lai. *The Sexual Teachings of the White Tigress: Secrets of the Female Taoist Masters*. Rochester, VT: Destiny Books, 2001.

Hutchison, Neil. *Money Number One: The Single Man's Survival Guide to Pattaya*. Pattaya, Thailand: Guru Trading Co., 2001.

Hwang, David Henry. *M Butterfly*. New York: Plume, Penguin Books, 1986.

Institute for Research on Household Economics, http://www.kakeiken.or.jp/english/index.html.

Isaacs, Harold R. *Images of Asia: American Views of China and India*. (*Scratches on Our Minds*). New York: Harper & Row Publishers, 1972.

Iwao Sumiko. *The Japanese Woman: Traditional Image and Changing Reality*. Cambridge, MA: Harvard University Press, 1993.

Iwasaki Mineko. *Geisha of Gion*. London: Pocket Books, Simon & Schuster, 2002.

Iyer, Pico. *The Lady and the Monk: Four Seasons in Kyoto*. London: Vintage Books, 1991.

_____. *Video Night in Kathmandu: And Other Reports from the Not-So-Far East*. New York: Alfred A. Knopf, 1988.

Jacobson, Dawn. *Chinoiserie*. London: Phaidon Press, 1999.

Jelen, Janos and Gábor Hegyi. *Angkor and the Khmers*. Budapest: Hegyi and Partner Publishing House, 1991.

Karnow, Stanley. *In Our Image: America's Empire in the Philippines*. New York: Random House, 1989.

Karnow, Stanley. *Vietnam: A History*. New York: The Viking Press, 1983.

Kelsky, Karen. *Women on the Verge: Japanese Women, Western Dreams*. Durham and London: Duke University Press, 2001.

Komroff, Manuel, ed. *The Travels of Marco Polo {The Venetian}*. New York: Liverlight Publishing Corp., 1926.

Kwon, Beth. "Me So Ornery." *Time Out New York*, no. 286, March 15–22, 2001.

Lacey, Liam, "The Eyes of a Stranger." *Globe and Mail* (Toronto), June 4, 2004, R7.

Lake, Morgan and Kristian Schirbel. *Love, $ex & Trust: Romantic Adventures in Thailand*. Phuket, Thailand: Meteve Phuket Co., 2000.

Larsen, Wanwadee. *Confessions of a Mail-Order Bride*. New York: Harper-Collins, 1989.

Lebra, William P. *Okinawan Religion: Belief, Ritual, and Social Structure*. Honolulu: University of Hawaii Press, 1966.

Lee, Charles. *Cowboys and Dragons: Shattering Cultural Myths to Advance Chinese-American Business*. Chicago: Dearborn Trade Publishing, 2003.

Lee Kwan Yew. *From Third World to First: The Singapore Story: 1965–2000*. New York: HarperCollins Publishers, 2000.

Lewis, Reina. *Gendering Orientalism: Race, Femininity, and Representation*. New York: Routledge, 1996.

Li Zhisu. *The Private Life of Chairman Mao*. New York: Random House, 1994.

Linao, Girlie. "Arroyo admits taking birth control pills as a young mother." *DPA*, March, 12, 2003.

_____. "Philippine leader said runaway population growth not too bad." *DPA*, October, 24, 2003.

Lloyd, Stuart. *Hardship Posting Vol. 1: True Tales of Expat Misadventure*. Victoria, Australia: Sid Harta Publishers, 2001.

Ma, Karen. *The Modern Madame Butterfly*. Tokyo and Rutland, VT: Charles E. Tuttle Co., 1996.

Mahbuhani, Kishore. *Can Asians Think? Understanding the Divide Between East and West*. South Royalton, VT: Steerforth Press, 2002.

Mahel, Barbara. *The Situation of Filipino Women*. Manila: Guaranty Press Inc., 1988.

Manchester, William. *American Caesar: Douglas MacArthur: 1880–1964*. Boston: Little, Brown, and Co., 1978.

Marchetti, Gina. *Romance and the "Yellow Peril": Race, Sex, and Discursive Strategies in Hollywood Fiction*. Berkeley, Los Angeles, and London: University of California Press, 1993.

Maslin, Janet. "Seeing and Believing: A Movie's Power Over Attitudes and Action." Week in Review, *New York Times*, February 22, 2004.

Mason, Richard. *The World of Suzie Wong*. London: William Collins Sons & Co., 1957.

Maugham, W. Somerset. *Collected Short Stories*. Vol. 4 (Twentieth Century Classics). New York: Penguin Books, 1995.

McCloskey, Kevin, "Heartthrobs: Lucy Liu." www.prevuemagazine.com, 2002.

Michener, James A. *Sayonara*. New York: Ballantine Books, 1953 (paperback ed.).

Milton, Giles. *Samurai William: The Englishman Who Opened Japan*. New York: Farrar, Strauss & Giroux, 2002.

Min, Anchee. *Becoming Madame Mao*. Boston, New York: Houghton Mifflin Co., Mariner Books, 2000.

Morgan, Stephen L. "Economic Growth and the Biological Standard of Living in China, 1880–1930." *Economics and Human Biology* 2, no. 2 (June 2004).

Morohashi, Taiki. "Nihon no taishu zasshi ga egaku jenda to 'kazoku.'" In *Media ga tsukru jenda*, edited by Muramatsu Yasuko and Hilaria Gossmann. Tokyo: Shinyosha, 1998.

Mulder, Niels. *Inside Thai Society: Interpretations of Everyday Life*. Amsterdam: The Pepin Press, 1996.

Nakashima, Ellen and Edward Cody. "Filipinos Take 'Going Places' Literally." *Washington Post*, May 26, 2004, A15.

Ng, Mei. *Eating Chinese Food Naked*. New York: Scribner, 1998.

Norindr, Panivong. *Phantasmatic Indochina*. Durham and London: Duke University Press, 1996.

Nothomb, Amélie. *Fear and Trembling (Stupeur et Tremblements)*. New York: St. Martin's Press, 2002.

Ochiai Emiko. *The Japanese Family System in Transition*. Tokyo: Yuhikaku Publishing Co., 1994.

Odzer, Cleo. *Patpong Sisters*. New York: Arcade Publishing, Blue Moon Books, 1994.

O'Neill, Hugh B. *Companion to Chinese History*. New York: Facts on File Publications, 1987.

O'Rourke, Dennis. *The Good Woman of Bangkok*. VHS. 1991.

Palmer, Martin and Zhao Xiaomin. *Essential Chinese Mythology*. London: Thorsons, HarperCollins Publishers, 1997.

Pan, Lynn. *The New Chinese Revolution*. Chicago: Contemporary Books Inc., 1988.

Preston, Diana. *The Boxer Rebellion*. New York: Penguin Putnam, Inc., 1999.

"Probable Developments in China." *ORE* 45–49, Central Intelligence Agency, June 16, 1949 (declassified for release October 21, 2004).

Ramaswamy, Kannan. *Singapore International Airlines: Preparing for Turbulence Ahead* (The Garvin School of International Management case study). Thunderbird Institute, 2004.

Rauch, Jonathan. *The Outnation: A Search for the Soul of Japan.* Cambridge, MA Harvard Business School Press, 1992.

Rosenthal, Elisabeth. "Suicides Reveal Bitter Roots of China's Rural Life." *New York Times*, January 24, 1999.

Said, Edward. *Orientalism.* New York: Vintage Books, Random House, 1994.

Sato, Barbara. *The New Japanese Woman: Modernity, Media, and Women in Interwar Japan.* Durham and London: Duke University Press, 2003.

Schaefer, Gary. "Divorces Hit All Time High." Associated Press, September 17, 2003.

Schell, Orville. *Virtual Tibet: Searching for Shangri-La from the Himalayas to Hollywood.* New York: Henry Holt, Metropolitan Books, 2000.

Schwarz, Adam. *A Nation in Waiting: Indonesia in the 1990s.* Boulder, San Francisco: Westview Press, 1994.

Seabrook, Jeremy. *Travels in the Skin Trade.* London, Sterling, VA: Pluto Press, 1996, 2001.

Seagrave, Sterling. *Dragon Lady: The Life and Legend of the Last Empress of China.* New York: Random House, 1992.

Short, Philip. *Mao: A Life.* New York: Henry Holt, 1999.

Shreve, Jenn. "America's most bitchin' broadcaster." *www.salon.com*, July 10, 1999.

Simpson, Caroline Chung. "Out of an Obscure Place: Japanese War Brides and Cultural Pluralism in the 1950s." *differences: A Journal of Feminist Cultural Studies* 10, no. 3 (1998).

Spence, Jonathan D. *Chan's Great Continent: China in Western Minds.* New York: Norton, 1998.

Steps Towards Gender Equality in Japan. Tokyo: Gender Equality Bureau, Cabinet Office, 2002.

Stober, Dan and Ian Hoffman. *A Convenient Spy: Wen Ho Lee and the Politics of Nuclear Espionage.* New York: Simon & Schuster, 2001.

Sugimoto, Yoshio. *An Introduction to Japanese Society.* Cambridge: Cambridge University Press, 2003.

Sun Tzu. *The Art of War.* Boston & London: Shambhala Pocket Classics, 1991.

Tan, Amy. *The Joy Luck Club.* London: William Heinemann Ltd., 1989.

Tan, Ming. *How to Attract Asian Women.* New York: BridgeGap Books, 2001, 2002.

Tanaka, Tomoyuki. "Disparity in Asian/white Interracial Dating FAQ." Usenet, [soc.couples.intercultural] (last-modified March 1, 1995).

Taylor, Sandra C. *Vietnamese Women at War*. Lawrence, KS: The University Press of Kansas, 1999.

Te Lin. *Chinese Myths*. London: Hodder Headline, 2001.

Templer, Robert. *Shadows and Wind: A View of Modern Vietnam*. New York: Penguin Putnam, 1998.

Tsao Hsueh-Chin. *The Dream of the Red Chamber*. Garden City, NY: Double-day Anchor Books, 1958.

Veneracion, Jaime B. "From Babaylan to Beata: A Study on the Religiosity of Filipino Women." *Review of Women's Studies* 3, no. 1 (Dec. 1992).

Wadler, Joyce. *Liaison*. New York: Bantam, 1993.

Walker, Dave and Richard S. Erlich. *"Hello My Big Big Honey!" Love Letters to Bangkok Bar Girls and Their Revealing Interviews*. Bangkok: Dragon Dance Publications, 1992.

Waley, Arthur, trans. *The Tale of Genji by Lady Murasaki*. Garden City, NY: Doubleday Anchor Books, 1955.

Walsh, Joan. "Asian Women, Caucasian Men: It's a Growing Trend in the Bay Area's New Multicultural World." *San Francisco Examiner*, Sunday supplement, December 2, 1990.

Wei Hui. *Shanghai Baby*. New York: Washington Square Press, Simon & Schuster, 1999.

Wile, Douglas. *Art of the Bedchamber: The Chinese Sexual Yoga Classics Including Women's Solo Meditation Texts*. Albany, NY: State University of New York Press, 1992.

Williams, Louise. *Wives, Mistresses & Matriarchs*. London: Orion Books, 1998.

Wiltshire, Trea. *Encounters With China: Merchants, Missionaries and Mandarins*. Hong Kong: Forum Asia, 2003.

Winchester, Simon. *In Hong Kong: Here Be Dragons,* edited by Rick Brown and James Marshall. New York: Stewart, Tabori & Chang, Inc., 1992.

Women in Japan Today. Tokyo: Gender Equality Bureau, Cabinet Office, 2003.

Xin Ran. *The Good Women of China: Hidden Voices*. New York: Pantheon Books, 2002.

Index